The Collected Works of
James M. Buchanan

VOLUME 15
*Externalities and Public
Expenditure Theory*

James M. Buchanan, Nobel Laureates Forum,
Tokyo, Japan, November 1988

The Collected Works of

James M. Buchanan

VOLUME 15

Externalities and Public Expenditure Theory

LIBERTY FUND

Indianapolis

05 04 03 02 01   C   5 4 3 2 1
05 04 03 02 01   P   5 4 3 2 1

Library of Congress Cataloging-in-Publication Data
Buchanan, James M.
Externalities and public expenditure theory / James M. Buchanan.
p.   cm. — (The collected works of James M. Buchanan ; v. 15)
A collection of 29 journal and book articles
previously published 1961–1990.
Includes bibliographical references and index.
ISBN 0-86597-241-9 (alk. paper). — ISBN 0-86597-242-7 (pbk. : alk. paper)
1. Externalities (Economics)   2. Expenditures, Public.
I. Title.   II. Series : Buchanan, James M.   Works.   1999 ; v. 15.
HB846.3.B83   2001
336.3'9—dc21   99-41678

LIBERTY FUND, INC.
8335 Allison Pointe Trail, Suite 300
Indianapolis, IN 46250-1684

Contents

4. Public Goods Theory

5. Applications—City, Health, and Social Security

6. Distributive Norms and Collective Action

Foreword

The core of James Buchanan's work in mainstream economics lies in the theory of public expenditure and externalities. For example, what are almost certainly Buchanan's two most famous articles—"Externality," with William Stubblebine, and "Economic Theory of Clubs"—are firmly located in this area. Both are included in this volume. For reasons outlined in the foreword to volume 1, we chose to reserve these famous papers for inclusion in this volume rather than include them in the introductory volume, so that they could be set alongside other, similarly technical, papers to which they are most closely related. As a result of this decision, the papers in this volume represent a coherent set of pieces focused on aspects of public expenditure theory and constitute all of Buchanan's papers in this area. However, readers should be alerted to Buchanan's book-length treatment of public goods theory, *The Demand and Supply of Public Goods*, which deals with some of the same questions as are engaged in this volume.[1]

The theory of public expenditure in economics purports to provide an answer to the question, What should governments do? And the answer to that question revolves around what is *necessary* for government action—namely, some element of market failure. As Buchanan himself and a subsequent generation of public choice scholars have been at pains to emphasize, a necessary condition is not a *sufficient* condition. Indeed, the corresponding analysis of *political* failure has been one of the important motivating elements in public

1. James M. Buchanan and Wm. Craig Stubblebine, "Externality," *Economica* 29 (November 1962): 371–84; James M. Buchanan, "An Economic Theory of Clubs," *Economica* 32 (February 1965): 1–14; *Demand and Supply of Public Goods* (Chicago: Rand-McNally, 1968), volume 5 in the series.

choice scholarship. Nevertheless, the analysis of market failure remains an integral part of the economist's theory of the (productive) state, and the exploration of "the anatomy of market failure" (to use Francis Bator's nice phrase) remains an indispensable exercise to set alongside crucial public choice results. Indeed, understanding when and why markets "fail" also provides insight into why markets *succeed* and thereby into a broader range of institutional design issues.[2]

Market failure analytics in the economics literature has revolved around a variety of related concepts—externalities, collective consumption, nonexcludability, public goods—all of which command somewhat independent attention. For example, public goods are those goods that are (must be?) consumed in common, such that each individual consumer consumes the total output. Examples commonly offered include lighthouse services, international deterrence, outdoor circuses, and environmental degradation. In each case, if the service is provided to one consumer, it is made available to all other potential consumers in the relevant group. Public goods exhibit in an extreme form the two independent properties of nonrivalness and nonexcludability. To say that a good is "nonrival" is to say that consumption by an individual does not reduce the amount available for consumption by other individuals. A good is nonexcludable if (and only if) it is not possible to exclude any particular individual (for example, one who does not pay for the good) from consuming it. Accordingly, a theatrical performance is "nonrival" in that the consumption of the performance by one observer does not reduce consumption by other observers, up to the limits of theater size. But the performance is totally excludable in that those who do not pay the entrance price do not gain admittance. Alternatively, the blackberries that grow on the common land are fully rival, in the sense that the more blackberries I pick, the fewer are left for you. But the blackberries are also nonexcludable in that access to them is not subject to any pricing device. Economists routinely conceive of fully private goods as both fully excludable and fully rival. Public goods lie, therefore, at the opposite pole of a two-dimensional spectrum, the two dimensions being thought of as the degree of rivalness and the

---

2. Francis Bator, "The Anatomy of Market Failure," *Quarterly Journal of Economics* 72 (August 1958): 351–79.

degree of excludability. And it is proper here to conceptualize the distinction between public goods and private goods as a spectrum, because both the excludability and rivalness can be present in degrees. Intermediate cases may involve partial nonrivalness or partial excludability. For example, congestion costs may be positive but not sufficient to make collective consumption of each unit produced by multiple consumers less economical than fully individual consumption: the swimming pool at the local resort may be subject to congestion, but the congestion is not sufficient to induce every family to purchase its own backyard pool. Hence we have *partial* nonrivalness in consumption. Similarly, crop dusting my crops will provide some protection against insect pests to the crops of neighbors, both because some of the dust spills over onto neighbors' crops and because the fact that pests cannot breed on my land reduces the supply of insects to the neighbors.

Samuelson's famous articles on "public goods" demonstrated conclusively that for the pure public good case the Pareto optimum is *not* a market equilibrium. But Samuelson does not derive that market equilibrium and is not, therefore, capable of specifying the *degree* of market failure. Some such specification is clearly necessary if the extent of market and political failure is to be compared. Because Buchanan recognizes that this comparison is critical to any complete normative analysis, Buchanan's approach involves an attempt to derive, in any particular case of alleged market failure, what the market equilibrium will be and, hence, the extent and nature of the market failure.[3]

Several questions arise in this connection. One question is whether the market failure associated with the pure public good is more attributable to nonrivalness or nonexcludability. Samuelson is more inclined to emphasize the nonrivalness attribute because that attribute is sufficient to generate the "optimality conditions" that he derives for public goods and hence also sufficient to demonstrate market failure in general. But in particular special cases—for example, that in which every individual's marginal demand for the public good is identical—no market failure will occur *unless* the public

---

3. Paul A. Samuelson, "The Pure Theory of Public Expenditure," *Review of Economics and Statistics* 36 (November 1954): 387–89; "Diagrammatic Exposition of a Theory of Public Expenditure," *Review of Economics and Statistics* 37 (November 1955): 350–56.

good is also nonexcludable. That is, an identical price to all users would be sufficient to achieve optimality in this special case, provided that the payment of the price is necessary for a consumer to be admitted. For that reason, the nonexcludability dimension—the capacity of nonpaying individuals to "free ride"—seems to be the more critical element in the market's failure to achieve Pareto optimality. The same considerations suggest that *differences* in individual marginal evaluations will be relevant in determining the extent of that element of market failure attributable to nonrivalness. Indeed, Samuelson suggests that, even if it were *feasible* to exclude, it could never be "Pareto optimal" to do so, since those excluded could be admitted to the public good at no extra cost *ceteris paribus*. But this conclusion is misleading at best, and downright wrong at worst. One can easily construct cases in which charging a uniform price Pareto dominates charging no price at all within a *market* context, since clearly in that context a *zero* price implies *zero* output. And it can easily be that charging a uniform price *in the market* is more efficient than public provision (with a zero user price) if there is any political failure *at all*.

More generally, in the whole range of intermediate cases, a host of considerations enter that are not present in the pure public goods case. For example, in the polar extreme case, the absence of price excludability creates a presumption that market failure consists in too little of the public good being produced. This presumption translates into a rule of thumb that the proper outcome of government intervention—whether by subsidizing private provision or by direct government provision—will be to increase the output of the good in question. However, as Buchanan shows in the paper with Milton Kafoglis in part 4, this conclusion does not necessarily follow in more complex intermediate cases. If, for example, my immunization shots are a partial substitute for yours in providing you with protection from disease, and vice versa, then the efficient arrangement has to attend to the distribution of immunization shots between us. In a private market equilibrium, generally this distribution will be inefficient and may well lead to more immunization shots in total than would be taken in the efficient outcome where the distribution of shots is such as to maximize gains from exchange. Moreover, when there is government intervention, there will, in general, also be some market response so that, in deriving the final consumption/production equilibrium, account will need to be taken of the interaction between public and private supply. These issues are engaged in the papers that follow in this volume. Indeed, it is largely Buchanan's work that has exposed them as issues.[4]

Buchanan's general strategy is to explore the multiple dimensions of possible market failure with an eye to delineating clearly the equilibrium outcome and distinguishing that outcome from that in which all possible gains from exchange have been appropriated by the relevant parties. There are two messages that emerge from this work: one is that a proper sense of the *extent* of market failure, rather than its mere *presence,* is relevant in all cases; the other is that "correcting" for such market failure is often a complex multidimensional business not captured by direct public provision at zero price and not necessarily involving expansion of market output.

The volume begins with three general introductory pieces, *The Bases for Collective Action,* "The Evaluation of Public Services" (written with Francesco Forte), and an extended essay, " 'La scienza delle finanze': The Italian Tradition in Fiscal Theory." This latter piece has a broad coverage and could have been as plausibly included in the previous volume on debt and taxes. As we noted in the introduction to volume 14, Buchanan's approach to fiscal theory follows the Italian (and, more generally, Continental) tradition in its rejection of the sharp divide between tax and expenditure sides of the budget that remains something of a feature of Anglo-American public finance outside the Buchanan stable.[5]

The next set of five papers, part 2, focuses directly on the externality topic. Beginning with the previously mentioned classic paper with Stubblebine, this group of papers explores a range of issues associated with the functioning of markets when externalities are present, both in the absence of government-imposed "corrective" taxes (as in "External Diseconomies in Competitive Supply," written with Charles Goetz) and in the presence of corrective taxes (as in "Public and Private Interaction," written with Gordon Tullock, and "External Diseconomies, Corrective Taxes and Market Struc-

---

4. James M. Buchanan and Milton Z. Kafoglis, "A Note on Public Goods Supply," *American Economic Review* 53 (June 1963): 403–14.

5. James M. Buchanan, *The Bases for Collective Action* (New Jersey: General Learning Press, 1971); James M. Buchanan and Francesco Forte, "The Evaluation of Public Services," *Journal of Political Economy* 69 (April 1961): 107–21; James M. Buchanan, " 'La scienza delle finanze': The Italian Tradition in Fiscal Theory," in *Fiscal Theory & Political Economy: Selected Essays* (Chapel Hill: University of North Carolina Press, 1960), 24–74.

ture").[6] This section concludes with an analysis of the "institutional structure" of externality relations based on a taxonomy of small-number and large-number cases.[7] There is a family connection between this latter paper and "Ethical Rules, Expected Values, and Large Numbers" included in volume 1, since both are concerned with the role of numbers of agents involved in the interaction.

Part 3 contains two papers dealing with joint supply or collective consumption. In the famous "clubs" paper, Buchanan examines the optimal conditions for a good that can be jointly consumed by all members of the relevant group but where the good is perfectly excludable. The analysis focuses on specifying the optimal size of the "club"—that is, the optimal numbers of consumers—and the way in which output levels and numbers are interrelated in cases where there is some degree of congestion in consumption. The "joint supply" paper deals with the relation between collective consumption and externality problems.[8]

In part 4, we have assembled six papers that are expressly focused on public goods in the sense that "public goods" is mentioned in all the titles. The extremely close connection with other papers in this volume will, however, be evident. For example, the paper with Kafoglis, which is designed to illustrate the possibility of overexpansion of public goods supply in market equilibrium, has an obvious analytical connection to the "reciprocal externality" paper with Tullock in part 2. Some of the papers in this section are quite brief. Their brevity reflects the fact that they were written as comments on exchanges between other scholars or on some paper by another author. However, these little papers provide considerable insight into Buchanan's

6. Buchanan and Stubblebine, "Externality"; James M. Buchanan and Charles J. Goetz, "External Diseconomies in Competitive Supply," *American Economic Review* 61 (December 1971): 883–90; James M. Buchanan and Gordon Tullock, "Public and Private Interaction under Reciprocal Externality," in *The Public Economy and the Urban Community,* ed. Julius Margolis (Resources for the Future, 1965), 52–73; James M. Buchanan, "External Diseconomies, Corrective Taxes, and Market Structure," *American Economic Review* 59 (March 1969): 174–77.

7. James M. Buchanan, "The Institutional Structure of Externality," *Public Choice* 14 (Spring 1973): 69–82.

8. James M. Buchanan, "An Economic Theory of Clubs," *Economica* 32 (February 1965): 1–14; "Joint Supply, Externality, and Optimality," *Economica* 33 (November 1966): 405–15.

views on various aspects of the public goods issue and no collection of his thoughts on this topic would be complete without them.[9]

Part 5 contains eight papers that constitute specific applications of these public goods ideas to various budget areas—with "financing the metropolis," with the health service provision arrangements in Britain, and, more generally, with social security.[10]

The final section, part 6, provides Buchanan's thinking on the redistributive aspects of government activity. These five papers should be read in association with the paper "The Political Economy of Franchise in the Welfare State," which appears in volume 13, since the latter paper gives an account of the "supply" side of the democratic redistributive process. Readers may also wish to consult the eighth chapter of *The Reason of Rules*, which deals with redistribution in a more explicitly constitutionalist way.[11]

---

9. James M. Buchanan, "Cooperation and Conflict in Public Goods Interaction," *Western Economic Journal* 5 (March 1967): 109–21; Buchanan and Kafoglis, "A Note on Public Goods Supply"; James M. Buchanan, "Public Goods in Theory and Practice," *Journal of Law and Economics* 10 (1967): 193–97; "Breton and Weldon on Public Goods," *Canadian Journal of Economics and Political Science* 33 (February 1967): 111–15; James M. Buchanan and A. Pinto Barbosa, "Convexity Constraints in Public Goods Theory," *Kyklos* 33, Fasc. 1 (1980): 63–75; James M. Buchanan, "Public Goods and Natural Liberty," in *The Market and the State: Essays in Honour of Adam Smith*, ed. Thomas Wilson and Andrew S. Skinner (Oxford: Clarendon Press, 1976), 271–86.

10. James M. Buchanan, "Public Goods and Public Bads," in *Financing the Metropolis: Public Policy in Urban Economics*, ed. John P. Crecine, vol. 4 (New York: Sage Publications, 1970), 51–71; "Principles of Urban Fiscal Strategy," *Public Choice* 11 (Fall 1971): 1–16; *The Inconsistencies of the National Health Service*, Occasional Paper no. 7 (London: Institute of Economic Affairs, 1965); *Technological Determinism Despite the Reality of Scarcity: A Neglected Element in the Theory of Spending on Medical and Health Care* (Little Rock: University of Arkansas Medical School, 1990), 3–17; "The Budgetary Politics of Social Security," in *Social Security's Looming Surpluses: Prospects and Implications*, ed. Carolyn L. Weaver (Washington, D.C.: AEI Press, 1990), 45–56; "Social Security Survival: A Public Choice Perspective," *Cato Journal* 3 (Fall 1983): 339–54; "Social Insurance in a Growing Economy: A Proposal for Radical Reform," *National Tax Journal* 21 (December 1968): 386–95; "Commentary," *Income Redistribution*, ed. Colin Campbell (Washington, D.C.: American Enterprise Institute, 1977): 99–101.

11. James M. Buchanan, "What Kind of Redistribution Do We Want?" *Economica* 35 (May 1968): 185–90; "Distributive and Redistributive Norms," in *Liberty, Market, and State: Political Economy in the 1980s* (Brighton, England: Wheatsheaf Books, 1986), 159–64; "Government Transfer Spending," in *Government Controls and the Free Market: The U.S. Economy in the 1970s*, ed. Svetozar Pejovich (College Station: Texas A&M University

Mention should be made here of those applications of the externalities and clubs ideas that Buchanan exploits in the context of the theory of federalism. Externalities often have a spatial dimension; political jurisdictions can be thought of as spatially based "clubs." However, as Buchanan and Goetz point out in "Efficiency Limits of Fiscal Mobility," the application of clubs theory to the study of federalism is not direct and requires a significant supplementation. The relevant papers are gathered with other papers on federalism in volume 18 in the series, *Federalism, Liberty, and the Law.*[12]

Geoffrey Brennan
Australian National University
1998

Press, 1976), 122–40; "Who Should Pay for Common-Access Facilities?" *Public Finance* 27, no. 1 (1972): 1–8; "Who Should Distribute What in a Federal System?" in *Redistribution through Public Choice,* ed. H. Hochman and G. Peterson (New York: Columbia University Press, 1974), 22–42; "The Political Economy of Franchise in the Welfare State," in *Capitalism and Freedom: Problems and Prospects,* ed. Richard T. Selden (Charlottesville: University Press of Virginia, 1975), 52–77; Geoffrey Brennan and James M. Buchanan, *The Reason of Rules: Constitutional Political Economy* (Cambridge: Cambridge University Press, 1985), volume 10 in the series.

12. James M. Buchanan and Charles J. Goetz, "Efficiency Limits of Fiscal Mobility," *Journal of Public Economics* 1 (1972): 25–43.

PART ONE

Public Services
and Collective Action

The Bases for Collective Action

Economic Foundations for Potential Collective Action

The natural ecological "economy" is anarchistic. It is an economy without law. Individual members of separate species interact with other individuals, both within species categories and among species. Each unit attains its own equilibrium, and the whole ecology can be described in terms of adjustment toward intra- and interspecies equilibriums. These results emerge from natural forces, and they do not require collective action on the part of separate species. There are no rulers and none are ruled; despite the fairy tale, there is no King of the Beasts. Nevertheless, even in the absence of "government," the ecology can be described as orderly in a scientific sense. Individual units as well as whole species seem to adhere to certain predictable and stable patterns. Ecology is a fully legitimate science.

To my knowledge, no one has fully developed the theory of an anarchistic economy in which human beings interact with each other and with other species without law. This theory could be developed as a branch of ecology. If humans were analyzed precisely as animals are analyzed, the natural forces leading to positions of both individual and species equilibriums could be described. Mankind probably would not vanish from the planet, and even his wholly uncontrolled behavior would not destroy other life in all its forms.

Thomas Hobbes deserves credit for providing a reasonably good and surely brief description of man's life in such an anarchistic setting. He argued that life would be "nasty, brutish, and short," a phrase that modern anarchists,

From *The Bases for Collective Action* (New Jersey: General Learning Press, 1971), 1–18. Copyright 1971 by General Learning Corporation. Reprinted by permission of Addison Wesley Educational Publishers, Inc.

along with the more enthusiastic "nature boys," neglect at their peril (and our own). Man escaped from this anarchy, quite literally, because he agreed to abide by *law*. And he continues to live pleasantly, humanely, and long largely because he remains a law-abiding animal. Law, which may be summarized as "rules for living together," finds its elementary justification in its ability to increase man's material well-being.

In its broadest definitional sense, collective action is the enactment and enforcement of law. The justification for all collective action, for government, lies in its ability to make men better off. This is where any discussion of the bases for collective action must begin.

This is not, of course, to suggest that all laws accomplish this purpose, that all collective action makes men better off, that all governments are "good," or that there cannot be bad laws, stupid political leaders, and corrupt and authoritarian regimes. As Hobbes properly recognized, however, almost any government is better than no government. The problem is where to draw the line between too much government, too many laws, and too little government, too few laws—a problem that will never be fully resolved, and about which reasonable men will surely continue to disagree.

In one sense, however, the logic for collective action at any margin of decision remains identical to that which arises in the first leap out of anarchy. It is essential that this logic be understood in some depth before commencing the arguments over drawing the appropriate limits.

LAW AS A PUBLIC OR COLLECTIVE GOOD

In conceptualized anarchy there are no individual rights, human or property, because there is no law defining these rights and no government to enforce them once they are defined. In such a system each person must devote much of his time and effort to defending what he claims as his own. Men are required to defend their staked-out territory and their females, as indeed animals are observed to do. But the resources used in this way could be used alternatively to produce goods and services. It should not take human beings long to recognize that in such an anarchy inconceivable gains for all concerned could be secured from the establishment of some sort of enforceable legal structure.

By one means or another, an "establishment" then emerges. It might take place through the enslavement of some men by other men; it might arise from a general agreement among all men to abide by a set of enforceable rules, which can be called a constitution or social contract; it might be represented by submission of all men to some sovereign government, organized explicitly to enforce the laws. The particular origin of collective action in laying down the law need not concern us, nor need we discuss in detail the historically descriptive accuracy of any theory of government formation. The emphasis here is quite different. The point is that government exists in the sense that it offers a sovereign agency for enforcement of laws that are also observed to exist. This is true for all times, all places, all human societies.

The existence and enforcement of laws, defined as rules for the interaction among men, are "public" or "collective," in the sense that these terms are used in modern economics. By this we mean that the laws, the whole legal structure, are simultaneously applicable to *all* participants in the social order. This generality in application of law is a characteristic of a free society. An acknowledged norm for such a society is that it should be impossible for one group of individuals in the community to be bound by one set of laws while other groups adhere to a different legal framework. When these norms are met, and law is generally applied, it may be analyzed as a genuine or pure "public good." Technically, a good or service is defined to be purely public when that amount available to any one person in the community is simultaneously available to all other persons.

The extension of this concept to the legal structure can be indicated by comparing it to the most familiar example of a purely public good, a national defense component. Just as all United States citizens, regardless of the value they might place on it, have available the protection of the Polaris submarine on patrol, so they also have available the federal statutes on narcotics, again regardless of the value they might place on these statutes. A characteristic feature of public goods is the absence of excludability; that is to say, if the Polaris submarine is on patrol, there is no way in which one individual may be excluded from its deterrent protection. Quite similarly, there is no way that particular individuals can be exempted from particular laws. To do this would violate the very meaning of law in a free society.

There are, of course, many differences among separate legal systems. But these are not of interest here. For our purposes, a legal structure contains a set of more or less well-defined rights which allow individuals to take certain types of action. These include the right to contract freely with one another for some subset of rights, notably to property, and the enforcement of these contracts by the sovereign agency, along with the policing of rights and contracts against fraud, deceit, destruction, and theft. Our analysis is confined to a legal system that is based on freedom of contract. It has been argued, convincingly, that this legal structure is one of the primary reasons for the economic superiority of Western civilization.

THE DISTRIBUTION OF RIGHTS

The legal structure describes a set of rights that allow individuals to take certain actions and a set of wrongs that proscribe other actions. These rights and wrongs pertain both to the usage of physical goods and property and to the treatment of or behavior toward other persons. Any discussion of the economic bases of government action presumes the existence of a specific legal structure that defines individual rights and wrongs.

Since the legal structure, "the law" as such, is equally applicable to all members of the society, it qualifies as a "public good." And there should be little or no quarrel with the assertion that everyone benefits from a legal structure, almost regardless of its specific details, by comparison with the situation that would prevail in its total absence. This is not to say that the legal framework that exists need be ideal or optimal in any sense. To a large extent, "the law" at any particular time in any particular society is arbitrary. As he grows into adulthood in a social setting, the individual finds himself subjected to "the law," a constitutional-legal setting, that he has had no part in making or accepting. To the individual this is no different from the "state of nature"; it becomes a part of his environment. For any particular person the rights that he is accorded by "the law" may not be those that he would most prefer. (Most of us would prefer more of many things.) Nor need he look with positive favor on the overall structure of rights as these are distributed among all persons, quite apart from his own personal share. He may seek to change the distribution of rights, to change the basic laws of the land. Even in this effort, however, the individual must adhere to those laws that control the manner of changing the law—that is, to constitutional processes. If he does not do so, if he becomes a revolutionary and chooses to subvert constitutional processes in attempting to change the structure of rights, he violates the implicit "social contract" with other members of the community. An individual may choose to become a revolutionary, but as a revolutionary he has no rights, since by his own behavior he denies the rights of others as defined in the legal structure. There is no basis for continuing inclusion in the community of those who claim political rights under law.

These comments about the distribution of rights and the legal structure generally are a necessary introduction to any analysis of the economic bases for collective or government action. In what follows we shall assume that a legal structure exists, along with a defined constitutional procedure for modifying this structure. We shall assume that individuals are free to make contracts one with another within broad limits and that there exist legal protections against fraud and deceit. The legal structure also defines a set of individual property rights, and these can be freely traded among persons and groups, again within very broad limits. Under these assumptions we can analyze the logical origins for the activities of governments at all levels. Once the protective function of the state or the government is established, why is there need for further specific collective action?

IDEALIZED LAISSEZ FAIRE

In a setting where the sole function of government consists in the definition and enforcement of private personal and property rights, which include the enforcement of voluntary contracts and the policing against fraud and deceit, an orderly economic process would emerge in the natural course of events. It is important that this be recognized. So long as men differ from one another in tastes and/or basic endowments, and so long as they are free to negotiate enforceable contracts with one another, trades will be made. Individuals will find it in their own interest to exchange goods and services (including productive services such as their own labor) with each other. "In their own interest" here means simply that individuals can increase their ultimate command over real goods by trade. Exchange becomes essentially equivalent to production; it provides an efficient means of transforming less desired into more desired goods and services.

So long as the possibilities of communication exist, and with no overt prohibitions against exchange behavior, men in such an environment will organize trades among themselves. One farmer who devotes half his land to apples and half to peaches may produce two hundred bushels of apples and one hundred bushels of peaches. If he produces nothing but apples and exchanges half of these for peaches, he may get one hundred and fifty bushels of peaches. His trading partner, whose land is differentially productive in peaches, secures more apples. For both, trade is a means of producing more. The whole set of trades, along with the productive processes that may be carried out prior to trade and which may be aimed at facilitating trade, can be called *an economy,* or an *economic process.*

The first point to be emphasized is that this economy or economic process will be tolerably efficient in performing the economic functions of the society. Goods and services will get produced, and resources will be combined in the production process in tolerably efficient ways. Goods and services will get distributed to ultimate users or consumers in a nonarbitrary fashion. The trading or exchange process will accomplish these functions through the placing of relative evaluations on goods and services, evaluations (prices) to which persons engaging in trade may adjust. (Other essays in this series discuss the detailed operation of the economy, which justifies the extremely brief treatment in this section.)

The results would not be chaos, even though no central agency and no single person or group makes overall allocative and distributive decisions. There is no central plan. No single person or group, government or otherwise, decides how many shoes will be produced in such an economy. But shoes get produced in a tolerably efficient way, and the trading process insures that those shoes find their way into the hands of those persons who place the highest relative value on them. Observations would reveal that there are no goods that are valued highly that are not being produced in this economy and also that no glut of undesired goods is produced. And all of this occurs despite the absence of a centralized decision-making structure, despite the absence of a central plan.

It is essential to recognize this principle of the operation of a pure-market or exchange economy before considering the appropriate range for collective action over and above that which is limited to the definition and enforcement of property rights. The pure exchange economy that would naturally emerge under this regime is characterized by what has been called a system of *spontaneous order.* Through their trading and exchange activity, individual participants in this sort of economic process will adjust their separate activities in such a way that coordination occurs in the absence of any central direction.

The genius of Adam Smith and other eighteenth-century philosophers lay in their recognition of this coordinating characteristic of the exchange process, and in their explicit analysis of the precise manner in which such an economy would work. Smith showed that such an economy, if only allowed to work freely, in contrast to the network of mercantilist controls that governments of Europe imposed on their economies in the sixteenth and seventeenth centuries, would indeed increase the "Wealth of Nations."

This is what laissez faire is all about. And it would be naive in the extreme to discuss the bases for collective action without some rudimentary understanding of laissez faire. The central notion cannot be repeated too often: it is simply that if men are left alone to organize their own trades and exchanges markets will emerge, and the wants of ultimate consumers will be tolerably well met. This is perhaps best summarized in Adam Smith's famous argument that it is not out of his benevolence that we get our meat from the butcher but out of his regard for his own self-interest. An economy organized on laissez-faire principles, that is, an economy where collective or government action is limited largely if not exclusively to the definition and enforcement of personal and property rights, uses the driving force of individual self-interest to secure socially desirable objectives. It is important to recognize this subsidiary principle at this point, because later we discuss possible avenues for reforms in government programs, one of which embodies this approach.

The major advantages of this system of organization lie in its maximization of the freedom it allows for individual choices, given the defined structure of rights, and in its tendency to minimize the costs of decision making and information. The laissez-faire or pure-market organization of an economy dispenses entirely with the necessity for any person to worry about and make decisions about what is indeed "good for the country," whether in his role as a dictator or as a participant in democracy. For example, since a consumer needs information only about his own demands, he does not have to undergo a costly process of finding out what anyone else wants. Decision making is decentralized. The individual is required to choose only what he will exchange, where, and with whom. To make this decision, he requires relatively limited information, and his actual trades may be implemented without unduly high costs of transaction itself. Decision making is decentralized, but the overall allocative and distributive process is effectively coordinated. This is a major advantage of the market order in an efficiency sense.

Perhaps more important than any efficiency advantage, however, is the market organization's minimization of man's power over man. His trading prospects define the range of options available to the individual participant in the pure-market economy. To the extent that he can choose among several persons with whom to trade, he is not subjected to the control or power of any one person. Free trade is an advantage to the individual precisely to the extent that it is free. If an individual desires to trade money for apples, his freedom is related directly to the number of apple sellers that he confronts. If there should be only one apple seller, the potential buyer's freedom depends strictly on the availability of close substitutes. The single apple seller's power over the potential buyer becomes quite small when there are other sellers of peaches and oranges. In an idealized laissez-faire economy, in which markets are perfect, no individual participant has any power over any other participant. Each buyer faces a large number of sellers of each good, and each seller confronts a large number of buyers. Every person has available to him a large number of alternative trading options.

This major advantage of a pure-market economy has perhaps been underemphasized in modern discussion, which has tended instead to concentrate on the efficiency properties of alternative organizational structures. As we move away from idealized models of the pure-market economy, the efficiency advantages of laissez faire may disappear in many specific cases. The personal freedom of the individual participant that a free-trade or free-exchange (free-enterprise) economy guarantees remains a major advantage of this organizational structure, even when the real-world departures from the conditions required for markets to work perfectly are acknowledged.

Personal or individual freedom is conditioned, of course, by the limits of power. The personal freedom that the market economy tends to maximize is that which is limited by the distribution of economic power among participants. This is, in turn, defined by the legal structure of property rights. The person who has little or no property, little or no human or nonhuman capacity to earn income in the market process, has available to him market options, but his freedom to choose among these may remain relatively meaningless because of his limited economic power. The pure-market economy as such has little to do, at least directly, with the distribution of economic power. This is determined, ultimately, by the natural distribution of talents along with the legal definition of rights, and a good dose of luck as well, in an uncertain world. Within these limits, the market economy allows for maximal freedom of individual choice.

SIMPLE AND COMPLEX EXCHANGE

Economists have a magic number—two. In all exchange or trading relationships there is a buyer and a seller. When Mrs. Jones purchases a dozen eggs from the A&P supermarket, the transaction, the trade of money for eggs and vice versa, involves Mrs. Jones and the A&P, and no one else. Mrs. Jones need not get authorization from Mrs. Smith, and the A&P does not have to clear the deal with Kroger's grocery. Because of the elementary fact that all economic exchanges can ultimately be reduced to two-person relationships, economic theory is greatly facilitated. As we indicated earlier, the power that the A&P has over Mrs. Jones depends on whether or not she has Kroger's available as an alternative source of supply, but the existence of alternative buyers and sellers exerts its influence on the conditions of the exchange and does not interfere with the bilateral characteristics of the exchange itself. We may say that the exchange is simple when only two persons are involved.

If all exchange, all economic interactions among buyers and sellers, could be reduced to simple two-person trades, there would be no basis for collective or governmental action beyond those protective functions already mentioned. Individuals could go about their business of trading goods and services, including the exchange of productive services for incomes. Production would be organized, values would be settled, and goods would be distributed to users. But not all potential exchanges can be factored down readily into two-person trades. There may be trading gains to be secured from the simultaneous economic interaction of more than two persons, more than two buyers or more than two sellers. This introduces *complex exchange*.

One traditional example, noted as early as David Hume, deals with several families who live on the edge of a meadow that needs draining. Since the owner of a dredge is quite willing to do the work, there is a single seller ready and willing to engage in trade. No single buyer, however, will find it worth his while to purchase the services. If all exchange must be strictly two-person, the meadow will not get drained. But it is likely that several of the families may benefit from the dredging if they join forces and share the expenses. The total benefits may well exceed the total costs. What is required here is complex exchange which involves the agreement of more than one person or unit on the buying side. Those entering the agreement must reach some decision as to how much dredging to purchase and how the total costs shall be shared.

Transactions costs and free riders

Complex exchange would cause no difficulty if it were possible to organize the necessary agreements quickly. If *transactions costs* were absent, any gain from trade that exists would be exploited by rational persons seeking to maximize their own utilities. This would be as true for those exchanges requiring multiparty agreement among a group of buyers as those requiring only the decisions of a single buyer and seller. In the world where transactions costs were zero, or even in a world where they were very low, government action could be limited to establishing and enforcing the legal rules.

In this setting collective agreement would be observed in the multiperson trading arrangements that take place. There would be no reason for these arrangements to involve political or governmental processes, however, since all exchanges could be worked out voluntarily. This would extend even to those complex exchanges which encompass all members of the community. All meadows would get drained that were worth draining, and no person would suffer the burden of paying taxes that he did not voluntarily accept as a part of his bargain.

It seems obvious, however, that when the potential gains from exchanges can be captured only after the agreement of many persons, transactions costs will not be negligible. Agreements must be negotiated among several persons, and each person will find it advantageous to invest some resources in strategic bargaining. Delays will be encountered, and potential gains may not be captured at all in certain cases. The several neighbors surrounding Hume's meadow may worry so much about who shall pay for the costs that the meadow will remain undrained, despite the potential net benefit to the community.

The problem of securing voluntary agreement among persons in this sort of setting is often called the *free-rider problem*. Although each person in the group may recognize that he would benefit from paying his share and having the meadow drained, he may not voluntarily make the payment. He may think that he could benefit still more if his neighbors pay the full cost while he enjoys a "free ride" at their expense. If there are potential "free riders" in the community, however, their behavior may, in its turn, dissuade others from contributing voluntarily or from reaching agreement. Even the person who might not, himself, exploit others through "free-rider" tactics may refuse to pay a share unless others are observed to do so. In the brief treatment here, all these problems have been included in the comprehensive term *transactions costs*.

One means of reducing transactions costs is for the group to take genuinely collective action through government or political organization. If the village is organized politically, and if there is a constitutional rule indicating how political decisions are to be made, the village government unit can make a specific decision about how much draining to undertake. More importantly, it can allocate the costs among the members of the community by levying taxes, which must be compulsory. Reaching decisions through governmental or political process can, in itself, be costly. But it may be considerably less so than the comparable process that would be required under purely voluntary organization.

It is relatively easy to see some of the determinants here. If the required agreement in a potential complex exchange involves only a small number of persons out of the whole community, transactions costs will probably not be significant. Ordinary market dealings will emerge, and efficient exchanges will be organized voluntarily. If, however, the required agreement in a complex exchange involves all or nearly all of the members of a community, transactions costs under voluntary arrangements may become almost prohibitive. In these cases resort to political action may be one means of dramatically reducing transactions costs, even when the costs of making political decisions are fully taken into account.

When are complex exchanges beneficial?

We have isolated a basic reason for political or government action in the possible reduction in transactions costs in situations where benefits can be secured only from large-number exchanges. The immediate question now becomes: under what conditions are such trades likely to be needed?

Consider once again Hume's meadow that needs draining. What is the situation here? It is relatively easy to see that the whole problem emerges only because individual property rights have not been defined so that all activities are included. The meadow is presumably common property. It is owned by no one, or, to put the same point in another way, it is owned by everyone. This absence of private ownership is what creates the problem. Common ownership is the same as no ownership when it comes to motivation for private action. If the meadow should be assigned to a single private owner, who would then secure the full benefits of drainage, no problem would arise. Ordinary two-person trading arrangements could be expected to secure efficient results.

It is important to recognize that the failure of private property arrangements to include common properties creates precisely the same set of problems as the absence of law in the first instance. In a genuine sense, to say that a piece of property is owned in common among all persons in the community is to say that "there is no law" concerning who shall do certain things with the property. It becomes appropriate for the government unit to lay down the law with respect to the usage and development of commonly owned property in the same manner that it is proper for the government to lay down the rules for personal interaction in the first place. Government action in respect of property that is held in common is equivalent, therefore, to a rather straightforward extension of the rules of contract.

This suggests that one of the important determinants for the appropriate range of government or political action is the degree of specificity with which private property rights are defined. If individuals and families, or voluntarily organized groups generally, are carefully assigned rights that are inclusive of most personal interactions, there is little left over to be held "in common." Relatively few additional collective rules need be laid down beyond the broad legal framework that defines and enforces the legal rights in the first place. By contrast, if private property rights are vaguely defined, and for many aspects of human endeavor not defined at all, we should surely expect government action to be required in laying down many supplementary rules and regulations.

This relationship of government rules to the specificity of property rights may be illustrated by another familiar example. Suppose that in one society all land is held in private ownership. If the owner of grazing animals seeks pasture, he must either purchase or rent land for this purpose. And, once he has done so, he can exclude the grazing animals of others from this land. Under these arrangements, we should expect that individual self-interest would insure that the land would not be overgrazed. There would be no need for government regulations about land use. Government action could be limited to enforcing contracts among persons except, of course, in those cases where more complex interdependencies arise.

By contrast, a society in which all land is held in common, where there is no private property in land—a description applicable to several underdeveloped areas of the world—the owners of grazing animals do not need to purchase or to rent land from other persons before allowing their animals to graze. By the same token, the owner of the grazing animals cannot keep other persons from allowing their own animals to graze the common land. As a result, there will be a persistent tendency to overgraze the land. Self-interest will fail as a means of limiting the number of grazing animals to the optimal capacity of the land. To prevent overgrazing, government action may be required to lay down the rules and regulations concerning the specific use of the common property.

EXTERNALITIES

Our discussion suggests that specific collective or government action over and above the minimal protection of property rights and enforcement of contracts may be required when private property rights are not well defined. This is, as we noted, the same thing as saying that government action may be required when there is no law. We may look at the problem in a somewhat different light if we examine the interaction of individuals themselves.

In, once again, the example of grazing land held in common rather than under private ownership, an individual owner of animals to be pastured will impose costs on all other owners of animals; his goats will eat the grass that could be used for other men's cattle. The commonality of the land insures that users impose *external* costs on each other, costs that are not covered by either receipts or payments for damages. Economists refer to such effects as *externalities,* and these may include effects on the benefits as well as the costs side. In the problem of draining the meadow, if one person should undertake to get it drained on his own account, he will provide an external benefit for his neighbors.

Somewhat more formally, we can define an externality as being present whenever the behavior of a person affects the situation of other persons without the explicit agreement of that person or persons. The relationship between exchange and externality is important. In trade or exchange, persons influence each other but are fully compensated for all costs that are suffered and fully pay for all benefits received. Trade can be considered to be a reciprocal exchange of effects upon which the two parties directly involved agree. An externality, by comparison, implies that a person either suffers a cost or receives a benefit from the actions of another person without entering into trade. If he suffers a cost, he secures no compensation for it. If he secures a benefit, he pays nothing for it. His agreement with the person exerting the effect is not involved. Hence, the term *externality;* the action is taken external to the person or persons affected.

Let us now look at externalities in terms of the simple and complex trading classification previously introduced. If there should be only two persons involved in an externality relationship, this would mean only that a simple trade or exchange opportunity is not exploited. If only two persons are pasturing cattle or goats on the land, when each one uses the commonly shared resource, the pasture, he imposes an external cost on the other. It is clear that possibilities might exist for mutually beneficial agreements on rules for using the commonly shared resource. And transactions costs between the two persons should not be prohibitive. We can, therefore, predict that an ordinary trading process would take place, with each person trading his agreement on usage of the common land. The same thing would be true on the external benefit side. We can summarize this point by saying that *small-number externalities* will tend to be eliminated by voluntary exchangelike agreements among the parties directly affected. Bargaining costs will still be present; individuals will try to secure differential gains. If the numbers are small, however, some agreement should be attained.

Suppose, however, that many persons are involved in an externality relationship. If, for example, there are a thousand owners of goats and cattle, all of whom use the common land for pasture, then each person, as he allows his animals to eat the grass, imposes external costs on all other users—999 of them. It is evident that in this *large-number externality* the transactions costs involved in achieving agreement among all persons involved might be very high indeed. What is required here is a complex rather than a simple exchange. And it is in such cases as this that collective action through governmental or political auspices may be the only means of securing tolerably efficient resource usage.

EXTERNALITIES AS A BASIS FOR POSSIBLE COLLECTIVE ACTION

The concept of externality provides a basis for considering collective or government action over and beyond that limited to the protection and enforcement of private personal and private property rights. We must, however, recognize that the extent of externalities depends both on the existing structure of private rights and on the existing behavior patterns of individuals. Under differing legal structure and/or differing behavior patterns, externalities would be different. We should, therefore, specify that there exists a given definition of rights to private property and that individuals are assumed to behave largely in accordance with narrowly defined self-interest criteria. Under these restrictions, we can discuss specifically the areas of human interaction where the need for government action is likely to be most severe—bearing in mind that in all cases this will be where the externalities are characterized by large numbers of persons.

External Defense. Perhaps the most obvious function of government over and beyond the mere definition of rights is some provision for defense of the community against external enemies. The logical basis for collective action through political auspices here is equivalent to that discussed with respect to draining the meadow. Each person or family might be expected to undertake some protection privately, but each person exerts an external economy on all others as he does so. Further, and more importantly, the gains from joint action are so large that individual or private actions would clearly be inefficient. There are likely to be major economies of scale present. The case for collective action by the political unit acting for all members of the group seems overwhelming.

This conclusion does not, however, say anything at all about *how* the political action should be taken. The collectivity as such may take on the task of organizing a defense force, and it may finance this, in turn, through taxes levied on members of the community. Alternatively, the state's role may be limited to one that requires all members to participate directly in a commonly organized effort. We shall discuss the selection of alternative methods of organizing collective action later.

Internal Defense and Law Enforcement. The provision of internal defense may also be brought under the externality basis for collective action, although it should be apparent that in a more fundamental sense this function is really an extension of the government's role in defining the legal framework. The enactment of laws, including the definition of personal and property rights, remains relatively empty until and unless *enforcement* is also provided.

Why is law enforcement needed? This can best be answered by posing the circumstances when such a need would be absent. If all members of the community could be relied upon to respect the legally defined rights of other persons at all times, there would arise no demand for internal defense. This suggests, and rightly so, that the need for explicit law enforcement depends directly on the behavior of members of the community. In a society where large numbers of its members voluntarily accept and adhere to the personal and property rights of other members, police protection may be minimal. By contrast, in a society where respect for the legally defined structure of rights is not widely or almost universally held, police protection, along with the accompanying court and penal system, may command a relatively large share of governmental resources. If there were no crime, there would be no need for policemen. There is perhaps no more clear example of the direct relationship between the behavior of individuals and the scope for collective action than that which is offered in this case.

If no collective or government action in the enforcement of personal and property rights should be taken, individuals would, of course, devote private resources to this purpose. Individuals would carry guns, install burglar alarms, and hire private guards. This method of arranging for law enforcement would be highly inefficient, and it is here that the externality argument for collective action can be introduced. If Mr. Smith hires a private guard, he probably imposes an external benefit on his next-door neighbor, Mr. Jones, whose property is also protected. On the other hand, by driving potential criminals from the neighborhood, Mr. Smith may well be imposing an external cost on Mr. Brown, who lives on the other side of town. Clearly, all three persons will find it advantageous to enter into some collective agreement to support the financing of a common police force empowered to protect all members of the community, including potential criminals (from other criminals).

There were reportedly more privately employed policemen in the United States in 1970 than publicly employed policemen. This represented a major inefficiency in resource use, although the rapid increase in private employment of police during the 1960's is readily explained by the increasing crime rates. The political popularity of "law and order" slogans in the late 1960's provides further evidence that collective government action in providing for law enforcement was less than that which the general public demanded.

EXTERNALITIES AND THE ABSENCE OF LAW

In its broadest interpretation, the concept of externality gives us an explanatory principle for possible collective action even when we limit consideration to the enforcement of existing legal rules. The criminal imposes an external cost on the man from whom he steals, and since every member of the community is a potential victim, there is an external benefit to be derived from any action to prevent crime. In imposing the external cost on society, however, the criminal explicitly breaks the law by violating a well-defined right of another man, a right that is supported and enforced by the collectivity.

A distinction must be made between this situation and that in which no law exists. This latter case provides the most common reason for introducing the externality concept into discussion of collective action. Here the action of one person affects the economic position of others without their agreement but there is no explicit violation of law involved.

Environmental Quality. This situation is well illustrated in the familiar set of issues summarized under the rubric "environmental quality," which includes all the problems of congestion and pollution. An individual who dumps garbage in the stream normally breaks no law, but he does impose an external cost on all other potential users of the stream, and without their agreement.

We are saying that the structure of legal rights has not been specified in such a way as to allow all potential interpersonal interactions to be coordinated through simple exchanges.

All issues of environmental quality can be reduced to a model analogous to the simple case of the grazing of the common land. The individual who dumps garbage into the stream has a legal right to do so, and he finds it to be in his interest to do so. He secures a "private good" by polluting; he does not pollute because he deliberately seeks to harm others. In saying that the polluter normally has a legal right to act, we are also saying that those persons damaged have no legal right to prevent him from acting or to assess damages against the action. At the same time, however, the person who pollutes the stream cannot prevent others from acting similarly and in this way reducing the value of the water for his own uses. In terms of excludability, no one possesses the legal right to keep others from using the stream as they desire, including the actions of pollution. This amounts to saying that the property rights in the usage of the stream have not been fully defined. There is no law with respect to the activities of potential users. This points toward one evident solution: property rights may be redefined in such a way as to eliminate the possibility of externality. (This solution will be further discussed at a later point.)

The water pollution example suggests that a basis for some form of collective action may be derived in those cases where externalities emerge within the law. This category includes most of the currently popular issues of air and water pollution, traffic congestion, and even such issues as population control. If the model is extended somewhat more broadly, however, many other existing or proposed collective or government programs can be brought under the environmental-quality rubric. For example, in considering the possible basis for collective support for education, an activity that commands a lion's share of state and local financial resources, we must presume that an increase in the educational attainments of children improves the environmental quality of the community in some inclusive sense. In order to justify general taxation in support of educational finance, it must be presumed that each taxpayer in the community has some positive interest in insuring that the child of each family gets educated to the extent of its abilities and, further, that this positive interest remains even at the margin of voluntary educational purchase that would be sought by the family itself. If such interest does in fact exist (and the empirical evidence suggests that such an interest, or at least the illusion of one, must also be widely shared), it seems clear that it would be extremely difficult for each person to arrange for a simple exchange with each family designed to subsidize the extension of its child's educational intake. The possible failure of the Smith family to secure more education for its child becomes equivalent to the pollution of the stream in the earlier example. Failure to create a "public good" is identical in effect to the creation of a "public bad," and the community is presumably "polluted" by the failure of the Smith family to extend the education of its child.

Precisely the same logical analysis may be applied to the possible need for collective action in the provision of various amenity goods and services, including parks, recreational facilities, preventive health care, and slum clearance.

The relief of poverty

Extending the notions of externality and environmental quality even more broadly, we can also encompass the potential role of collective action in providing for the relief of primary poverty. In one sense, the mere existence of very poor members reduces the overall environmental quality of any community. Any action aimed at removal of this poverty will impose an external benefit on all members of the community. There are clear gains to be made from cooperative or collective efforts to eliminate or at least to reduce poverty.

In more normal economic policy and public finance discussion, however, the possible role of the collectivity in redressing extreme inequalities in incomes and wealth is discussed separately from the more direct support of public goods. To the extent that poverty relief takes the form of direct transfers of money between the taxpayers, via the collectivity, and the recipients, no public sector usage of resources is involved. Precisely because the action here involves redistribution among members of the community, more or less directly, care must be taken to distinguish between government policy that can legitimately be derived from the individual preferences of potentially all of the members of the community and government policy that reflects political exploitation of certain classes by other classes and groups. It is important to recognize that this distinction does not arise directly in any other area of collective or government action. In the possible government policies aimed at improving environmental quality, for example, there will, of course, be differential benefits provided to specific occupational and locational groupings of persons. Such persons and groups will, predictably, be more interested in promoting such policies than those who secure less benefits. Furthermore, some persons may consider the changes in property rights to be equivalent to exploitation. The sense in which all members of the community share both the costs and the gains of government actions for improving the environment becomes quite impossible in pure transfer activity, where funds provided to recipients must be drawn from funds provided by taxpayers. There must be gainers on the one hand and losers on the other. In the context of game theory, income and wealth transfer may take on the properties of a politically determined zero-sum game. By contrast, the provision of public goods of the standard sort will normally be expected to constitute a political positive-sum game.

This is not to suggest that all government programs that embody direct income transfers from taxpayers to recipients must reflect political exploitation. As I indicated at the outset of this section, we may extend the externality concept to include some direct redistributional activity. Those taxpayers who finance the income transfers may secure a net utility gain from the improvement in the well-being of their fellow citizens. To the extent that they do so, the direct income transfers may be based on an economic argument that is in harmony with other collective action. The important point is that it remains extremely difficult to differentiate, in practical politics, between those income transfers that may represent net gains to all parties and those which represent offsetting gains and losses. For the latter there is no economic basis, and the derivation of government policies must be sought in terms of some externally derived ethical rule or norm.

Within the general category of redistribution, a further distinction must be made between direct income and wealth transfers and transfers in kind. The poor may be provided with money income in the former and with food stamps or other claims to real goods in the latter. To the extent that the utility levels of the recipients are considered, the transfers of generalized purchasing power are more efficient. When the preferences of the taxpaying members of the community are also taken into account, however, the transfer of income in kind may secure more comprehensive support. Taxpayers may be interested in supporting poverty relief not so much for the elimination of poverty as such but, rather, for the elimination of the overt manifestations of such poverty—for example, substandard housing and starving children. On this basis, such taxpayers may lend support to transfers in kind while opposing transfers of income. Much of the argument concerning the negative income tax as a replacement for other welfare programs has neglected this important distinction.

THE CONTROL OF MONOPOLY

As with the case of poverty relief, a broad interpretation of the externality concept would allow us to derive a logical basis for collective or government action aimed at controlling monopolies and improving the competitiveness of the economy. It is best not to stretch our concepts too far, however, and we shall discuss the enforcement of competition and the regulation of monopoly as a separate area for possible government intervention in the exchange economy. Earlier we examined the emergence of the institutions of a market or exchange economy in an idealized laissez-faire setting where the government role is limited to establishing and enforcing legal rules concerning property and personal rights. These exchange institutions will work efficiently, however, only while the pressures of actual or potential competition remain strong. So long as the individual buyer is confronted with competing sellers, existing or potential, all of whom are free to seek out his custom, he is insured against undue exploitation. The same point holds for the other side of exchange: the individual seller must be faced with competing buyers, existing or potential, if exploitation is to be avoided.

In most sectors of the economy, the existence of competitive pressures can be depended on to secure tolerable efficiency. There may be a role for government action in fostering more vigorous competition through antitrust laws, in prohibiting certain types of collusion, and so on. Other government activities may contribute positively toward improving market performance. There is also scope for such activities as the provision of information about market alternatives.

For some sectors of the economy, the existence of what have been called "natural monopolies" reduces the scope of competitive pressure considerably and suggests the possible introduction of some form of collective control. A natural monopoly is said to exist when the advantages of large-scale production are such that relative to the market demand that is faced only one (or a few) firms can reach a position for lowest-cost operation. If average costs fall throughout the range of output that may be potentially demanded by the whole market, it is evident that a single firm can produce more efficiently (at lower cost) than any one of several smaller firms that might be required to insure competitive effectiveness.

The single firm can produce most efficiently, but it can also use its monopoly position to charge higher-than-competitive prices. When this situation exists, a role for collective action may be indicated. There are several ways in which such control may be exercised, at least in theory. Those that are most familiar in the United States involve attempts to regulate the pricing of natural monopoly products and services (the public utilities) through regulatory commissions or boards. At the national government level, the Interstate Commerce Commission, the Federal Power Commission, the Federal Communication Commission, and the Civil Aeronautics Board derive their economic foundations at least in part from the natural monopoly control that may be needed in the industries that they regulate. Most state governments also have one or more regulatory commissions or boards. At the local level, an alternative method of control is often employed; such public utilities as the systems of water distribution, sewage disposal, and, in some cases, electricity distribution are organized as government enterprises. European countries rely more heavily on this method than the United States.

THE MONETARY FRAMEWORK

We shall make no attempt to catalogue all of the specific activities which might be collectivized in modern society, even of those that might find some logical bases in economic analysis. (Specific discussion of many of these will be found in other studies in this series.) Up to this point, we have presented some of the broad categories of potential collective action; many of the varied activities of governments can be placed within these. In its broadest sense, all of the economic bases for collective action stem from the public good concept, which translates, in its turn, into the externality relationship. The first of the categories mentioned included the provision of an overall

legal framework, that set of rules and institutions within which privately acting individuals and groups can carry through contractual arrangements of
many types.

If this category is made inclusive, it may encompass the collective maintenance of a monetary framework that will insure reasonable stability along
with adequate growth in the total economy. These broad macroeconomic
objectives can be treated as public goods, and individual demands for these
goods can be examined in the same way as the demands for other collectively
provided goods and services. Economists do not normally follow this path,
however, and the attainment of these macroeconomic objectives tends to be
discussed as a separate sphere of government activity, the demand for which
is often wholly divorced from the desires of citizens. Furthermore, economists often discuss these objectives as if government responsibilities in this
area have only come to be recognized since the depression of the 1930's.

The depression, along with the subsequent inflations, should serve as a
continuing reminder that in practice collective action in this sphere has been
far from satisfactory. Nonetheless, government's role in providing a suitable
monetary framework has long been acknowledged. Some economists would
suggest that the collectivity's responsibility in achieving macroeconomic objectives goes beyond the limitations imposed by the operation and maintenance of a monetary framework. The argument here depends in large part
on what is meant by a suitable monetary framework, and there will also be
disagreement on the specific structural and policy steps that are required to
implement a genuine monetary constitution. The details of such controversies cannot be summarized here. We should emphasize only that, if desired,
a logical basis for collective action in the macroeconomic sphere can be
found in the concepts of externality and public goods.

The Political Economy of Collective Action

Our general discussion of the economic bases for possible collective or political action showed that for the activities falling within certain categories
individuals can expect to secure benefits from ideally organized joint action. Fully efficient collective organization could be expected to produce results that are more desirable, to all members of the community, than the
alternative that might be predicted under a regime of wholly voluntary be-

havior. In a regime of genuine anarchy, as we noted, life would be "nasty, brutish, and short" so long as individuals behaved in accordance with narrow self-interest. Interaction is required to move out of this dilemma, and this, in its turn, requires the establishment of and adherence to social rules, including the joint provision of collective goods and services. It will be useful to discuss briefly alternative methods or means of securing these desired results.

TOWARD SOCIAL BETTERMENT: BEHAVIORAL REFORM

The plausible presumption that persons behave largely in accordance with their own interests need not imply that all persons act selfishly in all of their dealings with their fellows. The standard behavioral model for economic theory suggests only that there does exist a difference, a possible conflict, between the benefits to the acting party and the benefits to others in the community. In the simplest possible example, the standard economic model assumes that I shall secure more benefit from the consumption of an apple if I eat it than if you do. Unless some such presumption is made and plugged into the analytical model, there could be no such thing as an externality, at least in any conceptually observable sense of the term. If any other man's enjoyment of the stream is valued equally with his own enjoyment, the man who dumps the garbage is not really imposing an external cost on others. He is, instead, internalizing all of the costs through his own suffering for his fellow men. At the same time, his fellows are internalizing the benefits secured by the polluter; they treat these as their own. Under these conditions, rational private or individual behavior should produce efficient results, despite the presence of the apparent large-number externalities.

This immediately suggests that one way of securing collectively desired results when complex exchange relationships are required lies in some modification of the behavior patterns of individuals. Economists tend to assume that behavior is immutable, but the role of ethical standards in promoting social cooperation should not be overlooked. In one sense, both Christian and Kantian ethics can be interpreted as attempts to secure social harmony (to produce "public goods") through changing the behavior of ordinary men rather than through the introduction of collectively imposed and coercive rules.

Consider, once again, the pollution example. If acting individuals and managers of firms can be induced to take the interests of others into account, to treat others as themselves or to follow some version of the Kantian generalization principle, pollution would not tend to extend beyond socially efficient limits. Empirical evidence suggests that this voluntary method of control has not been effective, but we must admit that the propaganda campaigns against litterbugs have probably had significant influences on behavior. If individuals could be led to act out of genuine love for their neighbor, as the Christian ethic commands, or to act out of mutual self-respect, as the Kantian ethic dictates, some of those activities which might otherwise require government or political provision or prohibition would be properly extended through voluntary actions.

This is not to suggest that an ethical revolution, even if this were within the realm of reality, would convert genuine anarchy into a viable social system. Men would still disagree on what "goods" are to be provided, and the most authoritarian personalities are often those with a complete absence of narrow self-interest. The more limited point is that behavioral adjustments in the direction of mutual tolerance can reduce the pressures toward and the need for collective intervention in society. Unfortunately, the empirical evidence in 1971 suggests behavioral shifts in the opposing direction. As men come to be less and less tolerant of the interests of others, the basis is laid for an extension of coercive action by the collectivity. If men will not voluntarily abide by the rules for social interaction, they must, perforce, be made to adhere to such rules by external power of the collectivity. There is no way in which this elementary principle of social balance can be refuted.

TOWARD SOCIAL BETTERMENT: REDEFINITION OF PROPERTY RIGHTS

Economists normally leave detailed discussion of ethics to other scholars. The models of economic theory and policy incorporate the behavior of men who act from self-interest, at least in some average or representative sense. Even with this restriction, however, there are two distinct routes toward securing collectively desired results. As we noted earlier, the need for collective action depends directly on the way in which the law defines private property rights. If these rights are carefully and specifically delineated, the self-interest of individuals can be relied upon to produce socially desired results. This was the great discovery of the eighteenth century, and it provided the philosophical basis for the whole laissez-faire movement. As with other great movements in history, the laissez-faire advocates tended to overreach themselves and to neglect the complex exchange relationships that would not be effectively consummated under unrestrained freedom of contract.

It remains nonetheless true that, for many of the externality problems, where complex and large-number exchanges would seem to be required for any effective solution, a redefinition of private property rights could resolve the issue without direct and continuing collective action. In the familiar pollution example, as we suggested earlier, the polluter presumably has the "right" to dump garbage in the stream, but he has no "right" to exclude others from doing likewise. In a real sense, the whole problem arises because no one "owns" the stream. If property rights could be so defined as to place commonly owned and commonly used resources in private hands, freedom of contract could accomplish much of the results that collective action might otherwise seek to secure. If the stream were "owned" in the sense that the would-be polluter were required to pay for the damages that his action produces, contractual arrangements between the owner and the polluter might secure efficient results.

Some of the modern scholars who have been most concerned about the deterioration in the quality of the environment call for a much more comprehensive delineation of private property rights. E. J. Mishan in particular has proposed that individuals be granted a whole set of "amenity rights," by which he apparently means rights to such things as clean air, clean water, freedom from noise, and other amenities. Much can be done in this direction, but the possibilities should not be overemphasized. It is precisely in those areas where private property rights have proven to be difficult to define that the familiar basis for more specific collective action emerges. It is exceedingly difficult, in practice, to redefine private property rights to air, sound waves, or water courses so that large-number externality problems will be eliminated. This approach becomes even less suitable in those cases where external economies rather than diseconomies are encountered. How could private property rights be rearranged to insure that individuals would, voluntarily, provide for the socially desired quantity of external and internal defense, education, preventive health care, fire protection, and so on?

COLLECTIVE CONSTRAINTS ON PRIVATE CHOICES: A PARTIAL REDEFINITION OF PROPERTY RIGHTS

For the reasons noted, it may be impossible to redefine private property rights in such a manner that voluntary market exchanges can be expected to generate fully satisfactory solutions. Some of the more important current issues of social policy may, however, be approached through a partial redefinition of property rights. Water pollution is a good example. Although it may prove impossible to define precisely the private rights to waterways in such a way that the market would yield desired results, there may nonetheless be no reason to go to the opposite extreme and require explicit collective action. Property rights could be redefined so as to impose charges on those individuals and firms that are observed to impose external costs on the public at large. With stream pollution, effluent charges could be based roughly on the estimate of social damage caused. Under this general approach, which has received much attention since the early 1960's, the potential polluter retains the "right" to dump effluents in the stream, but it is now available to him at a higher cost. He will, as a result, discharge less into the stream. His conditions of choice are modified, and if the charges are properly assessed, he may be led by his own self-interest to further the social interest. This approach can be applied to several of the environmental-quality issues, and it may incorporate bribes or payments to those who generate external benefits as well as charges on those who impose external costs.

EXPLICIT COLLECTIVE ACTION

In complex social interactions of many sorts, we must acknowledge that neither behavioral reform nor changes in the structure of private property rights, including the use of bribes and charges, can be expected to accomplish the desired results. This suggests that in such cases more explicit collective action may be required. And collective action must take a governmental or political form, even if the conceptual bases for such action may suggest general consensus. It is relatively easy to show that all members of the relevant community may, conceptually, be made better off by collective action in the face of a large-number externality. Hume's drainage of the meadow in the village is an example. Although all residents of the village presumably may benefit from the drainage scheme, different persons may secure differing value improvements, depending on their locations and on their own preferences. The criterion for social improvement that emerges from modern welfare economics, called the Pareto criterion, is the conceptual possibility of improving the well-being of all members of the group, or at least improving the well-being of some members while harming none of the others. If this criterion is met, then voluntary cooperative action would seem to be indicated. As we have previously noted, however, the transactions-costs barrier may prevent such action in those cases where large numbers of potential beneficiaries are involved. Privately, individuals who are potential beneficiaries may find it advantageous to spend resources seeking strategic positions in the cooperative bargain that would have to be struck. As a result, action that is in the genuine interest of all parties may be long delayed and possibly not ever accomplished. Disputes over the distribution of the gains—the "free-rider" problem again—may prevent the gains from being realized.

Collective Decision Rules. In recognition of this, the community may agree on the organization of a governmental or political unit, and coercive powers may be granted to this unit in some constitutional process. Once individuals find themselves members of such a unit, they must abide by the decisions it imposes on them. The coerciveness of any government or political structure reduces the relative efficiency of collective action by comparison with individual freedom of contract that characterizes the market exchange process. The outcomes produced under governmental process depend directly on the rules through which collective decisions are made. It should be evident that collectivization of an activity may prove highly desirable under one set of decision rules and highly undesirable under another. For example, if most persons feel that the national government is subject to genuine popular control, they may consider a national (as opposed to a local) police force beneficial. On the other hand, these same persons would probably oppose any outlay for a national police force if the federal government should be controlled by a dictator.

Extending our meadow drainage example, the effect of collective decision rules on the final positions of separate members of the community may be easily understood. Suppose that there are nine residents of the village, and that the total cost of the drainage project is $900. Suppose further that each person is subjected to a pro rata or equal share in the total tax, and that collective decisions in the village are reached by simple majority voting rules. Assume now that the benefits from the drainage project are as shown in table 1. It is clear that the total benefits from the drainage project exceed the total costs. It is equally clear that a majority of the citizens of the village (individuals 1 through 5) would vote in favor of the project, given the tax system that we have assumed to be in existence. Note, however, that the minority which opposes the project (individuals 6 through 9) will actually be harmed by the collective action. A more revealing example is shown in table 2: note that the total benefits in this case sum to less than the total costs but that the project would still be approved by a majority of the citizens of the village.

The extremely simplified examples presented in tables 1 and 2 reveal much about potential collective action. Table 1 suggests that even for those projects that yield higher total benefits than they cost there is no guarantee that all members of the group will find their own positions improved as a result of

Table 1

Individual		Value of Benefit		Tax Cost		Net
1		$ 200		$100		$100
2		200		100		100
3		200		100		100
4		200		100		100
5		200		100		100
6		50		100	(−)	50
7		50		100	(−)	50
8		50		100	(−)	50
9		50		100	(−)	50
	Total	$1,200	Total	$900		

Table 2

Individual	Value of Benefit	Tax Cost		Net
1	$110	$100		$10
2	110	100		10
3	110	100		10
4	110	100		10
5	110	100		10
6	50	100	(−)	50
7	50	100	(−)	50
8	50	100	(−)	50
9	50	100	(−)	50
Total	$750	Total	$900	

collective action. Table 2 suggests that under the decision rule and tax structure postulated collective projects may be undertaken that cost more in total than the benefits they provide.

These results depend, of course, on the particular assumptions of the example. If the collective decision rule requires a larger-than-majority approval, neither project could be approved unless the tax system is modified. If the tax system is modified so as to allow for a closer relationship between tax costs and individual demands, the project in table 1 could be approved by all members of the group.

Political Externalities. The simple analysis of collective action under majority voting is important largely because it draws attention to the necessity of examining collective action as an alternative to market process. The bases for some interference with the workings of the laissez-faire economy were discussed earlier. Economists have often referred to this sort of analysis as that of "market failure." This tends to be misleading terminology, however, until and unless the market organizational alternative is compared with its collective counterpart. The "failure" of markets to produce efficient results in the face of large-number externalities does not, in and of itself, justify explicit collective action. Since collective action also involves externalities of a similar sort, the problem becomes one of comparing two second-best organizational arrangements.

The inherent externality that is present in political decision making can be seen quite readily from the simple examples presented above. Referring again to table 1, when an individual member of the majority (individuals 1 through 5) votes in favor of the drainage project, he is participating in a decision that imposes a net cost of $50 on each person in the minority. This is fully analogous to the action of the polluter who in dumping garbage in the stream imposes external costs on other users. The transfer of activities that exhibit externalities in the private or market sector to the collective or public sector changes the form of the externality relationship. It does not eliminate externalities.

The Burden of Bureaucracy. Still another and quite different aspect of collective action further reduces the comparative efficiency of this organizational alternative. Our simple examples have implicitly assumed that once a collective decision is made, the outcome will be directly produced. Once the village majority made its decision to drain the meadow, the project could presumably be completed without delay. When we look at actual governmental processes, however, we recognize that there is a major barrier between collective decision and final collective or government action. We may summarize this barrier under the term *bureaucracy,* defined as the whole institutional structure through which political or government decisions, once made, are carried out or implemented. Some of the problems appear immediately when this definition itself is examined critically. Despite a general decision, the particulars of any policy are not made until the operation of the bureaucracy takes place.

Let us suppose that the United States Congress, along with the executive branch, decides that further federal action is required in water pollution. Legislation is enacted, and funds are appropriated. How are these funds normally expended? Either an existing federal agency or a new agency will be charged with the tasks of carrying out the legislation and spending the funds. In the process, individual decision makers within the bureaucratic structure often possess wide discretionary powers to lay down rules of procedure, allocate the funds among competing demands, or develop standards for performance. In each case, the bureaucrat who makes the decision will be motivated to some extent by his own private costs and private benefits rather than those of the Congress or those which might be genuinely defined as the public interest. Bureaucrats are themselves no different from anyone else, and they will act so as to preserve and to advance their own career prospects. Hence, unless these prospects are tied directly to the public interest, the inherent inefficiency in bureaucratic process will tend to dissipate, at least to some degree, almost any collective effort to achieve social betterment. It is largely the burden of bureaucracy that insures the continuation of collective-action programs long after they have ceased to be required or needed. For example, the Interstate Commerce Commission still exists in 1971, although the plausible basis (the natural monopoly position of railroads) upon which it was created in the late nineteenth century no longer exists. Surely this is partly because of the self-interest of those bureaucrats employed by the Commission. For the same reason, most agencies, bureaus, and departments tend to be larger than necessary for the tasks assigned to them. The power, prestige, and general emoluments of a government administrator tend to be directly related to the size of the working force he supervises and the budget he dispenses.

Financing versus Operation. The burden of bureaucracy arises largely in those cases where governments attempt directly to operate systems for collective provision of goods and services. Recognition of this burden, along with other factors, points toward the necessity of distinguishing between direct government operation of activities and government financial support of activities. When the market economy is observed to generate large-number externalities of significance, when collective action is considered to be indicated, there should be no implication that direct government operation of the activities in question should take place. Education provides perhaps the best example of this distinction: although it is widely accepted that there is some collective interest in insuring that all children receive adequate education, this does not at all imply that this education should be provided directly through governmentally operated school systems. The collective interest can be secured by financial support for the private purchase of education by families. In recent years much attention has been paid to the partial replacement of public school systems by schemes under which parents of school children will be provided directly with vouchers that might be spent only on the purchase of educational services.

The advantage of limiting government action to financing lies in its reduction of the burden of bureaucracy. Equipped with education vouchers which may be used in any school meeting public standards, parents may call on the competitive forces of the market to insure at least tolerable efficiency in generating final product. The point here can be dramatized by asking the simple question: who is likely to try harder to educate his pupils, the instructor or school administrator who has a tenure position in a monopolistic public school system, or the instructor or school administrator employed in a privately organized school that competes with many other similar institutions for pupils?

COMPETITION IN COLLECTIVE ACTION: POLITICAL DECENTRALIZATION

When the political economy of collective action is considered, the possible "failures" of governmental process appear. Recognizing the limits of the market or exchange economy in securing desired results in the face of large-number externality relationships, we seem to be left with trying to choose between the best of two inefficient alternatives. The market economy will not generate the results that are desired, and neither will governments when the tasks are turned over to them. Are there alternative means of achieving desired results?

One important alternative has been ignored to this point. We know that the efficiency that characterizes market process is achieved largely through the working of competition between buyers and sellers. This suggests that one means of securing more efficient collective action might lie in the introduction of competition. Monopoly in collective or governmental operation has results similar to those in the private economy. It allows taxpayers and beneficiaries to be exploited. Competition may be introduced, even if indirectly, if individuals are allowed to choose among several political systems. To some extent, this result is accomplished by the freedom of individual migration among government units. If individuals are free to choose which of several communities they may join, the exploitation potential of any one community is limited. This suggests, of course, that there is a strong efficiency argument for encouraging collective action at the decentralized or local level in an economy, as opposed to collective action at the federal or central level.

The efficiency gains to be secured from retaining activities at the local level should not be overemphasized. "Voting with their feet" is a method through which individuals may keep government units efficient, but it is indirect and subject to significant thresholds of reaction and response. Furthermore, the efficiency aspects of decentralized action may be offset by the spillover externalities that remain among separate local units. For certain types of collective goods and services, local jurisdictions are surely the most practical supplying and financing units. For other collective functions, central government administration and finance is inescapable. Even where intergovernmental competition cannot be relied on as a means of improving the efficiency of bureaucratic operation, however, there may be a range for the introduction of intragovernment competition among separate bureaucratic units. This proposal has been made by William Niskanen but, to my knowledge, has not been put into practice in any government.

Effective decentralization in the actual provision of collective goods and services may be achieved without the accompaniment of financial decentralization. The efficiency-promoting properties are partially offset by the break between taxing and spending responsibility here, but the prospects for this sort of decentralization are much more real. Various proposals for federal revenue-sharing and bloc grants were made in the late 1960's, and enactment on a limited scale seems likely to take place in the early 1970's. Under these schemes, state and local units of government would be provided with some shares in the federal government's tax collections. These funds would relieve the burden on local taxpayers and, more importantly, allow the state and local units to expand the provision of certain goods and services that might otherwise be shifted to direct federal supervision and control.

Drawing the Line

It should not be surprising that no hard and fast conclusions emerge from either our general discussion of the bases for possible collective action or our analysis of some of the problems that are necessarily encountered when action is taken collectively rather than privately. No attempt has been made to lay out an agenda for political or government action. Perhaps the most important point was the irrelevance of any such agenda that is derived independent of the form of the governing process itself. That is to say, the dividing line between the private and the public sectors of the economy must be influenced by the sort of collective decision making that is predicted to take place.

In one sense, the general discussion may be considered as a provisional shopping list, analogous to that carried around in her mind by the housewife in the furniture store. Some items that she possesses seem a bit out-of-date and rundown, but she need not purchase replacements unless she is convinced that these will be a net improvement over what she has. The exchange process, the market economy, does supply some of most goods and services, provided that the collectivity fulfills its minimal role in defining and enforcing a set of legal rules. The question about public or government extension of activity is always one of comparison. There are economic arguments which indicate that the exchange economy falters when large-number externality relationships exist, when complex exchanges are required for genuine social betterment. But equally convincing economic arguments suggest the limits on the efficiency of potential collective alternatives to market arrangements.

Regardless of one's ideological predispositions, there is no escape from the fact that there are no principles which dictate the most efficient means of organizing the provision of particular goods and services. The line between the public or collective sector and the private or market sector must always be settled on a case-by-case, pragmatic evaluation. In a setting where the extent of collectivization is sharply limited, or where the possibility of individual shifts to alternative governments are not unduly costly, the inefficiencies of market provision can be seriously considered as legitimate bases for some sort of collective action. By contrast, in a setting where collectivization is already extensive, and/or where individuals can shift to alternative collectivities only at extremely high personal sacrifice, the tolerance limits for market inefficiencies may be wide indeed.

We know that over the last century the range of collective action has been gradually expanded in most countries. There is no way of determining whether or not this trend has reached its apogee or when it may be reversed. We do not, as individual members of a collectivity, participate in such aggregate decisions. It is useful to recognize this. The relative size of the public sector and the private sector in a national economy depends on the day-by-day, year-by-year decisions to expand this or that collective activity. Small changes cumulate to large ones if the direction remains the same.

BIBLIOGRAPHY

William J. Baumol, *Welfare Economics and the Theory of the State,* rev. ed. Harvard University Press, 1965.

James M. Buchanan, *The Demand and Supply of Public Goods.* Rand McNally, 1968.

James M. Buchanan and Gordon Tullock, *The Calculus of Consent.* University of Michigan Press, 1962.

F. A. Hayek, *The Constitution of Liberty.* University of Chicago Press, 1960.

Wilhelm von Humboldt, *The Limits of State Action.* Cambridge University Press, 1969.

E. J. Mishan, *The Costs of Economic Growth.* Staples Press, 1967.

William A. Niskanen, *Bureaucracy and Representative Government.* Aldine-Atherton, 1971.

Mancur Olson, *The Logic of Collective Action.* Harvard University Press, 1965.

Gordon Tullock, *The Politics of Bureaucracy.* Public Affairs Press, 1965.

The Evaluation of Public Services

Francesco Forte and James M. Buchanan

Specialists in the construction and use of national income and product accounts have been unable to agree upon the appropriate evaluation of public or governmental goods and services. In a recent conference, this problem was said to represent "the chief and perhaps the only really serious point of disagreement" among these specialists, and the lines of communication among the adversaries were said to be "notoriously defective."[1] Despite the general recognition that the issues are conceptual in nature, the fact that specialists in national accounting have been so closely associated with instrumental problems of measurement per se may have served to prevent the clarification that seems so obviously to be required. Non-specialists may be able to contribute toward such a clarification because of their very detachment from the complexities of statistical estimation.[2]

Although generalizations concerning the two sides of any debate are difficult to support, the fundamental cleavage in this particular case seems to be based on the fact that the adversaries are approaching the whole issue of

From *Journal of Political Economy* 69 (April 1961): 107–21. Copyright 1961 by The University of Chicago. All rights reserved. Reprinted by permission of the publisher, the University of Chicago Press.

1. National Bureau of Economic Research, Conference on Research in Income and Wealth, *A Critique of the United States Income and Product Accounts: Studies in Income and Wealth,* 22 (New York: National Bureau of Economic Research, 1958), 17, 304.

2. R. A. Musgrave's recently published treatment may be taken as a case in point. His analysis has advanced the state of the debate, but controversial issues remain, and additional clarification of some of the conceptual problems seems possible; see R. A. Musgrave, *The Theory of Public Finance* (New York: McGraw-Hill Book Co., 1959), chap. 9.

measurement with two separate purposes or goals in mind. National income or national product can, on the one hand, be taken to reflect an evaluation of *existing* output for the purpose of making comparisons of "welfare" among communities and through time. On the other hand, national income or product can be taken to measure the value of *potential* output that might be produced with existing inputs of resources. In either case, consistent procedures for measurement can be developed, but only after the purpose is made definite. The distinction between these two approaches will, we hope, be made clear in what follows.

If the circular-flow conception of the economic process is accepted, income payments received by factor owners must equal the value of total output produced. This dual manner of conceiving national income or product has served to introduce an important element of confusion into national accounting, a confusion that directly affects the evaluation of public services. Income, as received by factor owners, has been measured at factor costs, whereas output or product has been measured at market prices. Despite these two distinctly different means of valuation, the attempt has been made to force the aggregative results into the equality suggested by the circular-flow identity. There seems to have been some failure to recognize that costs do not measure the same thing as do market prices. Costs provide a measure of the market value of resources in *alternative* uses; only indirectly do cost values provide some measure of the value of resources in existing uses. And there is no reason why a measure of national income at genuine factor costs need be equal to national product at market prices. The circular-flow identity can be assured only if all residual rents are included in costs. But this procedure makes the whole distinction between market prices and factor costs meaningless. As Bowman and Easterlin point out, consistent evaluation at cost *or* at market price can restore the definitional identity between the two sides of the account.[3]

The particular discussion concerning the evaluation of the public services does not seem wholly to have escaped from the confusion and the ambiguities of the diamond-water paradox. Participants have not consistently em-

---

3. R. T. Bowman and R. A. Easterlin, "The Income Side: Some Theoretical Aspects," in *Critique of United States Income and Product Account,* 170. Some of the inconsistencies that arise from the use of the factor-costs approach have been pointed out by Douglas Dosser in his unpublished paper, "The Status of National Income at Factor Costs."

bodied in their measurement proposals adequate recognition that economic values for output are set at the margins and that a market price always reflects the purchasers' evaluation of a little more or a little less of a good or service rather than any evaluation of a total quantity. Prices multiplied by quantities and summed over all goods and services provide an evaluation of the *particular* composition or output mix that is purchased and nothing more.

The fact that both sides in the debate have chosen to discuss the evaluation of public services within an overly restricted frame of reference has prevented progress toward a solution. First of all, discussion has been centered on the proper treatment of those goods and services, provided collectively, that serve as *intermediate* products or inputs to private business firms or upon those governmental activities that supply environmental or framework services for the private production process. If an attempt had been made to extend the analysis to the evaluation of public services generally, a more satisfactory meeting of minds, if not an agreed-upon solution, might have been achieved. A second weakness has been the widespread reliance on the application of the so-called invariance test. Argument has proceeded on the assumption that the net product of the economy should not be changed by the shift of an activity from the private to the public sector, or vice versa. However, when it is recognized that the institutional shift of an activity from private production, which embodies a positive output price, to public production, if this embodies free provision of the service in question, must generate some reallocation of economic resources, the change in the output mix and its distribution must be expected to involve some change in the real value of net output. The whole problem of appropriate quantity weighting for deflating money measures of output to obtain real values is introduced.

In Sections II and III we shall examine critically the two opposing positions: first, that taken by the Department of Commerce in its actual measurement procedures and stoutly defended by departmental spokesmen and, second, that taken by Professor Simon Kuznets and his followers. We shall demonstrate that neither of these positions is fully satisfactory. In Section IV we shall present an alternative proposal that is valid for the evaluation of both intermediate and final public services. Finally, in Section V, we shall try to show that the Department of Commerce position can be rationalized more readily if we shift the purpose from that of measuring the value placed on existing output to that of measuring the potential output value that might be produced from existing resource inputs.

II

The Department of Commerce, in estimating the total value for net national product, adds the cost value of all governmentally provided goods and services (except for those that are directly priced) to the values for final output of privately produced goods and services. This practice has been subjected to a long and continuing criticism. The method has been said to be based on the assumption that all public goods are equivalent to final products for consumers. The spokesmen for the Department have responded by stating that the relevant distinction, for the public sector of output, is not that between intermediate and final goods; it is, instead, whether or not the goods are "resold" through ordinary market channels. If the goods provided by government are not resold (that is, if they do not again enter the market process), they are freely consumed and must be considered, in this sense, as final goods and services. Departmental spokesmen have illustrated this position with reference to the now familiar example of free flour. If the government should provide free flour to all bakers, the bread subsequently produced would be sold to consumers at prices which *do not* include a cost-price for flour. The consumer would receive the value of this flour free of direct charge. The baking firms would serve only to "transmit" this final good to consumers. Therefore, every publicly provided good or service that is not directly priced, that is provided free, becomes final. And, since the acknowledged final goods and services received by individuals from government are to be included in estimates of national product, there is no reason why the so-called intermediate goods and services should be treated differently.

This analysis seems unsatisfactory, but not primarily for the reasons advanced by its opponents. The value of goods sold in the market, when computed at market prices, is the value placed upon them by purchasers *at the margin*. What is the value at the margin for public goods and services that are provided to purchasers free of direct charge?

At the risk of oversimplification, we propose to examine the evaluation of intermediate goods and services supplied by government in carefully restricted analytical models. For the time being, we shall assume a fully competitive economy. Resources are assumed freely mobile as among alternative employment opportunities; no specialized resources exist, and all production is carried out under conditions of constant returns. Now let us assume that, through an international agreement with another country, the government purchases a technological advisory service affecting a particular industry and embodying a cost-reducing innovation. It then makes this service freely available to the firms in the domestic industry. This is clearly an *intermediate* service provided by government. Under the circumstances described, the mechanism of competitive adjustment will insure that more resources enter the industry affected. Prices of output to consumers will fall by the full value of the freely provided service. At the new industry and firm equilibriums, the product price will be fully exhausted by marginal productivity payments to *priced* resource inputs. No imputable value for the free technical service will remain in the price of final output.

Intuitively, this analysis seems consistent with the position of the Department of Commerce. The firms in the industry act merely as "transactors" that pass along the free service to final consumers. The departmental spokesmen are in error, however, in that they reach wrong conclusions from a position that can be made internally consistent. They have been quite correct in emphasizing that the values of freely provided intermediate products *do not show up* in final product prices under the competitive adjustment model *because they are free.* But this also suggests that precisely because the services are free they are not positively valued by users at the relevant margins. The free provision of services by government, under the conditions of this model, guarantees that resources will be adjusted in such a manner that the services will be treated *as if* they were, in fact, "free" in the broader, zero-cost sense. And, since "free" goods have no economic value, they should not be counted in estimates for national output. The fact that the government actually uses up resources in acquiring these services and, in order to finance this acquisition, levies charges on the general taxpayer is not relevant at all. For purposes of measuring national output at market values, these services must be treated in the same way that any genuinely free good, say air, is treated.

On one point the Department of Commerce spokesmen are quite correct: that there are no reasons for treating the intermediate services provided by government any differently from final services. The analysis above can be applied without change to freely provided final goods and services. We may demonstrate this by the introduction of a simple illustration. Let us assume that a municipality provides water to residential consumers free of direct charge and that it places no restrictions upon the amount of water that each consumer may use. Despite the fact that this water will cost something in resources and that this cost will be distributed among individual citizens through the tax system, the utilization of water in the community will proceed *as if* it were genuinely *free* in all respects. The individual consumer will use water to the point at which the marginal utility becomes zero, since there will be no marginal price connected with his own decision to use a little more or a little less. It is relatively easy to see that, under circumstances such as these, the individual will place no marginal value on the water provided by the municipality. Water will be treated in precisely the same way that a genuinely costless (free) good is treated. To impute a value to water by measuring it at some cost-price for purposes of including this value in estimates of community output would amount to measuring a part of "consumers' surplus," something that is not done for other goods and services. Since the individual will use the freely available water to such an extent that one unit has no value, the total valuation of water would be zero.

These conclusions suggest that both intermediate and final goods and services supplied by government without charge should be excluded from estimates of national output at market values insofar as they are made available to consumers (individuals or firms) in unlimited quantities. But there remains the question concerning those intermediate or final goods and services provided by government without direct charge to consumers but in limited amounts. In this case, despite the fact that the goods or services are not directly priced, a positive marginal utility may exist in any final equilibrium. Let us continue, for now, to assume a fully competitive economy with resources freely mobile among separate employments and all production carried out at constant returns.

First we may examine a model in which a limited quantity of a public good is made available; this good is known to generate differential effects on the separate sectors of the economy but is made freely available to all firms that might potentially employ it.[4] Here we may rely on the famous Pigou-

---

4. Samuelson has provided a rigorous definition for a purely collective good, although he discusses collective consumption goods only; see Paul A. Samuelson, "The Pure The-

Knight "narrow but good road" for all illustrations.[5] Competition among the using firms will act so as to increase the non-collective inputs in the affected industry. The market price charged to consumers will fall to some extent, but not by the full amount of the costs of the collective input. This stems from the fact that, relatively, too many private resources will be drawn into the industry for efficient operation. At a final equilibrium, output price in the industry will be barely sufficient to pay for the services of the privately supplied resource inputs employed. No part of the input price can be imputed to the publicly supplied input that is made available without charge. The total production of the industry differentially affected will, of course, be larger after the instrumental public good is made available than before. The marginal value of this production will be smaller than before, and this value will be fully exhausted in meeting marginal productivity payments to priced resource inputs. The publicly supplied input has no marginal value. The only means of including the value of this publicly supplied input in estimates of national output is to include the value of the larger private production in differentially affected industries at the new prices. This is accomplished, of course, simply by counting the whole value of private output at market prices.

Let us now examine a different model. Return to our former example and assume that, instead of making water available without charge in unlimited quantities, the municipality provides each resident with a definite quantity of water. Assume further that the freely provided public water amounts to less than the average residential use in the case of unlimited availability. Under these circumstances water will, of course, have some positive marginal utility to the average or the representative consumer. If water rights to this

---

ory of Public Expenditure," *Review of Economics and Statistics,* 36 (November, 1954), 386–89. J. Margolis has shown that the purely collective-good case of Samuelson is a limiting case ("A Comment on the Theory of Public Expenditure," *Review of Economics and Statistics,* 37 [August, 1955], 347–49). Even services like external defense do have usually differential effects on separate sectors of the economy.

5. A. C. Pigou, *The Economics of Welfare* (1st ed.; London: Macmillan & Co., 1926), 196; F. H. Knight, "Fallacies in the Interpretation of Social Costs," *Quarterly Journal of Economics,* 38 (August, 1924), 582–606, reprinted in pp. 217–36 of *Ethics of Competition* (London: George Allen & Unwin, 1935). Note that the road case may be used to study both "intermediate" and "final" public goods, because roads are used both for purposes of production and for final consumption.

limited quantity are allowed to be marketed freely among separate individuals, a price will come to be established for these rights. Note, however, that this valuation, which should be included in output estimates, will be wholly divorced from the costs of supplying the water to the municipality. These prices for water rights will depend on the amount of water that is made available freely by the municipality and on the marginal evaluation of water by the citizens. In this case, it seems clear that a cost valuation for the municipally supplied water should not be added to the market valuation of water rights. Only the latter should be included in national output estimates. If the rights to free water are not marketable, however, this positive utility will not be represented in a market value. The evaluation of water in national output should, however, be wholly divorced from the average cost or the marginal cost of providing this free public good.

Let us now consider an intermediate good or service that is made available without direct charge, that does generate some differential effects among the separate industries, and that is not freely accessible to all potential users. We may think of the government making some good available to all firms in a perfectly competitive industry but rationing the limited quantity among the firms. Water for irrigation purposes might be the example. In this case, the provision of the free inputs will result in the creation of differential rents for those producers who receive the ration coupons that enable them to utilize the free inputs. This rent may serve to reduce the costs of production for the benefited producers. Because of the free public good, the productivity of priced resources will be greater for the affected firms. But this increased productivity will not be reflected through an increase in resource prices because the marginal productivity of priced resources in "non-subsidized" employment will tend to determine resource prices.

This model, embodying the formation of differential rents as a result of free provision of a public intermediate good, may seem somewhat extreme under the assumptions of an ideally competitive economy. However, when this latter assumption is dropped, the differential rent model becomes perhaps the most general one. If the mechanism for competitive adjustment is imperfect, if monopoly is allowed to be present, in greater or lesser degree, the creation of differential rents as a result of governmental provision of intermediate goods and services must be carefully considered. Even if an input service should be made available in unlimited amounts, or if a fixed amount should be made freely accessible to all potential users, the failure of full competitive adjustment to take place may allow some of the benefits from the free government input to be retained by producing units. The full benefits may not be shifted forward to final consumers, and, as a result, some part of the final product value will tend to reflect the marginal value of the government input.[6]

When we combine all these models, we must conclude that the procedure for evaluating public goods and services that is followed by the Department of Commerce is conceptually incorrect. Insofar as public goods and services are made available without direct charge in unlimited quantities and competitive adjustment takes place, the value of these goods and services at the margins of use becomes zero. There is no reason to include any cost valuation for these goods and services in any proposed measurement for the market value of national output. Insofar as public goods and services—intermediate or final—are provided to users free of direct charge, but either they are unequally distributed among users or fully competitive adjustment does not take place—or both—producers' rents may be created. Such rents may arise for firms in industries supplied with a governmental intermediate product or for firms in industries supplying goods that are complementary with a freely provided final good or service. To the extent that such rents replace private costs of production, at the margin, as imputable distributive shares, the market value of the free public goods is included in the market value of private output. Double-counting or duplication is indeed involved here when the cost value of public goods is added to the market value of final output.

There remain situations in which public goods, although provided without direct charge to consumers, retain a positive value at the margin and in which this value is not included in the market value of some final output.

---

6. Once the assumption of full competitive adjustment is dropped, the free provision of intermediate goods and services can result in the elimination as well as the creation of producers' rents. If, for example, some firms receive a free input service and as a result are led to expand production, this may cause a general reduction in rents previously enjoyed by those resource owners not directly benefited by the government action. Insofar as the availability of free water reduces the cost of producing new crops on marginal lands, the price of the agricultural products concerned will fall, the rents of previously existing inframarginal lands will be reduced, and the benefits of the free public good will be transmitted forward.

These situations are represented in those cases where the quantity of the public good is limited but where the benefits of this limitation are transmitted forward to final consumers. Even for these cases, however, an inclusion of the public goods at values at the margin has no relation to the cost of production, and the unit value may be above or below marginal or average cost. This is reminiscent of Jevons: cost can influence marginal value only through its influence on supply; and, in this case, the supply of the public good made available is not directly influenced by cost considerations.

III

Simon Kuznets has been the most important and persistent advocate of the thesis that intermediate and environmental public goods and services should be excluded from estimates of national product.[7] In his view, current procedures of measurement result in an overstatement of the contribution of the public sector because of the failure to introduce some downward adjustment for the value of the intermediate goods supplied by government. The inclusion of the publicly provided "intermediate" goods and services involves a clear case of double-counting; these goods and services do not represent net additions to national output.

This general position has perhaps been most clearly outlined by Bowman and Easterlin.[8] In specific reference to the line of reasoning advanced in opposition by Department of Commerce spokesmen, the double-counting argument has perhaps been most fully developed by Shoup and Musgrave.[9] To counter the Department's argument that firms act merely to "transmit" the values of freely provided intermediate goods to final consumers, these writers rely on the deflation of money measures of output to offset collectively induced changes in output prices. If, as in the example of free flour, the mar-

7. See especially his "National Income: A New Version," *Review of Economics and Statistics,* 30 (May, 1948), 151–79; and his "Government Product and National Product," in *Income and Wealth,* Ser. 1 (Cambridge, Mass.: International Association for Research in Income and Wealth, 1951).

8. R. T. Bowman and R. A. Easterlin, "An Interpretation of the Kuznets and Department of Commerce Income Concepts," *Review of Economics and Statistics,* 35 (February, 1953), 41–50.

9. Musgrave, op. cit., chap. 9; and C. S. Shoup, *Principles of National Income Analysis* (Boston: Houghton Mifflin Co., 1947), chaps. 4, 7.

ket price of bread should fall as a result of the initiation of collective provision of an intermediate good, flour, the general price level is presumed to fall. Thus, when measured values for output are appropriately deflated to reflect real values, national product should remain invariant under the particular change postulated.

A somewhat broader approach has been taken by Kuznets with reference to those environmental or framework services that are not fully analogous to inputs in the private production processes but which nevertheless constitute a part of the setting essential for private production. (Typical examples are external defense and the administration of justice.) Kuznets' argument for excluding any valuation for these "environmental outputs" from national income is that these goods and services, by making private production possible, must be reflected in the value of final output for the private sector. In other words, private output assumes a certain size because of the existence of collective provision of defense, justice, etc. To count both the preconditions of production and the production itself, argues Kuznets, involves duplication.[10]

Let us consider these arguments: first, that of "adjusted income" employed in opposition to the inclusion of those strictly intermediate goods and services supplied by government, for example, free flour. If the flour is provided to firms in the baking industry without charge, the results may be represented in one of two limiting cases or any combination thereof. In the first extreme, no competitive adjustment takes place at all because of monopolistic or other conditions. The price of bread (final product) may remain invariant. In this case there is no reason to include the value of the flour at cost in estimates of national output, since this value will already be embodied in the price of bread, being now imputable as a distributive share to producers and classified properly as producers' differential rents. In the second extreme, the full competitive adjustment will take place, and the market price of bread will fall by the full amount of the value of the free government input. Here, the proponents of the "adjusted income" argument say, the general price level also goes down. If national production in any given year (or community) has to be compared with that of another year (or community), money measures for output must be deflated by some appropriate

10. Kuznets, "Government Product and National Product," 192–96.

price index in order to obtain comparable "real" incomes. When two situations are compared—one in which a good, say flour, is provided free of charge and in which the price of output, bread, is lower; another situation in which the same good is priced through the market and the price of output, bread, is for this reason higher—*if the same amount of bread is produced in both situations,* the proper deflation will yield identical "real" incomes for both situations. To add a cost value of the free flour to the value of the bread in the public-good situation, continues this argument, will result in double-counting because the value of this free input is reflected in the price-deflator that must be applied to reduce money values to real values.

The important, and essential, step in this analysis is the assumption of invariance, that is, the assumption that the production of the differentially affected commodity or service remains the same when the intermediate good is provided free and when it is priced through the market. It is, however, clear that this invariance assumption is not supportable. When an intermediate good is provided freely to firms in an industry, surely the output of the industry must be increased, provided only that there is some variation in the coefficients of production. If, in fact, output could not increase, then the price could not fall and the whole idea of adjusted real income to reflect price changes would be meaningless. If the production of the differentially affected commodity is increased as a result of the free provision of a single input, the production of other goods and services normally must be decreased. The whole output composition of the community is modified. And, once this is allowed to happen, the central problem of index numbers is introduced. Weighting with the output mix of one situation will lead to a different result from weighting with the output mix of another situation. *Ceteris paribus,* weighting an index with the quantities of final output produced in the situation in which the intermediate good is priced through the market will tend to produce, relatively, a lower "real" income for the public-good situation than will the weighting of the index by those quantities of output produced in the situation when the intermediate good is provided freely by government.[11]

11. An additional difficulty in the invariance approach involves the implicit assumption that it is possible to compare situations with and without public goods and services. But a perfectly anarchistic model is wholly unrealistic. The relevant comparisons must be

Let us turn to the broader argument of Kuznets for the exclusion of the "framework" intermediate public services from output measures. If the purpose is that of measuring "welfare" by the market evaluation of present consumption and capital goods useful for future consumption—Kuznets holds—all items of expenditure that are not in themselves final consumption or investment must be excluded. But the dividing line between framework goods and other public goods, as traced out by Kuznets, seems arbitrary. He asserts that those goods, with counterparts in the private sector, which are provided freely by government are not part of the "framework" of production. But it seems questionable to classify public schools, which do have counterparts in private schools, as falling without the "framework" and external defense, which has no private counterpart, as within the "framework." Logically, this argument suggests that the institutional structure of the country, which will determine the presence or absence of many counterparts to public goods and services, may affect the evaluation procedures.

From the discussion of Section II, and from what follows in Section IV, it should be clear that, for some purposes, we should support Kuznets' recommendations as improving currently employed measurements procedures, but both the adjusted income and the framework arguments in support of these recommendations seem to be of questionable conceptual validity. Neither the specific recommendations of Kuznets nor the arguments in their support lead to a wholly satisfactory resolution of many of the difficulties inherent in the evaluation of public services.

IV

As we have said, the methods of evaluating social income and, through this, the contribution of the public sector depend upon the purposes that the evaluation is designed to accomplish. J. R. Hicks has distinguished two ends or goals of income measurement: welfare and productivity.[12] If either of these is to be adopted, some value scale must be introduced through which

---

between situations in which different amounts of public goods and services are provided. No deflator is able to exclude fully the impact on prices of money caused by the public services existing in the initial base situation.

12. J. R. Hicks, "The Valuation of Social Income," *Economica*, 7 (May, 1940), 105–24.

a whole set of heterogeneous goods and services may be compared and summed. Market-established prices provide the basic value scale in an enterprise economy. Since the individual consumer presumably adjusts his behavior to an established set of prices, the total expenditure that he makes on all goods and services reflects his evaluation of the whole pattern of his consumption. The total expenditure of all consumers thus provides us with some composite evaluation of the whole output mix, and, because of this, we can accept this as an indicator of "welfare" in one highly restricted sense.

We propose to exclude all valuation for government product that is not directly priced. This seems to follow directly from this "welfare" criterion. Since individual users (firms and final consumers) are not charged for public goods and services, their behavior is adjusted to *zero* prices for these services. Hicks accepts the proposal that publicly provided goods and services should not be valued in national output if they are made available in unlimited quantities (our first model). He does not accept this procedure when the total supply of the goods and services is limited. The legitimacy of extending the exclusion even to these cases can, perhaps, best be shown by analogy. There are many "free" goods in nature that are strictly limited in supply. The sun shines only four hours per day on the average in some communities; clearly, "welfare" could be increased by more sunshine. But no effort is made to place a positive value on sunshine because no market transaction can produce more of the output. Instead, we assume implicitly that the adjustment processes of the economy act so as to take the differential availability of such "free" goods into account. Publicly supplied but limited goods and services seem no different. If the individual secures the enjoyment of these goods without direct charge and cannot resell them through some sort of a market transaction, no value should be included in national output estimates.

The two supposedly contradictory arguments that have appeared in the debate—the first that government intermediate services should not be counted (double) in national product and the second that "free" intermediate and final services cannot be distinguished and should not be differently treated—are not contradictory at all when considered properly. Both extend to the logical conclusion that all free public goods and services must be excluded from any consistent evaluation of national product for the purpose of measuring "welfare" in the restricted sense. From one point of view all public goods and services are, in fact, intermediate. From another point of view they are all final. They are intermediate because being freely provided they must to some extent be reflected in the values of other goods and services. In this sense, their inclusion in measurements of output implies overstatement. From another point of view all public goods are final because they must be considered to provide some measure of satisfaction to the population. This remains true despite the fact that, in many cases, they may provide zero marginal value to consumers. But any attempt to measure the extent of this total satisfaction by including these public goods at cost is not consistent with valuing private goods at their marginal (market) prices. In those cases where the freely provided goods retain positive marginal values, there are no means of determining what these values are and to what extent they are reflected in the market prices of other goods and services. The inclusion of public goods supplied free of direct charge at some cost valuation implies, therefore, both an inconsistency and an overstatement. Total exclusion, on the other hand, may imply an understatement of "welfare" in a certain sense. But it must be kept in mind that even the valuation of privately produced goods and services at market prices measures "welfare" in a very restricted definition of this term since only marginal values are incorporated. A measure of "total welfare" is unattainable. We are reduced to using the measurement of output valued at market prices because it is internally consistent and because it does have *some* significance for welfare. This consistency as well as the limited significance for welfare that is present is lost when the market values of privately produced output are added to the cost values for publicly supplied output. The only consistent measure of national output with current welfare significance at all seems to be that which includes only the valuation of goods and services actually sold on markets at positive prices.

It is important to note that this approach does not prevent useful comparisons of "welfare" between communities with different amounts and kinds of goods provided free through the collectivity. The exclusion of those goods and services provided free from the total value of output at market price means only that the items in question have zero prices. A total valuation of zero is put on such goods, but the quantities of these goods provided are not necessarily excluded from the collection of items that may be relevant for purposes of making comparisons with communities in which these same goods have a positive price because they are sold through organized markets.

Again, let us proceed by simple examples. Community 1 is assumed to have no public police force; certain private individuals and firms hire police services through ordinary market channels. Community 2, assumed to be similar to Community 1 in other respects, taxes its citizens in order to provide police protection collectively. Under our proposals for the evaluation of community real output, the value of police protection would be included in the measurement of real product in the first community but excluded in the second community. Community 1 would, therefore, seem to show a higher real output solely due to the difference in organization. This implication is not correct, however, even in this specific example. To show that it is not, take the extreme assumption of invariance. Assume that private individuals in Community 1 hire the same number of policemen that the whole community does in 2. Assume further that the whole scheme is financed by income taxes that do not alter prices (another extreme assumption). Measured output in Community 1 would exceed that in Community 2 by the amount of the valuation placed on police services. But the price level is lower in Community 2 by virtue of the fact that police services *are priced at zero*. With the income generated in Community 2, consumers should be able to purchase, at Community 2 prices, all the goods consumed in Community 1, including police services that may be secured at zero prices. Obversely, with the income generated in Community 1, at Community 1 prices, consumers should be able to purchase all goods purchased in Community 2, including police services which are available only at market prices.[13]

In the normal case, however, with police protection being assumed genuinely collective, Community 1 would tend to utilize fewer police services than would Community 2. The "private" solution for Community 1 would, therefore, involve fewer resources devoted to police protection and more resources devoted to other uses than in Community 2. How does this change influence the problem of comparing real incomes in the two communities? Since the composition of production is no longer identical, the problem of

---

13. Note that our employment of the invariance test in this extreme model is not inconsistent with our earlier criticism of this test as it has been normally introduced in the discussion. In a sense, our approach here considers all government output as final product but includes this at zero prices in computations of index numbers. This is wholly different from assuming that government intermediate product, insofar as its value is transmitted forward to consumers, will reduce final prices of products on the market. In this latter case output cannot remain invariant.

quantity weights is introduced. The output of Community 1 will contain fewer police services and more alternative goods and services. If the quantities of goods and services actually consumed in Community 2, *including the amount of police services freely provided,* could be purchased by the income generated in Community 1, at Community 1 prices, *which must include some positive price for police services,* then Community 1 clearly has a real output at least as great as Community 2 has. On the other hand, if the quantities of goods and services actually consumed in Community 1, including the amount of police services purchased by private individuals and firms, could be purchased at Community 2 prices, which must include a zero price for police services, by the money income generated in Community 2, then real output in Community 2 must be at least as great as that of Community 1. By this procedure, Community 2 can, of course, show a lower money income but a higher real income than Community 1.

Unambiguous results could be expected to follow from such direct procedures only in limiting cases. Beyond these, nothing definite can be said about the relative size of real incomes in the two separate communities without the introduction of an explicit value judgment concerning the appropriate weights to be employed. Our purpose here is not, however, that of discussing the complexities of index-number construction and application to the evaluation of real product in making comparisons among countries or through time. The simple examples presented here have been designed to show only that no bias in such comparative measurement needs to be systematically introduced by our proposals for treating the governmental sector of output. Although resources are, of course, utilized in the production of governmental output, the exclusion of any valuation for this output from estimates of national product does not necessarily affect the comparison among communities that may organize their economic structures differently. That is to say, no difficulties that are not already present when such comparisons are attempted are introduced by the exclusion of any evaluation of public services.

V

A wholly different approach is suggested if the aim is that of measuring, not "welfare," even in the limited sense embodied in the attempts discussed above, but the value of the *potential* output that might be produced by the resource bundle in existence at any period of time. In this approach the relative evaluations placed on final goods and services are irrelevant except insofar as product prices reflect genuine marginal costs of production. Ideally, this approach would involve the addition of genuine resource or factor costs for all goods and services produced, including public as well as private goods. Immensely difficult problems arise, however, when any attempt is made to break down final product prices into the separate components of resources costs and true rents. Recognizing this difficulty, the analyst is tempted to adopt the simplifying assumption that in competitive economies product prices do, in fact, tend to approximate marginal costs. For the private sector, therefore, the addition of output values, yielding total expenditure, provides a measure of productive capacity.

Something of this approach seems to be implicit in current Department of Commerce practices, or, at least, this enables us to rationalize these practices more easily. If, in fact, market prices in the private sector could be assumed to equal marginal costs, the total value of privately marketed goods and services, minus indirect taxation, *plus* the cost values of publicly provided goods and services would yield one acceptable measure for productive capacity of the economy. Market prices will, in this pure model, reflect only *private* marginal costs to firms; no cost value for publicly supplied intermediate or environmental services could possibly be included in market price. Therefore, no adjustment along the lines of Kuznets' theory would need be made for these. But indirect taxes would clearly act to insert a wedge between product prices and genuine marginal costs; hence, some downward adjustment must be introduced to account for this. Since resources are also employed in producing governmental output, consistency requires that a direct cost-valuation be added to the indirect cost-valuation (through market price) for those resources employed in the private sector.

Conceptually, this is a consistent approach, and comparisons between separate communities or through time could be made. If consistent practices are followed in measuring the relevant magnitudes in each of two separate communities, meaningful comparisons of real productive potential should be possible despite the differences in the organizational breakdown between the public and the private sectors in the two communities. Note here, however, that the price index which should be used to deflate measured income estimates must include the quantities of publicly supplied output *valued at cost-prices*, not zero prices, as in the other "welfare" measurement approach.

But let us now try to see precisely what such a "productivity" measure means. If, when appropriately reduced to constant-dollar totals, Community 1 is shown to have a higher "productive capacity" than Community 2, what does this suggest? In the purely private economy (without any collective action) the answer seems clear. A "higher" productive potential means that if the market economy should be "optimally" organized total output will be greater in Community 1 than in Community 2. The production surface over the relevant area lies outside that for Community 2. When we introduce a public sector of the economy, however, the analysis becomes more complex. If it is legitimate to employ market prices, net of indirect taxes, to reflect marginal (equal average) costs of goods and services produced in the private sector, and if it is legitimate to use average cost to reflect marginal cost of public goods and services, the transformation curve between private and public goods and services must be linear. A shift of resources from private to public production could never change average and marginal costs under the restrictive assumptions required by this model. Thus, even at this purely conceptual level, the highly restricted nature of this model must serve to reduce seriously the value of any comparative results that might be obtained.

The primary difficulty with this cost model, however, lies in its practical failure to measure real opportunity costs. Market prices, even after these are adjusted for indirect taxes, do not reflect marginal costs except in a very rough sense in the real dynamic world economy of less-than-perfect competition. Some improvements might be made by viewing the separate components of cost from the factor side and trying to isolate genuine opportunity costs from true rents. This would be a most difficult task. The failure of any realizable measurement procedures to incorporate the required adjustments in market prices that would make this costs approach fully acceptable makes any unambiguous estimation of "productive capacity" practically impossible.[14]

Quite apart from the difficulties that arise from any attempt to measure opportunity costs in the market sector alone, the different treatment of en-

---

14. On some of these problems, see G. Warren Nutter, "On Measuring Economic Growth," *Journal of Political Economy*, 65 (February, 1957), 51–63, esp. 57 ff.

trepreneurial remuneration in the private and the public sectors creates complex theoretical and practical problems. The practical result of any overall cost approach must surely be some bastard combination of a "welfare" and a "productivity" measurement which tends to compound the theoretical difficulties of both.

The "welfare" approach that we have advanced, in which the values of all publicly supplied services are excluded except those that are directly priced, is internally consistent. No addition of cost values and market values need be made, directly or indirectly. No problem arises of classifying public goods into final, intermediate, and environmental. And, with this approach, meaningful, even if somewhat restricted, international and intertemporal comparisons of real output, with some "welfare" significance, can be made. The "cost" approach covers a wider range of questions; but in its practical application it is less consistent and much more ambiguous. It seems reasonable to suggest that this latter approach be introduced, on grounds of expediency, only when the first, and more rigorous, approach is not considered sufficient for the task at hand.

We find the current practices of measuring national output justifiable on neither theoretical nor practical grounds. No effort is made to eliminate the inconsistency of adding the value of public goods at costs to the value of private goods at market prices. The admitted correction for the indirect tax wedge is meaningless, unless current practices are assumed to follow the costs approach suggested. In any attempt to measure the total market value of existing output, such a correction is clearly not in order. The only significant measure of national output at market prices is that which we have suggested: the price value of output that is effectively sold in organized markets. The addition of the private and the public sectors may have meaning, in a rough and ready sense, only when made in terms of input or cost values and when designed for the purpose of approximating to the total opportunity costs of producing the existing output mix.

"La scienza delle finanze"
The Italian Tradition in Fiscal Theory

I. Introduction

Now that the important early Swedish contributions on monetary and cycle theory have been made available, it may be asserted that the single most important national body of doctrine which remains largely unknown to and unappreciated by English-language economists is the Italian work in fiscal theory. The linguistic barrier has served effectively to prevent the dissemination of the Italian contribution in this area of applied economics, an area which has been an Italian speciality for at least a century. The only book which has been translated is de Viti de Marco, *First Principles of Public Finance.*[1] While this book is perhaps the most outstanding single work, its contribution cannot readily be appreciated by those not familiar with the Italian tradition.

From *Fiscal Theory & Political Economy: Selected Essays* (Chapel Hill: University of North Carolina Press, 1960), 24–74. Copyright 1960 by the University of North Carolina Press. Used by permission of the publisher.

Much of the research upon which this paper is based was conducted while the author held a Fulbright research scholarship in Italy. I am especially indebted to Professors Giannino Parravicini and Sergio Steve for their assistance in facilitating this research as well as for their helpful comments on earlier versions of this paper. I also gratefully acknowledge the helpful suggestions made by Professors Luigi Einaudi and Gustavo del Vecchio, both of whom read earlier versions of this paper. Their intimate acquaintance with the whole body of doctrine discussed here has made these suggestions especially valuable. Errors of fact, interpretation, and analysis remain, of course, entirely my own.

1. Antonio de Viti de Marco, *First Principles of Public Finance,* tr. E. P. Marget (London: Jonathan Cape, 1936).

A few additional essays have recently been translated and are included in *Classics in the Theory of Public Finance,* ed. R. A. Musgrave and A. T. Peacock (London: Macmillan, 1958). Essays by Pantaleoni, Barone, Montemartini, and Mazzola are included.

This explains the extremely divergent reactions of Henry Simons and F. C. Benham to the book, Simons calling it a "monument to confusion," while Benham was acclaiming it as the best book ever written in public finance.[2]

A whole body of doctrine, extending over a hundred years and including literally hundreds of contributions by scores of scholars, cannot adequately be summarized and critically discussed in a single essay. In spite of this, I shall attempt in this paper to sketch the broad outlines of the Italian tradition, to isolate a few of the important contributions, and to relate these to the present state of fiscal theory.

Procedure

I shall limit my discussion largely to what may properly be called the "classical" Italian tradition in public finance theory. Chronologically, this covers approximately a sixty-year period extending from 1880 to 1940. With the exception of the work of Francesco Ferrara, which is extremely important, although its influence was exerted in an indirect way, I shall not consider precursors of the main figures in Italian thought. I shall not discuss contemporary works of the post–World War II period except insofar as these may serve to clarify older contributions and controversies.

After a brief survey of the institutional setting of Italian public finance, I shall first attempt to identify some of the background factors which appear to have exerted some influence on the main Italian ideas and to have produced certain general characteristics in Italian thought. There follows an effort at classifying the Italian works into two broad categories, a classification which is necessarily somewhat incomplete. The second half of the paper begins with the discussion of what I consider to be the important contributions of the Italians. Properly following this, I shall conclude with a summary comparison of the Italian with the Anglo-Saxon tradition.

The institutional setting

Contrary to the conventional practice in England and the United States, the study of public finance in Italy is an independent branch of scholarship. It is

2. H. C. Simons, *Journal of Political Economy*, 45 (1937), 712–17; F. C. Benham, *Economica*, 1 (1934), 364–67.

not a part of the economics curriculum in the universities; it has a separate curriculum and a separate existence all its own. Normally it is taught and discussed as the science of finance and financial law. Political and legal aspects of finance have been considered integral parts of the discipline, equally important with the economic aspects.

This status has not been entirely a happy one. The doctrinal independence of public finance has been attacked and defended in a continuing controversy. One group, represented by the late Professor Benvenuto Griziotti, has defended the separateness of public finance on the basis of the subject matter. This position follows the Germanic tradition of "Staatswissenschaft." In this view, finance should be studied in its total setting, which includes the legal, political, administrative, and economic aspects. These various disciplines are included insofar as they are relevant to the consideration of problems of financing state services. The approach taken by this group has something in common with the American institutionalists, notably with the position of John R. Commons.

The opposing group has tried to emphasize the economic approach to state fiscal activity. While this attitude admits differentiation in the subject of study, it holds that the fundamental distinction should be in method. The importance of the non-economic aspects of fiscal problems is not denied; but proponents of this view are willing to allow these to be considered by non-economists.

The whole controversy over the independence of finance as a separate branch of scholarship has contained much that is sterile. The controversy has, however, served to emphasize certain methodological issues which have been neglected or glossed over in the English-language tradition. These will be discussed in some detail at a later point. But perhaps the most important influence of the doctrinal independence itself has been that public finance, as a branch of scholarship, has attracted many of the better scholars. The science of finance has probably been even more widely respected than general economic theory, and the best Italian economists have felt themselves compelled to do some work in the field. With the single exception of Pareto, who was not without major influence although he was not a direct contributor, all of the outstanding Italian economists have devoted some time to finance theory.

A disadvantage of the doctrinal independence has been that an excessive amount of work has been done in this field relative to others. Although there probably exist external economies to scholarly research in the specific sub-branches of economics, surely the Italians have, in many cases, gone beyond the limits of the full exploitation of such economies. But having established chairs in public finance at many institutions, and having a literal "publish or perish" rule for selection and promotion, Italian scholars have been sometimes forced into relatively unproductive work.

II. Background Influences

FERRARA AND CLASSICAL ECONOMICS

The influence of classical economics upon Italian fiscal thought cannot be separated from that of Francesco Ferrara. The important classical writings were made available to Italian scholars in translation in the 1850's through the famous series *Biblioteca dell' economista*. Ferrara selected the works to be translated, supervised the translations, and himself wrote lengthy prefaces to the individual selections. In these prefaces, as in his courses of lectures, Ferrara was intensely critical of many aspects of classical thought. On the whole, his criticisms are excellent by modern criteria, and he anticipated many of the neo-classical contributions. He anticipated, and in some respects surpassed, the subjective-value theorists. He was forceful in his emphasis that value theory must be based on individual behavior, his whole construction departing from what he called "the economic action," the author of such action being the individual who feels, thinks, and wants. The classicists were criticized for their attempts to construct an objective theory of value, and Ferrara was perhaps the first economist completely to shed all of the mercantilist trappings in his rejection of economics as the science of wealth. Value was determined by both utility and cost, with exchange value representing a comparison of these two forces. As a single principle, he developed the idea of the cost of reproduction as a measure of value, meaning by this the cost which would have to be incurred *if* the unit in question were to be reproduced. This principle was extended to apply to goods and services which were not physically reproducible by the introduction of the idea that it is the utility produced by the good, not the good itself, which determines value. Ferrara does not appear to have explicitly discussed diminishing marginal utility as such, although its acceptance is clearly present in his work, as Pareto recognized.[3]

The Physiocratic and classical distinction between productive and unproductive labor was all but demolished by Ferrara. In very persuasive fashion, he showed that the particular form of a good is unimportant, and that immaterial goods or services are equally valuable with material goods. He also rejected the Ricardian rent theory on the basis of a surprisingly modern argument. The idea of differential rent is held to be an undesirable and incorrect heritage of the Physiocratic concept of net product. Rent, or net product, is held to accrue to all factors, not to land alone, and rent, as a distributional share, is attributed to the superior productivity of the productive inputs which receive it.

With this general approach to economic theory, Ferrara was able to reach a profoundly different conception of fiscal activity from that reached by the English classical economists or implied in their works. First of all, he recognizes that social or collective action as well as individual action must be based on individual choice. The state is conceived ideally as a natural outgrowth of the division of labor, and the government is considered as a "producer" of such services as justice, defense, etc. . . . In its pure form, the tax is held to be a payment for such state-supplied services which provide positive utility to the individual.[4] The expenditure for these public services may be as productive as that for private goods and services. In this recognition of the tax as a price and of the productivity of public services, the foundation stone for the whole Italian fiscal tradition is laid. The whole of society enjoys the fruits of state services; specific mention is made of schools, port facilities, roads, asylums, and hospitals. It is to the advantage of each citizen to cede a portion of his private goods to the state in exchange for such services.

This broad view of the fiscal process might suggest that Ferrara was less libertarian than the English classicists. Such is, however, not the case. The

---

3. V. Pareto, "Per la verità," *Giornale degli economisti*, 2 (1895), 424. Pareto was an admirer of Ferrara, and traces of much of the Paretian theoretical construction can be found in Ferrara's works.

4. ". . . the tax, in its pure significance, would represent neither a sacrifice nor a violence exercised on the contributor by some superior; it would represent a price . . . for all the great advantages which the state provides for us." (F. Ferrara, *Trattato speciale delle imposte* [1849–1850], contained in *Lezioni di economia politica* [Bologna: 1934], 2, 551.)

"economic" conception of fiscal activity was, to Ferrara, an ideal. In the actual state of the world, Ferrara considered that the levy of taxes tended to be oppressive and constituted the "great secret through which tyranny is organized." Although his analysis is not developed in terms of the specific contrast, Ferrara's distinction between the philosophical or "economic" concept of fiscal activity and the historical or "oppressive" concept may also be considered as an early statement of the more refined distinctions which were later to be very important in Italian fiscal thought.[5]

Although recognizing that public services may be productive, Ferrara was intensely critical of the view, which had been expressed by German writers, that merely because tax revenues are transformed into public spending and are returned to the economy, society does not undergo a net loss. He emphasized the necessity for spending the tax proceeds productively, and he constantly referred to the required comparison between utility and cost.[6] The tax is the instrument by which the consumption of one type of good (public) comes to be substituted for another (private). The test of efficiency is always to be found in a comparison of these two consumptions.

Interestingly, Ferrara's influence on the development of Italian fiscal thought appears to have been rather indirect. Until the publication of his lectures in 1934, Italian scholars made little reference to his works. Yet the similarity between the basic conceptual framework developed by Ferrara and the subsequent development in Italy suggests that his ideas were instrumental. The explanation is probably provided in the direct influence which Ferrara exerted on the thinking of the early writers, notably Pantaleoni and, through him, on de Viti de Marco. Thus it came to be that subsequent Italian scholars looked to Pantaleoni and de Viti as the sources of their discipline, only to awaken in the 1930's to find that Ferrara had been the genuine fountainhead of ideas.

Regardless of the means through which they were transmitted, Ferrara's ideas muted the impact of the classical implications at precisely those points

5. Einaudi has stated that this is the major contribution of Ferrara to fiscal theory. See Luigi Einaudi, "Francesco Ferrara," in *Saggi bibliografici e storici intorno alle dottrine economiche* (Rome: 1953).

6. "The tax itself is neither a good nor an evil. To make an adequate judgment, one needs to compare the sacrifice with the utility which is promised." (Ferrara, loc. cit., 469.)

where these implications could bear on fiscal theory. In Anglo-Saxon fiscal thought, this sort of influence has been absent. Here is explained, at least in part, several important differences in the two developing bodies of fiscal doctrine.[7] It explains why the Italians have from the beginning recognized the spendings side of the fiscal account as an integral part of fiscal activity, whereas, even today, this has not yet been fully incorporated into the English tradition. As a corollary to this, the greater Anglo-Saxon emphasis on sacrifice theories of taxation is more readily understandable. The concept of net sacrifice as a result of the fiscal process has been almost completely absent from Italian works. The Ferrarian influence also explains why the single tax has had little support in Italy.

THE THEORY OF UTILITY

While the Ferrarian model was influential in taking some of the rougher edges off classical economics, it was equally important through its positive contribution in preparing the groundwork for a ready acceptance of the subjective-value approach and the theory of marginal utility. And it is only after Ferrara's major work was completed, and also after the subjective-value decade of the 1870's, that Italian fiscal theory emerged in its fullest sense. The origins of "classical" Italian theory, represented in the works of Pantaleoni and de Viti de Marco, appeared in 1883 and 1888, respectively. These represent attempts to apply the theory of marginal utility to the activity of the public entity. While this attempt to explain state action in terms of the marginal calculus was but natural to the Italian familiar with Ferrara's works, it was foreign and unnatural to the Englishman or the American imbued with Ricardo's principles, and therefore was never carried out.

Interestingly, Pantaleoni first applied the marginal calculus to the theory of public expenditure rather than to the theory of taxation. He tried to construct a theory of public spending analogous to the theory of consumption for the individual with the decision-maker being the average or representa-

---

7. Einaudi, in his review of Pigou's *Study in Public Finance*, makes the telling point that if Ferrara's ideas had been accepted outside of Italy, this would have prevented all such efforts as Pigou's attempted distinction between productive and transfer expenditure. (Luigi Einaudi, *La riforma sociale*, 39 [1928], 164.)

tive member of the legislative assembly. Public revenues were to be distributed among the various possible employments so as to equalize the marginal
yields from equivalent units in the minds of the average legislator.

De Viti was more ambitious. He attempted to show that an "economic"
theory of the whole fiscal process could be developed. His fundamental early
work, *Il carratere teorico del' economia finanziaria* (1888), was conceived independent of the work of Emil Sax which appeared in Austria one year earlier, and it is, in many respects, vastly superior to the Sax effort. The stated
purpose of de Viti's monograph is that of extending the principles of theoretical economics to fiscal activity. The extension is accomplished by accepting the state as the subject for study in lieu of the individual. The task of the
economist is held to be that of studying the behavior of the state in fulfilling
its tasks, not that of determining the ends of state activity. While the motives
for state action may be different from those of individual action, the overriding principle remains that of "minimum means," and, on this principle, de
Viti tried to erect his theory. Public activity is held to be eminently productive, and it serves to satisfy collective needs. But the production of public services is costly, and there is required a comparison of satisfaction and cost;
this comparison is the essence of the financial calculus.

THE THEORY OF GENERAL EQUILIBRIUM

With the work of Pantaleoni and de Viti de Marco in the 1880's, Italian fiscal
theory achieved an independent status. As the tradition developed, however,
the emerging Walrasian-Paretian work on general equilibrium was to exert
substantial influence. This explanation of the economic process served to reinforce the Ferrarian orientation toward generality in approach and to draw
attention away from the study of particular problems. Thus, except for an
early work by Pantaleoni, the theory of tax shifting and incidence, which was
largely born in the Marshallian tradition of partial equilibrium, is relatively
unimportant. The general-equilibrium approach exerted further influence
in forcing Italian theorists to recognize both sides of the fiscal account. The
influence of general-equilibrium analysis on Italian fiscal thought came
through an acceptance by the Italian writers of the Walrasian-Paretian construction and not through any direct contribution on the part of Walras or
Pareto. Walras constructed his model in abstraction from the state, and Pa-

reto removed collective action from economics by his claim that completely different principles of choice are applicable.

THE THEORY OF THE RULING CLASS

The fourth major idea or conception which appears to have affected Italian fiscal theory in a significant way is that of the ruling class. This owes its origin to both Mosca and Pareto. The ruling-class conception of government, which was perhaps born out of the Italian political turmoil, has been formulated in almost complete independence of the Marxist conception, although clearly the two approaches have much in common. The "ruling class" in Italian political thought need not be historically determined by the laws of production; it can be an hereditary class, an intellectual élite, a political party temporarily in power, or the proletariat. It may be permanent or it may be shifting; it may exert its power through autocratic or democratic forms and institutions. This conception is, therefore, broader and more general than the Marxist. The essential characteristic is the denial of the democratic process in the reaching of social or collective decisions. Social decisions are always made by a group smaller than the total citizenry. The Anglo-Saxon idea of universal participation in the processes of social or collective choice, either directly or through representation, does not appear to have dominated Italian thought or even to have been widely accepted.

The ruling-class conception has forced Italian thinkers, even those who do not accept its validity, to devote greater attention to the form of the state. In this respect the conception has proved to be of great value for the development of fiscal theory. It has made Italian fiscal theorists more explicit as regards their political presuppositions. By contrast, in the non-Italian tradition the political assumptions have rarely been stated with the resultant inherent inconsistencies and contradictions. As Wicksell so acutely noted, the implicit assumption has often been that of benevolent despotism.[8]

---

8. Knut Wicksell, *Finanztheoretische Untersuchungen* (Jena: Gustav Fischer, 1896). An English translation of the important part of this work has been published in *Classics in the Theory of Public Finance*, ed. R. A. Musgrave and A. T. Peacock (London: Macmillan, 1958).

See also Pierre Tabatoni, "La rationalité économique des choix financiers dans la théorie contemporaine des finances publiques," *Économie Appliquée*, 8 (1955), 158.

SCIENTISM

A final influencing factor in Italian fiscal thought has been the insistence that work in this field remain purely "scientific," or, in current methodological terminology, "positivistic." In the Italian context this characteristic of scholarship is synonymous with objectivity or impartiality, and it carries with it no precise operational connotations. The task of the scholar is solely one of observation; only by a rigorous adherence to the role of the detached observer of the social scene can a genuinely experimental science be constructed. This view, expressed most clearly by Pareto in his works on sociology, has been present in most of the Italian fiscal work.

This positivism has been useful in some respects. It has served to eliminate from the Italian literature the lengthy normative discussions on fiscal "justice" which have plagued this field of study elsewhere. The net effect of this approach, however, must be judged as negative. No observer of the social scene can remove himself from the observed, and personal and subjective attitudes necessarily color all activity, including the scientific. The Italian scholar, in his attempt to avoid an open admission of this, tended to become enmeshed in excessive generality. And propositions which he presented as explanatory or descriptive turn out, in some cases, to be valid only on the acceptance of his set of values.

By and large, this attempt at positivism has caused Italian fiscal theory to be much further removed from actual policy issues than is the case in either England or the United States. With rare exceptions, the Italians have not been greatly interested in fiscal reforms, or perhaps better stated, they have tried to conceal what interest they have possessed. This appears to have been unfortunate, because it is precisely from an open and direct interest in reform that many new insights have been, and can be, achieved and new truths attained—truths which will fully stand up to the most severe scientific tests.

Barone and Einaudi, among the important figures, appear to have come closer to escaping this debilitating influence. Both extended the scholar's task beyond that of mere intellectual observation and speculation. But no Italian

---

An important recent American book develops an approach to collective decision-making which has much in common with that propounded by the "ruling-class" conception. See Anthony Downs, *The Economic Theory of Democracy* (New York: Harper, 1957).

theorist appears to have approached his task on the basis of an outright and explicitly stated set of personal value judgments. The simple recognition that in the social sciences the observer is necessarily among the observed nowhere shines through.

III. Principal Features

THE BASIC DUALISM

Perhaps the most important single characteristic of Italian fiscal thought is its dualism. From the contrasting models of the "philosophical" and the "oppressive" states of Ferrara, and the first explicit development in the de Viti de Marco models of the "cooperative" and the "monopolistic" states, Italian contributions can be classified on the basis of the nature of the political entity or, more specifically, on the basis of the location of the decision-making power. The first alternative involves the fundamental premise of democratic choice to the effect that *all* members of the social group participate conceptually in the reaching of collective decisions. This alternative may be called the "cooperative," the "democratic," or the "individualistic," and it stems from the contractual conception of the state itself. As applied to fiscal theory, this approach tends to concentrate on the individual-choice processes and to emphasize the basic similarity between individual behavior in choosing public goods and that in choosing private goods. This has sometimes been labeled the "economic" approach because individual decisions on collective or public goods and services are normally conceived as being ruled by the economizing principles of choice. As Borgatta states, the central hypothesis is simply that "the application of income to the payment of taxes is a particular case of the general law of the allocation of income."[9] The voluntary aspects of fiscal action are stressed, and the tax is considered as a price in the broadest philosophical sense. The general productivity of public services is a central feature. Although he develops his theoretical structure in terms of the two contrasting models, de Viti de Marco is essentially the source of this approach, and his cooperative state model is his standard construct.

9. Gino Borgatta, "Prefazione," *Nuova Collana di Economisti*, Vol. 9, *Finanza* (Turin: 1934), xxxi.

His central idea is that in the cooperative state the producers and the consumers of public services are identical. Therefore, it is erroneous to conceive the tax as other than a form of price, a "season ticket." Although he recognizes the inherent struggle among individuals concerning the distribution of the common burden, this is viewed as a problem of political choice-making. The essence of the fiscal action per se is the marginal equivalence between the two sides of the account, which must hold for the totality if not for the specific individual member of the group. De Viti does not attempt to develop a purely "individualistic" theory in the sense of Wicksell and Lindahl, nor does he appear to have been impressed by the work of Sax and his Italian followers.

Einaudi is the most distinguished follower of de Viti de Marco in this cooperative or democratic tradition, which has not been the dominant one in terms of number of adherents. Fasiani, clearly the most important figure to emerge in the inter-war period, followed de Viti de Marco in the sense that he developed his theory in terms of the contrasting models of the cooperative and the monopolistic state. However, while de Viti de Marco's major stress was placed in the cooperative model, Fasiani's was placed in the monopolistic model.

The alternative model of state activity owes its continuing importance to Pareto and stands directly opposed to the "democratic" model. Ferrara and de Viti conceived society as moving progressively from the tyrannical or monopolistic state toward the democratic and cooperative state. Pareto was successful in shifting completely this evolutionary emphasis. As of any given period of time, a specific group exerts political power, and the individual members of the whole group may be classified into two broad categories, the governing and the governed. Fiscal activity is to be explained solely in terms of the behavior of the ruling group. The important figures in this tradition are Puviani, Pareto, Murray, Borgatta, Barone, Fasiani, and Cosciani.

Within this group a further classification may be made. Certain theorists, especially Borgatta, the most direct follower of Pareto, reject any attempt to use economic analysis in the explanation of fiscal activity. To Pareto and to Borgatta state decisions are made by a different sort of calculus, and there is no such thing as a "science of finance" analogous to economic science. The explanation of fiscal activity should be sought instead in the murky science of sociology. This Paretian emphasis led Borgatta to search for a socio-political theory of the fiscal process without much success.[10] This socio-political approach, which is still accepted by some writers in Italy, leads to the vagueness and indeterminancy which surround such concepts as "countervailing power" which have recently been advanced in other connections in the United States.

Another more important group has tried to construct an economic theory of fiscal activity of the ruling class. This group includes Puviani, Barone (for whom the political assumption is relatively unimportant), Fasiani, and Cosciani. This approach has tended to stress the coercive aspects of fiscal choices, and excellent criticisms of the individualistic approach have been advanced. The individual "versus" the state has been the center of the discussion, and the efforts of the state to conceal its activity through the creation of fiscal illusions has been an important part of the analysis. On the other side, the reactions of individuals, singly or in groups, to the fiscal power of the collectivity (the ruling class) have been emphasized.

Both of the above-mentioned variants of the ruling-class conception remain "individualistic" in terms of decision-making. The idea of any *über-individual* or organic decision-maker is explicitly denied. The characteristic feature is that decisions are made by a limited group of individuals, which the system of relationships called "the state" has placed in power, perhaps only temporarily. Little influence is attributed to the actual form of the state or the actual process of choice, and in this respect the vision is closely akin to that of the Marxist.

The genuinely organic conception, in the explicit sense in which the interests of the individual are presumably incorporated in the general social will as embodied in the state, was almost wholly absent from the Italian fiscal literature before the 1930's. During this decade it appeared in the work of Masci, P. Ricca-Salerno, and others influenced surely by the dominant Fascist ideology.

---

10. Borgatta adopted a different approach when he examined practical problems in fiscal theory. Here he applied economic analysis in the usual sense and neglected his sociology.

GENERALITY

In many respects, "la scienza delle finanze" resembles philosophy more than it does Marshallian economics. The goal of Italian fiscal theorists has been that of providing generalized or philosophical explanations of the fiscal process. Research has been concerned with the "nature of things" rather than with finding operational propositions in the modern scientific sense. Italian scholars have been interested, by and large, in constructing complete, integrated systems, and the criterion for success has been logical consistency rather than usefulness for making predictions, actual or conceptual.

To many of the modern-day Italian specialists, this traditional approach appears sterile, and there is now a tendency to admire and to emulate the Anglo-Saxon problem-solving approach. At the forefront of this reaction was Fubini, who, writing in the 1930's, sharply criticized the overly philosophic emphasis, which he attributed to the excessive influence of Ferrara. He contrasted this with the Ricardian-Marshallian tradition which he held to be superior.

In contrast to this understandable and natural reaction on the part of modern-day Italian scholars, the philosophical emphasis has a great deal of value for the Anglo-Saxon scholar who has been trained in the Ricardian-Marshallian tradition and who has been substantially influenced, albeit unconsciously in some cases, by pragmatic-institutionalist ideas.

IV. Specific Contributions

GENERAL METHODOLOGY

Because of the influencing factors and the central characteristics noted, Italian fiscal theory is strongest in precisely those areas where Anglo-Saxon theory is weakest, and *vice versa*. If the Italians, on occasion, seem to have overlooked the fundamental purpose of fiscal economics, problem-solving, the English-language scholars have also failed to recognize that the analysis, and thus the solutions of particular problems, is conditioned by the methodological framework. And it is because the Italians have concentrated on general principles, on internally consistent systems, that their work can be of immense value.

From the outset and with a few notable exceptions, Italian fiscal theory has been developed in general-equilibrium terms. For the Italian, fiscal theory is concerned with the activity of the state, and not primarily with that of the individual as he is affected by the fisc. This is true equally for the "economic" and "non-economic" approaches. The theory is rarely individualistic in the sense that the individual or private economy is the central subject of the analysis.

The general-equilibrium aspects are more inclusive than a mere superimposition of taxes and expenditures onto a Walrasian model. The Italian model includes the state, and the more important feature has been the tying-together of the two sides of the state fiscal account, taxation and expenditure, and the general recognition of the limited usefulness of any one-sided analysis.[11] It is but natural that this feature should stem from the so-called "economic" approach (de Viti de Marco, Einaudi). But somewhat surprisingly it is also accepted by those who specifically reject the economic aspects of fiscal choice (notably Borgatta).[12]

Pantaleoni held that insofar as the tax exceeds that which the individual would freely sacrifice for the public service, the results of taxation were identical to those of brigandage or plunder. De Viti and Einaudi, through the development of their productivity theory of state expenditure, showed that the Pantaleoni view of a tax could be applied only to an individual or group. For the whole community the estimated net benefits must be at least equal to the costs, or the public service would never be performed under the assumption of any sort of rational choice-making for the collectivity.

Perhaps some credence may be given to the claims of the semanticists here, for it seems that by an extremely fortunate choice of words, Einaudi did much to overthrow the brigandage conception of the tax. He labeled the assumption which neglects the effects of the expenditure that of the "imposta grandine." Literally translated, "grandine" means hailstorm. The tax must be considered as something which destroys economic resources or otherwise removes them from the economy once and for all, without further repercussions or effects. By thus laying bare the implications of fiscal analysis limited

11. As del Vecchio has stated: "The history of the science has proved that theoretically there is no possibility of applying partial theories to the science of finance. Any finance problem, even particular ones, presupposes the whole system of economic relationships." (Gustavo del Vecchio, *Introduzione alla finanza* [Padua: 1954], 10).

12. See Gino Borgatta, "Contributi alla teoria della spesa dell' imposta," *Studi in memoria di Guglielmo Masci* (Milan: 1943), 1, 29–46.

to the tax side alone, Einaudi was instrumental in forcing Italian theorists to devote specific attention to this aspect of fiscal methodology.

The analysis of the spendings side corollary with that of the tax side was systematically incorporated into the treatment of de Viti de Marco. In his criticism of the traditional doctrine which neglected the effects of spending, de Viti perhaps went too far. For just as the traditional doctrine had unconsciously employed assumptions applicable, if at all, only to partial-equilibrium problems, de Viti conceived the fiscal process only in its most general framework. Here the tax can best be considered as a "price," but he failed to recognize the tremendous difficulties involved in any complete integration of the tax and expenditure sides, and his specific analyses are often oversimplified. De Viti failed to recognize the usefulness of the "imposta-grandine" assumption in analyses aimed only at partial-equilibrium results.

It remained for Fasiani and Cosciani to complete the Italian methodological contribution.[13] Fasiani attempted to identify those cases in which the "imposta-grandine" assumption could be legitimately employed, correctly stating that the real test was the fruitfulness in allowing accurate predictions to be made, not the correspondence of the assumption to apparent reality.

The most important and relevant of these cases were (1) when the purpose is that of deliberately isolating partial effects with the incompleteness fully acknowledged; and (2) when the tax is small and the proceeds are spread over many items of expenditure as opposed to the concentrated effects of the tax. The second case is, of course, the traditionally assumed setting for partial-equilibrium tax analysis, and many useful results have been obtained from this model. However, this model or framework has also been used to reach general-equilibrium conclusions, and this has been the source of much error and confusion. One of the most familiar examples of this is, of course, the so-called "excess burden" analysis which compares the effects of an income tax and an excise tax. Another is the analysis which attempts to trace the influence of general excise taxes on product prices. Only in the postwar

---

13. Mauro Fasiani, "A proposito di un recente volume sull' incidenza delle imposte," *Giornale degli economisti,* 18 (1940), 1–23; "Sulla legittimità dell' ipotesi di un imposta-grandine nello studio della ripercussione dei tributi," *Studi in memoria di Guglielmo Masci* (Milan: 1943), 1, 261–79; Cesare Cosciani, *Principii di scienza delle finanze* (Turin: 1953), 326–31.

period have economists come to recognize the extreme limitations which must be placed on partial-equilibrium analysis if it is to be useful and to attempt to place their analyses in a more general setting. Precisely because of this welcome shift in perspective, the Italian contribution should only now come to exert its proper influence in fiscal theory. If general-equilibrium or general-welfare conclusions are sought, Fasiani's second case no longer is an appropriate one, for in "macro-economic" or "income" terms the summed effect of the use of the tax yield in many different expenditure categories will be dimensionally equal to the concentrated effect of the tax levy. Therefore, the expenditure side must be reintroduced. There remains only the first case, that in which no conclusions can be reached at all, except on an acknowledged preliminary basis, conclusions which are, perhaps, better not even published if the ultimate purpose is that of influencing policy decisions in any desirable way. If fiscal theory is to be of any real usefulness in solving problems of political economy, the Italian conception of the fiscal process must perforce be employed.[14]

PUBLIC SERVICES AS PRODUCTIVE FACTORS

Many of the more specific contributions which Italian fiscal theory contains are derivative from the general methodological approach. One of these is the recognition of the general productivity of public expenditure, a contribution which has been developed by those who adopt the "economic" conception of fiscal activity, notably by de Viti de Marco and Einaudi. The essential idea was present in Ferrara, but it remained for de Viti to develop it and to use it as a basis for a principle of taxation.

The de Viti vision of public services goes beyond the mere acknowledgment of the usefulness of such services in a general and unspecified sort of way. Many students accept this view, but still conceive public services as *consumption* services, similar in many respects to bread and buttermilk. While such services may or may not be essential for existence, it is difficult to im-

---

14. Any model which incorporates some recognition of offsetting changes, for example in the level of alternative taxes or in the absolute price level, should be classified as equivalent methodologically to the Italian model.

pute to them a share in the income-creating or productive processes of the economy. De Viti looked at public services differently; to him these were productive services, that is, inputs in the whole productive operation of the economic mechanism. Public services are instrumental to the production of final goods and are on an equal basis with labor and capital. Therefore, it becomes conceptually possible to impute to such services an appropriate distributive share.

If the productive contribution of such services is specific to particular types of activity, these services will be priced in the ordinary manner. It is only when the contribution is not differential among the separate activities that the fiscal problem in a real sense arises. The existence of the tax rather than the price indicates that the contribution of the services so financed is general for all income-producing activity. Therefore, the properly imputed share assignable to the publicly supplied input is equal for each unit of income produced. As he put it, each unit of real income is born with a tax claim against it. From this it follows that if some units of income should escape this tax claim, other units must necessarily be charged with more than their properly imputed share of government cost.

This argument is more subtle than it at first appears, and it represents perhaps the most complete attempt to develop a purely economic theory of public activity. Its validity depends, however, on the acceptance of either one of two specific assumptions. Either all public services that affect different lines of activity differently must be assumed to be financed by direct pricing arrangements, or, alternatively, the differential effects exerted on each line of activity must be assumed to be mutually canceling when all public services are considered. Neither of these assumptions seems to be empirically supportable. If either one of them should prove to be realistic, however, the de Viti approach might prove acceptable. It could then with some legitimacy be argued that the ideal tax system is one that subtracts an equal share from each unit of income produced, that is, a purely proportional income tax.

Going beyond the distribution of the tax payment, a means is also provided for the determination of the aggregate amount of public activity. The necessary condition is provided in the equality between the marginal productivity of the public services and the marginal productivity of the resources in private employments. Conceptually, the test for this condition is a simple one. Would real income of the community increase, decrease, or remain unchanged by an incrementally small variation in the amount of government activity? Or, to state the criterion more correctly, would the present value of the community's future income stream be increased, decreased, or remain unchanged by an incrementally small change in the amount of government? It should be noted that the evaluation of real income here need not involve any assigning of values to the public services. This problem is eliminated by the device of assuming that these are purely instrumental and that their value shows up in final goods and services.

The grand design of de Viti was thus to apply the marginal-productivity theory of distribution to the fiscal problem. This theory is, however, an explanation of the workings of the private market economy, given the appropriate institutional framework. Resources will tend to be paid in accordance with their marginal productivity. But the extension of this sort of analysis to the fiscal problem introduces another dimension. There is nothing inherent in the workings of the collective choice-making process to cause the marginal-productivity criteria to be met. This is the great failure of the de Viti model. If, in fact, individuals could respond voluntarily in their purchases of public services, some such theory might provide an explanation. Separate individuals might freely choose the margin between the public and the private employment of resources. But what de Viti failed to see is that despite the objectivity with which real income might conceptually be measured this is not the appropriate criterion upon which private individuals will choose. Given any assumed value scale, real income for the community may conceptually be measured. But it is the distribution of such income among individuals which is relevant for individual choices. The criterion of social real income can be made objectively meaningful only if the decision-making power is located in some particular individual, group, or class who chooses to accept this criterion. Once this is admitted, the productivity conception loses much of its appeal and merit.[15]

De Viti's theory can be rescued only if it is changed into a normative one. It must be presumed to define a goal toward which collective action should strive. This involves the acceptance of certain value judgments concerning social welfare. It must state that the only correct evaluation of real income is

---

15. This point is made by Papi. See G. U. Papi, *Equilibrio fra attività economia e finanziaria* (Milan: 1942), 17.

that provided by the currently existing value scale established. Thus the de Viti attempt to apply the marginal-productivity theory of distribution to the fiscal problem goes beyond the mere acceptance of marginal-productivity payments as the ethically justified system of distribution for the private economy. It proposes to extend this norm to the public economy as well.

If the de Viti analysis is considered as explanatory, it is open to objections on analytical grounds; if it is considered as normative, it need not be accepted on ethical grounds. In spite of this, the approach is highly useful because of the insights it offers. First of all, it indicates that if specific public services are really in the nature of productive inputs and do affect certain lines of production differentially, the allocation of economic resources will tend to be affected adversely unless such public services are directly priced. The direction as well as the degree of resource distortion will vary in each case, depending upon, among other things, the elasticity of demand for the final product in question. Only within the last few years has this point come to be widely recognized; only recently has it been made clear that if we do not "price" highway services properly, we shall get too many resources devoted to automotive transportation; if we do not "price" the services of firemen, we shall get too little investment in fire protection devices, etc.

The de Viti conception also offers interesting insights on the whole idea of the neutral fiscal system. In the English-American tradition, strongly influenced by Pigou, the neutral tax system is supposed to require a set of lump-sum taxes. Any other system will have positive announcement effects. It is obvious that this line of thought stems directly from an undue concentration on the tax side to the neglect of the expenditure side. The de Viti approach indicates that the neutral tax structure is dependent upon the distribution of expenditures which is assumed, and that neutrality can be defined only in terms of both sides of the fiscal account.

Einaudi's conception of public activity closely follows that of de Viti. He suggests that the "optimal" tax, defined as that which leads to the maximum production of real income for the community, is that which bears on each particle of real income equally.[16] His treatment is superior to that of de Viti, however, in that his analysis per se does not depend upon his conception of

---

16. See Luigi Einaudi, "Contributo alla ricerca dell' ottima imposta," *Annali di economia*, 5 (1929).

the fiscal process. He explicitly states his principle of equality as a normative statement for the distribution of taxation. Each particle of real income, defined in the flow sense, *should* be equally taxed. His conclusions follow from this premise. Einaudi is almost alone among the Italians in adopting this methodological procedure.

CRITIQUE OF SACRIFICE THEORIES

As the discussion of the previous section indicates, the Italian approach can perhaps contribute more in a negative or critical sense than it can in any positive way. We find the Italians assuming the front ranks among the critics of the sacrifice "theories" of taxation, normative "theories" or "principles" which have dominated the Anglo-Saxon tradition, and which remain influential enough to justify whole works being written to dispel them.[17] No important Italian theorist has advanced propositions of the Mill, Edgeworth, Cohen Stuart, Pigou type, which state that the best tax system is achieved when individual sacrifices are equal or equi-proportional or when aggregate sacrifice is minimized. The Italian contribution has been rather in excellent critiques of these propositions, for the Italians follow the developments in the English-language publications quite closely. Notable critics are Barone and Einaudi, both of whom wrote on this subject as early as 1912.

Barone, always a clear thinker, was at his best when he demolished all versions of the sacrifice principle.[18] He applied essentially the same reasoning to all versions. The principle was invalid for two reasons. First, the utility of income for Tizio is not comparable with that of Caio. Second, even neglecting the problem of inter-personal comparability, a general pattern of tax distribution could be indicated only if the utility functions for the individuals were found to be of specific forms. By modification of the shapes of these

---

17. The recent study of Walter J. Blum and Harry Kalven, Jr., *The Uneasy Case for Progressive Taxation* (Chicago: 1953), is largely devoted to an attack on the sacrifice theories. And, although fiscal theorists might consider the argument as flogging a dead horse, the fact that the book was published and has received favorable reviews in the professional journals is sufficient proof of the point made in the text.

18. Enrico Barone, *Le opere economiche*, Vol. 3, *Principii di economia finanziaria* (Bologna: 1937), 149–60. The relevant portions of this work were originally published in *Giornale degli economisti* (1912).

functions, a progressive, proportional, or regressive tax system could be justified. As for the Edgeworth principle of minimum aggregate sacrifice, Barone acknowledged its superiority over the others in its being neat and precise both in its premises and in its conclusions. He showed, however, that this principle also required the comparability of utilities among individuals. But he went further and asked the question: Does the principle really minimize aggregate *social* sacrifice? Redistributive measures may be applied, without apparent harm to the social structure, in the short run, but the results may well be different if longer-run considerations are taken into account. Finally Barone concluded: "This doctrine of minimum sacrifice represents one of the major aberrations which may be reached by the arbitrary calculus of pleasure and pain."[19]

Barone concluded further that all theories of taxation based in any way on the marginal utility of income to the individual are inadequate and purely arbitrary. A system of taxation should be clear and predictable, and it should not be made to depend on the particular psyche of the individual which cannot possibly be examined in any objective way.

The Barone critique is substantially complete, and today, some forty-five years after it was written, it remains superior to all but a handful of contributions in the Anglo-Saxon literature.

Einaudi developed a critical argument on much the same grounds in his course of lectures in 1910–11 which were not published.[20] Starting with a simplified arithmetical model which shows how the assumption of a diminishing marginal utility of income could lead to an argument for progressive taxation, Einaudi then asks: Is it possible to sum utilities over separate individuals? He answers by stating that the sacrifices are individualized sensations which each person is able to measure and compare, but that it is impossible to add the sensations of Tizio and Caio. The minimum sacrifice principle is, therefore, of no significance.

Italian fiscal thought has never been plagued with the heritage of utilitarianism which has so influenced the development of fiscal theory in England

---

19. Ibid., 158.

20. He repeats his argument in Luigi Einaudi, "Il cosidetto principio della imposta produttivista," *La riforma sociale* (1933), reprinted in *Saggi sul risparmio e l'imposta* (Turin: 1941), 286–88.

and America. The minimum sacrifice principle, and its more ambiguous cousin, the ability-to-pay principle, is still a part of our fiscal doctrine. Perhaps the latter principle owes its popularity to its very ambiguity; it can be used to criticize, or, alternatively, to support, almost an infinite number of distributions of the tax load.

TAX CAPITALIZATION

One contribution that is peculiarly attributable to Professor Luigi Einaudi and which also stems directly from the productivity conception of public activity is contained in the analysis of tax capitalization. Einaudi was successful in overthrowing the so-called "classical" views. This was accomplished in a series of essays written between 1912 and 1934.[21] The "classical" or orthodox view held that whereas a partial tax was subject to capitalization, a general tax was not due to the effects of the general tax upon the rate of interest. Italian representatives of this theory were Gobbi and Ricci.[22] This view was discussed in America some forty years ago by T. S. Adams and E. R. A. Seligman, and it has recently been advanced again in a series of articles by J. A. Stockfish.[23]

Einaudi correctly showed that the orthodox view on tax capitalization depended upon the acceptance of the "imposta-grandine" assumption concerning the other side of the fiscal account. He showed that if the government's use of the tax proceeds is taken into account the effects of the rate of interest may be different in different situations depending on the relative efficiency of government's use of the revenues.

The dominant theory stated that if the tax covered an important field of resource return—that is, if the tax was of the type usually referred to as

21. These essays are all reprinted, along with others, in Luigi Einaudi, *Saggi sul risparmio e l'imposta* (Turin: 1941).

22. See U. Gobbi, *Trattato di economia*, 2nd ed. (Milan: 1923), 2, 129; U. Ricci, "La taxation de l'épargne," *Revue d'économie politique*, 16 (1927), 878–79.

23. J. A. Stockfish, "The Capitalization and Investment Aspects of Excise Taxes under Competition," *American Economic Review*, 44 (1954), 287–300; "The Capitalization, Allocation, and Investment Effects of Asset Taxation," *Southern Economic Journal*, 22 (1956), 316–29. See my "The Capitalization and Investment Aspects of Excise Taxes under Competition: Comment," *American Economic Review*, 46 (December 1956), 974–77, for an application of Einaudi's argument to the Stockfish analysis.

"general"—it must exert some effect on the rate of yield on capital resources. If completely general, the tax will reduce the rate of yield on all earning assets. This would appear to affect capital values; but when it is recalled that capital values are determined by both the yield and the rate of interest, the simple conclusion does not follow. For, accepting a productivity theory of interest-rate determination, the capitalization rate is reduced *pari-passu* with the yield. Therefore, capital values remain unchanged.

Einaudi did not accept this theory, and he showed that it contained the standard fiscal fallacy of neglecting the effects of the expenditure of the tax revenues. Presumably the government plans to use its tax revenues. If so, then the effects upon the rate of interest cannot be determined *a priori*. Einaudi said that if the funds were used as advantageously by the state as they would have been if left in private hands, the real income of the community will not change, and the rate of interest will tend to remain unchanged. Thus, the general tax will tend to be capitalized. Capital values will be reduced.

On the other hand, if the state uses the funds more advantageously than they would have been used in private employments, a premise of the economic theory of state activity, real income of the community would be increased. Additional savings would be forthcoming, and probably the rate of interest would diminish. As a third possibility, the state may use the proceeds of the tax in some manner less efficient than would be the case if the funds were left in private employments. In this case, the community's real income would be diminished. Savings would be reduced, and presumably the rate of interest would be increased. Thus, if the "grandine" assumption is fully accepted, said Einaudi, the conclusions drawn from the orthodox theory are wrong. Griziotti, in an important early article, substantially supported and reinforced the Einaudi thesis.[24]

The details of the Einaudi-Griziotti argument need not be accepted to recognize the value of this contribution, which reduces to an application of the Italian methodological position to the particular problem of tax capitalization. The error in the orthodox position on tax capitalization regarding the impossibility of capitalizing a general tax stems from the failure to extend

---

24. Benvenuto Griziotti, "Teoria dell' ammortamento delle imposte e sue applicazione," *Giornale degli economisti* (1918), reprinted in *Studi di scienza delle finanze e diritto finanziario* (Milan: 1956), 2, 275–391.

the analysis to a genuinely general-equilibrium framework. The effects of a generally imposed tax on resource yields is fully acknowledged; and the effect of the level of resource yields on interest-rate determination is also accepted. But the analysis stops one step short of the necessary generality. It must also include the effect of the expenditure of the proceeds on the rate of yield. In its most basic sense, Einaudi is stating that there can be no truly general tax. All income-producing sources cannot be simultaneously hit because government is also an income-producing source. The fiscal process is essentially a two-sided balance sheet sort of affair.

THE DOUBLE TAXATION OF SAVINGS

As mentioned above, Einaudi was one of the few Italian writers who explicitly stated a value premise at the start of his analysis. This was that each particle of income *should* be taxed equally. A significant portion of his work has been devoted to showing that the tax on personal income levied *in the ordinary way* does not meet this criterion. This argument involved an elaboration of the J. S. Mill–Irving Fisher thesis that the inclusion of income saved in the tax base involves double taxation. Therefore, Einaudi concludes, equity requires the exemption of income saved.[25]

A considerable portion of the Einaudi argument is simply arithmetic. He shows, clearly and precisely, that the present value of a specific amount of income devoted to saving (capital formation) becomes less than the present value of an equivalent amount of income devoted to current consumption if the income from the capital created is also to be taxed. The only way in which the present values of such equivalent units of current income can be equated is by the exemption of savings from current taxation. This is the only means by which savings can be prevented from being taxed twice, once originally as income and secondly on its yield.[26]

The close relation between this argument and the Einaudi argument on tax capitalization discussed above should be mentioned. If, in fact, the clas-

25. The main Einaudi works on this point are included in the volume cited above, *Saggi sul risparmio e l'imposta,* and in "Contributo alla ricerca dell' ottima imposta," *Annali di economia,* 5 (1929).

26. The Einaudi thesis has been made forcefully by Nicholas Kaldor. See his *An Expenditure Tax* (London: Allen and Unwin, 1955).

sical argument on the capitalization of a general tax were acceptable, there would be no double taxation of savings. For, if taxation did not serve to reduce capital values, there would be no difference in the present values of like amounts of income devoted to savings and to consumption.

Although Einaudi has not been without his supporters, notably Fasiani, the double taxation of savings thesis has not been widely accepted in Italy. The primary influence seems to have been that of de Viti de Marco who employed his own version of the productivity of state services to overthrow the Einaudi argument, much to the surprise of Einaudi. In its most general sense the totality of public services is considered by de Viti as a factor entering into the production of all economic goods and services, that is, all real income. Therefore, each portion of income has a tax claim against it. Recognizing this, it is erroneous to impute the whole of a future income stream to a current private investment of capital. The capital is productive due to the aid of the state environment; therefore, a portion of future income is to be attributed to public productive services. It follows that all units of current income must be fully taxed in order to compensate the state for its contribution; but it also follows that all units of future income must also be taxed. In other words, de Viti said that equality in present values is not the proper criterion for tax equity. He said that incomes of each period must be considered separately for tax purposes. Einaudi argued that capital and income are simply different dimensions of the same magnitudes. De Viti implied that this would be true only in an economy without the state. If the state is introduced, capital and income are not merely different in a dimensional sense; income carries with it a tax claim.

Thus taxing income as earned and then the yield on that portion saved does not involve double taxation at all, but is, on the contrary, necessary in order to achieve objective equality in the treatment of all income units.

In this rather ingenious way, de Viti was able to overcome the force of the tautological exactness of the Einaudi position. Although consistently holding an "*ertrag*" concept of income, he arrived at conclusions similar in many respects to those produced by the use of the "*einkommen*" concept.[27]

27. Cf. Henry Simons, *Personal Income Taxation* (Chicago: University of Chicago Press, 1938).

THE ITALIAN CONTRIBUTION TO DEBT THEORY[28]

The theory of public debt has been a central issue in Italian fiscal theory, and the contributions of Italian scholars are sufficiently unique, both in approach and analysis, to warrant a special discussion. The issue, in effect the debate, has been drawn almost exclusively in terms of the basic Ricardian proposition concerning the fundamental equivalence between extraordinary taxes and public loans.

The Ricardian thesis was elaborated and extended by de Viti de Marco.[29] Ricardo argued that the fully rational individual should be indifferent as between paying an extraordinary tax of $2,000 once-and-for-all and paying an annual tax of $100 in perpetuity, assuming an interest rate of 5 per cent. He extended this analysis to apply to all individuals and concluded that if the government borrows $2,000 and commits taxpayers to finance interest payments of $100 annually, the individual living in a future income period would find himself in an identical position with that which he would have enjoyed had the government chosen to impose the extraordinary tax of $2,000. The individual will fully capitalize the future tax payments when the debt is created, and he will write down the capital value of the income-earning assets which he owns by the present value of these future tax payments.

The limited life span of the individual does not affect the analysis. If an individual pays the once-and-for-all extraordinary tax, his heirs will receive capital assets reduced in value by this amount. If, on the other hand, the debt is created, his heirs will receive capital assets yielding a higher gross income. But when the interest charge is deducted, the net income stream is identical with that received in the tax situation.

The analysis would, at first glance, appear to apply only for those individuals possessing patrimony or capital. Its extension to individuals, members of professional or laboring groups, who own no income-earning assets is not

---

28. The discussion of this section closely parallels that contained in my *Public Principles of Public Debt* (Homewood: Irwin, 1958), Ch. 8, Appendix.

29. Antonio de Viti de Marco, "La pressione tributaria dell' imposta e del prestito," *Giornale degli economisti*, 1 (1893), 38–67, 216–31. Essentially the same analysis is contained in *First Principles of Public Finance*, tr. E. P. Marget (New York: 1936), 377–98.

initially evident. But Ricardo, and de Viti de Marco, anticipated this and made this extension. The individual who possesses no capital assets which he can sell to raise funds to meet his extraordinary tax obligation must of necessity borrow privately, thereby obligating himself to meet future interest charges on a private debt. In this case, provided only that the interest rates on the public and the private debts are the same, the individual owes an equivalent interest charge in each future period. The effect of the government's replacing the extraordinary tax with the public loan is nothing more than the replacement of a whole set of private loan arrangements with the public loan.[30]

It is at this point that Ricardo as well as de Viti de Marco became confused. Accepting the restrictive assumptions necessary for the analysis to be valid, how does this analysis affect the question as to whether the burden of the debt is shifted forward in time? Both Ricardo and de Viti suggested that the full burden of the debt must rest on individuals living at the time of debt creation.

But how may the "burden" of the debt be defined? In one sense we may define it as the sacrifice of goods and services which could have been consumed if the public expenditure which the debt financed had not been undertaken. It is clear that burden in this sense must rest on individuals living in future generations. They are the individuals who must sacrifice a portion of their income for debt service which they otherwise could have consumed. And the fact that bondholders receive the interest payments on internal debt does not modify this conclusion. If, however, the burden of the debt is defined in this manner, how can individuals living in future time periods be in equivalent positions in the two situations, with the debt and with the extraordinary tax? The answer can only be that individuals living in future time periods *must also bear the real burden of the extraordinary tax under the narrowly restrictive Ricardian–de Vitian assumptions.* It is true that, under these assumptions, the effects of the loan and the extraordinary tax are equivalent, but the correct inference is that the real burden of both is passed on to future

---

30. The most complete statement of Ricardo's position is to be found in *Principles of Political Economy and Taxation, Works and Correspondence* (London: Royal Economic Society, 1951), 1, 244–46.

time periods, not that this burden is borne in both cases by the individuals living during the initial period.

This rather paradoxical conclusion may be readily seen when the nature of the extraordinary tax required to make the Ricardian proposition hold is examined. Both Ricardo and de Viti assumed that such a tax would be drawn wholly from privately held capital assets, that is to say, that either individuals would sell off capital holdings sufficiently to finance the tax obligation or they would create private debts (incur capital liabilities) to the full amount of the individual share of the tax. In other words, the extraordinary tax was to be a capital levy *in fact,* regardless of the form which the fiscal authority chooses. If the full amount of the tax is financed from capital, then it becomes clear that the current generation does not suffer any real income reduction. The current generation essentially "draws on capital" in the form of the public project undertaken.

The failure to grasp this point appears to have been fundamental, but the reason for this is not difficult to find. The individuals who are coercively forced to give up resources, whether these are drawn from consumption or investment uses, are normally considered to "bear" the costs of the project financed. Taxes, of any sort, are held to impose a sacrifice on individuals during the period when the tax obligations must be met. This becomes a reasonable, and correct, inference when it is recognized that the ownership of capital assets itself provides some utility to the individual. This being the case, we can say that regardless of the source of the funds paid out in taxes, the individual undergoes a "sacrifice" of utility. It may also be claimed that if individuals fully discount future tax obligations the creation of future interest payments on a debt reduces the present value of an expected utility stream. Thus, both the extraordinary tax and the public debt of like amount must be "paid" by individuals during the time of the original transaction.

Thus, we have reached diametrically opposing conclusions; first we stated that the burden of both the extraordinary tax and the public loan rests, under the Ricardian–de Vitian assumptions, exclusively on individuals living in future time periods. This conclusion holds when we consider burden in terms of sacrificed real goods and services. Secondly, we stated that the burden of both the extraordinary tax and the public loan rests, under the full Ricardian–de Vitian assumptions, on the individuals living during the initial period. This conclusion holds when we try to measure sacrifice or burden in terms of the change in present value of an expected or anticipated utility stream and when we attribute some positive utility to the holding of income-earning assets.

The confusion of these two concepts becomes especially likely when it is recognized that the actual form of any conceivable tax levy, either extraordinary or normal, must differ from the Ricardian model in the direction which adds to the confusion. The Ricardian model overlooks the essential difference between the coercive levy of taxes and the voluntary subscription to public loans. Any coercive imposition of a tax seems certain to reduce both current consumption spending and investment spending. The assumption that only the latter is affected, that is, only private capital formation is reduced (private liability formation increased), is clearly incorrect. If we make the assumption that an individual attempts at any point in time to attain some marginal equalization between the present value of expected future enjoyments of income and the present value of current enjoyments of income, then any tax imposition will cause him to adjust both types of outlay downward. Some portion of any tax must come from current consumption spending, whatever the form that this tax takes. This being the case, some share of the extraordinary tax comes to rest on individuals living in the initial period, even if we consider only the real aspects and ignore the utility aspects altogether. On the other hand, the public loan operates through voluntary subscription. Individuals are likely to reduce current consumption outlay only insofar as the interest rate encourages an increased rate of saving, a questionable relationship. The major share of funds going into the purchase of government securities does come from private capital formation. The generation of individuals currently living sacrifices nothing in utility and little, if anything, in real goods and services in creating the loan. Therefore, in the real sense, there is a differential effect between the extraordinary tax and the public loan.

This differential effect is further widened when it is recognized that the full Ricardian assumptions do not hold on the utility side either. Individuals do not fully discount future tax payments. If the Ricardian–de Vitian reasoning is accepted for all individuals owning capital assets and receiving sufficient income to allow them to borrow privately, there still may be other large groups of individuals. These comprise the bulk of the lower income or laboring classes. It is impossible to levy extraordinary taxes on these individuals. The extraordinary tax must be levied on the first two groups. But, if the public debt is created, some portion of the annual interest charges may be placed on the third group. The lower income classes in future time periods may bear a portion of the burden of the public loan, whereas they must, by definition, escape fully the burden of the extraordinary tax. This is the objection which Griziotti raised to the de Viti elaboration of the Ricardian thesis.[31]

De Viti de Marco attempted to refute this objection, but he was not really successful. He tried to show that even the complete exemption of all non-propertied individuals from the extraordinary tax would not affect his conclusions. Here he introduced a long-run competitive model. He reasoned that such exemption would tend to increase the relative attractiveness of the professional non-propertied occupations. This would, in turn, cause more people to enter these occupations and to turn away from those activities such as management and administration of property. In the long run, the lot of the non-propertied classes would tend to be identical with that which they would enjoy even if they were taxed for the service of the public loan. As Griziotti suggested, this represents the stretching of the competitive model a bit too far.

Griziotti went further and argued that even for individuals owning capital assets discounting of future tax payments does not take place fully. Individuals do not act as if they live forever, and familial lines are not treated as being continuous. There is nothing sacred about maintaining capital intact, and individuals will not necessarily do so. The equivalence hypothesis requires continued abstinence from consuming capital on the part of those holding capital assets after public debt is created. Whereas the extraordinary tax effectively removes from an individual's possibilities the capital sum (once he has paid the tax he can no longer convert at least that portion of his capital into income), the disposition over this capital remains in his power in the public debt case. He may convert this capital into income at any time, without in any way removing the tax obligation on his heirs which is necessitated by the debt service.

---

31. Benvenuto Griziotti, "La diversa pressione tributaria del prestito e dell' imposta," *Giornale degli economisti* (1917), reprinted in *Studi di scienza delle finanze e diritto finanziario* (Milan: 1956), 2, 193–261.

Griziotti's claim that the creation of public debts does involve a shifting of the tax burden forward in time was not successful in overcoming the dominance of the de Viti de Marco elaboration of the Ricardian thesis in Italy. The prestige and apparent logical clarity of the de Vitian argument coupled with the changed conditions were successful in reducing the Griziotti influence. There have been isolated supporters of Griziotti,[32] but the de Viti formulation continues to dominate the Italian scene.

Additional elements of the de Viti de Marco conception of public debt may be mentioned, since he anticipated much of the "new orthodoxy," which came to be adopted in the United States only after the Keynesian revolution. To anticipate erroneous ideas is, of course, no great contribution, but de Viti's arguments concerning the problem of debt repayment are surprisingly modern in this respect. Included in his discussion of the public debt is what he called the theory of automatic amortization. De Viti used this to demonstrate that debt should never be repaid. De Viti started from his interpretation of the Ricardian argument that public debt merely serves as a substitute for private debts. He assumes a community of three individuals, only one of whom is a capitalist.[33] Now assume that the state requires a sum of 1,200,000 lire and levies an extraordinary tax, 400,000 on each individual. Individual 1 being the capitalist, individuals 2 and 3 will find it necessary to borrow from him in order to meet their tax obligations paying an assumed interest rate of 5 per cent. As these individuals save in future periods, they may amortize their debt to the capitalist.

Now assume that the government, instead of levying the tax, borrows the 1,200,000 directly from individual 1. The annual interest charge will be 60,000, and it is assumed to collect 20,000 from each of the three citizens. As in the first case, as individuals 2 and 3 save they may utilize this savings to purchase the government securities, which are assumed to be marketable, from individual 1. Their purchase of government securities in this case is identical in effect to their paying off private debts in the other case. Therefore, as the government securities are widely circulated among the population, the real debt is more or less automatically amortized. Individuals in

---

32. For example, see F. Maffezzoni, "Ancora della diversa pressione tributaria del prestito e dell' imposta," *Rivista di diritto finanziario e scienza delle finanze,* 9 (1950), 341–75.
33. This argument is developed in *First Principles of Public Finance,* 390–93.

purchasing debt instruments acquire an asset to offset their tax liabilities. The weight of the debt is effectively destroyed; hence debt need never be repaid, and there need be no fear that a country cannot bear the burden of public debts, however heavy these might appear to be.

This construction is both ingenious and misleading. Let us consider the private borrowing case carefully. Individuals 2 and 3, as they accumulate savings, increase their net worth, and they must also increase some item on the asset side, let us say, cash. When they accumulate sufficient cash to warrant paying off a portion of the private debt, the transaction is represented on their balance sheets as a drawing down of the cash item and a corresponding drawing down of their liability item. *Net worth does not change with debt repayment.*[34]

The construction is identical with the public loan. As individuals accumulate savings, these must take some form, cash, savings accounts, etc. Net worth is increased along with whatever asset item the individual chooses to put his savings into. At one point we assume that the individual accumulates sufficient funds to purchase a debt instrument. In so doing, he reduces his cash item and increases another asset item, government securities. He has, in this particular transaction, merely transformed one asset into another. *His net worth is not modified.* Therefore, the weight of having to pay the annual tax upon the debt instrument is precisely as heavy after as before his acquisition of the security.

De Viti de Marco is correct, in the extremes of his model, in saying that this transaction is equivalent to the repayment of private loans. In this sense the public debt is said to be amortized. But his error lies in inferring from this that public debt should not be repaid in fact. This error is based upon a misunderstanding of private loans. Implicit in the de Viti formulation is the idea that the repayment of private loans is necessarily beneficial to the individual. De Viti assumed that such repayment increases private net worth, and thereby reduces the weight or "pressure" of the loan. He failed to see that the new savings which go into private debt repayment have alternative employments. Whether or not private debt repayment reduces "pressure" on the individual economy depends solely upon the relative rates of return.

---

34. Cf. F. Maffezzoni, "Ancora della diversa pressione tributaria del prestito e dell' imposta," op. cit., 348.

The same is true for public debt. Having demonstrated that the transfer of public debt instruments might be similar in some models to private debt repayment, de Viti inferred that this "amortization" reduces the pressure or weight of the public debt. This is not necessarily true at all. The weight of debt remains as it was before, and the purchase of government securities can modify this only insofar as the relative rates of yield on government securities and other assets place the individual in a more preferred position.

This demonstration that the de Viti argument does not show that public debt should not be repaid cannot be applied in reverse. By saying that de Viti de Marco was wrong in making this extension is not to say that public debt *should be repaid.*

PUVIANI AND THE FISCAL ILLUSION

The contributions discussed so far have for the most part been due to the "economic" branch of Italian fiscal theory represented notably by de Viti de Marco and Einaudi. Several of the particular contributions are derivative from the general methodological approach, which recognizes the productivity of public services. The opposing school of thought has also made useful contributions, and, in some respects, these are more original and unique. Therefore, in some criteria, they should assume first rank. By far the most important of these is the idea of the fiscal illusion. It does not come directly from orthodox Italian fiscal theory, for it has scarcely been noted to a greater degree in Italy than elsewhere. The idea, vaguely expressed in the works of many writers, earlier and later, was crystallized in the work of one man, Amilcare Puviani, who wrote around the turn of the century.[35] In his time, his efforts were largely ignored, and it is only after his "rediscovery" by Fasiani that his ideas have now begun to exert some considerable influence on Italian thought.[36] Almost simultaneously, other continental writers are be-

35. Puviani's main work is *Teoria della illusione finanziaria* (Palermo: 1903). This book, which was published in a limited edition, is now extremely difficult to locate, and I have not been able to consult it directly. I am grateful to the late Professor Benvenuto Griziotti of the University of Pavia for the use of his personal copy of a somewhat older and equally rare Puviani book, *Teoria della illusione nelle entrate pubbliche* (Perugia: 1897).

36. Fasiani has thoroughly discussed and summarized the Puviani contribution in his treatise, and he includes direct quotations of the most important parts. See Mauro Fasi-

ginning to incorporate essentially similar ideas into their works on fiscal theory, although apparently independent of the ideas of Puviani.[37]

Puviani was, above all else, a political realist. He looked at the world around him and saw no sign of genuine democratic participation in the process of making collective choices. Such choices appeared to him to be made by the ruling or governing class, and he entertained no illusions about these choices being made in accordance with any vague criteria of general interest. The choices were not even conceived to be rationally made for the benefit of the governing class itself. Decisions as such were usually made on pragmatic grounds, and each was reached on the basis of causing the minimum of social friction.

From this approach Puviani constructed his hypothesis. He stated that the actions of the government could best be explained by the hypothesis that the government always acts to hide the burden of taxes from the public and to magnify the benefits of public expenditures. He was careful to state that governments do not actually do this as a deliberate plan. His hypothesis is, like all such similar ones, advanced as a working model, an *as if* sort of theoretical structure. When the governing group is successful in these attempts, fiscal illusions are created which effectively modify human behavior.

How do the separate parts of the modern fiscal structure fit the Puviani hypothesis? We may look first of all at the revenue, or tax, side. There is first the effort of governments to secure as much revenue as possible through the use of the public domain, that is, income-producing property owned by the state. Insofar as revenue can be raised from this source, private individuals do not consider themselves to undergo a net burden; the opportunity costs are not individualized, and no checks are imposed on government spending. The second and perhaps most obvious means of creating a fiscal illusion lies in the use of indirect taxes rather than direct taxes. The taxpayer-consumer is not able to isolate the public from the private part of his ordinary purchase price, and in this way the real value of his tax burden appears less than it

---

ani, *Principii di scienza delle finanze,* 2nd ed. (Turin: 1951), 1, 78–188. I should also mention the work of Vinci, written on the occasion of the fiftieth anniversary of the appearance of Puviani's main volume. See Felice Vinci, *La teoria dell' illusione finanziaria di A. Puviani nel suo cinquantesimo anniversario* (Milan: 1953).

37. See P. L. Reynaud, "La psychologie du contribuable devant l'impôt," *Revue de Science et Legislation Financiere,* 39 (1947), and 40 (1948).

might actually be. A third and equally evident means is provided in the raising of revenues through inflation of the monetary unit. Here the public clearly is hoodwinked, and it has been through the ages.

The remaining devices which governments use to create fiscal illusions are perhaps somewhat more subtle. Puviani said that the individual was not able to properly balance future income against current income. He will, therefore, consider the annual tax in perpetuity to be of less burden to him than the current capitalized value of that tax stream. Governments fully recognize this, and, as a result, public loans are always favored for extraordinary expenditures in preference to extraordinary taxes or capital levies.

Governments also recognize that taxes are more accepted by the taxpaying public if the moment of payment is associated with some pleasurable, and preferably unusual, event. Herein lies the explanation of gift taxation, according to Puviani, and, in fact, all taxes on transfers of wealth. The case of taxation of lottery winnings is clear. Similarly, taxes on non-ordinary consumption expenditures which are representative of the fulfillment of life-long desires are explained on this basis. Examples are taxes on the purchase of fine jewels or objects of art.

A device which always works, and which rings loud bells in application to fiscal structures today, is that of introducing taxes under the guise that they are temporary or expedient and then allowing them to become permanent fixtures of the system. Closely allied to this, of course, is the adage that the old tax is the good tax. This is a principle perfectly in accord with the basic Puviani hypothesis. The governing group will clearly consider the old tax as a good one because people have become accustomed to paying it, and, therefore, its payment does not create as much social disturbance as would a newly imposed tax of like amount.

Still another source of exploitation for the government is provided in the social conflict between classes. By playing off one class against the other, the government can secure the ready acceptance of taxes which would otherwise be difficult. As an example, Puviani states that the wealthy classes can be made to accept heavy taxes if the specter of the upheaval of the lower classes is presented to them. Or, if political and social forces should temporarily place one social class in great disfavor with the rest of the population, the government can take this opportunity to impose excessively heavy taxes upon the oppressed class or group.

Yet another Puviani example which strikes hard to the modern reader is the device of governments' posing the awful and dire consequences of the alternative to a proposed tax. Puviani says that the alternative of the destruction of the social system, for example, the breakdown of international relations, will habitually be posed when a new tax bill is proposed. Modern expenditures for national defense and for foreign aid are clear examples of this sort of attempt on the part of governments, even in nominally democratic societies such as our own.

Both the timing and the form of the tax can also foster fiscal illusions. If collected in small amounts and distributed over time, the tax will always appear to be less burdensome than one which is concentrated in time. Similarly, the collection of a given amount under the guise of many small taxes may well seem to exert less fiscal pressure than the collection of a like amount under one consolidated tax bill.

A final form of fiscal illusion involved in the levy of taxes comes about in the uncertainty concerning the actual incidence of the tax. Governments will try not to levy taxes for which the incidence is known. The aim will rather be to introduce as much uncertainty as is possible, thus keeping the individual in the dark concerning the actual amount of tax which he does pay in real terms.

The examples of fiscal illusions discussed above appear on the revenue side and act so as to make the taxpayer think that he is paying less than he actually does pay toward the cost of government. The fiscal illusion can be equally important, and is equally used, on the expenditure side. Here the procedure is that of making the taxpayer think that he is getting more from public services than he actually does get. Puviani points out that the taxpayers, through their representatives, have always demanded the right to approve taxes independent of and in advance of the demand for the right to make appropriations. And, even where the right of making appropriations has been won from executive authorities, the specialization of modern budgets prevents genuine control from being exercised. This provides the executive authority, the government, with an excellent opportunity to use fiscal illusions in the securing of legislative approval. For this reason, the executive tries to keep the budget as complex as is possible,[38] while fostering the belief

38. Although this is not the place for an extended discussion, the impact of the Puviani analysis on the very core of modern budgetary theory is evident. Budgetary theory has

among the taxpayers that they are participating effectively in the control of spending.

Although it is not stressed by Puviani, perhaps the most effective means through which the modern executive authority can distort public thinking concerning the efficacy of public expenditure lies in the use of generalized categories which are largely meaningless to the voter-taxpayer. In recent years in this country, almost all types of expenditure have been justified by the catch-all category "national defense," and active attempts have been made by the bureaucracy to render this budget category sacrosanct. If this goal could, in fact, be achieved, the fiscal illusion would be complete, and the executive authority would have effectively removed all public constraint. So long as the debate can be kept in terms of Air Force "Wings" without consideration of the make-up of such categories, the illusion will remain. The Puviani approach suggests, of course, that the most productive of all legislative activity in this age of budget specialization is precisely that of the much-ridiculed investigation into the "paper clips for the Navy." Only by the potential threat of detailed examination of budgetary items can the normal executive power be kept within reasonable bounds.

The importance of the Puviani-Fasiani idea of the fiscal illusion does not lie in any of the particular examples from modern fiscal practice which it does seem to explain. Its importance is rather to be found in the fact that such a large proportion of the modern fiscal system can be explained by a hypothesis which is directly contrary either to the de Viti–Einaudi conception of the public economy or to the classical Anglo-Saxon conception of a fiscal structure based on "ability-to-pay." Puviani asked two simple questions: (1) If a completely rational dictator or class desires to exploit the tax-paying public to the greatest possible degree, what sort of fiscal system will result? (2) To what extent do modern fiscal systems approach this model? As the above discussion indicates, the fit is a surprisingly good one, and certainly the Puviani hypothesis must take its place among the important contributions to fiscal theory. As Fasiani pointed out, this hypothesis does not serve as the single explanation, but neither does any other.

---

been formulated on the implicit assumption that some omniscient executive acts genuinely in the "public interest." Once the ruling class conception of the executive is raised or admitted, the whole budgetary conception must, of course, be drastically modified.

Puviani made no attempt to extend his analysis toward the development of normative principles for fiscal activity. He was merely explaining what happens in the autocratic state. If, however, democratic ideals are accepted, Puviani's analysis points the way toward a set of norms for fiscal activity.[39]

THE COERCIVE ELEMENT IN FISCAL CHOICE

It is but natural that those theorists who locate effective decision-making power in a directing class or group should also have emphasized the coercive elements which are involved in the fiscal process. In so doing they have been able to provide both an incisive critique of the "economic," or voluntary, theories of collective choice and a substantial contribution in their own right. Important figures in this tradition are Conigliani, Montemartini, Barone, Murray, and Cosciani.

These writers attempt to construct an economic theory of public finance along with those like de Viti and Einaudi and opposed to those like Pareto and Borgatta, who deny this as a possibility. But while the economic aspects of fiscal choice are central to this approach, the location of the choice-making power is no longer with the individual, who is both producer and consumer of the public services. The fiscal decisions are made by some directing, or ruling, class which is, by definition or implication, smaller than the total group. Once this is accepted as a premise, it is evident that fiscal decisions can only be carried out through coercion. It would be unreasonable to expect that individuals who do not participate in the choice process should voluntarily accept and comply with such decisions as may be made.

Montemartini is the apparent source of many of the ideas in this tradition, and his ideas are especially interesting.[40] He viewed the state as an enterprise which produces the service of coercion; the political entrepreneurs purchase this service in order to carry out economic aims. Such political en-

---

39. It is along these lines that I hope to do considerably more work. A whole set of fiscal principles can be developed on the presumption that fiscal choice should result from individual behavior which is as rational as is possible. Therefore, as a normative proposition, all fiscal illusions must be removed. On this basis, important criticism can be made against many elements of the existing fiscal structure.

40. G. Montemartini, "Le base fondamentali di una scienza finanziaria pura," *Giornale degli economisti,* 2 (1900), 555–76.

trepreneurs have available to them three means of meeting any given objective. They may, first of all, achieve it by individual action. Secondly, they may form a voluntary and private association and undertake cooperative action. Thirdly, they may ask that the state do it for them. In choosing among these alternatives, this group will be guided by least-cost criteria. If, by purchasing coercion from the state, the group is able to reduce its own cost, it will choose this means. But Montemartini was clear in his emphasis that the service of coercion itself was costly.

His numerical example is perhaps worth repeating. Suppose that we are considering a society of ten individuals with equal incomes of $10 each. Now suppose that eight of these desire that $56 be spent collectively for the provision of a public water supply. The other two desire that water be provided through individual private efforts. If the eight form a voluntary cooperative association, the cost to each will be $7. But if they can secure the service through a community effort which is financed by a general tax, this cost will be reduced to $5.60. From this example, Montemartini indicated that the lower-cost criteria may not always be relevant to the choosing of a collective action over a private one. But the example is not yet complete. The cost of imposing the necessary coercion on the two reluctant individuals has not been taken into account. And if these are fully considered, the public administration of the service may not be selected, even if the actual outlay necessary to finance the service is reduced by public action. Suppose that the public activity can reduce the cost from $56 to $50. If the costs of coercing the two minority members should be greater than $20, the majority of eight would still find it to their advantage to form the private association.

The Montemartini analysis clearly points up one of the major shortcomings of the de Viti–Einaudi analysis if the latter is considered to be explanatory rather than normative. This is the implication that the state's usage of the resources taken away from private employments by taxes must be at least as productive as private uses from which these resources are withdrawn. Unless unanimity is present in the choice (a point which Wicksell clearly perceived and upon which he based his tax theory), there is no assurance that, even in so-called "democratic choice processes," the real income of the community will be increased by the allocation of income to public uses.

The essential thesis of several writers in this tradition, notably Conigliani,

Murray, and Barone,[41] is that collective choices are by their nature different from individual choices. The basis for this argument is the distinction which was made by both Pantaleoni and Pareto between the problem of maximizing individual welfare and maximizing collective or social welfare. Pantaleoni argued that collective action need not imply coercion so long as it was aimed at the satisfaction of individual utilities. In this case individuals would freely and voluntarily contribute the necessary revenues to finance the public services.[42] In the terminology of modern welfare economics, this would indicate that some collective action could be carried out in accordance with the Paretian criteria for increasing general welfare. Conigliani, Murray, and the others were quick to point out, however, that this sort of action need not involve the state at all. If people will voluntarily contribute to finance state services, anarchism is the ideal social system. They argued that the very need for the state arose only because this was not the typical situation and that coercion was the one essential characteristic of all state action. Pantaleoni admitted the necessity of coercion when the state attempts to maximize in any way collective or social welfare. And he made a distinction between the maximization of individual welfare and the maximization of social welfare even within the choice pattern of the individual. This suggests that each individual acts in accordance with an individualized personal-utility or preference scale and at the same time with an individualized social preference scale. These may come into conflict at many points, and the individual may deliberately choose to be coerced and to coerce others if the social preference scale is overruling.

Pareto's distinction between the achievement of maximum utility *of* the society and the achievement of the maximum utility *for* the society is similar to that of Pantaleoni.[43] Murray, a close follower of Pareto, extended the Pa-

---

41. See C. A. Conigliani, "L'indirizzo teorico nella scienza finanziaria," *Giornale degli economisti,* 2 (1894), 105–29; R. A. Murray, "I problemi fondamentali dell' economia finanziaria," *Giornale degli economisti,* 1 (1912), 255–301; E. Barone, *Le opere economiche,* Vol. 3, *Principi di economia finanziaria* (Bologna: 1937).

42. M. Pantaleoni, "Cenni sul concetto di massimi edonistici individuali e collettivi," *Giornale degli economisti* (1891), reprinted in *Scritti varii di economia* (Rome: 1904), 281–340.

43. V. Pareto, "Il massimo di utilità per una collettivita in Sociologia," *Giornale degli economisti,* 1 (1913), 336–41.

reto analysis to the problem of fiscal choice. He tried to show that the achievement of any sort of collective or social maximum is impossible without the violation of some of the necessary conditions for the attainment of the individual maxima. State action necessarily implies some attempt in this direction; therefore, coercion is necessary.

Barone's conception of state activity was similar although somewhat more clearly stated. He pointed up the weakness in the voluntary theory of fiscal choice by showing that it is impossible to fix some distribution of the tax burden among individuals and then to say that the amount of public services is chosen voluntarily. The pre-fixing of the distribution of the tax burden, which is implicit in the work of de Viti and Einaudi, is essentially equivalent to choosing a social welfare function. Once this is chosen and action taken in accordance with it, no pretense of voluntary choice can be maintained. Coercion must be introduced. The individual is not allowed to calculate the utility of public services and to make his contributive choice accordingly. Barone sensed fully the necessity of the requirement of a Wicksellian unanimity in order to justify the use of any sort of voluntary theory of fiscal choice. But he denied the possibility of such unanimity being attained; therefore, the theory of finance reduces to the theory of the coercive distribution of the tax burden.

Cosciani is the modern interpreter of this tradition in Italian fiscal theory.[44] He states that the study of finance consists in the examination of the reasons for and the effects of the substitution of coercive collective choices for individual choices. Two sets of individual behavior are involved; first, that of the ruling class in making the decisions, and secondly, that of the taxpaying group in responding to the alternatives put before them. Anglo-Saxon fiscal theory has, of course, almost exclusively been concentrated on the second of these two sets of behavior. In a very real sense, therefore, our theoretical structure is more in keeping with the ruling-class tradition than with the voluntary tradition. The merit of the ruling-class conception appears to be its usefulness in forcing the separate consideration of these two aspects of fiscal action.

---

44. C. Cosciani, *Principii di scienza della finanze* (Turin: 1953).

MISCELLANEOUS CONTRIBUTIONS

Italian theorists have made several other, and more specific, contributions. A few of these may be noted briefly. The first consists in the application of the Paretian indifference curve apparatus to the classical problem of the relative burden of the income tax and the consumption tax. This application was first made by Barone in 1912, utilized again by Borgatta in 1921, and further developed by Fasiani in 1930.[45] It did not appear in English until the celebrated note by Miss Joseph was published in 1939.[46] This "excess burden" analysis has recently been criticized, and correctly so, on the basis of the attempts which have been made to extend the conclusions reached to any general statements relative to the merits of the general income tax and the excise tax. It is interesting to note, however, that this extension was not made by Barone or Fasiani. Both emphasized the partial-equilibrium nature of the conclusions reached and specifically warned that the analysis could not easily be applied to the community as a whole.

A second contribution closely related to the same analysis is that made by Gobbi. He argued that there is no difference in the burden of a consumption tax and an income tax of equal yield.[47] This was based on the alleged invalidity of the Marshallian concept of consumers' surplus. It seems clear that Gobbi was thinking in terms of the community as a whole, and that his rejection of consumers' surplus is based on an early recognition that this is not additive, and, therefore, it is of little use in general tax analysis. He stated that the consumers' surplus for all goods must be zero.[48]

A third contribution, made by Pareto and developed to some extent by Borgatta, consists in nothing more than some fragmentary ideas which seem to offer some insights into the process of fiscal choice. Clearly recognizing

45. E. Barone, "Studi di economia finanziaria," *Giornale degli economisti*, 2 (1912), 329–30, in notes; G. Borgatta, "Intorno alla pressione di qualunque imposta a parità di prelievo," *Giornale degli economisti*, 2 (1921), 290–97; M. Fasiani, "Di un particolare aspetto delle imposte sul consumo," *La riforma sociale*, 40 (1930), 1–20.

46. M. F. W. Joseph, "The Excess Burden of Indirect Taxation," *Review of Economic Studies*, 6 (1938–39), 226–31.

47. U. Gobbi, "Un preteso difetto delle imposte sui consumi," *Giornale degli economisti*, 1 (1904), 296–306.

48. Ibid., 301.

that all actual choices must be made by individuals, whether in their capacity as taxpayers-voters or as members of some ruling class, Pareto argued that the individual choices which go into the making of collective decisions are necessarily non-logical. It is therefore erroneous to attribute rationality to such choices and to judge them by any criteria of rational behavior. Non-logical action is not equivalent to purposefully irrational action. Rather it is action which may be ruled by mixed motives, which has no fixed objective, which involves many uncertainties. The chooser is not able to predict the results of his behavior with any degree of certainty, and even if he could do so, he would have little idea as to what goals he really seeks to maximize. Social man is essentially different from individual man. Out of the complex of actions which are taken, some logical, some non-logical, it may be possible to discover some uniformities, and it is here that a theory of finance must be discovered. It is not surprising that these ideas were not carried much further than this,[49] but any theory of collective choice must take the Paretian conception into account. It suffices to throw out both the voluntaristic approach, which assumes the taxpayer-voter to act similarly to his action in the private economy, and the organismic approach, which attributes some superior rationality to the collective entity.

V. A Comparative Summary

This discussion of the Italian tradition in fiscal theory may be concluded by a brief comparison with the Anglo-Saxon tradition. The latter is directly related to neo-classical economics and is specifically Marshallian in its essentials. Anglo-Saxon fiscal theory has analyzed the effects of particular fiscal measures (almost exclusively tax measures) upon the private economy. The analysis has normally been conceived in a partial-equilibrium framework, although recently the Keynesian influence has served to shift this emphasis somewhat. The usefulness of Anglo-Saxon thought depends upon, and is

---

49. See G. Borgatta, "Lo studio scientifico dei fenomeni finanziari," *Giornale degli economisti,* 1 (1920), 1–24, 81–116, for a good discussion of this point of view. For Pareto's own statement, see G. Sensini, *Corrispondenza di Vilfredo Pareto* (Padua: 1948), cited in M. Fasiani, "Contributi di Pareto alla scienza delle finanze," *Giornale degli economisti* (1949), 156.

limited by, this characteristic feature. Fiscal theory has been an adjunct of economic theory, and as such, it has been useful for many purposes, but it has been little else.[50]

It is appropriate to ask whether this is the proper role for finance theory. Surely the function of such theorizing must be that of analyzing and explaining the results of government action, however this action may be motivated. But government is co-dimensional with the whole economy and includes within its scope all of the individual units of this economy. Government action cannot, therefore, be limited in any genuine sense to any specific subsector. As del Vecchio wisely remarks, it is impossible to properly conceive fiscal theory in other than general-equilibrium terms. This does not suggest the necessity of using Walrasian-Paretian models for all fiscal problems, but it does imply that the interdependence among variables must be fully recognized. Spillover effects cannot simply be neglected in the faith that these will fade away and become unimportant as is the case in so many areas of applied economics. By their very nature fiscal problems are general welfare problems, not the problems of particular groups of persons, classes, or industries.

The great merit of the Italians is that they have placed fiscal theory in a broad framework in which the necessary interdependence has been fully recognized. By and large, their system is internally consistent. The weaknesses are much the same as those of Walrasian economics. Problem-solving has been relatively neglected. We find, for example, little discussion of the incidence of particular taxes or expenditures. But we should not measure contributions in terms of wordage on either side. A great deal of the Anglo-Saxon discussion on incidence has been of little value precisely because the general-equilibrium aspects of the problems have not been taken into account.

Contemporary Italian economists will freely admit that their tradition has suffered from an excess of "system" at the expense of "problem-solving." But all good Marshallians must acknowledge just as freely that the latter effort is fruitful only insofar as the "system" or the methodology is sound. While

---

50. This point is made by Earl Rolph, *The Theory of Fiscal Economics* (Berkeley: University of California Press, 1954), ix.

Fubini was correct in holding Marshall up as an idol to the Italian theorists, perhaps a good dose of Ferrara would be equally helpful to modern fiscal Marshallians.

The English-language tradition has almost completely neglected the second major problem of fiscal theory, that of collective choice. This has been introduced only in welfare economics, and this sometimes-rarified branch of study has rarely been tied to fiscal theory.[51] The Italian emphasis upon the state or the public entity as the subject of analysis, rather than the private economy, has forced attention to the problem of choice, in reference both to the collective unit and to the individual taxpayer-beneficiary. Much remains to be accomplished here, but students must look to the Italian and other continental sources, notably Wicksell, for any hints and directions; the Anglo-Saxons have defaulted, with the very recent exceptions noted above.

Finally, no reforming spirit has guided the Italians. This has made their arguments seem sterile and devoid of normative content. The normative elements which are present are usually clouded over, perhaps unintentionally, with pseudo-scientific pronouncements. This has not been a strong feature of the Italian tradition, but we can lay little claim to superiority here. Unconsciously trapped by our utilitarian heritage, we have accepted and promoted all of the nonsense which is contained in the theories of proportional, equal, and minimum sacrifice, etc. Only a handful of writers, such as Henry Simons, have been able to break through the enveloping fog.

Italian fiscal theory has many deficiencies, and it is certainly not lacking in its own varieties of nonsense. This "science" seems peculiarly addicted to the attraction of "fuzziness," whatever the land of origin. It may perhaps be charged that precious time is wasted in the attempt to sift old and foreign doctrines for good ideas. But if any progress is to be made, fiscal theory must break out of its current strait-jacket, and a hybridization may be required to accomplish this. Economists simply cannot neglect a fundamental re-examination of the whole orthodoxy upon which economic policy in this most important subject area has been, and continues to be, made.

51. The recent efforts by Bowen, Musgrave, and Samuelson provide notable exceptions.

BIBLIOGRAPHICAL NOTE

The student interested in a short history of the Italian work in fiscal theory should look first at G. del Vecchio, *Introduzione alla finanza,* 2nd ed. (Padua: 1957). A summary history of doctrine may also be found in L. Gangemi, *Elementi di scienza delle finanze* (Naples: 1948). For a single article summarizing the Italian contribution, Borgatta's introduction to the Italian translation of Wicksell's *Finanztheoretische Untersuchungen* and other essays is recommended (*Nuova Collana di Economisti,* Vol. 9, *Finanza* [Turin: 1934]).

The student interested in going to the original source for a surprisingly large proportion of the Italian ideas is directed to the work of Ferrara. Of all the Italians, Pareto included, Ferrara must assume first rank, and in his work may be found germs of later developments, not only in fiscal theory, but in all of economic theory as well. His complete works are only now in the process of being issued, volumes 1, 2, 3, and 4 having been published (Francesco Ferrara, *Opere complete* [Rome: 1955, 1956]). His work in fiscal theory is largely contained in his lectures, which were taken as notes (Ferrara, *Lezioni di economia politica,* 2 vols. [Bologna: 1934]).

Pantaleoni's works in public finance are scattered, and they have not been collected in a single volume. Barone's major writings on finance are available in volume 3 of his works *Le opere economiche* (Enrico Barone, *Principi di economia finanziaria* [Bologna: 1937]). The English translation of de Viti de Marco's *First Principles of Public Finance* is available, but this book does not, in itself, properly convey the Italian contribution. Einaudi's treatise is recommended: Luigi Einaudi, *Principii di scienza della finanza,* 3rd ed. (Turin: 1945), but his best work has appeared in his essays; the most important collection of his essays is *Saggi sul risparmio e l'imposta* (Turin: 1941).

Almost all of the important work in Italian fiscal theory appeared in the professional journals prior to later publication in book form. Prior to 1920, the *Giornale degli economisti* contained almost all of the important papers. After about 1920, Einaudi's review *La riforma sociale* began to attract important contributions.

At the present time, the most important Italian journal in public finance is *Rivista di diritto finanziario e scienza delle finanze,* which was founded by the late Professor Griziotti and which is issued at the University of Pavia.

The most important single work which appeared in Italy in the post-war period has been the second edition of the late Mauro Fasiani's treatise *Principii di scienza delle finanze,* 2 vols. (Turin: 1951).

PART TWO

Externalities

Externality

James M. Buchanan and Wm. Craig Stubblebine

Externality has been, and is, central to the neo-classical critique of market organisation. In its various forms—external economies and diseconomies, divergencies between marginal social and marginal private cost or product, spillover and neighbourhood effects, collective or public goods—externality dominates theoretical welfare economics, and, in one sense, the theory of economic policy generally. Despite this importance and emphasis, rigourous definitions of the concept itself are not readily available in the literature. As Scitovosky has noted, "definitions of external economies are few and unsatisfactory."[1] The following seems typical:

> External effects exist in consumption whenever the shape or position of a man's indifference curve depends on the consumption of other men.
>
> [External effects] are present whenever a firm's production function depends in some way on the amounts of the inputs or outputs of another firm.[2]

It seems clear that operational and usable definitions are required.

In this paper, we propose to clarify the notion of externality by defining it rigorously and precisely. When this is done, several important, and often overlooked, conceptual distinctions follow more or less automatically.

From *Economica* 29 (November 1962): 371–84. Copyright 1962 by London School of Economics and Political Science. Reprinted by permission of Blackwell Publishers Ltd.

1. Tibor Scitovsky, "Two Concepts of External Economies," *Journal of Political Economy,* vol. 62 (1954), 143.

2. J. de V. Graaf, *Theoretical Welfare Economics,* Cambridge, 1957, 43 and 18.

Specifically, we shall distinguish marginal and infra-marginal externalities, potentially relevant and irrelevant externalities, and Pareto-relevant and Pareto-irrelevant externalities. These distinctions are formally developed in Section I. As we shall demonstrate, the term, "externality," as generally used by economists, corresponds only to our definition of Pareto-relevant externality. There follows, in Section II, an illustration of the basic points described in terms of a simple descriptive example. In Section III, some of the implications of our approach are discussed.

It is useful to limit the scope of the analysis at the outset. Much of the discussion in the literature has been concerned with the distinction between *technological* and *pecuniary* external effects. We do not propose to enter this discussion since it is not relevant for our purposes. We note only that, if desired, the whole analysis can be taken to apply only to technological externalities. Secondly, we shall find no cause for discussing production and consumption externalities separately. Essentially the same analysis applies in either case. In what follows, "firms" may be substituted for "individuals," and "production functions" for "utility functions" without modifying the central conclusions. For expositional simplicity only, we limit the explicit discussion to consumption externalities.

I

We define an external effect, *an externality*, to be present when,

$$u^A = u^A (X_1, X_2, \ldots, X_m, Y_1). \tag{1}$$

This states that the utility of an individual, A, is dependent upon the "activities," $(X_1, X_2, \ldots, X_m)$, that are exclusively under his own control or authority, but also upon another single activity, Y_1, which is, by definition, under the control of a second individual, B, who is presumed to be a member of the same social group. We define an *activity* here as any distinguishable human action that may be measured, such as eating bread, drinking milk, spewing smoke into the air, dumping litter on the highways, giving to the poor, etc. Note that A's utility may, and will in the normal case, depend on other activities of B in addition to Y_1, and also upon the activities of other parties. That is, A's utility function may, in more general terms, include such variables as $(Y_2, Y_3, \ldots, Y_m; Z_1, Z_2, \ldots, Z_m)$. For analytical simplicity, however, we shall confine our attention to the effects of one particular activity, Y_1, as it affects the utility of A.

We assume that A will behave so as to maximise utility in the ordinary way, subject to the externally determined values for Y_1, and that he will modify the values for the X's, as Y_1 changes, so as to maintain a state of "equilibrium."

A marginal externality exists when,

$$u^A_{Y_1} \neq 0. \tag{2}$$

Here, small u's are employed to represent the "partial derivatives" of the utility function of the individual designated by the superscript with respect to the variables designated by the subscript. Hence, $u^A_{Y_1} = \partial u^A/\partial Y_1$, assuming that the variation in Y_1 is evaluated with respect to a set of "equilibrium" values for the X's, adjusted to the given value for Y_1.

An infra-marginal externality holds at those points where,

$$u^A_{Y_1} = 0, \tag{3}$$

and (1) holds.

These classifications can be broken down into economies and diseconomies: a marginal external economy existing when,

$$u^A_{Y_1} > 0, \tag{2A}$$

that is, a small change in the activity undertaken by B will change the utility of A in the same direction; a marginal external diseconomy existing when,

$$u^A_{Y_1} < 0. \tag{2B}$$

An infra-marginal external economy exists when for any given set of values for $(X_1, X_2, \ldots, X_m)$, say, $(C_1, C_2, \ldots, C_m)$,

$$u^A_{Y_1} = 0, \text{ and } \int_0^{Y_1} u^A_{Y_1} dy_1 > 0. \tag{3A}$$

This condition states that while incremental changes in the extent of B's activity, Y_1, have no effect on A's utility the total effect of B's action has increased A's utility. An infra-marginal diseconomy exists when (1) holds, and, for any given set of values for $(X_1, X_2, \ldots, X_m)$, say, $(C_1, C_2, \ldots, C_m)$, then,

$$u^A_{Y_1} = 0, \text{ and } \int_0^{Y_1} u^A_{Y_1} d_{Y_1} < 0. \tag{3B}$$

Thus, small changes in B's activity do not change A's level of satisfaction, but the total effect of B's undertaking the activity in question is harmful to A.

We are able to classify the effects of B's action, or potential action, on A's utility by evaluating the "partial derivative" of A's utility function with respect to Y_1 over all possible values for Y_1. In order to introduce the further distinctions between *relevant* and *irrelevant* externalities, however, it is necessary to go beyond consideration of A's utility function. Whether or not a relevant externality exists depends upon the extent to which the activity involving the externality is carried out by the person empowered to take action, to make decisions. Since we wish to consider a single externality in isolation, we shall assume that B's utility function includes only variables (activities) that are within his control, including Y_1. Hence, B's utility function takes the form,

$$u^B = u^B (Y_1, Y_2, \ldots, Y_m). \tag{4}$$

Necessary conditions for utility maximisation by B are,

$$u^B_{Y_1} \Big/ u^B_{Y_j} = f^B_{Y_1} \Big/ f^B_{Y_j}, \tag{5}$$

where Y_j is used to designate the activity of B in consuming or utilising some numeraire commodity or service which is, by hypothesis, available on equal terms to A. The right-hand term represents the marginal rate of substitution in "production" or "exchange" confronted by B, the party taking action on Y_1, his production function being defined as,

$$f^B = f^B(Y_1, Y_2, \ldots, Y_m), \tag{6}$$

where inputs are included as activities along with outputs. In other words, the right-hand term represents the marginal cost of the activity, Y_1, to B. The equilibrium values for the Y_i's will be designated as $\overline{Y_i}$'s.

An externality is defined as *potentially relevant* when the activity, to the extent that it is actually performed, generates *any* desire on the part of the externally benefited (damaged) party (A) to modify the behaviour of the party empowered to take action (B) through trade, persuasion, compromise, agreement, convention, collective action, etc. An externality which, to the extent that it is performed, exerts no such influence is defined as *irrelevant*.

Note that, so long as (1) holds, an externality remains; utility functions remain interdependent.

A potentially relevant marginal externality exists when,

$$u^A_{Y_1}\Big|_{Y_1 = \overline{Y}_1} \neq 0. \tag{7}$$

This is a potentially relevant marginal external economy when (7) is greater than zero, a diseconomy when (7) is less than zero. In either case, A is motivated by B's performance of the activity to make some effort to modify this performance, to increase the resources devoted to the activity when (7) is positive, to decrease the quantity of resources devoted to the activity when (7) is negative.

Infra-marginal externalities are, by definition, irrelevant for small changes in the scope of B's activity, Y_1. However, when large or discrete changes are considered, A is motivated to change B's behaviour with respect to Y_1 in all cases *except* that for which,

$$u^A_{Y_1}\Big|_{Y_1 = \overline{Y}_1} = 0, \text{ and}$$

$$u^A (C_1, C_2, \ldots, C_m, \overline{Y}_1) \geq u^A (C_1, C_2, \ldots, C_m, Y_1), \text{ for all } Y_1 \neq \overline{Y}_1. \tag{8}$$

When (8) holds, A has achieved an absolute maximum of utility with respect to changes over Y_1, given any set of values for the X's. In more prosaic terms, A is satiated with respect to Y_1.[3] In all other cases, where infra-marginal external economies or diseconomies exist, A will have some desire to modify B's performance; the externality is potentially relevant. Whether or not this motivation will lead A to seek an expansion or contraction in the extent of B's performance of the activity will depend on the location of the infra-marginal region relative to the absolute maximum for any given values of the X's.[4]

Pareto relevance and irrelevance may now be introduced. The existence of a simple desire to modify the behaviour of another, defined as potential

---

3. Note that $u^A_{Y_1}\Big|_{Y_1 = \overline{Y}_1} = 0$ is a necessary, but not a sufficient, condition for irrelevance.

4. In this analysis of the relevance of externalities, we have assumed that B will act in such a manner as to maximise his own utility subject to the constraints within which he must operate. If, for any reason, B does not attain the equilibrium position defined in (5) above, the classification of his activity for A may, of course, be modified. A potentially relevant externality may become irrelevant and *vice versa*.

relevance, need not imply the ability to implement this desire. An externality is defined to be Pareto-relevant when the extent of the activity may be modified in such a way that the externally affected party, A, can be made better off without the acting party, B, being made worse off. That is to say, "gains from trade" characterise the Pareto-relevant externality, trade that takes the form of some change in the activity of B as his part of the bargain.

A marginal externality is Pareto-relevant when,[5]

$$(-)u^A_{Y_1}\Big/u^A_{X_j} > [u^B_{Y_1}\Big/u^B_{Y_j} - f^B_{Y_1}\Big/f^B_{Y_j}]_{Y_1=\overline{Y}_1} \quad \text{and when}$$

$$u^A_{Y_1}\Big/u^A_{X_j} < 0, \text{ and } u^A_{Y_1}\Big/u^A_{X_j} > (-)[u^B_{Y_1}\Big/u^B_{Y_j} - f^B_{Y_1}\Big/f^B_{Y_j}]_{Y_1=\overline{Y}_1} \quad (9)$$

$$\text{when } u^A_{Y_1}\Big/u^A_{X_j} > 0.$$

In (9), X_j and Y_j are used to designate, respectively, the activities of A and B in consuming or in utilising some numeraire commodity or service that by hypothesis is available on identical terms to each of them. As is indicated by the transposition of signs in (9), the conditions for Pareto relevance differ as between external diseconomies and economies. This is because the "direction" of change desired by A on the part of B is different in the two cases. In stating the conditions for Pareto relevance under ordinary two-person trade, this point is of no significance since trade in one good flows only in one direction. Hence, absolute values can be used.

The condition (9) states that A's marginal rate of substitution between the activity Y_1 and the numeraire activity must be greater than the "net" marginal rate of substitution between the activity and the numeraire activity for B. Otherwise, "gains from trade" would not exist between A and B.

Note, however, that when B has achieved utility-maximising equilibrium,

$$u^B_{Y_1}\Big/u^B_{Y_j} = f^B_{Y_1}\Big/f^B_{Y_j}. \quad (10)$$

That is to say, the marginal rate of substitution in consumption or utilisation is equated to the marginal rate of substitution in production or exchange, i.e., to marginal cost. When (10) holds, the terms in the brackets in (9) mutually cancel. Thus, potentially relevant marginal externalities are also Pareto-relevant when B is in utility-maximising equilibrium. Some trade is possible.

---

5. We are indebted to Mr. M. McManus of the University of Birmingham for pointing out to us an error in an earlier formulation of this and the following similar conditions.

Pareto equilibrium is defined to be present when,

$$(-)u^A_{Y_1} \Big/ u^A_{X_j} = [u^B_{Y_1} \Big/ u^B_{Y_j} - f^B_{Y_1} \Big/ f^B_{Y_j}], \text{ and when}$$

$$u^A_{Y_1} \Big/ u^A_{X_j} < 0, \text{ and } u^A_{Y_1} \Big/ u^A_{X_j} = (-)[u^B_{Y_1} \Big/ u^B_{Y_j} - f^B_{Y_1} \Big/ f^B_{Y_j}] \quad (11)$$

when $u^A_{Y_1} \Big/ u^A_{X_j} > 0$.

Condition (11) demonstrates that marginal externalities may continue to exist, even in Pareto equilibrium, as here defined. This point may be shown by reference to the special case in which the activity in question may be undertaken at zero costs. Here Pareto equilibrium is attained when the marginal rates of substitution in consumption or utilisation for the two persons are precisely offsetting, that is, where their interests are strictly opposed, and *not* where the left-hand term vanishes.

What vanishes in Pareto equilibrium are the Pareto-relevant externalities. It seems clear that, normally, economists have been referring only to what we have here called Pareto-relevant externalities when they have, implicitly or explicitly, stated that external effects are not present when a position on the Pareto optimality surface is attained.[6]

For completeness, we must also consider those potentially relevant inframarginal externalities. Refer to the discussion of these as summarised in (8) above. The question is now to determine whether or not *A*, the externally affected party, can reach some mutually satisfactory agreement with *B*, the acting party, that will involve some discrete (non-marginal) change in the scope of the activity Y_1. If, over some range, any range, of the activity, which we shall designate by ΔY_1, the rate of substitution between Y_1 and X_j for *A* exceeds the "net" rate of substitution for *B*, the externality is Pareto-relevant. The associated changes in the utilisation of the numeraire commodity must be equal for the two parties. Thus, for external economies, we have,

$$\frac{\Delta u^A}{\Delta Y_1} \Big/ \frac{\Delta u^A}{\Delta X_j} > (-) \left[\frac{\Delta u^B}{\Delta Y_1} \Big/ \frac{\Delta u^B}{\Delta Y_j} - \frac{\Delta f^B}{\Delta Y_1} \Big/ \frac{\Delta f^B}{\Delta Y_j} \right]_{Y_1 = \overline{Y}_1}, \quad (12)$$

---

6. This applies to the authors of this paper. For recent discussion of external effects when we have clearly intended only what we here designate as Pareto-relevant, see James M. Buchanan, "Politics, Policy, and the Pigovian Margins," *Economica*, vol. 19 (1962), 17–28, and, also, James M. Buchanan and Gordon Tullock, *The Calculus of Consent*, Ann Arbor, 1962.

and the same with the sign in parentheses transposed for external diseconomies. The difference to be noted between (12) and (9) is that with infra-marginal externalities potential relevance need not imply Pareto relevance. The bracketed terms in (12) need not sum to zero when B is in his private utility-maximising equilibrium.

We have remained in a two-person world, with one person affected by the single activity of a second. However, the analysis can readily be modified to incorporate the effects of this activity on a multi-person group. That is to say, B's activity, Y_1, may be allowed to affect several parties simultaneously, several A's, so to speak. In each case, the activity can then be evaluated in terms of its effects on the utility of each person. Nothing in the construction need be changed. The only stage in the analysis requiring modification explicitly to take account of the possibilities of multi-person groups being externally affected is that which involves the condition for Pareto relevance and Pareto equilibrium.

For a multi-person group $(A_1, A_2, \ldots, A_n)$, any one or all of whom may be externally affected by the activity, Y_1, of the single person, B, the condition for Pareto relevance is,

$$(-)\sum_{i=1}^{n} u^{A_i}_{Y_1}/u^{A_i}_{X_j} > [u^B_{Y_1}/u^B_{Y_j} - f^B_{Y_1}/f^B_{Y_j}]_{Y_1 = \bar{Y}_1} \text{ when}$$

$$u^{A_i}_{Y_1}/u^{A_i}_{X_j} < 0, \text{ and, } \sum_{i=1}^{n} u^{A_i}_{Y_1}/u^{A_i}_{X_j} > (-)[u^B_{Y_1}/u^B_{Y_j} - \qquad \text{(9A)}$$

$$f^B_{Y_1}/f^B_{Y_j}]_{Y_1 = \bar{Y}_1} \text{ when } u^{A_i}_{Y_1}/u^{A_i}_{X_j} > 0.$$

That is, the summed marginal rates of substitution over the members of the externally affected group exceed the offsetting "net" marginal evaluation of the activity by B. Again, in private equilibrium for B, marginal externalities are Pareto-relevant, provided that we neglect the important element involved in the costs of organising group decisions. In the real world, these costs of organising group decisions (together with uncertainty and ignorance) will prevent realisation of some "gains from trade"—just as they do in organised markets. This is as true for two-person groups as it is for larger groups. But this does not invalidate the point that potential "gains from trade" are available. The condition for Pareto equilibrium and for the infra-marginal case summarised in (11) and (12) for the two-person model can readily be modified to allow for the externally affected multi-person group.

II

The distinctions developed formally in Section I may be illustrated diagrammatically and discussed in terms of a simple descriptive example. Consider two persons, A and B, who own adjoining units of residential property. Within limits to be noted, each person values privacy, which may be measured quantitatively in terms of a single criterion, the height of a fence that can be constructed along the common boundary line. We shall assume that B's desire for privacy holds over rather wide limits. His utility increases with the height of the fence up to a reasonably high level. Up to a certain minimum height, A's utility also is increased as the fence is made higher. Once this minimum height is attained, however, A's desire for privacy is assumed to be fully satiated. Thus, over a second range, A's total utility does not change with a change in the height of the fence. However, beyond a certain limit, A's view of a mountain behind B's property is progressively obscured as the fence goes higher. Over this third range, therefore, A's utility is reduced as the fence is constructed to higher levels. Finally, A will once again become wholly indifferent to marginal changes in the fence's height when his view is totally blocked out.

We specify that B possesses the sole authority, the only legal right, to construct the fence between the two properties.

The preference patterns for A and for B are shown in Figure 1, which is drawn in the form of an Edgeworth-like box diagram. Note, however, that the origin for B is shown at the upper-left rather than the upper-right corner of the diagram as in the more normal usage. This modification is necessary here because only the numeraire good, measured along the ordinate, is strictly divisible between A and B. Both must adjust to the same height of fence, that is, to the same level of the activity creating the externality.

As described above, the indifference contours for A take the general shape shown by the curves aa, $a'a'$, while those for B assume the shapes bb, $b'b'$. Note that these contours reflect the relative evaluations, for A and B, between money and the activity, Y_1. Since the costs of undertaking the activity for B are not incorporated in the diagram, the "contract locus" that might be derived from tangency points will have little relevance except in the special case where the activity can be undertaken at zero costs.

Figure 2 depicts the marginal evaluation curves for A and B, as derived from the preference fields shown in Figure 1, along with some incorporation

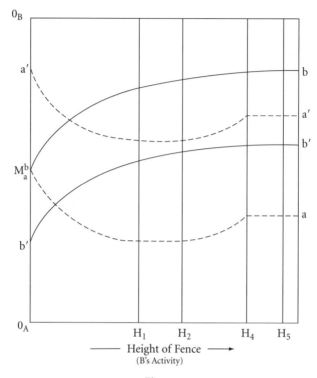

Figure 1

of costs. These curves are derived as follows: Assume an initial distribution of "money" between A and B, say, that shown at M on Figure 1. The marginal evaluation of the activity for A is then derived by plotting the negatives (i.e., the mirror image) of the slopes of successive indifference curves attained by A as B is assumed to increase the height of the fence from zero. These values remain positive for a range, become zero over a second range, become negative for a third, and, finally, return to zero again.[7]

B's curves of marginal evaluation are measured downward from the upper horizontal axis or baseline, for reasons that will become apparent. The derivation of B's marginal evaluation curve is somewhat more complex than that for A. This is because B, who is the person authorised to undertake the

---

7. For an early use of marginal evaluation curves, see J. R. Hicks, "The Four Consumer's Surpluses," *Review of Economic Studies,* vol. 11 (1943), 31–41.

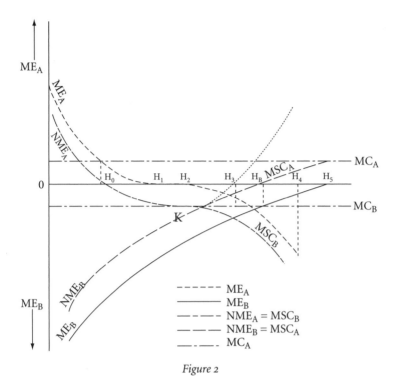

Figure 2

action, in this case the building of the fence, must also bear the full costs. Thus, as *B* increases the scope of the activity, his real income, measured in terms of his remaining goods and services, is reduced. This change in the amount of remaining goods and services will, of course, affect his marginal evaluation of the activity in question. Thus, the marginal cost of building the fence will determine, to some degree, the marginal evaluation of the fence. This necessary interdependence between marginal evaluation and marginal cost complicates the use of simple diagrammatic models in finding or locating a solution. It need not, however, deter us from presenting the solution diagrammatically, if we postulate that the marginal evaluation curve, as drawn, is based on a single presumed cost relationship. This done, we may plot *B*'s marginal evaluation of the activity from the negatives of the slopes of his indifference contours attained as he constructs the fence to higher and higher levels. *B*'s marginal evaluation, shown in Figure 2, remains positive throughout the range to the point H_5, where it becomes zero.

The distinctions noted in Section I are easily related to the construction in Figure 2. To A, the party externally affected, B's potential activity in constructing the fence can be assessed independent of any prediction of B's actual behaviour. Thus, the activity of B would,

1. exert marginal external economies which are potentially relevant over the range OH_1;
2. exert infra-marginal external economies over the range H_1H_2, which are clearly irrelevant since no change in B's behaviour with respect to the extent of the activity would increase A's utility;
3. exert marginal external diseconomies over the range H_2H_4 which are potentially relevant to A; and,
4. exert infra-marginal external economies or diseconomies beyond H_4, the direction of the effect being dependent on the ratio between the total utility derived from privacy and the total reduction in utility derived from the obstructed view. In any case, the externality is potentially relevant.

To determine Pareto relevance, the extent of B's predicted performance must be determined. The necessary condition for B's attainment of "private" utility-maximising equilibrium is that marginal costs, which he must incur, be equal to his own marginal evaluation. For simplicity, in Figure 2 we assume that marginal costs are constant, as shown by the curve MC. Thus, B's position of equilibrium is shown at H_B, within the range of marginal external diseconomies for A. Here the externality imposed by B's behaviour is clearly Pareto-relevant: A can surely work out some means of compensating B in exchange for B's agreement to reduce the scope of the activity—in this example to reduce the height of the fence between the two properties. Diagrammatically, the position of Pareto equilibrium is shown at H_3, where the marginal evaluation of A is equal in absolute value, but negatively, to the "net" marginal evaluation of B, drawn as the curve NME_B. Only in this position are the conditions specified in (11), above, satisfied.[8]

---

8. This diagrammatic analysis is necessarily oversimplified in the sense that the Pareto equilibrium position is represented as a unique point. Over the range between the "private" equilibrium for B and the point of Pareto equilibrium, the sort of bargains struck between A and B will affect the marginal evaluation curves of both individuals within this range. Thus, the more accurate analysis would suggest a "contract locus" of equilibrium

III

Aside from the general classification of externalities that is developed, the approach here allows certain implications to be drawn, implications that have not, perhaps, been sufficiently recognised by some welfare economists.

The analysis makes it quite clear that externalities, external effects, may remain even in full Pareto equilibrium. That is to say, a position may be classified as Pareto-optimal or -efficient despite the fact that at the margin the activity of one individual externally affects the utility of another individual. Figure 2 demonstrates this point clearly. Pareto equilibrium is attained at H_3, yet B is imposing marginal external diseconomies on A.

This point has significant policy implications, for it suggests that the observation of external effects, taken alone, cannot provide a basis for judgment concerning the desirability of some modification in an existing state of affairs. There is not a *prima facie* case for intervention in all cases where an externality is observed to exist.[9] The internal benefits from carrying out the activity, net of costs, may be greater than the external damage that is imposed on other parties.

In full Pareto equilibrium, of course, these internal benefits, measured in terms of some numeraire good, net of costs, must be just equal, at the margin, to the external damage that is imposed on other parties. This equilibrium will always be characterised by the strict opposition of interests of the two parties, one of which may be a multi-person group.

In the general case, we may say that at full Pareto equilibrium the presence of a marginal external diseconomy implies an offsetting marginal *internal* economy, whereas the presence of a marginal external economy implies an offsetting marginal *internal* diseconomy. In "private" equilibrium, as opposed to Pareto equilibrium, these net internal economies and diseconomies would, of course, be eliminated by the utility-maximising acting party. In Pareto equilibrium, these remain because the acting party is being compensated for "suffering" internal economies and diseconomies, that is, divergen-

---

points. At Pareto equilibrium, however, the condition shown in the diagrammatic presentation holds, and the demonstration of this fact rather than the location of the solution is the aim of this diagrammatics.

9. See Paul A. Samuelson, *Foundations of Economic Analysis,* Cambridge, Mass., 1948, 208, for a discussion of the views of various writers.

cies between "private" marginal costs and benefits, *measured in the absence of compensation.*

As a second point, it is useful to relate the whole analysis here to the more familiar Pigovian discussion concerning the divergence between marginal social cost (product) and marginal private cost (product). By saying that such a divergence exists, we are, in the terms of this paper, saying that a marginal externality exists. The Pigovian terminology tends to be misleading, however, in that it deals with the acting party to the exclusion of the externally affected party. It fails to take into account the fact that there are always two parties involved in a single externality relationship.[10] As we have suggested, a marginal externality is Pareto-relevant except in the position of Pareto equilibrium; gains from trade can arise. But there must be two parties to any trading arrangement. The externally affected party must compensate the acting party for modifying his behaviour. The Pigovian terminology, through its concentration on the decision-making of the acting party alone, tends to obscure the two-sidedness of the bargain that must be made.

To illustrate this point, assume that A, the externally affected party in our model, successfully secures, through the auspices of the "state," the levy of a marginal tax on B's performance of the activity Y_1. Assume further that A is able to secure this change without cost to himself. The tax will increase the marginal cost of performing the activity for B, and, hence, will reduce the extent of the activity attained in B's "private" equilibrium. Let us now presume that this marginal tax is levied "correctly" on the basis of a Pigovian calculus; the rate of tax at the margin is made equal to the negative marginal evaluation of the activity to A. Under these modified conditions, the effective marginal cost, as confronted by B, may be shown by the curve designated as MSC_B in Figure 2. A new "private" equilibrium for B is shown at the quantity, H_3, the same level designated as Pareto equilibrium in our earlier discussion, if we neglect the disturbing interdependence between marginal evaluation and marginal costs. Attention solely to the decision calculus of B here would suggest, perhaps, that this position remains Pareto-optimal under these revised circumstances, and that it continues to qualify as a position of Pareto equilibrium. There is no divergence between marginal private cost and marginal social cost in the usual sense. However, the position, if attained

10. This criticism of the Pigovian analysis has recently been developed by R. H. Coase; see his "The Problem of Social Cost," *Journal of Law and Economics,* vol. 3 (1960), 1–44.

in this manner, is clearly neither one of Pareto optimality, nor one that may be classified as Pareto equilibrium.

In this new "private" equilibrium for B,

$$u_{Y_1}^B \Big/ u_{Y_j}^B = f_{Y_1}^B \Big/ f_{Y_j}^B - u_{Y_1}^A \Big/ u_{X_j}^A, \tag{13}$$

where $u_{Y_1}^A / u_{X_j}^A$ represents the marginal tax imposed on B as he performs the activity Y_1. Recall the necessary condition for Pareto relevance defined in (9) above, which can now be modified to read,

$$(-)u_{Y_1}^A \Big/ u_{X_j}^A > [u_{Y_1}^B \Big/ u_{Y_j}^B - f_{Y_1}^B \Big/ f_{Y_j}^B + u_{Y_1}^A \Big/ u_{X_j}^A]_{Y_1 = \overline{\overline{Y}}_1},$$

$$\text{when } u_{Y_1}^A \Big/ u_{X_j}^A < 0, \text{ and } u_{Y_1}^A \Big/ u_{X_j}^A > (-)[u_{Y_1}^B \Big/ u_{Y_j}^B - \tag{9B}$$

$$f_{Y_1}^B \Big/ f_{Y_j}^B + u_{Y_1}^A \Big/ u_{X_j}^A]_{Y_1 = \overline{\overline{Y}}_1}, \text{ when } u_{Y_1}^A \Big/ u_{X_j}^A > 0.$$

In (9B), $\overline{\overline{Y}}_1$ represents the "private" equilibrium value for Y_1, determined by B, after the ideal Pigovian tax is imposed. As before, the bracketed terms represent the "net" marginal evaluation of the activity for the acting party, B, and these sum to zero when equilibrium is reached. So long as the left-hand term in the inequality remains non-zero, a Pareto-relevant marginal externality remains, despite the fact that the full "Pigovian solution" is attained.

The apparent paradox here is not difficult to explain. Since, as postulated, A is not incurring any cost in securing the change in B's behaviour, and, since there remains, by hypothesis, a marginal diseconomy, further "trade" can be worked out between the two parties. Specifically, Pareto equilibrium is reached when,

$$(-)u_{Y_1}^A \Big/ u_{X_j}^A = [u_{Y_1}^B \Big/ u_{Y_j}^B - f_{Y_1}^B \Big/ f_{Y_j}^B + u_{Y_1}^A \Big/ u_{X_j}^A]$$

$$\text{when } u_{Y_1}^A \Big/ u_{X_j}^A < 0, \text{ and } u_{Y_1}^A \Big/ u_{X_j}^A = \tag{11A}$$

$$(-)[u_{Y_1}^B \Big/ u_{Y_j}^B - f_{Y_1}^B \Big/ f_{Y_j}^B + u_{Y_1}^A \Big/ u_{X_j}^A] \text{ when } u_{Y_1}^A \Big/ u_{X_j}^A > 0.$$

Diagrammatically, this point may be made with reference to Figure 2. If a unilaterally imposed tax, corresponding to the marginal evaluation of A, is placed on B's performance of the activity, the new position of Pareto equilibrium may be shown by first subtracting the new marginal cost curve, drawn as MSC_B, from B's marginal evaluation curve. Where this new "net" marginal evaluation curve, shown as the dotted curve between points H_3 and K, cuts the marginal evaluation curve for A, a new position of Pareto equilibrium falling between H_2 and H_3 is located, neglecting the qualifying point discussed in Footnote 8.

The important implication to be drawn is that full Pareto equilibrium can never be attained via the imposition of unilaterally imposed taxes and subsidies until all marginal externalities are eliminated. If a tax-subsidy method, rather than "trade," is to be introduced, it should involve bi-lateral taxes (subsidies). Not only must B's behaviour be modified so as to insure that he will take the costs externally imposed on A into account, but A's behaviour must be modified so as to insure that he will take the costs "internally" imposed on B into account. In such a double tax-subsidy scheme, the necessary Pareto conditions would be readily satisfied.[11]

In summary, Pareto equilibrium in the case of marginal externalities cannot be attained so long as marginal externalities remain, until and unless those benefiting from changes are required to pay some "price" for securing the benefits.

A third point worthy of brief note is that our analysis allows the whole treatment of externalities to encompass the consideration of purely collective goods. As students of public finance theory will have recognised, the Pareto equilibrium solution discussed in this paper is similar, indeed is identical, with that which was presented by Paul Samuelson in his theory of public expenditures.[12] The summed marginal rates of substitution (marginal evaluation) must be equal to marginal costs. Note, however, that marginal costs may include the negative marginal evaluation of other parties, if viewed in one way. Note, also, that there is nothing in the analysis which suggests its limitations to purely collective goods or even to goods that are characterised by significant externalities in their use.

Our analysis also lends itself to the more explicit point developed in Coase's recent paper.[13] He argues that the same "solution" will tend to emerge out of any externality relationship, regardless of the structure of

11. Although developed in rather different terminology, this seems to be closely in accord with Coase's analysis. See R. H. Coase, loc. cit.

12. Paul A. Samuelson, "The Pure Theory of Public Expenditure," *Review of Economics and Statistics*, vol. 36 (1954), 386–89.

13. R. H. Coase, loc. cit.

property rights, provided only that the market process works smoothly. Strictly speaking, Coase's analysis is applicable only to inter-firm externality relationships, and the identical solution emerges only because firms adjust to prices that are competitively determined. In our terms of reference, this identity of solution cannot apply, because of the incomparability of utility functions. It remains true, however, that the basic characteristics of the Pareto equilibrium position remain unchanged regardless of the authority undertaking the action. This point can be readily demonstrated, again with reference to Figure 2. Let us assume that Figure 2 is now redrawn on the basis of a different legal relationship in which A now possesses full authority to construct the fence, whereas B can no longer take any action in this respect. A will, under these conditions, "privately" construct a fence only to the height H_0, where the activity clearly exerts a Pareto-relevant marginal external economy on B. Pareto equilibrium will be reached, as before, at H_3, determined, in this case, by the intersection of the "net" marginal evaluation curve for A (which is identical to the previously defined marginal social cost curve, MSC, when B is the acting party) and the marginal evaluation curve for B.[14] Note that in this model A will allow himself to suffer an internal marginal diseconomy, at equilibrium, provided that he is compensated by B, who continues, in Pareto equilibrium, to enjoy a marginal *external* economy.

Throughout this paper, we have deliberately chosen to introduce and to discuss only a single externality. Much of the confusion in the literature seems to have arisen because two or more externalities have been handled simultaneously. The standard example is that in which the output of one firm affects the production function of the second firm while, at the same time, the output of the second firm affects the production function of the first. Clearly, there are two externalities to be analysed in such cases. In many instances, these can be treated as separate and handled independently. In other situations, this step cannot be taken and additional tools become necessary.[15]

14. The H_3 position, in this presumably redrawn figure, should not be precisely compared with the same position in the other model. We are using here the same diagram for two models, and, especially over wide ranges, the dependence of the marginal evaluation curves on income effects cannot be left out of account.

15. For a treatment of the dual externality problem that clearly shows the important difference between the separable and the non-separable cases, see Otto Davis and Andrew Whinston, "Externalities, Welfare, and the Theory of Games," *Journal of Political Economy*, vol. 70 (1962), 241–62. As the title suggests, Davis and Whinston utilise the tools of game theory for the inseparable case.

Public and Private Interaction under Reciprocal Externality

James M. Buchanan and Gordon Tullock

Market organization fails to produce results that satisfy the necessary conditions for Pareto optimality when Pareto-relevant externalities remain in equilibrium. This statement is tautological, but it accurately reflects the content of significant portions of theoretical welfare economics. From this statement, a second, and quasi-tautological one emerges. Given the presence of Pareto-relevant externalities in market equilibrium, collectivization *could* modify the results so as to guarantee the attainment of the Pareto welfare surface. There are no grounds for disagreement here, although, of course, the following less familiar statement is also indisputable. Given the presence of Pareto-relevant externalities in political equilibrium, marketization *could* modify the results so as to guarantee that the welfare surface is reached.

We propose to extend the analysis of both market organization and collective organization in the presence of a specific sort of externality relationship. We shall demonstrate that this extension introduces complications that are not normally considered, despite their importance for any comparative evaluation of the two organizational alternatives.

We limit the analysis to those activities which involve reciprocal externalities. That is to say, the behavior of a single unit in a group exerts external

From *The Public Economy of Urban Communities*, ed. Julius Margolis (Washington, D.C.: Resources for the Future, 1965), 52–73. Reprinted by permission of the publisher.

effects on remaining members of the group, while, at the same time, the behavior of any other single unit in the group exerts external effects on the first unit.[1] Since the argument for collectivization rests largely on the presence of significant external economies, we shall consider only this case, neglecting external diseconomies. Given any activity that is characterized by relevant reciprocal external economies, private or market organization will result in the simultaneous undertaking of the activity by many persons. If a municipal government does not exist for the performance of such functions, private citizens will, independently, hire guards and night watchmen, vaccinate their dogs against rabies, install fire protection devices, plant flowers in the spring, keep boulevards clear of snow in winter, send their children to school, paint their own houses, feed the birds. The list could be lengthened readily. It is clear that, in many such activities, the private behavior of each person may exert relevant external economies on some or all of the other persons in the community.

There may or may not exist a determinate equilibrium as a result of the interaction of individuals responding independently in activities of this sort. This equilibrium, if it exists, may involve a greater or smaller resource outlay than that which is necessary to satisfy the necessary conditions for Pareto optimality.[2] The mutual adjustment process under independent behavior must be carefully examined before the efficacy of market organization can be compared with that of collectivization.

---

1. For a definition of an externality, and for a careful distinction between a Pareto-relevant and a Pareto-irrelevant externality, see James M. Buchanan and William C. Stubblebine, "Externality," *Economica* 29 (November 1962): 371–84. For an important paper that introduces some of the complications of the reciprocal externality case, and for an unpublished paper further developing some ideas related to those treated here, see Otto Davis and Andrew Whinston, "Externalities, Welfare, and the Theory of Games," *Journal of Political Economy* 70 (June 1962): 241–62, and "Some Foundations of Public Expenditure Theory," unpublished manuscript. Ralph Turvey summarizes the recent developments in "On Divergencies Between Social Cost and Private Cost," *Economica* 30 (August 1963): 309–13.

2. For a demonstration of the point that private adjustment may generate a greater than optimal outlay, see James M. Buchanan and M. Z. Kafoglis, "A Note on Public Goods Supply," *American Economic Review* 52 (June 1963): 403–14.

Private and Collective Adjustments

MARKET ADJUSTMENT

Consider a simple example. Immunization against communicable disease protects the individual who takes the shots, but, at the same time, it reduces the likelihood that others in the community catch the disease. If all persons other than one in a community are protected, the remaining member is un- likely to get the disease for the simple reason that there is no one from whom he may catch it. A situation of this sort under a world-of-equals model is represented diagrammatically in Figure 1.

First, consider a discrete case in which it is assumed that one shot provides complete protection to the person who takes it over some relevant time pe- riod. If an individual does not get a shot, his chances of contracting the dis- ease decrease as the numbers of others in the community who are inoculated increase. The disease is assumed to be painful; it "costs" something, but it is not fatal. Also, assume that being inoculated costs something. On the ver- tical axis of Figure 1, measure costs, in dollars, as either the cost of being

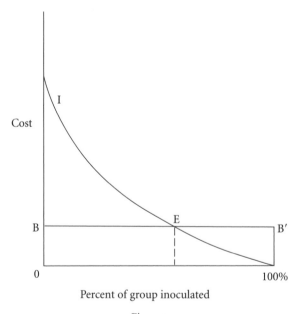

Figure 1

inoculated or the properly computed expected dollar equivalent of the pain and inconvenience of getting sick. Conceptually, one can think of the latter as the current insurance premium on a policy providing complete indemnification of illness from the disease.[3] On the horizontal axis is measured the percentage of the population in the group that is inoculated; the group is assumed to be closed. The cost to an individual of getting a shot is shown by 0B. The expected cost of the disease to the individual is indicated by the curve I, which may be labeled the "curve of external economies."

If all private decisions are to be made simultaneously, no position of stable equilibrium is present in this simple system. Initially, given the costs as depicted in Figure 1, all members of the group purchase inoculations. And, once having done so, all members seek to change their decisions. If it is assumed that immunity lasts for one period only, the simultaneous adjustment model would produce a cyclical swing between full inoculation and no inoculation. The model produces quite different results if the reasonable assumption is made that individuals make decisions in some temporal sequence, even though they may remain, for relevant purposes, essentially identical. In other words, one need assume only that "someone acts first." Under these conditions, individuals will continue to purchase inoculations so long as the discounted or expected costs of getting the disease exceed the costs of the shot. Equilibrium is reached at point E in Figure 1. Note that in this position persons who are inoculated and those who are not are in roughly equivalent situations. Those who purchase insurance policies pay premiums equal to the costs of the inoculations.

Point E represents a position of group equilibrium, when each individual acts independently. Note that although individuals act independent of each other they do take into account the presence of external economies in their behavior. The location of the individual along curve I depends, not on his own behavior, but on that of all others in the group. This location becomes the basis for his own decision. There is, of course, no means of identifying which individuals will become immunized and which will not.

---

3. If the world-of-equals assumption should be relaxed, there would, of course, be a different external economies curve for each person. This complicating factor would not change the basic conclusions of the analysis.

COLLECTIVE ADJUSTMENT

The position of group equilibrium attained under private adjustment must be compared with that which would be attained under collectivization, provided the underlying conditions of the model are not changed. Assume, as before, that all members of the group are identical for relevant purposes. How will collectivization of the activity affect the two cost functions confronted by the single individual, as drawn in Figure 1? Since individuals are assumed equal in this model, tax financing will impose on each person an equal charge. Hence, one can derive a tax-cost function, T, which runs from 0 to B' in Figure 2. Only if each person in the whole group is inoculated will the tax-cost per person equal the cost of purchasing one shot privately.

Under collectivization, it is assumed that the group, as a group, decides upon the percentage of the total number to be inoculated and that once this decision is made individuals to be immunized are chosen in some random fashion. Thus, regardless of the collective decision, an individual stands some chance of being in the immunized group. This fact must be taken into ac-

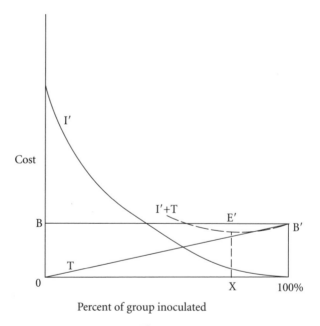

Percent of group inoculated

Figure 2

count in deriving the external economies curve under collectivization. For each level of inoculation for the group, it will be possible to compute the expected costs of the disease, costs that will become relevant to the individual as he participates in the collective decision process.[4] Because of some positive probability that he will be in the immunized group, at any percentage level, the external economies curve under collectivization, drawn as I' in Figure 2, will lie below the analogous curve, I, in Figure 1 throughout its range, assuming that the basic parameters of the model remain unchanged.

By utilizing the two cost functions in Figure 2, I' and T, it becomes possible to depict the position of group equilibrium under collective organization. This position is *not* indicated by the intersection of these two curves. These are total cost curves, and, in the collectivization model, as different from the private-adjustment model, the individual is able, through some political voting procedure, to choose the position for the "group." The optimal position for the individual is indicated by the low point in the curve of total cost, I' + T, which is derived by the vertical summation of the two components.[5] This "solution" is to the right of and below the position of equilibrium attained under private provision. In other words, collectivization produces both a greater degree of immunization and a lower cost per person than that which would be present under independent or market adjustment.

There is, of course, nothing at all startling about this result, which is strictly orthodox. The construction introduced does, however, allow attention to be focused on one or two features of the model that are not usually taken into account. Note that even in ideal collective equilibrium marginal external economies remain. What are eliminated are the Pareto-relevant externalities, not all externalities. Secondly, the model draws attention to the question as to why the ideal or optimal solution is not achieved under inde-

---

4. Note that this "external economies" curve is analogous to that derived in the private adjustment model, but that it is not identical. For each level of collective immunization it would be possible to derive a whole curve that would be identical in construction to that in Figure 1. In this context, the curve in Figure 1 is drawn on the basis of zero collective immunization. The composite "external economies" curve in Figure 2, I', traces out a locus of points on a whole family of such curves, drawn for each level of collective immunization.

5. The constructions here are similar to those that have been employed by Buchanan and Tullock in their analysis of political voting rules. See James M. Buchanan and Gordon Tullock, *The Calculus of Consent* (Ann Arbor: University of Michigan Press, 1962).

pendent adjustment. Return to the insurance premium version. Why does the rational insurance firm not subsidize some of its own clients, encouraging them to be inoculated? If there is only one firm, it could clearly increase profits by carrying out such subsidization to the point where the same amount of immunization that is present under collectivization would be achieved. One firm might, of course, go further and exploit its monopoly position. However, even if there should be a number of insurance firms, each would find it profitable to subsidize inoculation to some extent. One need not, however, rely on the insurance version of the model. Without insurance against the disease, it remains rational for individuals to "bribe" others in the group, each other, to secure inoculation, so long as Pareto-relevant externalities remain. It is, of course, the costs of organizing such bribes or compensations among large groups, and not the presence of externalities, *per se,* that provide the legitimate basis for collectivization.

Market for externalities

Such cost barriers to the organization of interpersonal markets point up a rather curious development in the theory of markets. Economists have often assumed that markets work perfectly for the exchange of goods and services, but that markets do not work at all for the exchange of those activities generating external effects. If, in fact, markets should work "perfectly" in a more inclusive sense, all gains from trade would be eliminated, including those that exist, by definition, when Pareto-relevant externalities are present. "Optimal" results are guaranteed by "perfect" markets in this broader model of trade. In the real world, of course, markets work, more or less, for the exchange of goods and services and for the exchange of externalities. The difference is one of degree, not of kind. Side payments for externalities do exist, and institutions are continually emerging to internalize these. Cost barriers to the organization of such interpersonal markets are more severe than those present for ordinary commodity and service markets, but these costs are not necessarily insurmountable.[6]

6. The fundamental paper by Ronald H. Coase ("The Problem of Social Cost," *Journal of Law and Economics* 3 [October 1960]: 1–44) should be noted in addition to those previously cited.

Distributional equity

The model suggests yet another important point that often tends to be overlooked. As the cost functions are drawn in Figure 2, collectivization, if ideally operative, will involve only some share of the total population securing inoculation. In the real world, this result may not be forthcoming. Generally accepted standards of equity may in such instances require that all persons be inoculated, or that inoculations be made free to all who choose voluntarily to take them. Under the assumptions made, these alternatives would produce the same results; everyone would be inoculated. Note that this solution will not represent any improvement over private provision. All persons will be inoculated; more resources will be devoted to vaccine and clinics; insurance costs will be zero; taxes will be high. Given any bias toward individual freedom of choice, this solution will be less satisfactory than private market adjustment. As compared with "ideal" immunization, this equity solution involves a relative overextension whereas the private adjustment process involves a relative underextension. The cost equivalence between these two inefficient results stems, of course, from the assumption that shots are available at constant costs. If increasing costs should characterize this service, the equity solution would be inefficient, even for the totalitarian. With decreasing costs, the equity solution would always be the efficient one.

The practical implication of this point is that it may be necessary, in order to achieve tolerable efficiency under collective organization, to devise some means of choosing those members of the total population who are to be directly benefited. This means must not appear to violate generally accepted standards of nondiscrimination. The desired results may be broadly attained by certain class distinctions, such as, for example, that only children or the aged shall be immunized. Alternatively, direct-user pricing could be introduced; inoculations could be made freely available to all who choose to pay a direct-user charge. This charge would be set at a level that would generate approximately the optimal outcome. In any case, either administrative rules or direct-user pricing must, if introduced, be substantially "correct." If not, there may arise particular institutional diseconomies that would have to be taken into account in any comparative evaluation of public and private organization.

COLLECTIVIZATION WITHOUT
RELEVANT EXTERNALITY

One useful benchmark case that is not normally considered, but which will be helpful, involves the collectivization of an activity that is not characterized by relevant externality in market organization. Suppose, for example, that through some error, inoculation against the communicable disease is not collectivized but that, instead, the medical treatment of the disease is. (The current practice of the National Health Service in Great Britain, which provides free hospital care but charges small fees for drugs, may be a partially applicable real-world example.) The situation is depicted in Figure 3, where the underlying conditions are assumed the same as before. The expected cost of the disease is reduced for the individual, since treatment is provided "free"; the external economies curve becomes I'', which is clearly lower than I in Figure 1 (drawn as dashed in Figure 3), and may be, although it will not

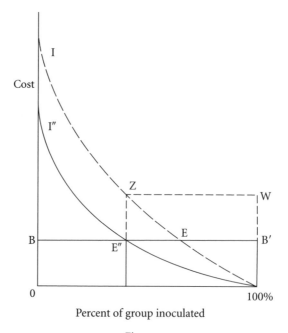

Figure 3

necessarily be, lower than I' in Figure 2. The cost of inoculation is not changed. Hence, independent adjustment will produce group equilibrium at E''. Note that under this scheme there will be fewer inoculations and more disease than under wholly private organization. Each individual will, however, bear the same direct cost as under wholly private provision. The tax-costs of treatment are wholly excess. The amount of these costs, for the group, is shown by the rectangle, E''ZWB'. This result need not be surprising. Treatment of disease is "free," and the individual adjusts his behavior to this fact. Since there are, by assumption, no relevant external economies involved in treatment, *per se*, only full-cost user pricing could eliminate the inefficiency under these arrangements. But, of course, such pricing would undermine the rationale for the collectivization.

The particular details of the example are not important. It should be noted, however, that when an activity that generates no significant external effects is collectivized, some distortion in resource use will necessarily result, unless goods and services are distributed through a system of voluntary purchases at market prices. This point is a familiar and obvious one, but it does represent one side of the whole externality-collectivization discussion that tends to be sidetracked. Arguments for decollectivization based on government failure in such cases are on all fours with arguments for demarketization based on market failure.

EXCESS BURDEN OF TAXATION

To this point, as is normal with economists who discuss topics such as these, we have assumed that tax-supported collective activities are financed with zero excess burden. If one is to complete the catalogue of externalities that must be relevant to any decision among alternative organizational forms, this element must be incorporated in the model. It is widely accepted that any tax, other than a purely hypothetical lump-sum construction, modifies the conditions for choice of the individual and, therefore, distorts his behavior to some extent. This possibility can be introduced into the simple geometrical model without difficulty. In Figure 4, Figure 2 is reproduced; only here allowance is made for some excess burden of taxation. The tax curve, T, is shifted upward to, say, T'. This, in turn, shifts the total cost curve, I' + T',

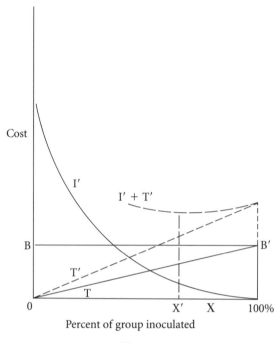

Figure 4

upward, and, with the configuration as drawn, this shifts the "optimal" position to the left. If the excess burden involved with raising tax revenues is sufficiently large, the final results achieved under collectivization may actually be less "efficient" than those achieved under market adjustment, despite the admitted presence of noninternalized and relevant reciprocal external economies in the latter. The implication is clear that the size of the excess burden of taxation should, in fact, be considered along with the other externalities in any choice of organization.

This point, like the others, is an obvious one. However, it seems rarely to have been made explicit in the discussion. Cost-benefit analysis, which is now becoming a popular pastime, has developed with very little attention being paid to the excess burden that might be involved in raising given revenue sums through taxation.

Multiple Alternatives

MARKET ADJUSTMENT WITH MULTIPLE ALTERNATIVES: THE UNEQUAL DISTRIBUTION CASE

In the simple model introduced in the first section, it has been assumed that each individual confronts only two alternatives of choice. He either gets inoculated or he does not. In the more general case, many alternatives will be open to him. Staying within the immunization model for the sake of expositional continuity, one can think of the individual either doing nothing or getting one shot, two shots, three shots, etc. Each additional shot will provide him with additional protection against disease and also generate external benefits for his fellows, but never reduce his risk to zero. Infantile paralysis vaccinations provide a partially applicable real-world example here. The reciprocal externality relationship is assumed to extend over the whole range of possible action open to each member of the group.

One means of illustrating this model is provided in the matrix of Figure 5. Here for consideration is a two-person group only, consisting of individuals A and B. Each person can get either no shots or any number of shots up

B \\ A	A_0		A_1		A_2		A_3		A_4	
B_4	30	70	12	62	4	64	2	72	0	80
	0	30	10	22	20	24	30	32	40	40
B_3	50	86	22	67.5	8	63	4	68	0	72
	0	50	10	32	20	28	30	34	40	40
B_2	62	96	27	70	12	64	5	63	0	64
	0	62	10	37	20	32	30	35	40	40
B_1	70	110	29	78	13	70	5.5	67.5	0	62
	0	70	10	39	20	33	30	35.5	40	40
B_0	75	150	30	110	14	96	6	86	0	70
	0	75	10	40	20	34	30	36	40	40

Figure 5

to a maximum of four per time period, producing a twenty-five cell matrix. For convenience, payoffs are measured negatively in terms of costs; hence, each "player" will attempt to minimize his relevant payout. In each matrix cell several entries are included. These are to be read as follows: In the upper left-hand corner of each cell is the expected cost of the disease computed from the probability of contracting it and the cost of suffering it once contracted. For simplicity, this may again be considered as the cost of an insurance premium per period. In the lower left-hand corner of each square is the cost of inoculations, assumed to be $10 per shot. These two costs are summed in the lower right-hand corner of each cell, giving the total cost to the individual, who is A in the payout matrix shown. Individual A will attempt to minimize the figure in the lower right-hand corner. Again for simplicity in exposition, it is assumed that A and B are identical in relevant respects. This makes the matrix confronting B the transpose of that confronting A. Thus, for example, the figure in the lower right-hand corner of the cell A_3B_1 gives a total cost to A of $35.50. This must be the same as the total cost to B in the cell B_3A_1. One can in this way compute the costs to B in each cell. Adding these to those for A, one obtains a total social cost figure, which is entered in the upper right-hand corner of each cell.

Consider now the adjustment process under private organization. Assume that no elements of strategic behavior are present, an assumption that will be justified later in the paper. Under these conditions, each person will purchase two shots per period. If, for any reason, some cell other than A_2B_2 is found to exist, one or both of the individuals will find it advantageous to shift his own behavior. Note, however, that the social optimum is located at A_4B_1 or A_1B_4. In this case, total costs can be minimized (total benefits maximized) by a significantly unequal distribution of services between the two persons. It is, of course, obvious that this particular result stems from the values assigned in the matrix illustration. The result is interesting, nevertheless, for it suggests one possibly important basis for collectivization that is seldom discussed. It is possible that the reciprocal external economies are such that only through collective organization can a sufficiently *unequal* distribution of services be implemented, so as to achieve efficiency. In this instance, collectivization allows a specific technological improvement in distribution to be made that is not possible under private provision. This seems reasonably common with some real-world public services. Police do not patrol every street with the same intensity. The national defense establishment concentrates its services at strategic points.

MARKET ADJUSTMENT WITH MULTIPLE ALTERNATIVES: THE EQUAL DISTRIBUTION CASE

Despite the importance of the unequal distribution of services in securing overall efficiency in particular situations, it will be profitable to return to the equal-distribution model since it is slightly more amenable to analysis. Continue to assume that individuals in the group are substantially identical. A matrix similar to that of Figure 5, but with different payoffs, is shown in Figure 6. Note that here each person would be motivated to take one shot, but neither would take a second, since he could not expect the other person to do likewise. However, if the two parties could make an agreement, each would be better off with both parties taking two shots. This is, of course, the traditional reciprocal external economies case, presented here as a version of the prisoners' dilemma game. Note, however, that if inoculation should be collectivized, with services being made free to individuals, that is, with the receipt of services wholly divorced from tax payments, both A and B would take four shots (Z). This position is less desirable than that reached under private adjustment, given the payoffs of the matrix. Such free provision of

B \ A	A_0	A_1	A_2	A_3	A_4
B_4	13 X 58 / 0 13	8 61 / 10 18	2 63 / 20 22	0 70 / 30 30	0 Z 80 / 40 40
B_3	15 X 52 / 0 15	10 55 / 10 20	3 56 / 20 23	2 64 / 30 32	0 70 / 40 40
B_2	21 X 50 / 0 21	12 O 49 / 10 22	4 O' 48 / 20 24	3 56 / 30 33	1 63 / 40 41
B_1	26 56.5 / 0 26	15 X 50 / 10 25	7 O 49 / 20 27	5 55 / 30 35	3 61 / 40 43
B_0	30 60 / 0 30	19.5 56.5 / 10 29.5	9 X 50 / 20 29	7 52 / 30 37	5 58 / 40 45

Figure 6

partially divisible services leads individuals to extend consumption to the point where marginal evaluation is zero, resulting in excessive utilization.[7]

Five cells in the matrix of Figure 6 are marked with X's. These represent simply the best situations for A, given each possible choice on the part of B. Note that the configuration of these "A optima" cells has specific characteristics. Its general direction is north-northwest, with the total costs for A becoming lower and lower as movement is made in this general direction. Call this locus of low points for A "the river," or "A's river," since one can think of these X cells as the locus of the lowest points on the third-dimensional cost surface of the matrix.

Three other cells on the matrix are marked with O's. These make up the set of positions that show lower social costs than A_1B_1, the position of independent adjustment equilibrium. The cell A_2B_2, marked O′, is the single "optimum," but for both individuals in the group, either of the O cells would be preferable to the private equilibrium position. This whole set may be called the "social provision area."

Continuous variation

It is relatively easy to shift from the matrix illustration that incorporates discrete and discontinuous alternatives to the more familiar case of continuous variation. Figure 7 simply converts relationships similar to those in Figure 6 to the continuous case. The "river" now becomes a smooth curve. Private equilibrium is shown by the intersection of the river, labeled R, with a 45-degree line drawn from the origin. The 45-degree line is, of course, the result of the assumption of identical persons and equal distribution of the activity. For B, it would be possible also to draw in a river curve, which would be the transpose of that drawn in for A under the stated restrictions. The two rivers would, of course, both cut the 45-degree line in the same point, labeled E, in Figure 7.

---

7. The leaders of the Soviet Union, presumably on ideological grounds, distribute bread at prices far below costs, and they often discuss making bread "free." This practice has led to weird, but predictable, results, including the feeding of cattle on bread rather than grain. Even the secret police have not been able to force consumers to behave in a Marxian manner toward bread.

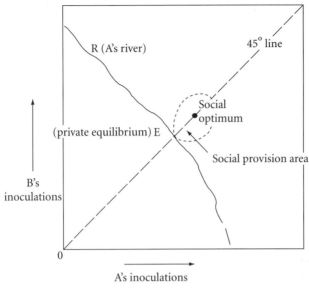

Figure 7

This construction has the advantage of facilitating the shift from the two-person case to the n-person case without difficulty. So long as one retains the assumption that all persons are identical in relevant respects, the analysis is not modified. On the one axis we simply measure the activity of "all others than A." Given appropriately defined scales, one can still utilize the 45-degree line construction. Any point along this line represents equal consumption of the service by all members of the n-person group.

In the two-person model, we have assumed, arbitrarily, that individuals did not engage in strategic bargaining behavior. The basis for this assumption can now be clarified, and with this assumption, two-person models may be used to attain results applicable to n-person groups. In an n-person group, a single individual, say A, will realize that the behavior of the n − 1 others in the group will influence his own utility. Recognizing this externality, he will adjust his own behavior to it. He will not, however, consider his own action to be sufficiently important as to influence the aggregate behavior of others. Hence, rational behavior consists in his adjusting or adapting his own activity to the situation in which he finds himself. This is, of course, fully analogous to the standard assumption concerning behavior of the individual buyer or seller in competitive markets.

Figure 8 illustrates the n-person model. This is identical with Figure 7 except for the fact that "all others than A" are substituted for B. A's river may be drawn in, as before, and the position of group equilibrium under wholly private adjustment, E, remains determined by the intersection of the river and the 45-degree line. This position will not be optimal. If joint action is possible, there must be points to the northeast of E that are preferable to E, for A and also for all others in the group. Topologically, the "river" represents the locus of low points on the third-dimensional cost surface, as this is confronted by A, acting independently. Remaining members in the group will confront similar cost surfaces, upon which similar "rivers" can be traced. The final position will be determined by the independent action of each person. Joint action is required to shift into the preferred area, which we have called the area of "social provision." Each point in this set is lower on the cost surface than E, for A and for everyone else in the group. But each point is dominated, for A and for everyone else, by points along the river, if independent adjustment is allowed.

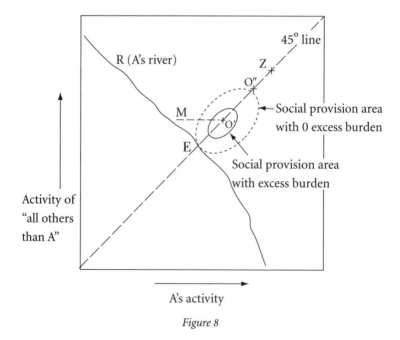

Figure 8

EXCESS-BURDEN QUALIFICATION

The excess-burden qualification must be incorporated into the geometrical model. If collectivization necessarily involves the imposition of taxes that have allocative-incentive effects, the "social provision" area is smaller in size than that which is indicated under the assumption of zero excess burden (shown by the dashed-circular area in Figure 8). It is possible, of course, that the external costs imposed by tax collection would eliminate altogether any net advantages of collectivization. However, the illustration is deliberately drawn to suggest that even with some positive excess burden of taxation a social provision area remains, as shown by the area enclosed by the solid line in Figure 8. Any position within this area represents some improvement, for A and all other members of the group, over E. A single optimal position, within this area, is shown at O'. This position will be located along the 45-degree line, from our assumption of equal distribution of the activity or service.

RATIONING DIFFICULTIES

Again we emphasize that there is nothing particularly new in this construction. It does help to point to some of the complicating features that must be taken into account. Refer to the area of social provision shown in Figure 8. The shift from private organization, which would attain position E, to collective or political organization, is efficient only if the group can insure a final location within the preferred area. There are, however, two separate problems that must be surmounted before such insurance is present. First of all, as previously suggested for the discrete case, unless either administrative controls or price rationing is introduced, collectivization may result in an excessive utilization of available facilities. Suppose, for example, that government finances the activity in question from general tax revenues, and, to stay with the example, then makes immunization shots free to all who want them in whatever quantity desired. The adoption of this "needs" approach to budgeting, which is not at all uncommon in real-world fiscal experience, would surely lead to some position such as that shown by Z in Figure 8, a position that may clearly be less desirable than E.

This problem becomes serious only insofar as individuals are able, by their utilization of a collectively provided service, to reduce the quantity available for others. Hence, for a purely collective good, defined in the strict Samuelson sense, this problem need not arise. It is known, however, that few goods or services are wholly indivisible. Most collective services embody both divisible and indivisible elements. To remain within the social provision area, therefore, something other than the mere collectivization of an activity must be introduced. The various administrative schemes for carrying out the necessary rationing are familiar. Police protection is provided generally, but a policeman cannot be asked to stand in front of every house. Firemen will respond to calls if fire breaks out, but only on occasion will they take pet cats out of trees, and severe fines are imposed for false alarms. Normally, only certain types of rubbish are picked up by municipal garbage collectors.

This first problem of keeping government efficient has been traditionally recognized in the theory of public finance. A time-honored principle states that governments cannot efficiently give away services for which the demand is price elastic over some range between cost price and zero. The treatment of the problem here is couched in different terms, but remains basically within the orthodox tradition.

Chiseling under collectivization

The second problem of government efficiency also brings up a familiar issue in price theory, which, to our knowledge, has not been developed with respect to the provision of public goods or services. The price theory analogue here is the enforcement of cartel agreements. Each partner to an agreement has an opportunity to "chisel," and, thereby, to secure differential profits for himself, although he recognizes that if all parties to the agreement do the same everyone will be damaged.[8] Competitive pressures are usually held to be sufficiently strong to guarantee that chiseling will take place in large-number groups until and unless severe sanctions are in some fashion imposed against all potential price-cutters.

8. G. Warren Nutter has recently developed a generalized "theory of chiseling" that does much to clarify the standard economic-theory treatment. See Nutter, "Duopoly, Oligopoly, and Emerging Competition," unpublished manuscript.

The same analysis is clearly applicable to the problem of remaining within the area of efficient social provision under collectivization of an activity. Refer to Figure 8. Note that by the construction of the river A will be motivated, always, to move in an east-west direction (the only way that he can move) so as to reach the lowest point on his cost surface. Assume now that the activity has been collectivized, and that the optimal position O' has been reached. Individual A finds himself located at O', on the 45-degree line. Clearly, if he retains any freedom of private action he would find it preferable to shift to point M, the lowest point in the plane cut horizontally through O'. If he should succeed in reaching M, he will be better off than at O'. But, since we assume that all individuals act similarly, the group will eventually end up again at E, where all will be worse off than at O'. In fact, they will be worse off than they were initially, since they will be bearing the excess burden of providing part of the activity in question by taxation.

WAGNER'S LAW OF INCREASING GOVERNMENT ACTIVITY

The point made in the previous paragraph is worth developing in some detail since it provides one explanation of Wagner's law of ever-increasing government activity. The question that arises is how and why will the individual shift from the social provision area? If the activity is collectivized, the individual will, presumably, be subjected to some coercive levy of taxes. Hence, he will not be able, by his own independent action, to reduce his own share of the cost of providing services for the group. If he were allowed purely private adjustment, he could shift to point M and reduce costs. Since he cannot do so, he will have no incentive to shift from O' to M. No problem of chiseling arises.

If the activity in question should be wholly independent of other activities within the adjustment possibilities of the individual, no process analogous to chiseling will take place. There would be no incentive for the individual to break the implicit agreement that collectivization enforces. It is known, however, that many separate activities, whether these are publicly or privately organized, are interdependent for the individual's decision calculus. Remaining within the immunization example, at E, the position of private equilibrium, assume that the individual is fully adjusted to the external actions of other persons. He will secure the indicated number of shots; he will also take certain other actions that may be closely related to direct immunization. Assume these include the maintenance of certain standards of sanitation in the treatment of garbage. Now assume that the immunization program in the community is collectivized, and the individual shifts to position O'. While he will have no incentive to modify his consumption of the service, assuming coercive tax payments along with ideal rationing schemes, he will not be in equilibrium with respect to those privately purchased services that are related to immunization. If, as has been assumed, individual A is in full equilibrium at E, then at O' he will find that he has an unnecessarily high level of sanitation. He will be able to, and he will have an incentive to, reduce his private spending on sanitation. As a result of this adjustment process, all individuals will find that position O', with respect to immunization from the disease, is no longer optimal. The effect of the private adjustment process is to increase the value of the external economies from direct immunization. Hence, position O', assumed to be optimal in relation to a determinate level of closely related activities, assumes nonoptimal properties. The group, despite the fact that it has collectivized inoculations, remains in an external-economies dilemma. Thus, there is an incentive to expand the immunization further, to, say, O''. The whole area of social provision shifts to the northeast, but this is not drawn in Figure 8. Once again a private adjustment process will take place, and, for the same reason, rational individual behavior in collective choice will further increase the level of the activity. The spiral-like process will continue, with public expenditures rising and private expenditures falling until some position is reached where the interdependence between immunization and other activities under the private control of the individual becomes insignificantly small.

If the excess burden resulting from public provision is taken into account, the possibility that the ultimate outcome may be undesirable is increased. Returning to Figure 8, suppose that the society has previously moved from E to O', and then that private adjustment has taken place in other activities making an extension of government provision desirable. For the move to O'' to be taken, it is only necessary that the *additional* excess burden be less than the gain expected. The process of adjustment may, through this effect, remove the net benefit from public provision. In order to avoid this result, the following steps would have to be taken: Before making each adjustment, not only the excess burden would have to be taken into account, but also the predicted private adjustment to each new arrangement of services.

Practical illustrations of the relationship noted here are surely abundant in emerging municipalities. Without collective fire protection devices, home owners buy fire extinguishers and introduce private sprinkler systems. Once collective fire departments are installed, these individual devices are not replaced. Rational home owners, and potential owners, depend upon municipally supplied protection, once it is provided, and, because they do so, investment in further expansion of municipal protection becomes necessary. In established municipalities it can be predicted that increased efficiency could be achieved by some substitution of individual or private fire protection devices for collective protection, provided that the institutional means could be found through which such a substitution would be possible. There would probably be a greater return, at the margin, from investment in more and better locks than in an addition to the police force.

In these illustrations, collectively supplied services stand in some substitute relationship to privately supplied services. This seems the most realistic case, although complementarity could also be present. The provision of a public park may, for example, encourage people to expand their private purchases of picnic supplies and equipment. This, in turn, makes them desire more picnics, for which some greater investment in public parks may be necessary. The outcome is the same; a spiral-like expansion of public expenditures until all of the secondary adjustments in private behavior produce some overall equilibrium.

INTERGOVERNMENTAL APPLICATIONS

The mechanism of adjustment analyzed here can be applied without difficulty to intergovernmental fiscal relationships. It is commonly observed that when the federal government begins to supplement state expenditures for particular functions there seems an inexorable tendency for state-local expenditures to be totally replaced by federal. This is, of course, readily explained by the fact that states and localities adjust to their own optimal levels, creating as they do still further need for expansion in federal outlay. Viewed in this light, matching provisions on the various conditional grants-in-aid may be seen as one device aimed at keeping state-local behavior restricted so as to guarantee that some position in the social provision area is maintained for the particular function. The matching grant would be analogous to an administrative requirement that all warehouses provide private sprinkler systems, even after the organization of a municipal fire department.

Collectivization and Growth

To be sophisticated in the mid-1960's, any discussion on matters remotely economic must, at some point, introduce the effects of the model on growth or the effects of growth on the model. Does the fact of growth affect the decision as to whether particular activities should, on efficiency grounds, be publicly or privately organized? There seems to be agreement on the fact that growth does modify the conditions of the problem, but there is also widespread disagreement as to the direction that the influence takes. It will be instructive to apply the models developed in this paper to this issue.

Return to the matrix illustration contained in Figure 6. Assume that as growth takes place personal incomes rise. With higher personal income levels, the money values for the opportunity costs of getting the disease increase. If, for purposes of this example, one can assume that these costs consist solely in time lost from the earning of salaries, a doubling of personal incomes will tend to double opportunity costs of illness. The number in the upper left-hand corner in each matrix cell of Figure 6 can then be doubled. Let it also be assumed that the cost of inoculations does not increase, but remains at $10 per shot. Figure 9 incorporates the necessary changes from Figure 6, changes that are due to growth in the manner postulated.

The rather dramatic change in results can best be noted by examining the cells marked with the X's in the two matrices. Figure 9 exhibits column dominance; regardless of what action B takes, A will find it advantageous to take two shots. Since the matrix confronted by B is merely the transpose of that facing A, he will also take two shots. Private adjustment will, therefore, attain the social optimum. There exists no position that is socially superior to the cell marked X', the position of private equilibrium. There is no social provision area.

Note that the external economies are not eliminated by the fact of income

B \ A	A$_0$	A$_1$	A$_2$	A$_3$	A$_4$
B$_4$	26 76 0 26	16 72 10 26	4 X 66 20 24	0 70 30 30	0 80 40 40
B$_3$	30 74 0 30	20 70 10 30	6 X 62 20 26	4 68 30 34	0 70 40 40
B$_2$	42 80 0 42	24 68 10 34	8 X′ 56 20 28	6 62 30 36	2 66 40 42
B$_1$	52 102 0 52	30 80 10 40	14 X 68 20 34	10 70 30 40	6 72 40 46
B$_0$	60 120 0 60	40 102 10 50	18 X 80 20 38	14 74 30 44	10 76 40 50

Figure 9

growth; these continue to exist as before. What the change has accomplished is the conversion of external economies that were Pareto-relevant at the private equilibrium solution of Figure 6 into external economies that are not Pareto-relevant at the private equilibrium solution of Figure 9. Individual A's situation continues to be affected by B's level of immunization; the more shots B takes, the better off A finds himself. Total costs for A fall as he moves north along any column of the matrix. The same holds for B, of course, in the transpose matrix; "rivers still run downhill." In the equilibrium position, X′, in Figure 9, however, A and B cannot, by mutual agreement, attain any other position that is preferred to X′. Each person would be willing to contribute up to $2 for either his own or his fellow's securing an additional shot. But this leaves a $6 deficit when benefits are compared with the $10 cost.

The matrix of Figure 9 represents, of course, only one simple numerical example that is deliberately constructed to make the point desired. The result derived can be made generally applicable if it is carefully applied. So long as the process of economic growth and development serves to increase the opportunity costs arising from failure of individuals to act privately more than it serves to increase the private cost of the activity itself, there will surely be some tendency for the independent or private adjustment equilibrium to shift toward the social optimum in the process, "optimum" being defined by the standard Paretian criteria. The external economies become less relevant as the society becomes more affluent. At some point in the process of development, these may become irrelevant, and, if they do, the activity should be returned to private organization providing it has been previously collectivized.

Practical examples are available to illustrate these general results. It is probably correct to say that the external or spillover benefits argument for governmental or collective support for elementary schooling becomes less and less relevant as the average level of income in a community rises. The case for socialized medicine is not so strong in 1964 as it would have been in 1938, on pure efficiency grounds, other elements of the problem remaining unchanged.

For completeness, it should be noted that the process of economic growth could make the external economies more significant in certain cases. If, for example, as personal incomes double, and opportunity costs of disease double (as between the situation in Figure 6 and Figure 9), the costs of inoculations should also double, the external economies remaining relevant. What is important here is the relationship between the opportunity costs (the benefits) of the action generating reciprocal external effects and the direct costs of carrying out the activity. With economic progress, it seems reasonable to suppose that the former should increase more rapidly than the latter, although peculiar circumstances may alter this relationship.

The analysis is not intended to suggest that, considered overall, the aggregate collectivization of the economy need decrease as economic development proceeds. Other elements of change surely introduce different, and, to an extent, offsetting factors. It seems safe to say that the external economies argument for expansion in the public sector will diminish over time, as this argument suggests. However, there will probably arise other interrelationships among persons, for the most part external diseconomies, which will require additional collective action in order for tolerable efficiency to be achieved. This may be summarized by saying that as people get richer they need to rely less and less on their neighbors to co-operate in securing the indivisible benefits of possible joint activities, but they may need to rely more and more on some collective mechanism to prevent themselves, and their neighbors, from imposing mutually undesirable costs on each other. In its broadest sense, "congestion" replaces "co-operation" as the underlying motive force behind collective action.

Analytically, external diseconomies and external economies are basically equivalent. There are important implications for the trend of public expenditure totals over time, however, if the thesis here is accepted. The collective action required in the case of Pareto-relevant external diseconomies can often be carried out by the introduction of simple administrative rules. Municipalities can simply prohibit transistor radios on public beaches, for example. By contrast, if the same municipality desires to see that all its school children get hot lunches, it will normally expend funds to provide such lunches. It could, of course, simply require that all children purchase hot lunches. But distributional considerations prevent the extension of administrative rules to the external economies side comparative with their application on the diseconomies side.

Nonsymmetrical Reciprocity

A WORLD OF UNEQUALS

There remains the task of extending the models so as to make them apply to a social group that contains persons who are *unequal* in respects relevant to the reciprocal externality relationships under consideration. As before, it is useful to begin with a two-person matrix illustration. Figure 10 duplicates Figure 6 in payouts confronting Individual A. Let us now assume that, instead of being equal with A, Individual B is, relatively, poor. The monetary value of benefits (opportunity costs) to B is, therefore, lower for B than for A. For simplicity, assume these to be one-half those for A. The matrix confronted by B is, in this case, no longer the simple transpose of that confronted by A, but instead is the transpose with the figures in the upper left-hand corner of each cell reduced by one-half. The payouts actually confronting B are shown in Figure 10 in the bracketed figures. Assume that the price of getting the shots remains the same as before.

The optimum values for A remain unchanged, as is shown by the cells marked by X's. Note, however, that the behavior of B will be substantially different. As the figures are computed for the example, B finds himself in a position of row dominance. Regardless of what A does or might do, B will not find it advantageous to get any immunization on his own. The cells marked with the B's trace the optimum values for B over all possible actions

B \ A	A₀	A₁	A₂	A₃	A₄
B_4	13 (2.5) X 55.5 (1.5) / 0 (40) 13 (42.5)	8 (1.5) 59.5 / 10 (40) 18 (41.5)	2 (.5) 62.5 / 20 (40) 22 (40.5)	0 (0) 70 / 30 (40) 30 (40)	0 (0) 80 / 40 (40) 40 (40)
B_3	15 (3.5) X 48.5 / 0 (30) 15 (33.5)	10 (2.5) 52.5 / 10 (30) 20 (32.5)	3 (1.5) 53.5 / 20 (30) 23 (31.5)	2 (1) 63 / 30 (30) 32 (31)	0 (0) 70 / 40 (30) 40 (30)
B_2	21 (4.5) X 45.5 / 0 (20) 21 (24.5)	12 (3.5) 45.5 / 10 (20) 22 (23.5)	4 (2) 46 / 20 (20) 24 (22)	3 (1.5) 54.5 / 30 (20) 33 (21.5)	1 (1) 62 / 40 (20) 41 (21)
B_1	26 (10) 46 / 0 (10) 26 (20)	15 (7.5) X 42.5 / 10 (10) 25 (17.5)	7 (6) 43 / 20 (10) 27 (16)	5 (5) 50 / 30 (10) 35 (15)	3 (4) 57 / 40 (10) 43 (14)
B_0	30 (15) B 45 / 0 (0) 30 (15)	20 (13) B 43 / 10 (0) 30 (13)	9 (10.5) XB 39.5 / 20 (0) 29 (10.5)	7 (7.5) B 44.5 / 30 (0) 37 (7.5)	5 (6.5) B 51 / 40 (0) 45 (6.5)

Figure 10

of A. In this case, cell A_2B_0 becomes the private adjustment equilibrium. Note, also, that this is the collective or social optimum under the revised set of payoffs. This result need not, of course, be a general one. It does indicate, however, that private adjustment may, in fact, generate the socially optimum solution, even in the presence of reciprocal external economies.

DISCRIMINATORY PRICING

When the world of unequals is introduced, and especially when the collectivization alternative is examined, the assumption that individuals will be confronted with uniform prices for the services in question becomes highly unreal. The poor may be allowed to purchase services at lower prices than the rich. One could, somewhat realistically in the particular example of medical care, assume that the private suppliers of inoculations made shots available to the poor at lower prices than to the rich. This would, of course, modify the private adjustment solution. This pricing change may or may not shift the solution closer to that which satisfied the necessary conditions for Pareto optimality. The relationship of the change to the Pareto frontier would depend upon the precise nature of the reciprocal externality in reference to the particular form of discrimination introduced.

DISCRIMINATION IN TAX-PRICES

A more interesting, and applicable, model, for the purposes of this discussion, is that which assumes the service to be collectivized, with the financing of the combination of services provided carried out on the basis of some familiar pattern of taxation. Suppose, for example, that the payout situation confronting A and B is that shown in Figure 10. However, the activity will now be under collective organization, and the direct outlay for inoculations is to be financed by the levy of a proportional income tax. Assume that A has an income that is double that for B. Hence, out of each aggregate outlay, A will pay two-thirds, and B only one-third. The results of this change are shown in Figure 11.

B \ A	A_0	A_1	A_2	A_3	A_4
B_4	13 55.4 (2.5) X 26.6 39.6 (13.3) (15.8)	8 59.4 (1.5) 33.3 41.3 (16.6) (18.1)	2 62.5 (.5) 40 42 (20) (20.5)	0 69.9 (0) 46.6 46.6 (23.3) (23.3)	0 79.9 (0) 53.3 53.3 (26.6) (26.6)
B_3	15 48.5 (3.5) X 20 35 (10) (13.5)	10 52.4 (2.5) 26.6 36.6 (13.3) (15.8)	3 54.4 (1.5) 33.3 36.3 (16.6) (18.1)	2 63 (1) 40 42 (20) (21)	0 69.9 (0) 46.6 46.6 (23.3) (23.3)
B_2	21 45.4 (4.5) B 13.3 34.3 (6.6) (11.1)	12 45.5 (3.5) B 20 32 (10) (13.5)	4 45.9 (2) BX 26.6 30.6 (13.3) (15.3)	3 54.4 (1.5) 33.3 36.3 (16.6) (18.1)	1 62 (1) 40 41 (20) (21)
B_1	26 45.9 (10) 6.6 32.6 (3.3) (13.3)	15 42.4 (7.5) C 13.3 28.3 (6.6) (14.1)	7 43 (6) X 20 27 (10) (16)	5 49.9 (5) 26.6 31.6 (13.3) (18.3)	3 56.9 (4) 33.3 36.3 (16.6) (20.6)
B_0	30 45 (15) 0 30 (0) (15)	20 42.9 (13) 6.6 26.6 (3.3) (16.3)	9 39.4 (10.5) XO′ 13.3 22.3 (6.6) (17.1)	7 44.5 (7.5) B 20 27 (10) (17.5)	5 51.4 (6.5) B 26.6 31.6 (13.3) (19.8)

Figure 11

The figures in the upper left-hand corner of each cell are the same as shown in Figure 10, since the opportunity costs of the disease have not changed. Similarly, the figures in the upper right-hand corner of each cell are not changed. Neither opportunity costs nor direct costs have been modified for the group as a whole. For each cell, however, the distribution of direct costs has been modified. Note, for example, cell A_0B_1; under the private adjustment situation, B pays $10 for one shot; A pays nothing since he gets no shots. However, in the proportional income tax model, for this same physical activity, B will pay only one-third of the total cost of $10, while A will pay two-thirds. The figures in the lower right-hand corner of each cell, indicating individual cost totals, are changed appropriately to reflect this modification in the allocation of direct costs.

It is clear that the individually desired positions will be modified by this imposed change in the allocation of costs. Individual adjustment is not, of course, possible since it is assumed that the activity is now collectivized. It is useful in evaluating the collective result that may emerge, however, to trace through the positions of individual optima under these modified conditions. The cells marked by X's trace out the positions that A would choose, given each level of B's activity. Similarly, the B cells trace out the same thing for B.

Now assume that both persons must agree on any collective solution, but that some constitutional rule requires proportional taxation. The position of political equilibrium in this case is that indicated by cell A_1B_1, marked as C. This may be shown by examining the process through which agreement is reached. Clearly, both persons would agree to move from A_0B_0, the no-activity cell, to A_1B_1. However, at least one person would object to any moves beyond this, in any direction. Note, however, that the political equilibrium solution is not the social optimum under the revised payoffs. This is shown, as in Figure 10, in the cell B_0A_2, marked XO' in Figure 11.

There is nothing especially new in this conclusion. Collective organization should not be expected to produce optimal results unless the structure of tax-prices should be such as to guarantee that the Pareto conditions are satisfied. And it should be evident that it would be, indeed, highly unlikely that the distribution of total taxes on the basis of any of the familiar institutions of taxation would produce optimal results. The model is helpful in that it does indicate the necessary correspondence between the structure of tax-prices and the political solution that might emerge.

In a more realistic setting, larger groups would have to be considered, along with different political rules for reaching collective decisions. The two-man model can be applied to a limited, but helpful, extent in this connection. Suppose, for example, that the poor were in the majority, and that majority rule prevailed, although the constitutional requirement of proportional taxation remained in force. In this case, a solution approximating that shown at A_0B_2 would be predicted. On the other hand, should the rich be in the majority under similar circumstances, cell A_2B_0 could be predicted as the result. It is, of course, pure circumstance that the latter would be, in the configuration of the numerical example, the socially most desirable result.

Conclusion

In this paper we have attempted to examine, with the aid of some very simple examples and some very elementary models, the adjustment process in the presence of reciprocal external economies. Several points have been developed which have not, possibly, been adequately recognized in the more hurried discussions of external economies and diseconomies. The importance of the social decision concerning the basic organizational structure of activities generating reciprocal external economies cannot be underestimated. Perhaps the major single point to be gained from this paper is that there are many more complications relevant to this social decision than might appear upon cursory examination. The results have been primarily negative; it is far easier to indicate that certain solutions fail to produce the ideally desired results than it is to indicate alternative institutional arrangements that will do so. Perhaps the greatest single need for improved analysis in theoretical political economy is for somewhat more careful recognition and analysis of the institutional processes through which people, publicly or privately, carry on economic activities.

External Diseconomies in Competitive Supply

Charles J. Goetz and James M. Buchanan

Economists have arrived at an understanding of how the competitive process eliminates the influences of irrelevant or pecuniary externalities on resource allocation.[1] They have not developed a comparably satisfactory understanding of how competition incorporates the influences of Pareto-relevant or technological externalities on allocative outcomes.[2] This paper aims to contribute toward such an understanding.

From *American Economic Review* 61 (December 1971): 883–90. Reprinted by permission of the publisher.

We are indebted to several critics at various stages of this paper. We should especially mention the help provided by Leland S. Case, Milton Kafoglis, H. E. Overcast, J. A. Stockfisch, and Gordon Tullock.

1. The famous neoclassical controversy on this point commanded the attention of such neoclassical "greats" as Alfred Marshall, A. C. Pigou, Allyn Young, D. H. Robertson, and Frank H. Knight. The central portions of the neoclassical controversy are reprinted in papers selected for inclusion in G. J. Stigler and K. E. Boulding, eds., *Readings in Price Theory* (Homewood, 1952), part 2. In particular, the paper by Howard Ellis and William Fellner, first published in 1943, provides an excellent summary treatment of the basic issues (H. S. Ellis and W. Fellner, "External Economies and Diseconomies," *American Economic Review* 33 (September 1943): 493–511, reprinted in *Readings in Price Theory*, 242–63.

2. Modern price theorists have recognized the complexities that remain in the analysis, and they have made progress in clarification. Specifically, note should be taken here of the contributions by E. J. Mishan, J. A. Stockfish, and D. A. Worcester, Jr. See E. J. Mishan, "What Is Producers' Surplus?" *American Economic Review* 58 (December 1968): 1269–82; J. A. Stockfish, "General Equilibrium versus Partial Equilibrium Supply Curves," 1962, mimeographed, and "A Study in the Theory of Cost and Supply," 1970, mimeographed;

Firms in competitive industries generally impose externalities on each other through interdependencies in their input or output prices and/or through alterations of the technological production relationships. We limit discussion to externalities in supply. We shall not consider the reciprocal externalities that firms impose on each other through influences on output prices. As a second major restriction, we assume that all externalities are contained within a well-defined industry category. Finally, we limit the specific analysis to external diseconomies, although much of the analysis is fully symmetric with respect to external economies.

We argue that familiar descriptions of the nonoptimality properties of competition in the presence of technological external diseconomies are misleading in that they focus exclusively on exchange inefficiency and neglect production inefficiency. A subsidiary purpose of the paper is to suggest that only through a more detailed understanding of the way that supply externalities affect allocative outcomes can the efficacy either of organizational alternatives such as centralized industry management or of corrective devices such as taxes be considered with sufficient sophistication to yield any hope for reasonably efficient results. When the precise way in which externalities enter the competitive process is clarified, the deficiencies in the standard corrective prescriptions such as Pigovian tax schemes become evident.

I. Optimality Properties—Pecuniary Diseconomies

We shall limit analysis to a two-good, two-industry economy.[3] Consider an amended version of Adam Smith's beaver-deer model in which each of two goods is produced by a fully competitive industry. In Figure 1, the convex set of points, *CC*, is defined in the two physical dimensions, beaver being mea-

---

D. A. Worcester, Jr., "Pecuniary and Technological Externality, Factor Rents, and Social Cost," *American Economic Review* 59 (December 1969): 873–85.

3. It is not fully legitimate to generalize a two-good model into one that is applicable for the *n*-good economy by treating one of the two goods as a composite measure for the *n* − 1 other goods. This familiar practice may be helpful in certain instances, despite the fundamental analytical error that is involved. The problem arises because of the non-uniqueness of the mix in the bundle of goods that the numeraire embodies. Once we move beyond a two-good setting, in the strictly physical sense, objective trade-offs between goods in production cannot be divorced from evaluations.

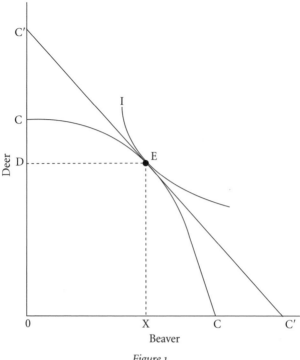

Figure 1

sured along the abscissa and deer along the ordinate. This curve is the locus of all possible equilibrium positions, similar to the one shown at *E*, which may be attained as demand shifts take place. Given any configuration of demand, equilibrium is reached when the market price of each good reflects both marginal cost to the producing firm and the marginal rate of substitution in consumption or use for all buyers (as reflected in the slope of the community indifference curve of Figure 1).

In the conditions depicted, each of the goods is produced under conditions of increasing supply price or average cost. At each position of full equilibrium, the familiar conditions that must be satisfied are

$$p_i = mc_i = ac_i, \qquad (1)$$

where the subscript *i* refers to the individual firm, and *p*, *mc*, and *ac* refer to output price, marginal cost, and average cost. The firm makes no profit or loss, and there is no incentive for entry or exit of firms from the industry.

Since the industry is merely the sum of all the firms that compose it, we also know that

$$ac_i = ac_I,$$ (2)

where the subscript I refers to the industry as a whole.

The construction of Figure 1 allows the function of rents in the general equilibrium context to be depicted readily. As demand patterns change, competitive adjustments have the effect of continuously converting the convex set of points traced out of CC into a series of linear price lines. At the equilibrium shown at E, the market price of beaver, in deer units, is represented by the slope of $C'C'$. If evaluated at this price, the supply of beaver, $0X$, is worth $C'D$ in units of deer. This is the total industry cost or outlay that is required to produce the $0X$ units of beaver. This total cost or outlay may be broken down into its two component parts, rents and nonrents. The amount $C'C$ measures rents, and CD measures nonrents. Note that at E the average cost to the industry, and hence to the individual firm, is represented by $C'D/0X$, which is equal to market price.

To this point we have deliberately refrained from making statements about the optimality properties of the economy represented. The conditions specified in (1) and (2) are those that are necessary for a position to qualify as one of full competitive equilibrium for an industry. These may or may not be consistent with those that must be met for Pareto optimality.

When there are no technological externalities among the separate firms in the industry, the increasing supply price for the industry, depicted by the convex set of possible equilibrium points, CC, arises solely because of the emergence of rents. The rents may reflect differential resource specialization, but this need not be present.[4] Rents take the form of increases in the prices of some inputs as industry output expands. Rents reflect pecuniary external diseconomies because the firm's influence on input prices is neglected. In expanding its own output, disregarding its own influence in driving up input prices, a firm imposes perfectly genuine external costs on all other firms in the industry. The error that both Marshall and Pigou made involved their

---

4. On this, see Joan Robinson, "Rising Supply Price," *Economica* 8 (1941): 1–8, reprinted in *Readings in Price Theory*, 233–41, and E. J. Mishan, "What Is Producers' Surplus?"

interpretation of these external costs to firms, and internal to the single industry, as *net* social costs which were properly to be included in determining allocative outcomes. This error was corrected by Allyn Young, D. H. Robertson, and Frank Knight. The correction involved the demonstration that these external costs suffered by firms in the industry whose output expands are precisely offset by the receipt of income gains to the owners of inputs. Therefore, although these rents are necessary costs to the firms and to the industry taken as a whole, they are, in the terminology of modern externality theory, Pareto-irrelevant.[5] In its failure to internalize these strictly pecuniary externalities, competition guarantees overall efficiency in resource use.

These generalizations may be discussed in terms of the geometrical representation. In the absence of technological externalities, the long-run supply curve is the *marginal social cost curve*. In Figure 1, the slope of the curve *CC* at any point is the marginal rate of transformation between the two goods for the society as a whole. This curve is the physically determinate *production-possibility* frontier as well as the locus of competitive equilibrium positions. Note that at equilibrium, which under the depicted demand configuration is located at *E*, all of the required conditions for Pareto optimality are satisfied. The marginal rate of transformation in production equals the marginal rate of substitution in consumption or use. Market price equals marginal social cost, which is also marginal cost to the producing firms in both industries of the model. Both industries are in long-run equilibrium in that there is no incentive for resource services to be shifted. All supply decisions are made by firms, and not by industries as units.

II. Technological External Diseconomies

It is widely acknowledged that the necessary marginal conditions for Pareto optimality are not satisfied when the external effects in production are technological, that is, when the action of one firm actually modifies the physical production relationships of other firms. To qualify as a position of competitive equilibrium, however, the conditions depicted in Figure 1 must be met. As demonstrated, price must equal average as well as marginal cost for each

5. This terminology is fully developed in J. M. Buchanan and W. C. Stubblebine, "Externality," *Economica* 29 (November 1962): 371–84.

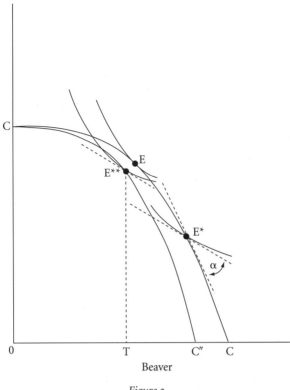

Figure 2

firm in each industry. The implications of these conditions appear to have been overlooked by many writers when they introduce technological externalities. The existence of such diseconomies is commonly considered to produce a nonoptimal equilibrium position at a point such as that shown at E^* on Figure 2 with E remaining the Pareto-efficient outcome as in Figure 1.[6] If beaver are produced under conditions of external diseconomies, each firm's marginal cost is less than the actual marginal cost to society in terms of fore-

---

6. Perhaps the most explicit examples of this reasoning as applied within an exact analogue to our Figure 3 are found in the international trade literature, including the well-known article by Gottfried Haberler, "Some Problems in the Pure Theory of International Trade," *Economic Journal* 60 (June 1950): 233–40, esp. pp. 236 and 237n. Also see J. Bhagwati and V. K. Ramaswami, "Domestic Distortions, Tariffs, and the Theory of Optimum Subsidy," *Journal of Political Economy* 71 (February 1963): 44–50, esp. pp. 45–46.

gone real opportunities. Hence, the effects of competition would seem to be those of shifting the equilibrium away from the potential optimal point at E and along the production-possibility frontier to such a position as E^*, where there are relatively too many beaver produced. From the geometrical configuration depicted, if E^* should be the location of the inefficient equilibrium, it would seem that an efficacious policy prescription might be the levy of a corrective Pigovian tax designed to eliminate the divergence, as represented by angle α, between the firm's and society's marginal rate of transformation.[7]

When the required conditions for full competitive equilibrium are incorporated into the analysis, however, the existence of such a position as E^* can be shown to be impossible. Indeed, if technological externalities exist, competitive equilibrium must be located on some *interior* locus, such as CC''. Production inefficiencies in addition to the exchange inefficiencies suggested in the more orthodox treatments must characterize competitive equilibrium under these conditions. The next step is that of indicating precisely how these production inefficiencies emerge.

Assume that a full competitive equilibrium is established at a beaver output of T units in Figure 2 and that the conditions for equilibrium are fully satisfied. Our problem is one of demonstrating that with technological externalities T is produced at E^{**} inside rather than on the *efficient* production-possibility frontier, CC. Since their existence generates somewhat different results, we shall distinguish two types of external effects on production: output-generated and input-generated.[8] Output-generated externalities occur when a firm's technological production function contains the output of other producers as one of its arguments. The original neoclassical discussion seems to be in these terms, and this case involves a strict interpretation of the phrase "external economies of industry [output] scale." Input-generated externalities occur when the externality argument in a firm's production function is based on other firms' use of one or more particular inputs. We will deal with these two cases successively.

---

7. Bhagwati and Ramaswami prescribe such a corrective tax for the analogous case of an external economy.

8. Murray Kemp, "The Efficiency of Competition as an Allocation of Resources; Part 1," *Canadian Journal of Economics* 21 (February 1955): 30–42, provides a separate analysis of these two classes of externalities. However, as indicated in the text below, our own analysis generates different conclusions.

OUTPUT-GENERATED EXTERNALITIES

Our demonstration involves examining the behavior of an individual firm in the affected industry. In order to emphasize the physical input-output relationship, cost is measured in units of a single homogeneous input or an input bundle whose use is to be minimized.[9] For simplicity, all firms are regarded as identical. Assume, then, that the cost function of any firm has the following specific functional form:

$$c_i = k + q_i^a + Q_i^b q_i \quad a > 1, b > 0, \tag{3}$$

where q_i is the firm's own output, where Q_i is the aggregate output of all *other* firms in the industry, and where $b > 0$ indicates the presence of the technological external diseconomy. As noted in (1) above, full competitive equilibrium requires that each firm operate where $mc_i = ac_i$, an output that corresponds to the minimum point on the firm's average cost curve. This equilibrium is depicted by point e_i in Figure 3. Average and marginal cost are derived straightforwardly from (3) as

$$ac_i = kq_i^{-1} + q_i^{a-1} + Q_i^b \tag{4}$$

and

$$mc_i = aq_i^{a-1} + Q_i^b, \tag{5}$$

with the externality variable, Q_i, regarded as a parameter by the firm. With all firms operating at a scale q_i, which equates (4) and (5), the industry produces the output T with n firms[10] such that

$$n = T/q_i. \tag{6}$$

The industry can, however, be reorganized with fewer firms each of which produces a larger output. Such a reorganization will lower average cost for

9. Conversion of cost into value terms requires only that we multiply both sides of (3) by input price. We neglect this complication since cost minimization for the firm implies an identical solution in either case. For the *industry,* cost minimization in value terms is clearly inappropriate since this would involve internalization of purely pecuniary, non-relevant externalities.

10. We adopt here the convenient expositional fiction that the number of firms is a continuous variable. In actuality, of course, the solution in the text must be modified to allow for n being always an integer. If n is large, this adjustment becomes negligible.

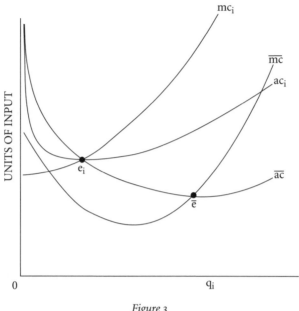

each firm in the industry, and, hence, a smaller quantity of industry inputs will be required to produce the same output, T.

In order to demonstrate this production-inefficiency of the competitive outcome, it is necessary to replace the *ceteris paribus* cost curves faced by the individualistic firms with *mutatis mutandis* cost curves which reflect Q_i as a variable rather than as a parameter.[11] The "other firms' output" externality variable is

$$Q_i = T - q_i, \tag{7}$$

for any constant industry output, T. Substituting (7) into (3) for Q_i, we get a *mutatis mutandis* total cost function,

$$\bar{c} = k + q_i^a + (T - q_i)^b q_i, \tag{3b}$$

where industry output is held constant at T by varying n inversely with q_i, according to the relationship implied in equation (6). The firm's *mutatis mutandis* average and marginal cost functions are:

---

11. Failure to recognize this sort of distinction seems to have led Kemp to reach conclusions quite different from those we reach in this section.

$$\overline{ac} = kq_i^{-1} + q_i^{a-1} + (T - q_i)^b, \tag{8}$$

$$\overline{mc} = aq_i^{a-1} + (T - q_i)^b - q_i b(T - q_i)^{b-1}. \tag{9}$$

The average costs in (4) and (8) are related as shown in Figure 3, with $ac_i > \overline{ac}$ for expansions and $ac_i < \overline{ac}$ for contractions from the firm's competitive equilibrium where $ac_i = mc_i$. Significantly, $\overline{ac}$ is not minimized where $ac_i = mc_i$ because, as (5) and (9) show, mc_i is always greater than $\overline{mc}$. The total resource cost of producing T units is minimized when firms produce at $\bar{e}$, the low point of $\overline{ac}$ in Figure 3, that scale of output which equates (8) and (9). Since (4) and (5) must be equalized for competitive equilibrium, and since (8) and (9) must be equalized for Pareto optimality, it is evident that competition is production-inefficient in that firm sizes are suboptimal and that there are too many firms in the industry.[12] Competitive equilibrium necessarily lies on an interior locus such as that shown by CC'' in Figure 2.

Our example may now be framed in completely general terms. Assume that the firm's total cost c_i is a function of its own output and external output,

$$c_i = f(q_i, Q_i). \tag{10}$$

Then the $ac = mc$ condition of competitive equilibrium requires

$$\frac{c_i}{q_i} = \frac{\partial f}{\partial q_i}. \tag{11}$$

But if industry output, T, has been constrained to be constant by equation (8) above, efficient firm operation demands that

$$\frac{c_i}{q_i} = \frac{\partial f}{\partial q_i} + \frac{\partial f}{\partial Q}\frac{\partial Q_i}{\partial q_i} = \frac{\partial f}{\partial q_i} - \frac{\partial f}{\partial Q} \tag{12}$$

for each firm.

An extremely important implication of this analysis is that any attempt to

---

12. As the geometrical construction suggests, the nonoptimality in firm size reflects the presence of an incentive for industry-wide internalization of decisions that is absent in the orthodox competitive equilibrium. Such an incentive always exists with respect to potential exploitation of monopoly-monopsony gains, but in the external diseconomy model with firm-size inefficiency there is some incentive over and beyond this. However, to the extent that individual firms behave parametrically, there will be no more tendency to depart from the equilibrium established in the external diseconomy case than there is in the more familiar model. In the absence of transactions costs, the inefficiency reflected by nonoptimal firm sizes could not, of course, remain.

impose a per unit corrective tax on the output of firms in the industry will fail. Such a tax will serve only to move the equilibrium to a different point on the inefficient interior locus. A per unit tax would simply shift the curves in Figure 3 upward in a parallel fashion. Or, in terms of the equations (11) and (12), adding a corrective tax t to each cost concept does nothing to modify the basic inconsistency of their solutions. Any fully corrective tax must be more complex than has been realized, since not only marginal cost but also the firm's perception of the *shape* of its average cost curve must be modified.[13]

INPUT-GENERATED EXTERNAL DISECONOMIES

The analysis above has been confined to "output-generated" external diseconomies. Similar conclusions are applicable for "input-generated" external diseconomies, those which are directly related to the use of one or more industry inputs and, through these, indirectly to the actual scale of industry output. In this case, the elements of our analysis are based upon a familiar adaptation of the Edgeworth-Bowley box construction to derive an economy's efficient transformation locus. To our knowledge, however, the implications have not been explicitly applied to externalities.

Wolfgang Stolper and Paul Samuelson used the box construction to demonstrate that the ratios of the marginal products of any two factors must be identical in each industry if the economy is to be production-efficient.[14] Competitive equilibrium implies the equalization of these ratios of marginal products to the *firm*. But the Stolper-Samuelson condition must be interpreted in terms of social marginal product, that is, *net* marginal product to the industry. Since these two concepts of marginal product diverge when technological externalities exist, it seems clear that in the standard case where

13. We hope to explore some of the complex issues involved in the determination of corrective taxes in a separate paper in process. We should note that our implied criticism of the simple corrective tax is different from, although related to, that of Davis and Whinston. Their analysis was developed exclusively in a small-number setting, and they did not consider the effects of the constraints imposed by the overall conditions for competitive equilibrium. See O. A. Davis and A. Whinston, "Externalities, Welfare and the Theory of Games," *Journal of Political Economy* 70 (June 1962): 241–62.

14. Wolfgang F. Stolper and Paul A. Samuelson, "Protection and Real Wages," *Review of Economic Studies* 9 (November 1941): 58–73.

factor prices are identical to all industries, input-generated external diseconomies lead to interior production-inefficient competitive equilibria. Specifically, the social marginal physical product of a diseconomy-producing input will be excessively low relative to the marginal physical products of other inputs. Consequently, such an input is over-used in the industry where it produces the diseconomies. A particularly clear illustration of this is provided when there exists an input whose marginal product to the firm is positive but whose externality-producing impact on the production of other firms causes its net (industry) marginal product actually to become negative.

The input-generated externalities are incorporated in inefficient input combinations for the firm regardless of the outputs chosen. It is not possible to draw conclusions about firm size similar to those previously stated with respect to output-generated externalities. With input-generated external diseconomies, firms may be either too small, the right size, or too large. The determination of efficiency-producing corrective taxes remains, however, a more complicated problem than has been generally acknowledged.[15]

III. Conclusions

Economies of space have prevented us from relating our analysis more directly to the neoclassical discussion and also from following up several of the implications in detail. Our objective here has been limited to presenting the analytical foundations for the theory of supply in environments that embody actual or potential external diseconomies. We have made no effort to provide a full taxonomy even of this subset of externalities. Specifically, we have restricted consideration to external diseconomies which are contained within a well-defined industry.

In this context, our results indicate that the standard description of misallocation in the presence of external production diseconomies is misleading.[16] The impact of production externalities has heretofore been conceived

15. One aspect of the difficulties involved in the correction of input-generated externalities has been described by Charles Plott, "Externalities and Corrective Taxes," *Economica* 33 (February 1966): 84–87.

16. The paper by John S. Chipman appeared only after the initially submitted version of this paper was provisionally accepted for publication. Accordingly, we have not mod-

of exclusively in terms of a suboptimal exchange equilibrium on the production possibilities frontier. We have shown, however, that this equilibrium must take place on a pseudo-frontier which lies interior to the efficient production possibilities locus. The resulting combination of exchange-inefficiency with production-inefficiency renders the construction of corrective devices much more difficult.

It is also possible that the output of a good produced under external diseconomies will actually be less than the Pareto-optimal quantity, in contrast to the standard expectation that such a good is always over-produced. It should be apparent from the construction of Figure 3 that utility functions embodying the standard properties could produce an externality-distorted competitive equilibrium that falls either to the right or to the left of the optimal quantity shown at E. The directional relationship between the competitive industry output and the socially optimal output depends strictly on the particular characteristics of utility functions as well as on the strength of the production externality component.

In summary, our analysis suggests that no real paradigm has existed in this area of the theory of competitive supply. To our knowledge, no one has explicitly traced the impact of externalities through their influence on the individual competitive firm's necessary conditions for competitive equilibrium. This approach has enabled us to describe more adequately the precise nature of a nonoptimal equilibrium in the presence of one form of technological externality.

---

ified the text to cover points raised by Chipman. His paper seems to be a sophisticated and modern presentation of the orthodox analysis. Our results differ from those reached by Chipman primarily because Chipman treats each firm's production function as a parametric approximation to the industry production. This simplification has unintended results. For instance, it does not generate U-shaped firm cost curves, nor does it allow the industry's resource cost to be affected by the distribution of output among firms. See Chipman, "External Economies of Scale and Competitive Equilibrium," *Quarterly Journal of Economics* 84 (August 1970): 347–85.

External Diseconomies, Corrective Taxes, and Market Structure

This note is presented as a contribution to the continuing dismantling of the Pigovian tradition in applied economics, defined here as the emphasis on internalizing externalities through the imposition of corrective taxes and subsidies. My central point is much more elementary than those advanced by some of the other contributors to the recent discussion. R. H. Coase demonstrated the inherently bilateral aspects of any externality relationship, and he showed that applying the Pigovian policy norms in neglect of the two-sidedness of the account may reduce rather than increase efficiency.[1] Davis and Whinston concentrated on the impossibility of determining the size of a corrective tax that would lead to an efficient outcome under conditions of reciprocal externalities when production functions are nonseparably related.[2] Plott called attention to the necessity of identifying properly the aspect of the production process that generates the externality.[3] I shall demonstrate that (1) even if the directional gains-from-trade are such that an orthodox corrective tax would increase efficiency, and (2) even if production functions are separable, and (3) even if no changes in the input mix are technically possible, the imposition of a corrective tax (under external diseconomy) will often

From *American Economic Review* 59 (March 1969): 174–77. Reprinted by permission of the publisher.

1. R. H. Coase, "The Problem of Social Cost," *Journal of Law and Economics* 3 (October 1960): 1–44.

2. O. A. Davis and Andrew Whinston, "Externalities, Welfare, and the Theory of Games," *Journal of Political Economy* 70 (June 1962): 241–62.

3. Charles Plott, "Externalities and Corrective Taxes," *Economica* 33 (February 1966): 84–87.

reduce rather than increase welfare in the Pareto-efficiency sense. Only when the industry generating the external diseconomy is competitively organized can the corrective tax be unambiguously hailed as welfare-improving, even in the presence of all of the other required conditions. Under monopolistic organization, the corrective tax may well lead to a reduction in welfare rather than an increase.

My criticism is aimed more at the "Pigovian tradition" than at Pigou himself. His whole analytics, and that of Marshall, was implicitly based on the assumption of competitive structures, as, indeed, some of the contributors to the externality literature seem to have recognized.[4] It is necessary to distinguish, however, between the relevance of market structure for the emergence of externality and the relevance of market structure for the application of the Pigovian policy norms. For example, Ellis and Fellner state that "the 'atomistic' character of one producer's output under competition, frequently thought to be crucial in the external economies-diseconomies context, is not decisive of itself."[5] Ellis and Fellner were referring here to the potential for the emergence of externalities, but it is relatively easy to see how this statement could be taken to imply that market structure also has little relevance to the application of the standard externality-correcting devices. And we know that the levy of corrective taxes under diseconomies and the provision of corrective subsidies under economies have been widely discussed without reference to market organization. This attitude is surely characteristic of modern treatments of pollution control. If, as I shall demonstrate, it is necessary to limit the Pigovian correctives on the tax side to situations of competition, much of the current discussion on these problems requires substantial revision. As we recognize, most of the problems falling under "congestion" as a general category involve external diseconomies.

My argument can be presented geometrically in the simplest of models, one in which constant cost is assumed. More complex models are not needed. An industry demand curve is shown as D in Figure 1, with the cost curve shown

4. Notably J. E. Meade, "External Economies and Diseconomies in a Competitive Situation," *Economic Journal* 62 (March 1952): 54–67.

5. H. S. Ellis and William Fellner, "External Economies and Diseconomies," *American Economic Review* 33 (September 1943): 493–511, reprinted in G. J. Stigler and K. E. Boulding, eds., *Readings in Price Theory* (Homewood, Ill., 1952), 242–63.

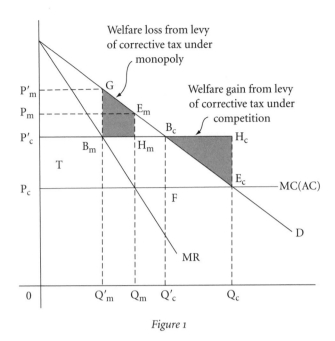

Figure 1

by $MC(AC)$. If the industry is competitively organized, equilibrium output is Q_c, and price is P_c. Let us now assume that a "bad" is suddenly discovered to be inherent in the output of this industry, an external diseconomy that is directly related to the number of units produced and not to any particulars of the input mix or to the rate of output for any other industry. This external diseconomy does affect the production functions of all firms in a second industry, also assumed to be competitively organized. The firms in the second industry have no legal claims to compensation for damages. Furthermore, for purposes of simplification, we assume that the costs of organizing firms in the second industry for the purpose of bribing firms in the first industry are prohibitive.

Given these restrictions, it is possible to indicate the size of a per unit tax to be imposed on the firms in the externality-generating industry. The orthodox Pigovian analysis suggests that the levy of this tax will induce behavioral changes that will move the economy to the efficiency locus. Let us suppose that the external diseconomy per unit is $P'_c P_c$, generating the unit tax T in Figure 1. Price will rise to P'_c, and industry output will fall to Q'_c.

How can the subsequent increase in welfare be measured? The rectangle $P_cP'_cB_cF$ represents a true "cost" that was previously treated as if it were consumers' surplus by the buyers of the first industry's product. If the proceeds of the tax are transferred to firms in the damaged industry, this now becomes consumers' surplus to the buyers of the product of this industry. If the proceeds are generally expended in the economy, these become diffused among all persons. Welfare gains and losses occur only with respect to the change in relative industry outputs. The buyers' evaluation of the quantity that was produced before the tax in the externality-generating industry but which quantity is eliminated by the tax is shown by the area under the demand curve over the range Q'_cQ_c, or by the area, $Q'_cB_cE_cQ_c$. The "cost" of this quantity to the community is indicated by the rectangle $Q'_cB_cH_cQ_c$. Hence, the welfare gain is shown by the shaded triangle, $B_cH_cE_c$.[6]

To this point, no problems are encountered given the restrictions initially placed on the model. However, let us now assume that the industry that generates the external diseconomy is organized as a monopoly, with a single profit-maximizing firm. Before the levy of any corrective tax, monopoly output is Q_m and price is P_m. As in the competitive case, Pigovian analysis suggests the levy of a corrective tax of T per unit of output. Monopoly output falls to Q'_m and price increases to P'_m.

It is easy to show that under the conditions as shown in Figure 1 welfare has *decreased*, not increased, as a result of the levy of the corrective tax. The cost of the change in quantity is measured, as before, by the rectangle $Q'_mB_mH_mQ_m$. The evaluation of the quantity is measured, as before, by the area under the demand curve, or by $Q'_mGE_mQ_m$. Since the latter area clearly exceeds the former, welfare has been reduced as indicated by the shaded area. The geometry makes clear that in this simple case this result must hold so long as the corrective tax, which we assume to have been estimated properly, is less than the difference between price and marginal revenue at the initial monopoly output.

As I have indicated, the point is a very elementary one. It is a particularly

6. If the damaged industry is identical in size to the industry that is generating the externality, and if demand and cost relationships are similar in the two industries, the welfare gain to the community can also be represented by the appropriate "welfare triangle" in a diagram depicting the situation of the other industry. The danger to be guarded against is double-counting of the same welfare gain in this procedure.

clear example of the theory of second-best. The monopolist simultaneously imposes two external diseconomies, at least in a general sense. He "pollutes" and hence increases costs of firms in the damaged industry. Also, however, he holds down output and hence increases costs of his product to buyers. So long as the second diseconomy is more highly valued than the former, any levy of a per unit tax on the monopolist's output will decrease total welfare. There are gains-from-trade here in two opposing directions, and there is no means of determining a priori which set of "trades" is potentially the more efficient. Conceptually, and ignoring costs of organizing, the firms in the damaged industry could bribe the monopolist to reduce output and thereby reduce "pollution." At the same time, again ignoring the costs of organizing, the buyers of the monopolist's product could bribe the monopolist to increase output. In some costless three-way negotiation process, the ultimate outcome under conditions such as those depicted in Figure 1 is the corrected equilibrium output at Q_c'.

As the construction as well as the discussion indicates, there is an important asymmetry between external diseconomies and external economies with respect to the possible offsetting welfare effects of market structure. With external economies, the provision of corrective subsidies reinforces the directional change in output that reforms in market structure would indicate to be desirable. In this case, buyers of the monopolist's own product could join forces with firms in an externally benefitted industry to bribe the monopolist to increase output.

As Coase has correctly emphasized, the whole approach of the Pigovian tradition is responsible for many confusions in applied economics that are slowly coming to be clarified. This approach involves an undue concentration on the decision-calculus of the firm or individual that is observed to be generating the external effects. Even if we disregard all problems of measurement, making the marginal private cost as faced by the decision-taking unit equal to marginal social cost does not provide the Aladdin's lamp for the applied welfare theorist, and the sooner he recognizes this the better.

The Institutional Structure
of Externality

I. Introduction

An emerging consensus on the theory of externality embodies a clear conceptual distinction between small-number and large-number interactions. When the parties to a potential externality relationship are few, market-like voluntary contractual arrangements are predicted to emerge.[1] Although bargaining difficulties are acknowledged, the contractual outcomes are predicted to satisfy broad efficiency norms. When the parties are many, prohibitive transactions costs are predicted to prevent the emergence of tolerably efficient voluntary agreements, and some resort to collective or governmental choice processes may be indicated when the externality exerts significant effects.

Subsidiary discussion has taken place within each of these major categories. Those who have concentrated on voluntary contractual internalization in the small-number cases have been fascinated, perhaps unduly, by the properties of the now-called "Coase theorem." This theorem states that in the absence of transactions costs *and* income effects the allocative results are invariant under changes in property rights. Regardless of the initial assign-

From *Public Choice* 14 (Spring 1973): 69–82. Reprinted by permission of the publisher, Kluwer Academic Publishers.

Work on this paper began as a direct result of a discussion with Professor J. G. Head of Dalhousie University in October 1970. It was presented in preliminary form in a seminar at the University of Chicago in February 1971. The paper was revised in early 1972.

1. Economists' recognition of this tendency toward contractual internalization of potential externality in the small-number cases stems from the basic paper by R. H. Coase, "The Problem of Social Cost," *Journal of Law and Economics,* 3 (October 1960), 1–44.

ment of rights in a potential externality interaction, the efficient allocative solution will be attained under the restrictive assumptions of the theorem. On the other hand, those economists who have sought to carry forward the neoclassical Pigovian policy prescriptions, and this includes most of those who have worked specifically on practical problems of environmental quality, have evoked the transactions costs rubric as a protective device that allows them to ignore the developments in the theory of small-number externalities. Their attention has turned to the specific formulation of corrective schemes which might ideally be introduced by collective or governmental agencies.[2]

My purpose in this paper is to demonstrate that the two-part classification of potential externality relationships into small-number and large-number cases obscures several considerations that are directly relevant to institutional rearrangements. Transactions costs are present in all potential exchanges, but these costs can vary greatly between one set of circumstances and another. In many of the large-number cases, a "publicness" aspect of an interaction is present, but in many others, this aspect is absent. The differences in transactions costs in these two subcategories can be significant. Concentration on two-party models in the small-number cases necessarily causes the publicness or joint-consumption aspects to be overlooked, but there seems to have been an implicit assumption that these aspects are always characteristic of large-number externalities.

It is widely recognized that all joint-consumption relationships are themselves externalities. In the strict sense, therefore, the failure of contractual arrangements to emerge may depend critically on the presence of *two* potential externality relationships rather than one. There may be an externality between the "producer" of an effect and the "consumer," but there may also be an externality *among* separate "consumers." The second of these may occur without the first, in which case we have the standard collective-goods paradigm. Or the second of these may accompany the first, in which case we have the collective- or public-goods paradigm plus an additional externality relationship, that between the group of joint consumers, considered as one party, and the producer or generator of the effects in question. Voluntary ac-

---

2. For a representative example of a paper in this general area, see William J. Baumol, "On Taxation and Correction of Externalities," *American Economic Review*, 62 (June 1972), 307–22.

tion will not produce fully efficient results in either of these two cases. By contrast, the externality relationship between producer and consumer of an effect may be present without the presence of any collective-goods externality. In this case, voluntary contractual internalization may occur regardless of the number of consumers.

II. Extending the Taxonomy

We need a somewhat more complete taxonomy of externalities. I propose to supplement the existing array only in terms of numbers affected by an interaction and by the presence or absence of joint-consumption efficiency or publicness. When this extension is made, we can show that the assignment of property rights may be critical in determining the efficiency of alternative institutional arrangements in some cases while not at all relevant in others.

I shall illustrate the analysis exclusively in terms of the example that was introduced by Coase and which has been much discussed since his paper was published. This involves the cattle raiser(s) or rancher(s) on the one hand and the owner(s) of growing crops [farmer(s)] on the other. The cattle are liable to stray, and in so doing they trample the wheat, hence destroying a part of the crop. There is no direct interaction between the separate cattle who might stray; the presence of one steer on the cropland does not affect the costs or benefits from other straying animals. The cattle that stray are as likely to trample one part of the total wheat crop as any other, regardless of particular location.

In this familiar setting, we can examine the possibilities for attaining allocative efficiency under alternative institutional arrangements. We allow the numbers on each side of the potential externality to vary along with the property-right arrangements. We can exhaust the range of possibilities in a four-by-two matrix illustration. The alternative ownership arrangements in terms of numbers are arrayed along the rows of Figure 1, while the two possible property-right arrangements are arrayed in the columns.

The approach taken by most economists has been to lump Cells I and II together in the small-number set (for which the Coase theorem is widely acknowledged to be correct within its restricted assumptions *and* to possess genuine predictive power) and all other Cells (III through VIII) into the large-number set, where transactions costs are alleged to prevent the attain-

	Cattle Raisers Have Legal Rights to Allow Animals to Stray	Cattle Raisers Have NO Rights in Croplands
One cattle raiser, one farmer	I. Bilateral bargaining toward efficient allocation.	II. Bilateral bargaining toward efficient allocation.
One cattle raiser, many farmers	III. Inefficient results due to "publicness" interaction among farmers.	IV. Inefficient results due to hold-out power of each farmer.
Many cattle raisers, one farmer	V. Efficient results with minor bargaining costs under competition. Possible inefficiencies under monopsony.	VI. Efficient results with minor bargaining costs under competition. Possible inefficiencies under monopoly.
Many cattle raisers, many farmers	VII. Inefficient results due to "publicness" interaction among farmers.	VIII. Inefficient results due to hold-out power of each farmer.

Figure 1

ment of efficiency through contractual arrangements. Several things become apparent from the matrix presentation. Note that efficiency may be attained by voluntary agreements in the settings described by Cells V and VI, despite the fact that there are many persons involved in the total externality relationship. Note, further, that the location of liability *does* influence the prospects for attaining efficiency in some situations. As we shall demonstrate, in all large-number interactions, the location of liability affects the ease with which bargaining among participants may move toward efficient final results.

The separate cells may be examined in turn. There is little need to treat the analysis of Cells I and II in detail, since these have been exhaustively covered in relationship to the Coase theorem. As the figure indicates, efficiency in allocation will tend to be produced if we disregard the possible difficulties that are inherent in bilateral bargaining negotiations. If we include bargaining costs as a part of transactions costs, we can then accept the version of the theorem that states the invariance of solution under the separate assignments of rights along with the efficient characteristics of this solution.

The situation depicted in Cell III is that which is often assumed to be descriptively relevant for many environmental quality issues such as air and water pollution. Attention here tends to be concentrated on the "antisocial" behavior of a person or firm which exerts external costs (diseconomies) on many other persons or firms. The classic illustration is, of course, the factory whose smoke fouls the laundries of the neighborhood housewives. As we have noted above, there are two externality relationships present in this setting. In the context of our cattle-raiser–farmer example, the straying cattle impose external diseconomies on each farmer. But, as among the several farmers, there is a joint-consumption external economy, at least in a potential sense. If a single farmer succeeds in negotiating with the rancher for a reduction in the number of straying cattle, *all* farmers secure equal benefits. The familiar "free-rider" dilemma emerges among the many farmers. The single farmer, acting privately and independently, may not be motivated to purchase the total reduction in cattle straying that is sufficient to satisfy efficiency norms. All farmers might be better off, along with the rancher, under some collective-cooperative agreement which would allow the farmers, as a group, to negotiate bilaterally with the rancher. Once such an organizational step is taken, the institutional setting becomes analogous to that depicted in Cells I and II. And if the straying cattle do, in fact, generate Pareto-relevant external diseconomies, some reduction in their numbers can be predicted to emerge from the bilateral bargaining that would ensue. A priori it is impossible to determine whether or not an initially apparent external diseconomy is or is not Pareto-relevant. In the absence of some collective bargaining unit which represents the farmers, we can say that the observed results will tend to be either (1) fully efficient, or (2) inefficient in the direction of too many straying cattle and too little wheat. This setting makes clear that the barrier to the achievement of efficiency through voluntary contractual arrangements lies in the publicness or joint-consumption interaction among the many farmers who are affected by the diseconomy.

Under the producer-consumer numbers of Row 2, a shift in the assignment of property rights *can* significantly alter the path toward tolerably efficient outcomes, provided that the initial situation is inefficient. Look now at the situation depicted in Cell IV, where there are many farmers and the single rancher, as before, but where the rancher no longer has a property right to allow his animals to stray over the croplands. Full ownership rights in the latter are now held by the farmers, separately and independently, and the rancher must purchase the permission of *all* farmers before allowing his cattle to roam. In this case, the publicness or joint-consumption interaction among the several farmers may generate allocative results that are just the opposite to those attained under Cell III. Since, by our assumptions, the rancher cannot specify in advance just whose crops will be damaged, and since the parcels of cropland are not separately fenced even though they are separately owned, he must secure the agreement of *all* members of the group before he can turn loose his cattle. This requirement places each and every farmer in a unique bargaining position that allows him to block or to veto any prospective agreement with the rancher, even one which has been accepted by all of his fellow farmers. The situation here is fully equivalent to operation of a unanimity rule for collective decision-making. This rule fails because it allows each person to be put in the strategic position of bargaining against all other persons in the group. Since it can be predicted that, in a many-person group, there will be at least one person who will exploit this strategic position, the producer of the external effect, in our example, the rancher, will not normally be able to secure the agreement that efficient results might require, almost regardless of the relative values that are placed on the alternatives. Even should the value which the rancher places on cattle straying substantially exceed the cost imposed on all farmers as a combined group, the agreement required for attaining efficient results may prove impossible to reach. In this setting, by contrast to that depicted in Cell III, therefore, we can say that the observed results in the absence of agreement will tend either to be (1) fully efficient, or (2) inefficient in the direction of too few straying cattle on the croplands.

This possible tendency toward an underproduction of the externality-generating good or service is the central flaw in the proposals to resolve environmental quality problems by the creation and assignment of new "amenity rights" to citizens. This term, along with the proposals, may be associated with the work of E. J. Mishan.[3] If, for example, each householder should be as-

---

3. See, for example, E. J. Mishan, *The Costs of Economic Growth* (New York: Praeger, 1967).

signed a property right to "pure air" and "noise-free sound wave," defined in such a way as to require his agreement before any "pollution" occurs, we should predict with a high degree of certainty that an inefficiently low level of polluting activity would take place.

The submodel depicted in Cell IV calls attention to the necessity of distinguishing carefully between the clear assignment of property rights to do things, to carry out specific acts, and the assignment of liability for damages once they are done. A right of a farmer to prevent cattle from invading his croplands can be voluntarily relinquished only through some explicit agreement with the rancher, the circumstances we have discussed above. This right of the farmer may be *violated* without his prior permission having been secured, and the rancher made liable for the damages done. This is an inherently different setting, however, because third-party adjudication of damage claims must be introduced. The modification of property rights to allow violation of rights with damages subsequently assessed would convert the setting into one analogous to the exercise of eminent domain by governmental units. The strategic bargaining or hold-out position of the individual farmer in our example would be eliminated by this procedure, but only at the expense of substantially extending the necessarily arbitrary power of third parties in an adjudication role. In this respect, there is a Cell III analogue to the liability-for-damage interpretation of Cell IV. If third-party adjudication is introduced, efficiency might be secured under the arrangements of Cell III by allowing some external agent to assign to farmers individual shares in the costs of securing the agreements required from the rancher.

MANY PRODUCERS, ONE CONSUMER

The settings described in Row 3, Cells V and VI, have not been widely discussed, but the understanding of these models may be important for certain directions of policy reforms. In our example, there are now many producers or generators of the external diseconomy, many cattle raisers, but there is only one consumer, one decision-maker who is subjected to the external costs. Also, because of the carefully specified assumptions in our illustration, there is no joint-consumption or joint-consumption efficiency in the interaction among the separate ranchers.

Consider, first, the setting depicted in Cell V, where the cattle raisers have an initial legal right to allow their animals to roam over the cropland, which is under single ownership. Since there is no "publicness" present, that is, since the external costs are exclusively concentrated on the single decision-maker, this farmer can negotiate separate agreements with cattle raisers if indeed such agreements are profitable to him. He can trade separately with each rancher, and aside from bargaining difficulties, we might predict that efficient outcomes would be forthcoming. If both the cattle industry and the farming industry are broadly competitive, in the sense that the prices of final products are established in a market larger than the interaction under consideration here, the position of the farmer as the single buyer, as a monopsonist, need not affect the generalized prediction that an efficient result will be produced voluntarily. He could not, in this situation, squeeze a monopsony rent by paying less to a rancher than the latter could earn in an alternative location for cattle raising.

In a more general model, the effects of the single purchaser's monopsony position should be taken into account. If the prices of reducing the external diseconomy increase as more units are purchased by the monopsonist, and if he cannot discriminate among separate sellers in price, he will tend to purchase a reduction in external diseconomies lower than overall efficiency considerations warrant. We can conclude that the contractual bargaining result which would emerge will either (1) be reasonably efficient, or (2) be inefficient in the direction of a remaining excessive generation of external diseconomies. If no bargaining is observed to take place, we can, of course, conclude that the initial situation is efficient.

The situation depicted in Cell VI involves a reversal of property rights. Here the single farmer holds full title to the croplands, and the ranchers have no rights to allow their animals to roam. If no bargaining is observed to take place, we can again conclude that the initial position is roughly efficient. If, however, bargaining is observed, we should examine the implications of this effort for allocative outcomes. The results are the obverse of those traced out for Cell V. If competition prevails in both industries, the single-seller or monopolistic position of the farmer cannot affect the price at which he may sell straying rights to ranchers. However, in the more general case, this monopoly position might allow him to exploit the several buyers. If he cannot discriminate among these buyers in price, but if he can exploit his monopoly power, we should expect that he would sell fewer straying rights than that number which strict efficiency conditions would dictate. We can conclude that the observed results of the bargaining process would either (1) be efficient, or (2) involve the production of a less than optimal amount of external diseconomies.

In Row 3, as in Row 2, there is a substantive difference in allocative results generated by the shift in property-right arrangements as between the two sides of the interaction. In both rows the direction of effect is the same; the assignment of rights to the acting party or "producer" of the external effect biases the outcomes in favor of an excessive supply of the diseconomy, whereas the reversal of this assignment biases the results toward an under-supply of the diseconomy. In this row, however, the inefficiencies stem from the potential monopsony and monopoly position of the single consumer in the two cases. In Row 2, by contrast, the inefficiencies that might arise are due to the publicness interaction among the separate consumers. This major difference can be turned to advantage in the institutional reforms that might be suggested.

Many producers, many consumers

Before discussing specific reform proposals, we should consider the institutional settings depicted in the two cells of Row 4 of Figure 1. In our familiar example, there are now many ranchers and many farmers. In Cell VII the ranchers initially hold property rights which allow their cattle access to the surrounding croplands owned by many farmers; in Cell VIII the farmers hold the rights of exclusion. The results are predictable from our analysis of the simpler cases. The complex interactions may be factored down into a set of Cell III and Cell IV models, in each of which many separate farmers confront a single rancher or producer of the external diseconomy. This factoring down is possible because of our initial assumption that there is no direct interdependence among the ranchers themselves. The straying of one rancher's cattle neither raises nor lowers the costs to other ranchers. With this restriction, the predictions made for Cell III and Cell IV settings become directly applicable in Cells VII and VIII. When the ranchers hold property rights in the range, inefficient results may be generated that take on equilibrium characteristics due to the publicness interaction among the separate consumers of the externality, the farmers in this example. This publicness is incorporated with respect to the straying of each rancher's cattle onto the croplands. For a single farmer, therefore, there is little or no incentive to enter negotiations with a single rancher for the purpose of reducing the damage to crops. Nor will a single farmer be able to accomplish much by entering into a bargaining coalition with only one or a few of his fellow farmers. A bargaining coalition of a size sufficiently large to insure gains to potential members (and nonmembers) may not be formed. Insofar as inefficiency persists, therefore, it will take the direction of relatively too much damage to the crops. There is likely to be too much of the external diseconomy.

When the property rights are reversed, the potential allocative error changes direction, as in the Cell IV comparison with Cell III. When the individual farmers are authorized to exclude cattle from the unfenced croplands which include their own holdings, no single rancher will be able to purchase all of the permissions that would be necessary to allow his cattle to roam freely, almost regardless of the relative benefits and costs to the parties involved. The reason is that each farmer is here placed in a position which allows him to block or to veto an agreement with any rancher. Hence, insofar as allocative inefficiency exists in this setting, the direction is surely that of preserving the croplands relatively free of straying cattle. There is likely to be too little of the external diseconomy.

III. Institutional Elements in Reform

The matrix presentation of Figure 1, along with subsequent discussion, allows generalized predictions to be made concerning the effects of institutional structure on allocative outcomes. To the extent that this structure itself is subject to collective modification and control, the analysis should suggest ways toward reform. In this respect, attention must be centered on the situations described in Cells III, IV, VII, and VIII. If the institutional setting depicted in these cells can be shifted so as to approximate the setting of Cell V or VI, the necessity for detailed correction of allocative inefficiencies may be eliminated. Such a shift will, in all cases, involve the internalization or elimination of the publicness aspect of the interaction. In our example, there must be some shift from a "many-farmers" to a "one-farmer" model. The number of ranchers or producers of the external diseconomy is irrelevant to the problem.

This indicates that some sort of collectivity or coalition should be formed among the many separate consumers of the external diseconomy, so long as the effects are nonexcludable among them. Once this step is taken, a single agent can act for the coalition, for the group, and as this single agent confronts the one or the many separate producers, tolerably efficient outcomes may be expected to emerge from the bilateral bargaining process.

This conclusion is simple enough, and it has, of course, long been recognized. It has not often been incorporated directly in specific proposals for reform. For the most part, reform proposals embody some collectively enforced modifications in the conditions of choice confronting the individual producers of the external effect. Corrective devices involve the levy of taxes directly on the participants, with the levels of these taxes being determined from some measure of the extent of spillover damage exerted. By comparison with this, the institutional reform suggested here eschews any attempt to determine optimal solution values, a step which is essential if the corrective taxes are to be efficiently levied. The institutional changes require only that a single bargaining agent be authorized to act on behalf of the consumers with no directions as to the specific outcomes which may be forthcoming in his negotiations with the separate producers.

Several advantages stem from this institutional approach. In the first place, attention is focused on the limits to the size of the effective coalition represented by the bargaining agent. The size of the coalition is determined by the limit of the publicness interaction. Nothing but inefficiency can result from the appointment of an agent which acts for a coalition of consumers that are not related through a genuine publicness interaction. In our example, if each farmer fences his croplands, and hence can privately exclude cattle, there is no problem of an agent to act for all farmers. We are in a Coase setting from the outset, and no coalition need be formed at all.

This elementary point has important implications for many of the problems of pollution control. There is, for example, surely no argument for *federally* imposed general standards of water purity. The consumers of the external diseconomy of water pollution are partners in a publicness interaction that is limited to the separate watersheds. It is for these separate groups of consumers that separate bargaining agents might be appointed.

The approach also draws attention to a second important, if also elementary, principle. The bargaining agent for the consumers of the external effect should be divorced from any and all pretense that its objective is to act in the "public interest." The interests of those who are externally affected by the diseconomy are not the interests of the whole public. This remains true even if all members of the community, as consumers or affected parties, should be included in the coalition. The essentially opposing interests of those who exert or impose the external diseconomy cannot be properly represented in the coalition.

Once empowered to act for those persons who bear the external diseconomy, the agent may bargain for either *more* or *less* of the externality-generating activity. A common fallacy is that of assuming that the genuine interests of consuming parties is always that of reducing the level of spillover damage that they suffer. This direction of change is, of course, desirable if there are no offsetting compensations. But if the value of extending the external diseconomy to the producer exceeds the damage value to the combined group of consumers, the latter's interests lie in agreeing to such an extension rather than preventing it. The power of the collective agency representing or acting for the group of consumers in either direction depends, of course, on some initial definition of property rights. If a Cell III setting is descriptive, the direction of change will tend to be that which involves the purchase of agreements to limit the degree of spillover damage. By comparison, in a Cell IV situation, the direction of reform may be the opposite.

In a generalized institutional reform, how should property rights be defined? It may be plausibly argued that the status quo provides a basis for explicit definition in those areas of emerging interaction. Producers and consumers might be granted rights to carry out activities in the same form and to the same limits as observed on a specific and unannounced date in some current period. This definition of rights along with the agency representing the sharers of the publicness interaction, acts to create an institutional structure from which changes would tend to be directionally efficient. If initial levels of the activity should be inefficiently high, the collectivity which acts for consumers could purchase agreements for reductions. For all increases, by contrast, the producers would be required to compensate the agency appropriately. In all cases, the final results will depend on the process of bilateral bargaining between the agency and the producer of the diseconomy.

The institutional changes discussed here do not, however, resolve the more difficult issues concerning individualized shares in the potential costs and benefits that might emerge from agreements reached between the consumers' agent and the producers of the external effect. How can the agent, acting on behalf of its members, properly assess aggregate costs and/or benefits from a particular agreement until and unless it is provided with some means of imputing shares to its members? Ideally, the evaluations of members must be used as the basis for such measurements. Some attempt might be made, at a practical level, to estimate these evaluations for adding-up purposes, but there remains the problem of *financing* and *disposition*. If the agent is to secure an agreement to limit the extent of spillover damage, financial outlays must be made. To secure funds, the agency would require taxing powers, and this will necessarily allow some determination of tax shares. Essentially the same problem arises when the agency's decision is to sell rights for extensions in the externality-generating activity. Funds will be collected, and these funds will have to be distributed to members of the consumer coalition in some fashion.

A SCHEME FOR TAX AND DIVIDEND SHARES

How could the agency secure accurate evaluation data from those persons whose interests it is supposed to represent, data which might be used both for the purposes of entering into exchange agreements with the producers of the diseconomies and for the imposition of tax shares on the one hand and for the disposition of dividends on the other? The problem of voluntary revelation of individual evaluations seems to be the familiar one that arises in all public-goods interactions, the "free-rider" dilemma. Individuals will find it advantageous to conceal their true preferences if they presume that other members of the group will provide sufficient funds to secure the public good. Consider how this applies to the present example. Individual consumers of the external diseconomy are, presumably, asked to state their evaluations of the "public good" that is represented by some limitation on the external diseconomy. These evaluations are, in turn, to be used as the basis for tax shares to be collected in the process of financing potential agreements with producers. In this unidirectional setting, the single person will have an incentive to understate his preferences; he will grossly undervalue the limitation on the diseconomy. As a result, the aggregation of individual evaluations will not reflect the true "social" value of the public good that is in question. Consider, however, the adjustment process in the other direction. Suppose that the agency also asks the separate consumers what values they place on the extension of the diseconomy, values which will be used both to measure the extent of the costs that a potential producer must cover in any agreement, and the disposition of the dividends of funds collected. In this case, the free-rider dilemma works in the opposing direction. Individuals will now have a strong incentive to overstate their true evaluations. In so doing they hope to secure a relatively large share of the dividends that potential producers might provide. The results are likely to be inefficient in that no exchanges will be made due to the aggregate overevaluations of the costs of extending the diseconomy.

The solution to the problem is suggested in the juxtaposition of the two effects discussed. If individuals are asked to reveal their evaluations of changes in the level of the diseconomy, with this evaluation required to hold for changes in both directions, the free-rider dilemma works in off-setting ways. For possible limitations on the activity, for which they will be subjected to tax, individuals will have a strong incentive to understate their true preferences. For extensions in the activity on the other hand, from which they will receive dividends, individuals will have a strong incentive to overstate their true evaluations. If they are now required to reveal their evaluations for determinable discrete changes in the level of the activity that generates the external effect with the direction of change to be determined by the negotiations between the agent and the producers, we should expect some rough approximation of an efficient outcome.[4]

Suppose that all persons should understate their evaluations on changes in the diseconomy, reflecting that the tax-side aspect of the free rider domi-

4. In a seminar presentation of this scheme, Professor Lester Telser of the University of Chicago objected strenuously to the implicit assumption that consumer evaluation schedules are linear over relevant decision ranges. To the extent that significant nonlinearity is characteristic, the valuation placed on increases in activity levels above the status quo may diverge from that placed on decreases in activity levels below this point. In this situation, when forced to state a single valuation on a proposed change in activity level, while remaining uncertain as to direction, the consumer may find himself in a position of lower utility after change, in either direction. This difficulty suggests that should the scheme be implemented, proposals for change should be made in terms of small, discrete steps rather than large ones.

nates the potential dividends side. In this case, the agency will be required to confront potential purchasers of rights to extend the activity with a relatively low aggregate evaluation. There would, in this case, be a strong prospect for an extension of the diseconomy. Individuals would find that their free-rider strategy has backfired on them; they would be subjected to further spillover damages for which they would secure inadequate compensation. On the other hand, suppose that all persons should overstate their evaluation on the dis-economy, reflecting that the potential-dividend side of the problem dominates the tax-payments side in their behavior. In this case, the agency will confront potential purchasers-sellers of changes in activity levels with a relatively high aggregate evaluation. These producers will find it advantageous to sell rights that they hold, hence reducing the level of the diseconomy. Individuals will find that the spillover damage exerted by the diseconomy is reduced; but they will be subjected to accompanying tax shares that exceed their own true eval-uations of the gains which are secured. In either of these two cases, the attempt on the part of individuals to behave strategically will be counterproductive. To the extent that this is recognized, persons will find it advantageous to submit evaluations which are based on their own best estimates of the true value of the diseconomy over the discrete changes that are defined as prospects.[5]

IV. Conclusions

The detailed operation of the institutional agent cannot be discussed in this paper. The set of institutional reforms sketched out will serve to insure that

---

5. Although independently developed, the scheme presented here is related variously to several other arrangements which have been invented, and elaborated in considerably more detail, to accomplish the same objective. Among those that have been brought to my attention are Edward H. Clarke, "Multipart Pricing of Public Goods," *Public Choice,* 11 (Fall 1971), 17–34; T. Nicolaus Tideman, "The Efficient Provision of Public Goods" (un-published manuscript, 1970); E. Malinvaud, "A Planning Approach to the Public Good Problem," *Swedish Journal of Economics,* 73 (March 1971), 93–112; Peter Bohm, "An Ap-proach to the Problem of Estimating Demands for Public Goods," *Swedish Journal of Eco-nomics,* 73 (March 1971), 55–66.

I should emphasize that my purpose here is not to advance a particular scheme or arrangement, and I am not interested in examining the operating characteristics in detail. My purpose is, instead, that of isolating the *institutional* setting that seems to be suggested for any approach to efficient outcomes.

some proximate solutions to the serious problems of environmental quality are attained. Major constitutional problems have been neglected. By what criteria is society to judge whether or not the environment as observed is sufficiently nonoptimal as to require the sometimes dramatic institutional reformation which the reform proposals may embody? When is a watershed or river basin so polluted as to require the establishment of an agent for all users of the river along with a precise delineation of pollution rights? Such steps are costly in themselves, and attempts at reforms could be justified only beyond some limits of inefficiency. These broader and more basic constitutional issues are too seldom mentioned in the familiar discussions of environmental quality.

This paper has been explicitly limited. The institutional structure of potential externality relationships was first examined. The analysis revealed that the presence of a "publicness" interaction among "consumers" or bearers of a potential external diseconomy is critical for the predicted failure of voluntary contractual arrangements. Once this point is accepted, the way is opened for the institutional reforms that are required. These involve the replacement of the many-person reactions on the consumer side by some agent or collectivity that is empowered to act on behalf of all consumers. This institutional agent is then placed in a position to negotiate directly with those individuals or firms who might find it privately profitable to generate the external effect. The agent may, on behalf of its constituent members, agree to sell or to purchase rights to carry on the activity, with the delineation of initial levels of activity being determined in accordance with some selected status quo position. Agency determination of the evaluation of its members on the public good–public bad involved in such limitations or extensions can be made on the basis of a specific scheme which exploits the two-sided prospects for directional change.

PART THREE

Clubs and Joint Supply

An Economic Theory of Clubs[1]

The implied institutional setting for neo-classical economic theory, including theoretical welfare economics, is a régime of private property, in which all goods and services are privately (individually) utilized or consumed. Only within the last two decades have serious attempts been made to extend the formal theoretical structure to include communal or collective ownership-consumption arrangements.[2] The "pure theory of public goods" remains in its infancy, and the few models that have been most rigourously developed apply only to polar or extreme cases. For example, in the fundamental papers by Paul A. Samuelson, a sharp conceptual distinction is made between those goods and services that are "purely private" and those that are "purely public."[3] No general theory has been developed which covers the whole spectrum of ownership-consumption possibilities, ranging from the purely private or individualized activity on the one hand to purely public or collectivized activity on the other. One of the missing links here is "a theory of clubs," a

From *Economica* 32 (February 1965): 1–14. Copyright 1965 by London School of Economics and Political Science. Reprinted by permission of Blackwell Publishers Ltd.

1. I am indebted to graduate students and colleagues for many helpful suggestions. Specific acknowledgement should be made for the critical assistance of Emilio Giardina of the University of Catania and W. Craig Stubblebine of the University of Delaware.

2. It is interesting that none of the theories of Socialist economic organization seem to be based on explicit co-operation among individuals. These theories have conceived the economy either in the Lange-Lerner sense as an analogue to a purely private, individually oriented social order or, alternatively, as one that is centrally directed.

3. See Paul A. Samuelson, "The Pure Theory of Public Expenditure," *Review of Economics and Statistics,* vol. 36 (1954), 387–89; "Diagrammatic Exposition of a Theory of Public Expenditure," *Review of Economics and Statistics,* vol. 37 (1955), 350–55.

theory of co-operative membership, a theory that will include as a variable to be determined the extension of ownership-consumption rights over differing numbers of persons.

Everyday experience reveals that there exists some most preferred or "optimal" membership for almost any activity in which we engage, and that this membership varies in some relation to economic factors. European hotels have more communally shared bathrooms than their American counterparts. Middle- and low-income communities organize swimming-bathing facilities; high-income communities are observed to enjoy privately owned swimming pools.

In this paper I shall develop a general theory of clubs, or consumption ownership-membership arrangements. This construction allows us to move one step forward in closing the awesome Samuelson gap between the purely private and the purely public good. For the former, the optimal sharing arrangement, the preferred club membership, is clearly one person (or one family unit), whereas the optimal sharing group for the purely public good, as defined in the polar sense, includes an infinitely large number of members. That is to say, for any genuinely collective good defined in the Samuelson way, a club that has an infinitely large membership is preferred to all arrangements of finite size. While it is evident that some goods and services may be reasonably classified as purely private, even in the extreme sense, it is clear that few, if any, goods satisfy the conditions of extreme collectiveness. The interesting cases are those goods and services, the consumption of which involves some "publicness," where the optimal sharing group is more than one person or family but smaller than an infinitely large number. The range of "publicness" is finite. The central question in a theory of clubs is that of determining the membership margin, so to speak, the size of the most desirable cost- and consumption-sharing arrangement.[4]

---

4. Note that an economic theory of clubs can strictly apply only to the extent that the motivation for joining in sharing arrangements is itself economic; that is, only if choices are made on the basis of costs and benefits of particular goods and services as these are confronted by the individual. Insofar as individuals join clubs for camaraderie, as such, the theory does not apply.

I

In traditional neo-classical models that assume the existence of purely private goods and services only, the utility function of an individual is written,

$$U^i = U^i (X_1^i, X_2^i, \ldots, X_n^i), \tag{1}$$

where each of the X's represents the amount of a purely private good available during a specified time period to the reference individual designated by the superscript.

Samuelson extended this function to include purely collective or public goods, which he denoted by the subscripts, $n + 1, \ldots, n + m$, so that (1) is changed to read,

$$U_i = U^i(X_1^i, X_2^i, \ldots, X_n^i; X_{n+1}^i, X_{n+2}^i, \ldots, X_{n+m}^i). \tag{2}$$

This approach requires that all goods be initially classified into the two sets, private and public. Private goods, defined to be wholly divisible among the persons $i = 1, 2, \ldots, s$, satisfy the relation

$$X_j = \sum_{i=1}^{s} X_j^i,$$

while public goods, defined to be wholly indivisible as among persons, satisfy the relation,

$$X_{n+j} = X_{n+j}^i.$$

I propose to drop any attempt at an initial classification or differentiation of goods into fully divisible and fully indivisible sets, and to incorporate in the utility function goods falling between these two extremes. What the theory of clubs provides is, in one sense, a "theory of classification," but this emerges as an output of the analysis. The first step is that of modifying the utility function.

Note that in neither (1) nor (2) is it necessary to make a distinction between "goods available to the ownership unit of which the reference individual is a member" and "goods finally available to the individual for consumption." With purely private goods, consumption by one individual automatically reduces potential consumption of other individuals by an equal amount. With purely public goods, consumption by any one individual implies equal consumption by all others. For goods falling between such extremes, such a distinction must be made. This is because for such goods there is no unique translation possible between the "goods available to the membership unit" and "goods finally consumed." In the construction which follows, therefore, the "goods" entering the individual's utility function, the X_j's, should be interpreted as "goods available for consumption to the whole membership unit of which the reference individual is a member."

Arguments that represent the size of the sharing group must be included in the utility function along with arguments representing goods and services. For any good or service, regardless of its ultimate place along the conceptual public-private spectrum, the utility that an individual receives from its consumption depends upon *the number of other persons with whom he must share its benefits.* This is obvious, but its acceptance does require breaking out of the private property straitjacket within which most of economic theory has developed. As an extreme example, take a good normally considered to be purely private, say, a pair of shoes. Clearly your own utility from a single pair of shoes, per unit of time, depends on the number of other persons who share them with you. Simultaneous physical sharing may not, of course, be possible; only one person can wear the shoes at each particular moment. However, for any finite period of time, sharing is possible, even for such evidently private goods. For pure services that are consumed in the moment of acquisition the extension is somewhat more difficult, but it can be made none the less. Sharing here simply means that the individual receives a smaller quantity of the service. Sharing a "haircut per month" with a second person is the same as consuming "one-half haircut per month." Given any quantity of final good, as defined in terms of the physical units of some standard quality, the utility that the individual receives from this quantity will be related functionally to the number of others with whom he shares.[5]

Variables for club size are not normally included in the utility function of an individual since, in the private-goods world, the optimal club size is unity.

---

5. Physical attributes of a good or service may, of course, affect the structure of the sharing arrangements that are preferred. Although the analysis below assumes symmetrical sharing, this assumption is not necessary, and the analysis in its general form can be extended to cover all possible schemes.

However, for our purposes, these variables must be explicitly included, and, for completeness, a club-size variable should be included for each and every good. Alongside each X_j there must be placed an N_j, which we define as the number of persons who are to participate as "members" in the sharing of good X_j, including the ith person whose utility function is examined. That is to say, the club-size variable, N_j, measures the number of persons who are to join in the consumption-utilization arrangements for good X_j over the relevant time period. The sharing arrangements may or may not call for equal consumption on the part of each member, and the peculiar manner of sharing will clearly affect the way in which the variable enters the utility function. For simplicity we may assume equal sharing, although this is not necessary for the analysis. The rewritten utility function now becomes,

$$U^i = U^i[(X_1^i, N_1^i), (X_2^i, N_2^i), \ldots, (X_{n+m}^i, N_{n+m}^i)].^6 \tag{3}$$

We may designate a numeraire good X_r, which can simply be thought of as money, possessing value only as a medium of exchange. By employing the convention whereby the lowercase u's represent the partial derivatives, we get u_j^i/u_r^i, defined as the marginal rate of substitution in consumption between X_j and X_r for the ith individual. Since, in our construction, the size of the group is also a variable, we must also examine, u_{Nj}^i/u_r^i, defined as the marginal rate of substitution "in consumption" between the size of the sharing group and the numeraire. That is to say, this ratio represents the rate (which may be negative) at which the individual is willing to give up (accept) money in exchange for additional members in the sharing group.

We now define a cost or production function as this confronts the individual, and this will include the same set of variables,

$$F = F^i[(X_1^i, N_1^i), (X_2^i, N_2^i), \ldots, (X_{n+m}^i, N_{n+m}^i)]. \tag{4}$$

---

6. Note that this construction of the individual's utility function differs from that introduced in an earlier paper, where "activities" rather than "goods" were included as the basic arguments. (See James M. Buchanan and Wm. Craig Stubblebine, "Externality," *Economica*, vol. 31 [1962], 371–84.) In the alternative construction, the "activities" of other persons enter directly into the utility function of the reference individual with respect to the consumption of all other than purely private goods. The construction here incorporates the same interdependence through the inclusion of the N_j's although in a more general manner.

Why do the club-size variables, the N_j's, appear in this cost function? The addition of members to a sharing group may, and normally will, affect the cost of the good to any one member. The larger the membership of the golf club, the lower the dues to any single member, given a specific quantity of club facilities available per unit time.

It now becomes possible to derive, from the utility and cost functions, statements for the necessary marginal conditions for Pareto optimality in respect to consumption of each good. In the usual manner we get,

$$u_j^i/u_r^i = f_j^i/f_r^i. \tag{5}$$

Condition (5) states that for the ith individual the marginal rate of substitution between goods X_j and X_r, in consumption, must be equal to the marginal rate of substitution between these same two goods in "production" or exchange. To this acknowledged necessary condition, we now add,

$$u_{Nj}^i/u_r^i = f_{Nj}^i/f_r^i. \tag{6}$$

Condition (6) is not normally stated, since the variables relating to club size are not normally included in utility functions. Implicitly, the size for sharing arrangements is assumed to be determined exogenously to individual choices. Club size is presumed to be a part of the environment. Condition (6) states that the marginal rate of substitution "in consumption" between the size of the group sharing in the use of good X_j, and the numeraire good, X_r, must be equal to the marginal rate of substitution "in production." In other words, the individual attains full equilibrium in club size only when the marginal benefits that he secures from having an additional member (which may, and probably will normally, be negative) are just equal to the marginal costs that he incurs from adding a member (which will also normally be negative).

Combining (5) and (6) we get,

$$u_j^i/f_j^i = u_r^i/f_r^i = u_{Nj}^i/f_{Nj}^i. \tag{7}$$

Only when (7) is satisfied will the necessary marginal conditions with respect to the consumption-utilization of X_j be met. The individual will have available to his membership unit an optimal quantity of X_j, measured in physical units, and, also, he will be sharing this quantity "optimally" over a group of determined size.

The necessary condition for club size may not, of course, be met. Since for many goods there is a major change in utility between the one-person and the two-person club, and since discrete changes in membership may be all that is possible, we may get,

$$\frac{u_j^i}{f_j^i} = \frac{u_r^i}{f_r^i} > \left.\frac{u_{Nj}^i}{f_{Nj}^i}\right|_{Nj=1} \; ; \; \frac{u_j^i}{f_j^i} = \frac{u_r^i}{f_r^i} < \left.\frac{u_{Nj}^i}{f_{Nj}^i}\right|_{Nj=2}, \tag{7A}$$

which incorporates the recognition that with a club size of unity the right-hand term may be relatively too small; whereas, with a club size of two, it may be too large. If partial sharing arrangements can be worked out, this qualification need not, of course, be made.

If, on the other hand, the size of a co-operative or collective sharing group is exogenously determined, we may get,

$$\frac{u_j^i}{f_j^i} = \frac{u_r^i}{f_r^i} > \left.\frac{u_{Nj}^i}{f_{Nj}^i}\right|_{Nj=k}. \tag{7B}$$

Note that (7B) actually characterizes the situation of an individual with respect to the consumption of any purely public good of the type defined in the Samuelson polar model. Any group of finite size, k, is smaller than optimal here, and the full set of necessary marginal conditions cannot possibly be met. Since additional persons can, by definition, be added to the group without in any way reducing the availability of the good to other members, and since additional members, could they be found, would presumably place some positive value on the good and hence be willing to share in its costs, the group always remains below optimal size. The all-inclusive club remains too small.

Consider, now, the relation between the set of necessary marginal conditions defined in (7) and those presented by Samuelson in application to goods that were exogenously defined to be purely public. In the latter case, these conditions are,

$$\sum_{i=1}^{s}(u_{n+j}^i / u_r^i) = f_{n+j} / f_r^i, \tag{8}$$

where the marginal rates of substitution in consumption between the purely public good, X_{n+j}, and the numeraire good, X_r, summed over all individuals in the group of determined size, s, equals the marginal cost of X_{n+j} also defined in terms of units of X_r. Note that when (7) is satisfied, (8) is necessarily satisfied, provided only that the collectivity is making neither profit nor loss on providing the marginal unit of the public good. That is to say, provided that,

$$f_{n+j}/f_r = \sum_{i=1}^{s}(f^i_{n+j}/f^i_r).\qquad(9)$$

The reverse does not necessarily hold, however, since the satisfaction of (8) does not require that each and every individual in the group be in a position where his own marginal benefits are equal to his marginal costs (taxes).[7] And, of course, (8) says nothing at all about group size.

The necessary marginal conditions in (7) allow us to classify all goods only after the solution is attained. Whether or not a particular good is purely private, purely public, or somewhere between these extremes is determined only after the equilibrium values for the N_j's are known. A good for which the equilibrium value for N_j is large can be classified as containing much "publicness." By contrast, a good for which the equilibrium value of N_j is small can be classified as largely private.

II

The formal statement of the theory of clubs presented in Section I can be supplemented and clarified by geometrical analysis, although the nature of the construction implies somewhat more restrictive models.

Consider a good that is known to contain, under some conditions, a degree of "publicness." For simplicity, think of a swimming pool. We want to examine the choice calculus of a single person, and we shall assume that other persons about him, with whom he may or may not choose to join in some club-like arrangement, are identical in all respects with him. As a first step, take a facility of one-unit size, which we define in terms of physical output supplied.

On the ordinate of Fig. 1, we measure total cost and total benefit per person, the latter derived from the individual's own evaluation of the facility in terms of the numeraire, dollars. On the abscissa, we measure the number of persons in possible sharing arrangements. Define the full cost of the one-unit facility to be Y_1, and the reference individual's evaluation of this facility

7. In Samuelson's diagrammatic presentation, these individual marginal conditions are satisfied, but the diagrammatic construction is more restricted than that contained in his earlier more general model.

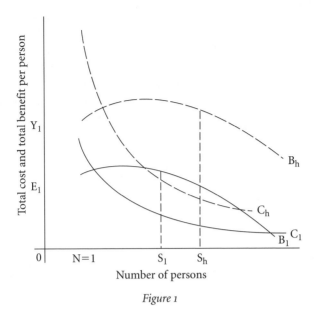

Figure 1

as a purely private consumption good to be E_1. As is clear from the construction as drawn, he will not choose to purchase the good. If the single person is required to meet the full cost, he will not be able to enjoy the benefits of the good. Any enjoyment of the facility requires the organization of some co-operative–collective sharing arrangement.[8]

Two functions may now be traced in Fig. 1, remaining within the one-unit restriction on the size of the facility. A total benefit function and a total cost function confronting the single individual may be derived. As more persons are allowed to share in the enjoyment of the facility of given size, the benefit evaluation that the individual places on the good will, after some point, decline. There may, of course, be both an increasing and a constant range of

8. The sharing arrangement need not be either co-operative or governmental in form. Since profit opportunities exist in all such situations, the emergence of profit-seeking firms can be predicted in those settings where legal structures permit, and where this organizational form possesses relative advantages. (Cf. R. H. Coase, "The Nature of the Firm," *Economica*, vol. 4 (1937), 386–405.) For purposes of this paper, such firms are one form of club organization, with co-operatives and public arrangements representing other forms. Generally speaking, of course, the choice among these forms should be largely determined by efficiency considerations.

the total benefit function, but at some point congestion will set in, and his evaluation of the good will fall. There seems little doubt that the total benefit curve, shown as B_1, will exhibit the concavity property as drawn for goods that involve some commonality in consumption.[9]

The bringing of additional members into the club also serves to reduce the cost that the single person will face. Since, by our initial simplifying assumption, all persons here are identical, symmetrical cost-sharing is suggested. In any case, the total cost per person will fall as additional persons join the group, under any cost-sharing scheme. As drawn in Fig. 1, symmetrical sharing is assumed, and the curve C_1 traces the total cost function, given the one-unit restriction on the size of the facility.[10]

For the given size of the facility, there will exist some optimal size of club. This is determined at the point where the derivatives of the total cost and total benefit functions are equal, shown as S_1 in Fig. 1, for the one-unit facility. Consider now an increase in the size of the facility. As before, a total cost curve and a total benefit curve may be derived, and an optimal club size determined. One other such optimum is shown at S_h, for a quantity of goods upon which the curves C_h and B_h are based. Similar constructions can be carried out for every possible size of facility; that is, for each possible quantity of good.

A similar construction may be used to determine optimal goods quantity for each possible size of club; this is illustrated in Fig. 2. On the ordinate, we measure here total costs and total benefits confronting the individual, as in Fig. 1. On the abscissa, we measure physical size of the facility, quantity of

9. The geometrical model here applies only to such goods. Essentially the same analysis may, however, be extended to apply to cases where "congestion," as such, does not appear. For example, goods that are produced at decreasing costs, even if their consumption is purely private, may be shown to require some sharing arrangements in an equilibrium or optimal organization.

10. For simplicity, we assume that an additional "membership" in the club involves the addition of one separate person. The model applies equally well, however, for those cases where cost shares are allocated proportionately with predicted usage. In this extension, an additional "membership" would really amount to an additional consumption unit. Membership in the swimming club could, for example, be defined as the right to visit the pool one time each week. Hence, the person who plans to make two visits per week would, in this modification, hold two memberships. This qualification is not, of course, relevant under the strict world-of-equals assumption, but it indicates that the theory need not be so restrictive as it might appear.

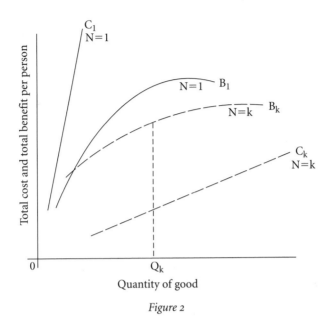

Figure 2

good, and for each assumed size of club membership we may trace total cost and total benefit functions. If we first examine the single-member club, we may well find that the optimal goods quantity is zero; the total cost function may increase more rapidly than the total benefit function from the outset. However, as more persons are added, the total costs to the single person fall; under our symmetrical sharing assumption, they will fall proportionately. The total benefit functions here will slope upward to the right, but after some initial range they will be concave downward and at some point will reach a maximum. As club size is increased, benefit functions will shift generally downward beyond the initial non-congestion range, and the point of maximum benefit will move to the right. The construction of Fig. 2 allows us to derive an optimal goods quantity for each size of club; Q_k is one such quantity for club size $N = k$.

The results derived from Figs. 1 and 2 are combined in Fig. 3. Here the two variables to be chosen, goods quantity and club size, are measured on the ordinate and the abscissa, respectively. The values for optimal club size for each goods quantity, derived from Fig. 1, allow us to plot the curve N_{opt} in Fig. 3. Similarly, the values for optimal goods quantity, for each club size, derived from Fig. 2, allow us to plot the curve Q_{opt}.

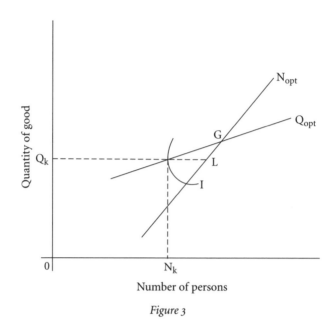

Figure 3

The intersection of these two curves, N_{opt} and Q_{opt}, determines the position of full equilibrium, G. The individual is in equilibrium both with respect to goods quantity and to group size, for the good under consideration. Suppose, for example, that the sharing group is limited to size N_k. The attainment of equilibrium with respect to goods quantity, shown by Q_k, would still leave the individual desirous of shifting the size of the membership so as to attain position L. However, once the group increases to this size, the individual prefers a larger quantity of the good, and so on, until G is attained.

Fig. 3 may be interpreted as a standard preference map depicting the tastes of the individual for the two components, goods quantity and club size for the sharing of that good. The curves N_{opt} and Q_{opt} are lines of optima, and G is the highest attainable level for the individual, the top of his ordinal utility mountain. Since these curves are lines of optima within an individual preference system, successive choices must converge in G.

It should be noted that income-price constraints have already been incorporated in the preference map through the specific sharing assumptions that are made. The tastes of the individual depicted in Fig. 3 reflect the post-payment or net relative evaluations of the two components of consumption at all levels. Unless additional constraints are imposed on the model, he must move to the satiety point in this construction.

It seems clear that under normal conditions both of the curves in Fig. 3 will slope upward to the right, and that they will lie in approximately the relation to each other as therein depicted. This reflects the fact that normally for the type of good considered in this example there will exist a complementary rather than a substitute relationship between increasing the quantity of the good and increasing the size of the sharing group.

This geometrical model can be extended to cover goods falling at any point along the private-public spectrum. Take the purely public good as the first extreme case. Since, by definition, congestion does not occur, each total benefit curve in Fig. 1 becomes horizontal. Thus, optimal club size, regardless of goods quantity, is infinite. Hence, full equilibrium is impossible of attainment; equilibrium only with respect to goods quantity can be reached, defined with respect to the all-inclusive finite group. In the construction of Fig. 3, the N curve cannot be drawn. A more realistic model may be that in which, at goods quantity equilibrium, the limitations on group size impose an inequality. For example, in Fig. 3, suppose that the all-inclusive group is of size N_k. Congestion is indicated as being possible over small sizes of facility, but, if an equilibrium quantity is provided, there is no congestion, and, in fact, there remain economies of scale in club size. The situation at the most favourable attainable position is, therefore, in all respects equivalent to that confronted in the case of the good that is purely public under the more restricted definition.

Consider now the purely private good. The appropriate curves here may be shown in Fig. 4. The individual, with his income-price constraints, is able to attain the peak of his ordinal preference mountain without the necessity of calling upon his fellows to join him in sharing arrangements. Also, the benefits that he receives from the good may be so exclusively his own that these would largely disappear if others were brought in to share them. Hence, the full equilibrium position, G, lies along the vertical from the $N = 1$ member point. Any attempt to expand the club beyond this point will reduce the utility of the individual.[11]

---

11. The construction suggests clearly that the optimal club size, for any quantity of good, will tend to become smaller as the real income of an individual is increased. Goods

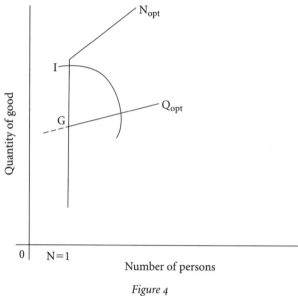

Figure 4

III

The geometrical construction implies that the necessary marginal conditions are satisfied at unique equilibrium values for both goods quantity and club

---

that exhibit some "publicness" at low income levels will, therefore, tend to become "private" as income levels advance. This suggests that the number of activities that are organized optimally under co-operative–collective sharing arrangements will tend to be somewhat larger in low-income communities than in high-income communities, other things equal. There is, of course, ample empirical support for this rather obvious conclusion drawn from the model. For example, in American agricultural communities thirty years ago, heavy equipment was communally shared among many farms, normally on some single owner-lease-rental arrangement. Today, substantially the same equipment will be found on each farm, even though it remains idle for much of its potential working time.

The implication of the analysis for the size of governmental units is perhaps less evident. Insofar as governments are organized to provide communal facilities, the size of such units, measured by the number of citizens, should decline as income increases. Thus, in the affluent society, the local school district may, optimally, be smaller than in the poor society.

size. This involves an oversimplification that is made possible only through the assumptions of specific cost-sharing schemes and identity among individuals. In order to generalize the results, these restrictions must be dropped. We know that given any group of individuals who are able to evaluate both consumption shares and the costs of congestion there exists some set of marginal prices, goods quantity, and club size that will satisfy (7) above. However, the quantity of the good, the size of the club sharing in its consumption, and the cost-sharing arrangements must be determined simultaneously. And, since there are always "gains from trade" to be realized in moving from nonoptimal to optimal positions, distributional considerations must be introduced. Once these are allowed to be present, the final "solution" can be located at any one of a sub-infinity of points on the Pareto welfare surface. Only through some quite arbitrarily chosen conventions can standard geometrical constructions be made to apply.

The approach used above has been to impose at the outset a set of marginal prices (tax-prices, if the good is supplied publicly), translated here into shares or potential shares in the costs of providing separate quantities of a specific good for groups of varying sizes. Hence, the individual confronts a predictable set of marginal prices for each quantity of the good at every possible club size, independent of his own choices on these variables. With this convention, and the world-of-equals assumption, the geometrical solution becomes one that is relevant for any individual in the group. If we drop the world-of-equals assumption, the construction continues to hold without change for the choice calculus of any particular individual in the group. The results cannot, of course, be generalized for the group in this case, since different individuals will evaluate any given result differently. The model remains helpful even here, however, in that it suggests the process through which individual decisions may be made, and it tends to clarify some of the implicit content in the more formal statements of the necessary marginal conditions for optimality.[12]

---

12. A note concerning one implicit assumption of the whole analysis is in order at this point. The possibility for the individual to choose among the various scales of consumption-sharing arrangements has been incorporated into an orthodox model of individual behaviour. The procedure implies that the individual remains indifferent as to

IV

The theory of clubs developed in this paper applies in the strict sense only to the organization of membership or sharing arrangements where "exclusion" is possible. Insofar as non-exclusion is a characteristic of public-goods supply, as Musgrave has suggested,[13] the theory of clubs is of limited relevance. Nevertheless, some implications of the theory for the whole excludability question may be indicated. If the structure of property rights is variable, there would seem to be few goods the services of which are non-excludable, solely due to some physical attributes. Hence, the theory of clubs is, in one sense, a theory of optimal exclusion, as well as one of inclusion. Consider the classic lighthouse case. Variations in property rights, broadly conceived, could prohibit boat operators without "light licenses" from approaching the channel guarded by the light. Physical exclusion is possible, given sufficient flexibility in property law, in almost all imaginable cases, including those in which the interdependence lies in the act of consuming itself. Take the single person who gets an inoculation, providing immunization against a communicable disease. Insofar as this action exerts external benefits on his fellows, the person taking the action could be authorized to collect charges from all beneficiaries under sanction of the collectivity.

This is not, of course, to suggest that property rights will, in practice, always be adjusted to allow for optimal exclusion. If they are not, the "free-rider" problem arises. This prospect suggests one issue of major importance that the analysis of this paper has neglected, the question of costs that may be involved in securing agreements among members of sharing groups. If individuals think that exclusion will not be fully possible, that they can expect to secure benefits as free riders without really becoming full-fledged contributing members of the club, they may be reluctant to enter voluntarily into cost-sharing arrangements. This suggests that one important means of

---

which of his neighbours or fellow citizens join him in such arrangements. In other words, no attempt has been made to allow for personal selectivity or discrimination in the models. To incorporate this element, which is no doubt important in many instances, would introduce a wholly new dimension into the analysis, and additional tools to those employed here would be required.

13. See R. A. Musgrave, *The Theory of Public Finance,* New York, 1959.

reducing the costs of securing voluntary co-operative agreements is that of allowing for more flexible property arrangements and for introducing ex-cluding devices. If the owner of a hunting preserve is allowed to prosecute poachers, then prospective poachers are much more likely to be willing to pay for the hunting permits in advance.

Joint Supply, Externality, and Optimality[1]

The relationship between Marshallian joint supply and external economies has been noted, especially in connection with the theory of public goods, but this relationship has not to my knowledge been explicitly treated in a general setting.[2] In this article, externalities are classified as one sub-category of joint supply. The necessary conditions that must be present for joint supply to be efficient with and without externality can be stated straightforwardly. This joint-supply approach to the externality relationship concentrates attention on the "externality mix," an aspect that seems to have been neglected. This mix is shown to be equivalent to the Marshallian mix among final-product components in orthodox joint-supply situations. In either case, the problem of determining the necessary conditions for optimality in this mix arises when the proportions are not technologically fixed. These conditions, once

From *Economica* 33 (November 1966): 405–15. Copyright 1966 by London School of Economics and Political Science. Reprinted by permission of Blackwell Publishers Ltd.

1. The central points developed in this paper were first presented in seminars at North Carolina State University and York University, England, during the Spring term, 1965, and at Boston College during the Fall term, 1965. I am indebted to J. R. Norsworthy, Charles Plott, W. C. Stubblebine, and Andrew Whinston for helpful comments and suggestions.

2. The extensive discussion by J. G. Head represents a partial exception, despite its limitation to the public-goods framework. Head's conclusion to the effect that jointness and externality are separate and distinct characteristics is, however, different from that reached in this article. See J. G. Head, "Public Goods and Public Policy," *Public Finance/Finances Publiques,* vol. 17 (1962).

For a discussion that concentrates on the joint-supply characteristics of public goods, see Carl S. Shoup, "Public Goods and Joint Production," *Rivista internazionale di scienze economiche e commerciali,* vol. 12 (1965), 254–64.

defined, become required supplements to the more familiar necessary conditions for efficiency in the extension of production.

The relevance of this analysis to the modern theory of public goods is apparent. The joint-supply approach to external economies and diseconomies provides, in a precise sense, an "economic theory of non-exclusion."[3] The definition of the necessary conditions for optimality in the externality mix suggests, in its turn, the conceptual answer to mundane practical questions of the sort: Where should the municipal fire station be located?

In Section I the setting for the analysis will be described, and the notation to be employed will be introduced. Section II sets out the requirements for efficiency in joint supply, the necessary conditions for full trading equilibrium and for Pareto optimality, and the subsidiary marginal conditions for non-discrimination. The analysis here demonstrates that a relaxation of the non-discrimination conditions destroys the uniqueness of the trading solution but that it does not, in any way, modify the remaining properties. In Section III external economies and diseconomies are shown to be special cases of joint supply, and a means of classification is presented. The conditions for determining optimality in the externality mix are analysed in Section IV. The concluding section of the article extends the analysis and relates it to some of the existing literature.

I

Most of orthodox micro-economic theory has been developed in application to exchanges of goods and services that are purely private in consumption and that are produced separately, not jointly. In such exchanges, it is not necessary to distinguish between a unit of good *in production* and a unit of good *in consumption*. Because there is a one-to-one correspondence here, the same generic name can be used in discussing both production and consumption. One additional apple that is produced implies one additional apple available for consumption, by one person privately. It is not confusing to discuss "apples" as being both produced and consumed.

Even within the private-goods restrictions the orthodox convention is strained when conditions of Marshallian joint supply are encountered.

---

3. The non-exclusion characteristic of genuinely public or collective goods has been stressed by R. A. Musgrave. See his *The Theory of Public Finance*, New York, 1959, chapter 1.

Here the unit of production embodies two or more final-product components, these being jointly, not separately, produced or supplied. In the classic Marshallian example, the cattle breeder produces steers, each unit of which embodies both meat and hides. Discussion can be clarified if a distinction between production units and consumption units is made explicit. In this article x's will be employed to refer to production units and y's to consumption units. The y's attached as subscripts to the x's indicate the consumption-component content of the production unit, with quantities appropriately defined. Hence, the notation x_{y_1} indicates that the consumption unit y_1 is embodied in the production of x, which is, of course, identified by the consumption components. This notation is, to an extent, redundant for goods and services that are separately produced, but it will be helpful in analysing joint supply. The latter relationship can now be written as x_{y_a, y_b}, where a unit of production x (a steer) embodies both y_a (meat) and y_b (hides), with the quantities of the latter two being defined on the production unit.

We assume that individual utility and cost functions take the standard forms. The utility function for any individual, i, in the community of persons, $i, j = 1, 2, \ldots, m$, is written as[4]

$$U^i = U^i(y_1^i, y_2^i, \ldots, y_n^i). \tag{1}$$

The transformation possibilities confronting any individual, i, are summarized as[5]

$$F^i = F^i(x_{y_1}, x_{y_2}, \ldots, x_{y_n}; x_{y_t, y_u}; x_{y_t, y_u, y_v}; x_{y_1, y_2, \ldots, y_n}). \tag{2}$$

4. As written here (1) includes as arguments in the individual's utility function only consumption components available to him, actually or potentially. A more general form of this function would include some y^j's, since the individual's utility may be affected by the consumption components available to others than himself. An alternative, and more complex, formulation of the whole analysis could be presented which incorporates a utility function of this more general form.

5. Let S denote a set with n elements $(1, 2, \ldots, n)$. For any z one forms the set of all $\binom{n}{z}$ combinations of z elements in S_n which we note as I_z. The transformation possibilities in (2) are then defined where,

$$(t, u)\varepsilon I_2, \ (t, u, v)\varepsilon I_3, \ \text{and} \ (1, 2, 3, \ldots, n)\varepsilon I_n.$$

This general form allows for the possibility that any and all consumption units may be jointly produced, in any combination, including, at the limit, all consumption units being produced in the same process.

II

If joint rather than separate supply characterizes the relatively efficient organization of exchange, the marginal cost of supplying the two or more consumption components jointly must be less than the marginal cost of supplying these same units separately. If we adopt the notation where the lower-case u's and f's stand for partial derivatives of the utility and transformation functions, and if we postulate that x_{y_r} in production (y_r in consumption) is the numeraire or money commodity, the condition for joint-supply efficiency in the two-component case can be written

$$f_{x_{y_a}, \, y_b} \Big/ f_{x_{y_r}} < f_{x_{y_a}} \Big/ f_{x_{y_r}} + f_{x_{y_b}} \Big/ f_{x_{y_r}}. \tag{3}$$

Note that super-scripts identifying the individuals are not required in (3) since, if these conditions hold for *any* single person, joint supply will tend to emerge.

Following Marshall, we may define the necessary marginal conditions for full trading or exchange equilibrium when all consumption or final-product components are purely private and divisible among users. In the two-component case, these conditions are

$$f_{x_{y_a}, \, y_b} \Big/ f_{x_{y_r}} = P_{y_a} + P_{y_b}, \tag{4}$$

the P's representing the prices for the appropriately defined quantities of final products, y_a and y_b. This states, of course, that so long as $x_{y_a}, \, y_b$, the unit of production, is supplied under competitive organization, the marginal cost must be brought into equality with the summed prices of the consumption components that are embodied in a single production unit.

In the standard Marshallian model an additional and supplementary set of marginal conditions will also be satisfied in full trading equilibrium. Since individuals are free to adjust quantities purchased, and since re-trading among separate demanders is possible, the prices that confront all buyers must be identical. These conditions, which may be called the requirement for non-discrimination, may be written

$$P_{y_a} = u^i_{y_a} \Big/ u^i_{y_r} = u^j_{y_a} \Big/ u^j_{y_r},$$

$$P_{y_b} = u^i_{y_b} \Big/ u^i_{y_r} = u^j_{y_b} \Big/ u^j_{y_r}, \ (i, \, j \, = \, 1, \, 2, \dots, \, m). \tag{5}$$

Note that so long as (5) holds, the ratios of marginal utilities may be substituted for prices in (4), without identifying super-scripts.

I now propose to introduce only one variation on this familiar Marshallian model of joint supply. Instead of goods, consider now jointly supplied services which cannot be re-traded among separate purchasers. These services may be descriptively quite different, analogous to the Marshallian joint products, for example, theatre performances in the theatre itself and at home over closed-circuit television. Or, alternatively, these services may be descriptively similar, even identical, for example, garbage collection for separate households.

For the purpose of introducing at a later point the externality relationship as one category of joint supply, I shall consider here jointly supplied services that are presumably identical in some physical sense. An example will be helpful. The owners of the two sides of a duplex are potential demanders for the services of an exterminating firm to rid their properties of termites. Condition (3) seems likely to hold here: while separately supplied services might be purchased, joint supply is probably much more efficient. If the industry is competitively organized, we should expect that something approximated by (4) will still describe full trading equilibrium. Note, however, that it would now be necessary to redefine the terms in (4) so that the two prices refer to separate *charges* made to the two purchasers of the service. There is nothing in the exchange process that will insure equality in these two charges, despite the fact that, in terms of physical characteristics, the services actually enjoyed by each customer are identical.[6] In one sense, therefore, analogous conditions to those defined by (5) are no longer satisfied. Price discrimination, as this is usually defined, can occur. In yet another sense, however, no genuine discrimination exists here, since the two jointly supplied services remain quite distinct one from the other, regardless of their possible descriptive identity. In any case, a range of indeterminacy is introduced, and there will now be some scope for possible bargaining between the two purchasers over their respective shares in the total cost of the services defined in production units.

The ratios of the marginal utilities, which must now be identified by persons, can be incorporated in an analogue to (4), and the consumption components which are now distinguishable only because they are supplied

6. Some pressures toward equalization will arise through possibilities of indirect exchange. In the example, this might involve the re-sale of properties among separate owners.

to *different* persons can be rewritten as: y^i_k, y^j_k, with the sub-script denoting the descriptive identity (in terms of inputs) of these components. Making these changes, (4) may be transformed into (4A):

$$f_{x_{y^i_k},\ y^j_k} \Big/ f_{x_{y_r}} = u^i_{y^i_k} \Big/ u^i_{y_r} + u^j_{y^j_k} \Big/ u^j_{y_r}. \tag{4A}$$

Despite the restriction of this model to the Marshallian joint supply of purely private and divisible services, (4A) becomes equivalent in all respects to the familiar Samuelson conditions for efficiency in the supply of purely public goods.[7] These conditions can, of course, readily be generalized to include any number of demanders for jointly supplied services.

III

The classification of externalities as a special category of joint supply is a logical extension of the analysis. In the most general terms, an externality is present when an activity on the part of one person (his production or his consumption of some good or service) affects the utility or cost function of a second person.[8] If the affected person is neither compensating nor compensated through trade, and if the effect is exerted at the margin, the externality becomes Pareto-relevant. Its very presence indicates that the necessary marginal conditions for Pareto optimality are not satisfied.

In the terminology introduced in this article, any externality becomes a joint-supply relationship. An individual's act of consuming or producing a good or service is, at the same time, *jointly* supplying at least one other person with a "good" (or a "bad"). If an individual, i, produces a good for his own consumption, measured here in units of y^i_k, and, at the same time, supplies consumption units, measured in y^j_k, to a second person, j, we can discuss i's production of units defined by $x_{y^i_k},\ y^j_k$. The advantage of the approach lies in its concentration on the decision process of the person who exerts the potentially relevant externality.

7. See Paul A. Samuelson, "The Pure Theory of Public Expenditure," *Review of Economics and Statistics*, vol. 36 (1954), 387–89.

8. For a general discussion, see James M. Buchanan and Wm. Craig Stubblebine, "Externality," *Economica*, vol. 29 (1962), 371–84.

The analysis may be clarified by an illustrative example, one which may involve potentially relevant external economies. Suppose that an individual, i, engages in the activity of growing flowers for his own enjoyment, consumption units of which we label y_k^i. These are units measurable in some physically distinct sense such as colour intensity. We may assume that joint supply of his own and his neighbour's consumption is relatively more efficient than separate supply. Condition (3) above is likely to be satisfied, which can now be re-written as

$$f_{x_{y_k^i},\, y_k^j} \Big/ f_{x_r^y} < f_{x_{y_k^i}} \Big/ f_{x_{yr}} + f_{x_{yk}} \Big/ f_{x_r^y}. \tag{3A}$$

We now want to distinguish two sets of relationships within this joint-supply category, those in which there is no relevant externality, and those with such externality. When will an individual behave so as to supply, without compensation, consumption units to a second person (or more) jointly with his own? What are the marginal conditions for Pareto-relevant external economies and diseconomies? Clearly, (3A) alone is not sufficient, since its satisfaction is not inconsistent with

$$f_{x_{y_k^i},\, y_k^j} \Big/ f_{x_{yr}} > f_{x_{y_k^i}} \Big/ f_{x_{yr}}. \tag{6}$$

When (6) holds, no externality will be observed since individual i will not undertake to supply y_k^j, along with y_k^i, until and unless he is appropriately compensated for so doing.[9] An external economy or diseconomy emerges only when the acting individual, i, finds it relatively efficient to supply his own consumption units by producing, at the same time, consumption units for other persons. In our notation, the condition may be written as

$$f_{x_{y_k^i},\, y_k^j} \Big/ f_{x_{yr}} \leq f_{x_{y_k^i}} \Big/ f_{x_{yr}}. \tag{7}$$

Note that all situations which satisfy (7) also satisfy (3A); hence, any exter-

---

9. If some y_k^j's enter directly as arguments in i's utility function, this conclusion will not be valid. In this analysis we have restricted the utility function so as to rule out this possibility. Note, however, that this restriction does not rule out effects on i's utility resulting from the various activities of "others." The restriction merely limits the interdependence to effects on the flows of goods and services to i.

nality may be treated as a case of joint supply. The reverse is not true; joint supply need not imply the presence of externality, as the Marshallian examples demonstrate.

The necessary marginal conditions for Pareto optimality remain those defined in (4A) above; these hold for all cases of joint supply. These conditions will not be met through independent private adjustment when relevant externalities are present, by definition of the latter. In this case, individual i will behave so as to satisfy

$$f_{x_y i, \; y^j_k} \Big/ f_{x_{yr}} = u^i_{y^i_k} \Big/ u^i_{yr}. \tag{8}$$

When (7) and (8) are fulfilled, however, opportunities for mutually advantageous trade exists, and in the small-number example here discussed, individual j may be led to offer compensation to individual i in exchange for the latter's agreement to extend production (or to contract production in the case of external diseconomies). Trade will tend to take place until the conditions defined by (4A) are met so long as the interacting group remains small, and so long as bargaining difficulties do not delay the attainment of equilibrium. If the externality affects some critically large number of persons, the "free-rider" problem arises to prevent voluntarily organized shifts toward the optimality frontier. In limiting cases, full trading equilibrium in the ordinary sense will remain non-optimal, although pressures for rules changes through the mechanism of "political trade" will remain.

IV

To this point the analysis summarizes recent developments in the theory of externality in slightly modified terminology. The joint-supply approach leads to a further step in the theory that does not seem to have been developed explicitly. This concerns the "externality mix," and the determination of the necessary marginal conditions for optimality in this mix. Previous analysis, both in the theory of externality proper and in the theory of public goods, has been based on the assumption that the activity that generates an external economy or diseconomy embodies a mix among separate components that is "technologically" fixed. Trade, actual or potential, has been assumed to involve compensations only for extensions or contractions in a single dimension.[10]

In terms of our flower-growing illustration, the size of the flower garden has been the variable under consideration, not its location with respect to the two persons sharing its potential benefits. In the theory of public goods, the gross quantity of fire protection has been the adjustable variable, not the location of the fire station with respect to the citizens to be protected.

Once the question is raised, however, it becomes clear that any assumption of "technological fixity" is unduly restrictive. A fully general statement must include reference to the mix among components in the production unit of joint supply. The analogy with the Marshallian analysis is direct; the determination of the equilibrium or optimal mix here is identical with the determination of the equilibrium or optimal mix between meat and hides when fixity of proportions is dropped.

At this point, the analysis can best be discussed by geometrical illustration. In Figure 1, the consumption component enjoyed by individual i, the individual who is presumed to be the one who acts, is measured along the abscissa. In the flower-growing example, these are units of "final consumption" physically available to i, which may be objectively computed in terms of colour or scent intensities. If the externality conditions hold, i's activity in growing flowers will involve the provision of final consumption units to j. These are measured along the ordinate. So long as joint supply is relatively efficient, the optimal position will lie in the north-east quadrant, regardless of the presence of externality. However, if no externality is involved, independent adjustment behaviour on the part of i, before trade with j, will always lead to some position along the horizontal axis in Figure 1. He will not supply spillover benefits (or impose spillover harm) to j unless the conditions summarized in (7) are met. When these conditions are fulfilled, inde-

---

10. The discussions of Coase, Turvey and Plott provide partial exceptions. Coase and Turvey discuss the possibility of adjustments being made in alternative ways, but they do not develop the analysis rigourously. Plott concentrates on the necessity of making input-output distinctions explicit. In each case, however, the objective or criterion for compensated adjustment remains extension or contraction in the uni-dimensional externality. See R. H. Coase, "The Problem of Social Cost," *Journal of Law and Economics*, vol. 3 (1960), 1–44; Ralph Turvey, "On Divergencies Between Social Cost and Private Cost," *Economica*, vol. 30 (1963), 309–13; Charles Plott, "Externalities and Corrective Taxes," *Economica*, vol. 33 (1966), 88–91.

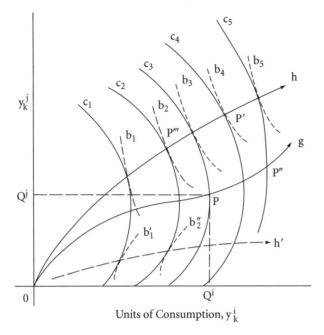

Figure 1

pendent adjustment by i will generate a position somewhere along a path, say, g, which will be determined strictly by the private-cost–private-benefit situation that he faces. Under the restrictions on his utility function that we have postulated, individual i will try to produce each quantity of his own consumption, y_k^i, at its lowest possible cost. The "privately efficient" mix between the two components can, therefore, be traced as the locus of points along vertical segments of a set of iso-cost curves or iso-outlay curves, shown by the c's in Figure 1. At P, the quantity Q^i of the consumption units enjoyed by i, units of y_k^i, can be supplied most efficiently by i through a production process that jointly supplies the quantity Q^j of the consumption units y_k^j to j, which the latter cannot avoid consuming.

Initially, let us assume that i attains a position of private independent equilibrium at P. It seems clearly to be in j's interest to secure more of his own consumption units, y_k^j, which we assume that he values positively in this case of external economies. He may find it profitable to offer compensation to i in exchange for a greater output directed along the path g. This will be the case, for example, if the path should define the only possible mix for each output level. Along any such ray, trade would continue until the conditions defined by (4A) are satisfied, say, at P''. The construction suggests, however, that unless some fixity in proportions is required, more effective trades may be organized which involve changes in the externality mix. Individual i may be compensated by j, not exclusively for extending production, but, also, for shifting the ratio between y_k^i and y_k^j in favour of the latter.

To stay within the flower-growing illustration, individual j may compensate i not only for growing more flowers, but also for shifting the location of the flower garden so that it lies closer to j's property.[11] The production path that defines the privately efficient mix will not normally be the path that defines the jointly efficient mix.

What are the necessary marginal conditions which must be satisfied to insure optimality in this respect? The geometrical construction is helpful in presenting these in the two-person model. The slopes of the iso-cost curves represent the marginal rate of transformation between components on the production side. It is also necessary to derive iso-benefit curves, the slopes of which will reflect marginal rates of substitution on the consumption side. If we make the assumption that individual marginal evaluations of the consumption units are made in money or numeraire terms and are conceptually measurable on a third-dimensional axis extending toward the viewer in Figure 1, the two "benefit mountains" may be added in this dimension. And, from this total evaluation or total benefit surface, iso-benefit contours may be mapped onto the plane surface of Figure 1. This procedure will generate a family of curves, shown by the b's in the figure.[12,13] The locus of tangency

11. For purposes of analysis, "location" here can represent a surrogate for any and all changes that involve variation in the mix between final consumption components.

12. Note that the derivation of the b curves here is not analogous to the derivation of "social indifference curves." The difference lies in the fact that in this model both individuals must adjust to the same quantities of both components.

13. This geometrical derivation of the optimal path, h, neglects income-effect feedbacks on the shapes of the benefit or evaluation surfaces. This allows us to derive these surfaces independent of the division of cost shares over the relevant bargaining range. If these income-effect feedbacks are incorporated in the model, the division of cost shares over infra-marginal bargaining ranges will influence not only the extension of production along any given path but also the path itself. This complexity, one that is common to all public-good problems, need not be damaging when the purpose of the model is taken to

points between these curves and the iso-cost curves determines the path of optimal mix, h. Attainment of the Pareto-optimality surface requires that production take place along this path until the conditions defined by (4A) are met.

For the two-dimensional, two-person case, these necessary marginal conditions for optimality in the mix can be stated more formally as follows:[14]

$$\frac{f_{y_k^i}}{f_{y_k^j}} = \frac{u_{y_k}^i}{u_{y_r}^i} \Big/ \frac{u_{y_k}^{j\,j}}{u_{y_r}^j}. \tag{9}$$

As Samuelson's formulation of the conditions defined in (4A) demonstrates, no problems arise in extending the one-dimensional public-good analysis over n persons, so long as the group is of fixed size. Once a second dimension is introduced, however, this extension cannot be made readily. Conceptually, the conditions defined in (9) for the two-dimensional, two-person model can serve as an analogue for those that must be present in a multi-dimensional, large-number model. The mathematical statement for the latter conditions cannot, however, be made in terms of the familiar equalities among marginal rates of substitution, and the precise statement becomes a formidable undertaking.[15]

Before leaving the construction of Figure 1, a paradox of sorts may be

---

be that of demonstrating the characteristics of equilibrium and not that of finding or locating it.

14. A more general form of (9) would allow for some reciprocal evaluation of the other's consumption flow by each person. This generalization has been neglected throughout this paper for purposes of expositional clarity.

15. The problem becomes analogous to one in which *all* goods are purely public. No trade can take place in an explicit sense, and uniform quantities must be available to all persons. If the size of the group is larger than two, even if there are only two goods, Pareto optimality is not necessarily characterized by equalities in marginal rates of substitution between *any two* persons, and more than simple summations procedures are required for defining necessary conditions. For the two-good, three-person case, the Pareto-optimal set of positions is represented geometrically by a triangular area connecting three optima; this is comparable to the contract locus connecting two individual optima in the two-person case.

For a rigorous statement of the necessary conditions in the n-person, n-public-goods model, see Charles Plott, *Generalized Equilibrium Conditions Under Alternative Exchange Institutions*, Research Monograph No. 9, Thomas Jefferson Center for Political Economy, University of Virginia, December 1964. Also, see Ragnar Frisch, "On Welfare Theory and Pareto Regions," *International Economic Papers*, No. 9 (1959), 39–92.

noted. If, as we have assumed, P is the position of private equilibrium before trade in the externality, then P''' is clearly a position of possible equilibrium after such trade, given the required configurations. Note, however, that at P''' the acting individual, i, secures a smaller quantity of consumption units, y_k^i, than he does at P, despite the fact that his action exerts a relevant external economy on j, and at P''' he is receiving compensations from j. By changing the mix, he reduces the quantity of his own consumption component in physically measurable terms. He will, of course, be on a higher level of utility than before the trade takes place. The compensations from j will more than offset the reductions in his own consumption of y_k^i. This result is not, of course, necessary; a more normal one would involve increased quantities of consumption by both parties, as shown in the possible equilibrium position P'.

Our concern here has been with determining the necessary conditions for optimality in the "externality mix." It should be evident that precisely the same analysis applies for joint supply without externality. In this case, the ray of private adjustment before trade will lie along the abscissa; the optimal path will, however, still lie in the general position indicated by h in Figure 1, and the same conditions will have to be met in full trading equilibrium. With appropriate notational changes, the conditions defined in (9) provide a supplementary set of requirements under orthodox joint supply when the mix is subject to variation.

The geometrical analysis, along with the illustrative example, has been limited to jointly supplied "goods," either external economies or positively valued goods and services in the more orthodox sense. No changes are required in the algebraic statements of the necessary conditions when the analysis is extended to include "bads," or external diseconomies. The construction of Figure 1 can also be adapted readily to this case. The iso-benefit contours take on the shape of the b', b'' ones; the path of optimal mix is represented by h'. One difference is to be noted, however, which makes the analysis somewhat asymmetrical. Unless (7) holds, joint supply will never embody "bads." Therefore, on this side the very existence of joint supply implies external diseconomies, and *vice versa*. The reason here is, of course, that if (6) holds, and if y_k^i is a "bad" rather than a "good," no one will offer the positive compensation that would be required in order to induce joint rather than separate supply.

V

The joint-supply approach to externality along with the extensions here developed seem to have some potential practical relevance. Through its concentration on the possible variability in the mix among jointly supplied components, the analysis suggests that a broad range of alternative adjustments should be considered when apparently relevant externalities are observed. In this approach, the externality relationship is necessarily multi-dimensional, and corrective measures should reflect some recognition of this fact. Optimality may require not more "parks" but a change in location, not less "smoke" but a change in chemical composition or hours of emission. Choosing the optimal location for any given amount of fire protection may be as important as, or even more important than, choosing the optimal gross supply in production unit terms.

The necessary conditions for optimality in an externality or public-goods mix have been derived exclusively from individual evaluations placed on the separate components along with the cost relationships. Conceptually, therefore, resort to external, non-individualistic criteria for selecting the precise characteristics of multi-dimensional public services is not required.[16] Practical application of the analysis in any specific sense would, of course, be extremely difficult. Even here, however, some conceptual predictions become possible to the extent that broad criteria of economic efficiency in the usual

16. The problem of determining the desired mix among separate components in a single municipal public service, crime protection, has recently been discussed by both Carl Shoup and Douglas Dosser. They examine the problem, however, in terms of postulated criteria such as number of crimes committed, marginal cost of prevention, and community indifference functions. They do not derive the latter from individual evaluations in the sense here developed, and they do not relate their treatment to the more general joint-supply, externality problem. See Carl S. Shoup, "Standards for Distributing a Free Governmental Service: Crime Prevention," *Public Finance*, vol. 19 (1964), 383–94; Douglas Dosser, "Note on Carl S. Shoup's 'Standards for Distributing a Free Governmental Service: Crime Prevention,' " *Public Finance*, vol. 19 (1964), 395–402.

While these two papers seem more closely related to the argument developed here than others, much of the literature in cost-benefit and systems analysis has been concerned with determining the appropriate trade-offs among separate components of multi-dimensional jointly produced goods, e.g., weapons systems. The discussion has almost always been based on the assumption that resort to non-individualistic criteria is necessary and/or desirable, both conceptually and in practice.

definition are accepted. The analysis allows us to "explain" the pressures toward equilibrium, through ordinary trading processes if the interacting groups are critically small, or through the working of the political process if the interacting group becomes critically large, provided that democratic institutions prevail. In the latter case, which is the one relevant for analysis of public-goods supply, the structure of decision rules can channel pressures in non-optimal directions, making the task of explanation more difficult. But this explanation of both market and political processes, and not a will-of-the-wisp search for "optimality" as determined by non-existent "social welfare functions," remains the objective of positive political economy.

PART FOUR

Public Goods Theory

Cooperation and Conflict in Public-Goods Interaction

I

An important feature of the modern theory of public goods is its emphasis on the failure of individuals to act voluntarily in accordance with socially desired results in the presence of public-goods interactions. If left to select their own contributions to the costs of providing commonly shared benefits, they will become "free riders"; they will conceal their true preferences.[1] By comparison and by contrast much of the discussion of the game situation descriptively called the "prisoners' dilemma," and especially that which examines the results of experimental sequential runs of this game, suggests that individuals tend to adopt cooperative patterns of behavior, even in the absence of explicit communication, when play is repetitive.[2] The interaction among individuals who share the benefits of a purely public good or service

From *Western Economic Journal* 5 (March 1967): 109–21. Copyright 1967 by Western Economic Association. Reprinted by permission of the Western Economic Association.

Mark Pauly, Roger Sherman, and Gordon Tullock offered helpful comments on earlier drafts of this paper.

1. See, for example, Paul A. Samuelson, "The Pure Theory of Public Expenditure," *Review of Economics and Statistics,* 36 (November, 1954), 388 f.; R. A. Musgrave, *The Theory of Public Finance* (New York: McGraw-Hill, 1959), 10 and 117.

2. For a general discussion of the prisoners' dilemma and of the "quasi-equilibrium," but highly unstable, cooperative outcome under repeated plays, see R. Duncan Luce and Howard Raiffa, *Games and Decisions* (New York: John Wiley and Sons, 1957), 97–102. For a comprehensive report on the results of experimental tests, see Anatol Rapoport and Albert M. Chammah, *Prisoner's Dilemma* (Ann Arbor: University of Michigan Press, 1965).

is an example of the prisoners' dilemma game, at least in certain essential respects, and the interaction is one that presumably continues over a sequence of time periods. This suggests the need for some reconciliation between the two apparently divergent strands of behavioral analysis. Both logic and experimental results suggest that after repeated plays a significant proportion of individuals caught in the two-person dilemma independently choose to behave so that the joint maximum, or Pareto-optimal, outcome is achieved.[3] Does this suggest that the public-finance stress on "anti-social" behavior in small-group settings is at least partially misplaced? Will the voluntary behavior of individuals who share a public good generate, after some sequence of trial-and-error teaching-and-learning periods, Pareto-optimal results? Must "free-rider" elements of behavior be reserved for individuals in effectively large groups, where direct considerations of strategy are not present?

These questions are examined in this paper. Strictly interpreted, the analysis applies only to interactions among small numbers of persons, and the actual models are limited to two-person groups. By extension, and in part by contrast, the results can be applied to individual behavior in large-group interactions. I shall demonstrate that the choice range of the individual in public-goods interaction is more extensive than that which is suggested by analogy with the simple prisoners' dilemma game. The expansion of the latter removes the dominance features that highlight the predicted one-play or terminal-play results. With an appropriately expanded choice matrix, the opposing pressures on the individual can be illustrated, those leading toward cooperation on the one hand and conflict on the other.

Although the analysis is concentrated on public-goods interaction, where the need for some connecting links seems apparent, some aspects of the discussion are relevant for other applications. Notably, the models introduced in the paper can be extended to the more familiar problem involving cooperation and conflict among oligopolists.

---

3. The precise results depend upon many variables, but in their conditions of the "pure matrix" and the "block matrix" games, Rapoport and Chammah found that the proportion of cooperative responses reaches approximately 70 percent after repeated plays. See Rapoport and Chammah, Ch. 5. For earlier experimental results that suggest roughly similar patterns of behavior, see Lester B. Lave, "An Empirical Approach to the Prisoner's Dilemma Game," *Quarterly Journal of Economics*, 76 (August, 1962), 424–36.

Section II presents the elementary two-person, two-good model in terms of familiar geometrical constructions. Section III presents the same model in a three-by-three game matrix in which the behavioral options open to the individuals are necessarily limited to discrete alternatives. Section IV extends the analysis to large-number groups. Finally, Section V briefly discusses the implications of the analysis for the theory of oligopoly.

II

Consider the simplest of models. There are two persons, identical with respect to tastes and resource endowments. For convenience in discussion, we shall call these persons Tizio and Caio. There are two goods, one of which is defined to be purely private and wholly divisible as between the two consumers. The other good is defined to be purely public, or collective. It is wholly indivisible, and a unit of the good enjoyed by one person is, by definition, equally available for the enjoyment of the second person. Each of the goods may be produced by either person on an outlay of labor time, and, for simplicity only, the transformation function between these two goods is linear, as shown by the line P in Figure 1.

Initially, assume that Tizio is wholly unaware of the presence of Caio and, hence, unaware of the public-goods externality that reciprocally makes them interdependent. Tizio knows only that he faces the transformation function between the two goods. He will plan for a consumption mix between the private good and the public good as shown at (3) in Figure 1; the necessary marginal conditions are satisfied at this mix. He will not, of course, attain this target, because, unknown to him, Caio will be making similar plans and acting upon them. In trying to attain position (3), each person will find himself at position (7), with double the amount of the public good that he had anticipated in isolation. We may, at this stage, continue to assume that each remains unaware of the other. Each recognizes only that there are additional units of public good available to him. The position at (7) will not be one of equilibrium. Finding himself in this position, each person will plan on reducing his own public-goods production. After a series of adjustments, both parties will converge toward an equilibrium position shown at (6) in Figure 1.

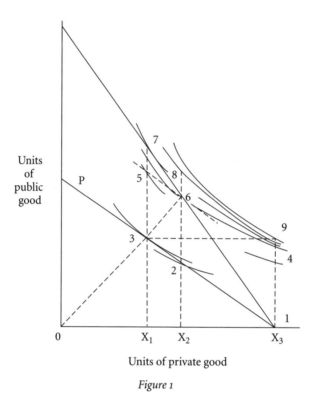

Units
of
public
good

Units of private good

Figure 1

This position, (6), can be called that of *independent-adjustment equilibrium*.[4] Each person is giving up private goods in the amount indicated by X_3X_2 in "exchange" for public goods in the amount indicated by the distance X_2 (6). Each person is in private equilibrium, since the ratio of marginal utilities, the slope of an indifference curve, is equal to the marginal rate of transformation that he privately faces, as shown by the dotted line drawn through (6) parallel to P. It is worth repeating that this position is attained when each person regards the behavior of the other as if the latter is simply a part of "nature." The behavior of the other is embodied as data in the choice

4. Although developed in slightly different terms and for a different purpose, the analysis here is related to that in James M. Buchanan and Gordon Tullock, "Public and Private Interaction Under Reciprocal Externality," in *The Public Economy of Urban Communities*, edited by Julius Margolis (Resources for the Future, 1964), 52–73.

calculus, but the other person is not considered to be subject to influence or control, positively or negatively. So long as this attitude informs behavior, position (6) retains its equilibrium qualities, even if we now drop the restrictive assumptions about mutual recognition. The two persons can be aware of each other's existence and also of the public-goods externality.

Such an "impersonal" attitude need not, however, be present. Each person may recognize, not only the presence of the other along with the public-goods interaction, but also the possibility of varying the other person's behavior by some modification in his own pattern of action. We shall continue to limit the analysis to independent behavior, and we shall not consider explicit undertakings to "trade" or "agree." Even within the limits of independent behavior, however, once the prospect of modifying the other's behavior by some action of his own is predicted, neither individual will remain in equilibrium at (6). The stability properties of this outcome no longer exist.

What departures from this position can be anticipated? If Tizio assumes that in response to his own (Tizio's) cutback in public-goods production Caio will expand production, then Tizio will shift away from public goods. In this setting, Tizio will treat the newly recognized relationship to be non-reciprocal. He will expect Caio to continue to adjust non-strategically to circumstances and to treat Tizio's behavior as a part of "nature." In the extreme, Tizio may, under such conditions, give up all production of the commonly shared public good hoping by so doing to achieve the position shown at (9) on Figure 1. In this position, Caio has expanded his own public-goods production from X_2 (2) to X_1 (3); his expanded production replaces, in part, Tizio's previous output. The expectation that such a position as that shown at (9) may be attained is what tempts each person to behave strategically by reducing his own output below the independent-adjustment equilibrium level, to act strictly as a "free rider." This element in individual behavior is that which public-goods theorists seem to have emphasized. Note that in trying to attain position (9) Tizio may find it advisable to conceal his true preferences from Caio. If he can convince Caio that his (Tizio's) interest in the public good is relatively low, Caio is more likely to carry a disproportionate share of the costs. When both persons in our model attempt to secure position (9), however, the actual outcome will be that shown at position (1) in Figure 1. Since each person will try to "ride free" by allowing the other to carry the public-goods burden, neither will secure the benefits, and both will be worse off than they would be in independent-adjustment equilibrium.

Before embarking on this much-discussed self-defeating course of action, however, Tizio may consider another, and opposing, direction of behavior. He may realize that position (7) would be more desirable to both persons than (6), although neither person could attain this position independently.[5] By increasing rather than by decreasing his own contribution, Tizio may hope that Caio will, over a series of learning and response periods, follow suit and cooperate in response, allowing attainment of position (7). To the extent that such hopes are met by Caio, or to the extent that he acts similarly, Pareto optimality is attained through independent behavioral adjustments. It is this tendency that has been stressed in the literature on the orthodox prisoners' dilemma game under repetitive play.

The simplified geometrical illustration shows the opposing pressures that are placed on the individual. The construction is, of course, drawn explicitly to illustrate the problem, but note that the utility function mapped in Figure 1 exhibits the standard properties. The relative strengths of the opposing forces will, of course, depend on the specific shape of the utility function, upon the subjective probabilities assigned to the different response patterns of his fellow public-goods beneficiary, and upon the cost of the public good.[6]

III

Additional insight into the individual's choice problem under discussion here may be secured if we convert the geometrical illustration into a simpli-

5. In order to simplify the geometrical construction, Figure 1 is drawn so that the position of Pareto optimality, (7), is coincident with the position that is attained when each person acts initially in the absence of knowledge of the other. The arbitrary nature of this assumption should be noted. The position of joint maximum, at (7), may involve more than, the same amount as, or less than double the amount of public good that an individual in full isolation would produce.

6. Under certain configurations, the ordinal utility levels attained by cooperative action may exceed those potentially attainable to the single person through deviant behavior. That is, the positions (7) and (9) in Figure 1 may be reversed. As the matrix illustration and discussion below will indicate, however, the ordinal rankings shown in Figure 1 are the only plausible ones when we shift attention to a large-group model.

fied matrix. Instead of continuous variation in production, implicitly assumed to be possible in the geometrical construction, we now assume that each individual can behave in only one of three ways. He can produce that quantity sufficient to attain the position of independent-adjustment equilibrium, (6) in Figure 1, one-half of X_2 (6), which is X_2 (2). He can produce nothing. Or, finally, he can produce one-half of that quantity of public goods required to attain the position of joint maximum at (7). In this case, each individual produces an amount, X_1 (3), of the public good. These restrictions allow us to concentrate on nine possible outcomes, and each person must find himself at one of these positions, three along each of the three verticals in Figure 1. Positions (1), (6), and (7) represent symmetrical behavior on the part of both persons in the model. The other positions, to be attained, require that the behavior of the two persons be different. The positions are numbered (1) through (9) on Figure 1 to correspond with the ordinal utility ranking of Tizio. These numbers may be used directly to measure utility payoffs to Tizio in the three-by-three matrix of Figure 2.

By limiting attention to the two-by-two matrix in the upper-left, or northwest, of Figure 2, the orthodox payoff structure of the prisoners' dilemma emerges. For Tizio, faced with this limited choice prospect, remaining in the independent-adjustment position, once attained, dominates cooperative be-

		CAIO'S BEHAVIOR		
		Produce pro rata share of joint optimum	Produce at independent-adjustment equilibrium	Produce nothing
TIZIO'S BEHAVIOR	Produce pro rata share of joint optimum	7	5	3
	Produce at independent-adjustment equilibrium	8	6	2
	Produce nothing	9	4	1

Figure 2. Payoff matrix confronting Tizio

havior. And, by assumption, since the appropriate payoff matrix for Caio is merely the transpose of that faced by Tizio, the one-play or terminal-play outcome is that shown at (6). As a series of repeated plays takes place, however, some attempts may be expected on the part of one or both of the parties to shift toward the cooperative behavior pattern, and, ultimately, a position at (7) may emerge. This outcome will be Pareto-optimal, but it will be highly unstable. So long as behavior is voluntary and wholly independent, the position at (7) exhibits at best quasi-equilibrium properties and only then in a setting where both players anticipate further rounds of play with an indefinite terminal point.

As the geometrical illustration makes clear, however, the two-by-two matrix does not include all relevant alternatives. Each person faces the prospect of behaving strategically so as to shift a major share of the burden onto the other while himself securing a share of the benefits. Once this additional opportunity for genuine "exploitation" of the other person is recognized, dominance no longer characterizes the utility payoff matrix. Tizio's optimizing choice now depends on the behavior that he predicts for Caio, even in the one-play case. Optimally, Tizio prefers the position where he secures the benefits of an amount, X_1 (3), of the public good, all of which is provided by Caio. This is shown by position (9) on Figure 1 and by the payoff 9 on Figure 2. On the other hand, if Tizio predicts that Caio's behavior is fixed at the independent-adjustment equilibrium and is unresponsive to his own behavior in either direction, Tizio, too, will find it advantageous to remain at (6). Finally, if he considers Caio certain to act strategically, Tizio will find it preferable to avoid the dog-in-manger outcome at (1) by producing the whole supply of the public good and moving to (3).

There is no determinate solution to this game. Dominance no longer exists as in the more limited game, and there is no saddle point. Some interesting features of the matrix may be noted. If each player is a risk averter and if each considers the other person to choose somehow at random among the alternatives open to him, a naive maximin strategy rule may lead each to produce one-half of the Pareto-optimal amount, and hence to a Pareto-optimal result. This is not, of course, a solution, since each player will have an incentive to modify his own behavior in the direction of a smaller contribution.

It may be argued nonetheless, and with some apparent legitimacy, that the cooperative outcome in this game, when played repeatedly, is more probable than in the more restricted prisoners' dilemma. In the latter, noncooperative behavior strictly dominates cooperation, for each player, in each round of play. In the expanded game of Figure 2, there exists at least one response of the opponent that will induce adherence by each player to the cooperative behavior pattern. Experimental evidence for this expanded, yet simple, game situation would be helpful.

The absence of strict dominance in suggesting the higher probability of a cooperative outcome is offset by the presence of the enhanced rewards to strictly strategic behavior, behavior that is not an alternative in the more limited game. To this point, the numerical payoffs in Figure 1 and Figure 2 have been used to represent ordinal levels of utility only, but it is clear that the predicted pattern of response will depend upon the intervals between the separate alternatives. If the expected reward from exploiting or defecting behavior should greatly exceed that which is enjoyed by the individual in the joint-maximum position, the likelihood of achieving the latter position is surely reduced.

In the pure public-goods interaction examined here, the shift in the size of the interacting group exerts an important influence on the relative reward to cooperative behavior on the one hand and to exploiting behavior on the other. This is true even when we limit analysis to critically small groups. As the number increases only from two persons to three, for example, the single person's behavior affects his own enjoyment of the good by one-third rather than by one-half when behavior is symmetrical. He will, therefore, have less incentive to initiate cooperative action and more incentive to behave contrary to the whole group's interest. Somewhat surprisingly, there have been relatively few experimental studies designed to reveal the extent of cooperative behavior in three- or four-person prisoners' dilemma situations, but the proportion of individuals who behave cooperatively, even after repeated plays, would surely fall dramatically below that found applicable in the two-person experiments. So long as the interaction is limited to small groups, however, there will remain some motivation for the individual to behave strategically. He will recognize that his own action can exert some influence on the behavior of others in the group. There will remain some incentive for the tacit cooperation found to be present in the two-person prisoners' dilemma, but as the group size grows this incentive becomes increasingly faint while the pressures toward "anti-social" behavior become increasingly strong.

IV

To be at all relevant for public-goods problems in the real world, the analysis must be extended from the small-number to the large-number case.[7] As the number of participants becomes critically large, the individual will more and more come to treat the behavior of "all others" as beyond his own possible range of influence.[8] At some point, the position of independent-adjustment equilibrium, shown as (6) in both Figures 1 and 2, becomes the determinate solution to the large-number public-goods game under wholly voluntary and independent behavior.

Once this position is reached, it will be stable so long as independent action provides the only means of securing public-goods benefits. No person, independently or privately, will have any incentive to modify his own behavior, either in a single play or in a repeated series of plays. Pressures for shifts toward the Pareto-optimal outcome will arise only in the efforts of individuals to organize themselves in group trading-agreements, either through governmental or non-governmental auspices.

The convergence toward this equilibrium remains to be examined in the large-number model. Suppose that initially all members of a large group contribute amounts to a commonly shared public good that are sufficient to generate Pareto-optimal results. Position (7) becomes the starting point. The matrix of Figure 2 may still be used to indicate the situation confronted by any member of the group, Tizio in our model. The single other person in the game becomes "all others." Ordinarily, the payoff matrix does not change, but descriptive realism for the large-number case may be provided by choosing an arbitrary scale like that of Figure 3. As a member of a large

---

7. This is true so long as individuals are the acting units considered, because most political jurisdictions include effectively large numbers of persons. Interactions among separate units of government may, however, involve small numbers, and the analysis developed above may have some direct relevance for the behavior of such units. For some of the problems of public-goods externalities among local units of government, see Alan Williams, "The Optimal Provision of Public Goods in a System of Local Governments," *Journal of Political Economy*, 74 (February, 1966), 18–33.

8. For an extended discussion of this point in relation to ethics, see my "Ethical Rules, Expected Values, and Large Numbers," *Ethics*, 76 (October, 1965), 1–13.

BEHAVIOR OF "ALL OTHERS"

		All produce pro rata shares in optimal quantity	All produce at independent-adjustment equilibrium	All produce nothing
	Produce pro rata share of optimal quantity	700	55	3
TIZIO'S BEHAVIOR	Produce at independent-adjustment equilibrium	714	60	2
	Produce nothing	730	40	1

Figure 3

group sharing a single public good, Tizio's own behavior will change his own net benefits much less than will a change in the behavior of his fellows, as a group.[9]

Faced with the choice situation shown in Figure 3, and finding himself, along with his fellows, in the upper left-hand corner, Tizio will clearly find it advantageous to reduce his own contribution to zero. In this large-number setting, no strategic elements of behavior enter in determining this response. Tizio will not assume that he has any influence on the behavior of "all others." His action in reducing his contribution to zero involves no concealing of true preferences, no bluffing, no threats. Given the choice situation that he confronts, he acts strictly on the basis of his own utility function.[10] If all members of the large group are identical, and if each acts simultaneously with the others, we should expect here a continuing and regular cycle between the Pareto-optimal result and that result in which none of the good is produced. In this extreme model, if either of these results is initially achieved, there

9. This conclusion holds, in the strict sense, only because we are limiting the analysis here to purely public goods, defined as being equally available to all persons. In the situation where there are both private- and public-goods aspects in behavior, the ordinary case of external economies, this relationship between the effects of an individual's own behavior and that of "all others" on his own utility can take any form.

10. This aspect of the problem was first explicitly discussed by Otto Davis and Andrew Whinston in an unpublished paper, "Some Foundations of Public Expenditure Theory," Carnegie Institute of Technology, November, 1961.

would be no convergence toward the independent-adjustment equilibrium. All that is required to remove such a cycle, however, is some modification in these extreme assumptions. Individuals may remain identical, both as to tastes and resource endowments. But in making adjustments, we can specify that some persons act more quickly than others. This change alone is sufficient to produce the necessary convergence toward the large-number solution.

The convergence may be illustrated by Figure 4. If everyone finds himself in the position where a joint maximum is being achieved, each person has an incentive to reduce his own contribution to zero, to act as a "free rider." As a few persons take this step, however, the net utility payoffs to others who follow suit are reduced, along with the net payoffs to those who have already departed from the optimizing pattern of behavior. As more and more members of the group opt out, as it were, some point, say Z, on Figure 4, is reached where it becomes no longer advantageous for further reductions in outlay even for those individuals who choose to act on the basis of short-term utility-maximization factors. Once this point is reached, however, the net utility payoffs to those who have already opted out are reduced to equivalence with those who stop at the independent-adjustment level. Behavioral changes will now set in for both the early "free riders" and for the lingering optimizers. Individuals in both these sets will find it desirable to shift toward the level of contribution indicated by the independent-adjustment outcome.

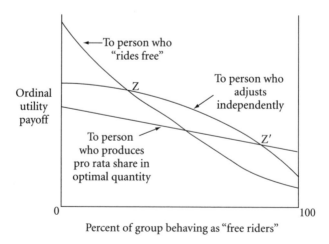

Figure 4

In this manner, all persons will eventually reach a final equilibrium, and in this world-of-equals model, all will be behaving in the same way. A similar convergence could be traced if all persons should find themselves initially in the non-production extreme. Here, as more and more parties respond by producing pro rata shares in the joint-maximum amount, the net payoff rises to some point, say Z', from which a gradual shift of all persons to the independent-adjustment level is indicated.[11]

The large-number solution is, of course, non-optimal, and in a limited sense already noted, it retains characteristics of the one-play outcome of the prisoners' dilemma. The n-person setting eliminates *both* the possible shifts toward cooperative patterns of behavior under repeated play and the strictly strategic behavior characteristic of small-number bargaining. It is important to note that an individual in the large-number equilibrium behaves neither cooperatively nor competitively vis-à-vis his fellows who share the public good. He simply treats them as if they are a part of his natural environment. Psychologically, there is no conflict; there are no game-theoretic elements in behavior. Much of the early literature in the modern theory of public goods has implied, even if sometimes indirectly, that game-theoretic elements of behavior are present, even in the large-number settings. Only this presumption can satisfactorily explain the repeated references to the tendencies of an individual to "pretend to have less interest in a given collective consumption activity than he really has . . ."[12]

---

11. Strictly interpreted, the construction of Figure 4 should be in three, rather than in two, dimensions, since there are three behavioral alternatives open to any person. The precise location of the three curves, as well as their points of intersection, will depend, not only on the percent of the group who behave as free riders, which is measured along the abscissa, but also on the mix between the "cooperators" and the "independent adjustors" in the non-free-rider set. For any specified mix, however, the general relationships among the three curves, as well as among their points of intersection, will remain those shown in Figure 4. For purposes of illustrating the convergence to equilibrium, therefore, the two-dimensional presentation seems preferable to the more complex alternative.

The equilibrium itself is not, of course, shown on Figure 4, since it requires similar behavior on the part of all persons. Conceptually, we might think of equilibrium as being attained by a shift of the vertical axis to the right to any point between Z and Z'.

12. Samuelson, "The Pure Theory of Public Expenditure," 388. See also Musgrave, *The Theory of Public Finance,* 116 f; William J. Baumol, *Welfare Economics and the Theory of the State,* Revised Edition (Cambridge: Harvard University Press, 1965), 21; J. G. Head, "The Welfare Foundations of Public Finance Theory," *Rivista di diritto finanziario e scienza della finanze* (May, 1963), 25.

V

The position of independent-adjustment equilibrium in large groups is analogous to that of full competitive equilibrium in an industry. The fact that competitive equilibrium, in its general conception, is Pareto-optimal, whereas the comparable position under public-goods interaction is non-optimal, suggests that the analogy must be used with caution. Competitive equilibrium is optimal for the inclusive group, embodying *both* producing-supplying firms and consumers-purchasers. For the first subgroup, that of the producers-suppliers only, the position at competitive equilibrium is identical to that confronted by individual beneficiaries of a commonly shared public good in the absence of organized cooperation.[13] If the group is large, the individual unit has no incentive to modify its own behavior despite its recognition that *joint* action toward restricting supply would increase total profits.

As the size of the producing group is reduced, small-group behavior patterns emerge. In the small-number setting, some of the models introduced in earlier sections of this paper may be extended to the familiar problems of oligopoly behavior. The prisoners' dilemma aspects of this problem have been widely recognized. Most of the analysis seems to have been, however, limited to analogues of the orthodox dilemma game. The tendency of firms to violate cartel agreements, to depart from patterns of behavior that maximize joint payoffs, to chisel, has been stressed in one body of literature,[14] while the offsetting tendency of firms to behave cooperatively so as to maximize joint profits has been stressed in another.[15] The range of outcome has been more or less implicitly held to be limited by the joint maximum on the one hand and the competitive result on the other.

This feature of the standard works has been effectively criticized in the Davis-Whinston paper previously cited. My indebtedness to this paper should be acknowledged, especially since it remains unpublished and not available to a wide readership.

13. Olson has particularly stressed this comparison. See Mancur Olson, *The Logic of Collective Action* (Cambridge: Harvard University Press, 1965).

14. For an extended development of the tendency toward price-cutting behavior, see G. Warren Nutter, "Duopoly, Oligopoly and Merging Competition," *Southern Economic Journal*, 30 (April, 1964), 342–52.

15. See, for example, Almarin Phillips, "A Theory of Interfirm Organization," *Quarterly Journal of Economics*, 74 (November, 1960), 602–13.

The models developed above suggest that under certain conditions oligopolistic behavior may produce results less satisfactory to participating firms in an industry than a fully competitive outcome. The matrix illustration of Figure 2 is reproduced in Figure 5 in terms of discrete alternatives facing a duopolist. Consider that an initial position at the joint maximum (7) has been achieved by independent behavior; each firm produces one-half of that output which will maximize joint profits. The single firm will, if it predicts that the other firm will hold to this restricted level of output, find it advantageous to produce *more* than one-half of the output that would be required to achieve competitive price-output levels. If both firms respond in this manner, position (1) will be reached, at which joint output will be above and price correspondingly below competitive levels. This result will, of course, be a temporary one, since it will immediately generate shifts back toward restricted output on the part of both firms. However, if duopolists in such a situation possess substantially complete information about their opponents and make certain assumptions about opponents' randomizing behavior, a mixed-strategy equilibrium can be found for any set of cardinal payoffs. For our purposes, it is useful to note only that any such mixed strategy would probably produce occasional outcomes beyond competitive output limits.

This result arises only because we have limited behavior to discrete quantum variations in output by a firm. If the firm is allowed to vary its output

BEHAVIOR OF "OTHER" FIRM

		Produce one-half joint-profit maximizing output	Produce one-half competitive output	Produce more than one-half competitive output
FIRM'S OWN BEHAVIOR	Produce one-half joint-profit maximizing output	7	5	3
	Produce one-half competitive output	8	6	2
	Produce more than one-half competitive output	9	4	1

Figure 5. Payoff matrix facing duopoly firm

by small steps, the familiar Cournot convergence to the independent-adjustment equilibrium output will take place. If quantum variations are not ruled out, however, the models suggest that a firm may deliberately choose them, provided it possesses sufficient information about its rival's payoff structure. It should be noted here that this model suggests the possibility of occasional higher-than-competitive output and lower-than-competitive prices independent of any explicit "threat" or "ruin" strategy on the part of either firm. Such strategy may, of course, be present, in which case an additional explanation for below-equilibrium prices is provided. A "bluffing," or "concealed preference," strategy may also be employed, similar to that commonly referred to in public-goods theory. The bluffing firm may attempt to convince its rival that the bluffer's own cost-revenue situation dictates a large output, even in joint-maximizing equilibrium; thus, it may hope to force a larger share of the restriction onto its rival.

As in the public-goods model, the shift from the two-firm, or duopoly, setting to the three-firm, four-firm, or other small-group setting will tend to increase the rewards expected from departures from joint-maximum quasi-equilibrium positions, even if strategic considerations remain relevant for behavior. In this case, the possibility of outcomes characterized by prices even below competitive levels is probably enhanced. The particular aspect of oligopoly strategy that this comparison with "free-rider" strategy emphasizes is not unfamiliar in price and rate wars, but this aspect seems to have been relatively neglected in the orthodox theories of oligopolistic behavior.[16]

The individual in a small-group, public-goods interaction and the firm in an oligopolistic industry face three broadly defined alternatives. He (or it) may behave cooperatively hoping that his (its) "rivals" will emulate his (its) action. He (or it) may behave independently, treating "others" as a part of nature. Or, he (or it) may behave strategically, hoping that "rivals" will be induced to carry the primary opportunity costs involved in securing the jointly available potential benefits. The individual in a large-group, public-goods interaction and the firm in a competitively organized industry face

---

16. In his discussion of duopoly, Shubik explicitly introduces a matrix illustration that produces a larger-than-competitive level of output (p. 61). He does not, however, integrate the particular illustrative matrix here with the more extensive discussion. See Martin Shubik, *Strategy and Market Structure* (New York: John Wiley and Sons, 1960), 60–64.

no such prospects. There is no pressure or incentive to behave either co-operatively or competitively so long as independent action is considered. As Professor Frank Knight has often noted: "In competition there is no competition." Applied to public-goods interaction in large groups, this becomes: "In the free-rider problem there are no free riders."

A Note on Public Goods Supply

James M. Buchanan and Milton Z. Kafoglis

The theory of economic policy upon which arguments for the collectivization of any activity must be based embodies the prediction that the behavior of individuals in markets does not produce socially desirable results. In the orthodox analysis, this prediction stems from the presence of significant externalities that the market is presumed unable to internalize. In his independent behavior, the individual is assumed to take into account only the effects of his actions on his own utility or that of his family group. From this it follows that if private behavior exerts Pareto-relevant external economies,[1,2] the market-generated supply of resources to the activity in question falls short of the "social optimum," as this is defined by the Paretian criteria. For example, if the citizens of a social group secure, generally, genuine benefit from the existence of a healthy, disease-free population, the behavior of individuals in purchasing health services independently in private markets appears to commit, relatively, too small a share of total community resources to the provision of such services.

From American *Economic Review* 53 (June 1963): 403–14. Reprinted by permission of the publisher.

The authors are indebted to W. C. Stubblebine and Gordon Tullock of the University of Virginia for their comments at various stages.

1. For a definition of Pareto-relevant externalities, see James M. Buchanan and Wm. Craig Stubblebine, "Externality," *Economica* 29 (November 1962): 371–84. Briefly an externality is Pareto-relevant when the party or parties enjoying an externally imposed benefit (suffering an externally imposed damage) can be made better off without the acting party or parties being made worse off. Favorable interpretation of the literature suggests that economists have, generally, meant to refer only to Pareto-relevant externalities when they discuss external economies and diseconomies. Otherwise, most of the orthodox analysis is seriously deficient.

2. The discussion here is limited to the external economies case, since it is upon this that the collectivization argument is normally based.

In this note, we shall demonstrate that this orthodox policy implication is not completely general, and that in certain circumstances it may be in substantial error. Independent or market organization of an activity that is acknowledged to embody relevant external economies need not result in an undersupply of aggregate resource inputs, relative to that amount required to satisfy the necessary marginal conditions for Pareto-optimality.

We shall examine alternative institutional arrangements through which one particular service may be provided. For expository purposes, we may consider the utilization of a type of medical care that will reduce the probability that the individual will catch a communicable disease. We analyze two separate cases. In the first, the consumption of the service by one person, say B, is assumed to exert relevant external economies on another person or persons, say A, but this relationship is *not reciprocal*. The consumption of the same service by A does not exert relevant external economies on B. For example, A, the "rich man," may find his utility affected by B's consumption of the service, whereas B, the "poor man," may not be affected marginally by the extent to which A himself purchases the service. The second case is that in which the relationship is *reciprocal*. The utilization of the service by B exerts relevant marginal economies on A, as in the first case, but, also, A's consumption of the same service exerts relevant marginal economies on B.

The first and most obvious point to be made is that if an individual receives external or spillover benefits from the activity of others, this affects his utility and may lead him to change his allocation of income among the various goods and services available. If the activity of others generating the spillover benefit is a substitute for some of his own, he will reduce the latter as the activity of others is increased. An increase in the level of immunization privately undertaken by B will tend to reduce the purchase of medical services, say vaccinations, by A. The degree to which the alternative institutional arrangements facilitate the mutually desirable adjustments of consumption in the presence of such substitutability determines their relative efficiency in the exploitation of the external economies. It will be convenient to discuss the nonreciprocal and the reciprocal cases separately and with different tools of analysis.

I. Nonreciprocal Case

We discuss the nonreciprocal case in terms of a two-person geometrical model. We shall, however, treat this model as representative of the *n*-person

model, and we shall not be concerned with considerations of strategic behavior. In Figure 1a, the curve D_a represents the marginal evaluation of individual A for a final output which, in this model, we label "healthy days per
year." Throughout the analysis, we neglect income effects, allowing us to use
marginal evaluation curves as demand curves. This demand curve, D_a, can
also represent the demand for health-service inputs, which we define in units
of the size necessary to provide one healthy day. The ordinate measures the
price of these inputs, along with A's marginal evaluation. Input units are
available at constant marginal cost. Assume, initially, that A considers himself to live in isolation from B. He will purchase a quantity, Q_m, of health-
service inputs, yielding an output, Q_m, of healthy days per year.

By assumption, B does not experience any spillover benefits from A's action. He will purchase a quantity, q, of health-service inputs, shown in Figure
1b, providing to him a like amount of final output. This is clearly not an equilibrium for the group, however, since A will recognize that B's performance
of the activity is providing him with certain spillover benefits at the margin,
and, under the assumptions of the model, these are substitutes for A's own
purchases of health services.

Initially, we assume that A considers B's utilization of an input unit to be

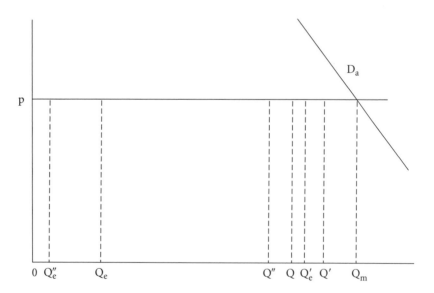

Figure 1a

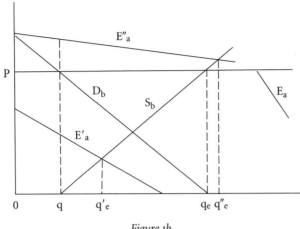

Figure 1b

a perfect substitute for his own direct utilization of a like unit. That is to say, B's use of one additional input unit allows A to maintain the same quantity of healthy days per year by reducing his own direct use by one unit. Thus, A will reduce his own direct consumption from Q_m to Q, as shown in Figure 1a, with this difference being exactly equal to q. This position, described by A's purchasing Q and B's purchasing q, is the equilibrium that is attained through wholly independent adjustment.

We now compare this position with that which might be attained under an alternative institutional arrangement that allows full advantage of the external economies to be taken. If interpersonal markets should become activated, this would provide a means of exploiting such externalities, and the analysis will be developed in terms of such markets. More traditionally, we may assume that some "ideally" operating collective arrangements produce the same results. Individual A will recognize that at the independent equilibrium, he can secure additional benefits through some extension of B's consumption. Retaining the assumption that B's use of an input is a perfect substitute for his own, we now examine A's evaluation of B's activity. In this instance, A would be prepared to pay any amount below the price of an input to himself in exchange for B's marginal extension of the activity. The marginal evaluation curve—that is, A's demand for B's activity—would lie along the horizontal marginal cost or price curve, out to the point at which this intersects with A's demand curve for final output.

How much compensation will be required to encourage B to extend his direct purchases of health-service inputs? The supply curve for B's services that confronts A may be derived by subtracting B's own demand curve from the marginal cost curve, constant at the given price per input unit in this model. This supply curve is shown as S_b in Figure 1b. Equilibrium is attained when B purchases q_e units of health service. A will, in this solution, reduce his own direct input purchases to Q_e, which is less than Q by exactly the difference between q_e and q.[3] The answer to our basic question in this set of circumstances is clear. The solution that allows the full exploitation of the external economies embodies the same total resource use as that which is involved in the independent market adjustment, provided that in the final solution A continues to utilize directly some positive quantity of inputs. The distribution of resource use and the total amount of final output are, of course, different in the two solutions. B enjoys more healthy days than under independent adjustment, and A enjoys the same amount, although his own direct purchases of inputs have been reduced *pari passu* with the expansion in B's purchases.

The analysis indicates that in this type of model it is necessary to distinguish carefully between *units of resources supplied* and *units of final output that may be consumed.* In ordinary market organization, because of the assumed divisibility of benefits in consumption, these two dimensions are equivalent; a unit supplied to the consumer by the seller is identical, physically, to the unit that is consumed. Thus, the total number of units supplied to all purchasers is equal to the total number of units consumed by all persons. This direct relationship between inputs and outputs is, however, modified when some interpersonal substitutability in consumption is allowed, as must be the case with external economies. The very word "economies" suggests that a greater quantity of final output can be achieved with a given quantity of resource inputs when these economies are exploited.

We may now extend the analysis to allow for either less-than-perfect or more-than-perfect substitution between the inputs by B and those by A, in the utility function of A. If A recognizes that B's utilization of health-service inputs will yield external benefits to him, but that these still are not so pro-

---

3. The analysis of individual adjustment in the presence of external economies has been developed in a somewhat different context by Milton Z. Kafoglis, *Welfare Economics and Subsidy Programs* (Gainesville, Fla., 1961), 33–38.

ductive of health as those stemming from his own utilization of inputs, his marginal evaluation curve for B's activity will lie below the price. One such curve is shown as E_a' in Figure 1b. In this situation, equilibrium is attained with B's purchase of the amount q_e' subsidized by A over the range beyond B's own desired independent purchases. In this case, A will find it possible to reduce his own direct purchases, but he will not reduce these sufficiently to offset the expansion in B's resource use. Hence, A will reduce his own direct resource use from Q', the position reached under independent adjustment in this case, to Q_e'. Total resource commitment will be expanded as a result of the exploitation of the externalities.

If, however, B's utilization of health services should prove to be more-than-perfect substitutes for A's own direct consumption, these results are reversed. The marginal evaluation curve of A for B's activity will lie above the price, as is shown by E_a'' in Figure 1b. Here equilibrium is attained with the amount q_e'' being provided by B. Individual A will, in this instance, reduce his own activity by more than the amount of additional activity undertaken by B. The final result will embody a smaller resource use, a smaller total expenditure, than that produced under independent adjustment. As in the other two models, A will continue to enjoy the same total quantity of final services, healthy days per year, and B will, of course, enjoy substantially increased amounts of final services as he utilizes directly more inputs. Because of the extreme substitutability that is present, however, this result can be attained with a smaller total outlay than before.[4,5]

4. It is, of course, possible that B's activity might be a more-than-perfect substitute for A's own at certain levels of provision and a less-than-perfect substitute at other levels. In this case, the appropriate E_a curve in Figure 1b would cut the marginal cost curve, and the final solution might embody either more or less aggregate resource use depending on the particular configuration.

5. In each of the models considered, individual A continues to enjoy the same quantity of final services, "healthy days per year," as indicated by Q in Figure 1a. As B's direct utilization of inputs is allowed to substitute for A's shots, the average price per unit of final service consumed by A falls. This decline in average price might suggest that A would move down his demand curve for the final service as this substitution takes place. His decision will depend, however, on marginal price, not average price, and, so long as he continues to purchase directly for himself any health-service inputs, "healthy days" are available to him only at the marginal price shown by P. Thus, since marginal price does

This third model is not nearly so implausible as it might initially appear. In the immunization example, it seems clear that under certain conditions private organization would generate an overextension of immunization on behalf of some groups in the population that might be more than proportionately reduced in response to an extension of immunization on behalf of other groups.

II. Reciprocal Case

We now turn to the case where reciprocal external economies are present. In the two-person model, the consumption of A yields relevant external economies to B, while, at the same time, the consumption of B yields relevant external economies to A. As we did in the analysis of Section I, we assume that there are no scale effects present in the utilization of inputs. That is, were A and B to act jointly they could not purchase the inputs more cheaply than they could with each acting privately.

As in the nonreciprocal case, we examine the process through which the various members of a group attain equilibrium when we assume that only independent action is possible. The individual will not take into account here the external benefits that his own decisions impose on others. However, he will adjust his own behavior in the light of actions taken by others. As in the earlier model, we limit analysis to the situation where the relationship is one of substitution. Each individual will extend his own independent activity in purchasing inputs in some inverse relationship to the quantity of activity that he expects others in the group to generate.

We have, in this model, an example of "nonseparable" externality, defined by Davis and Whinston,[6] and, as their analysis suggested, the familiar eco-

---

not change, total amount of final services demanded does not change, given our previous assumption that income effects may be neglected. If the relationships were such that as B's utilization of inputs substitutes for his own A could cease all of his own direct input purchases, marginal price would decline. In this case, the elasticity of A's demand for final services as well as the elasticity of substitution between B's resource use and his own would be relevant in determining the direction of change in resource outlay that the co-operative solution would generate.

6. Otto A. Davis and Andrew Whinston, "Externalities, Welfare, and the Theory of Games," *Journal of Political Economy* 70 (June 1962): 241–62. In an unpublished manu-

nomic policy analysis cannot be readily applied. In all such nonseparable cases, it is essential that the interactions among individual decisions be carefully examined. The tools of game theory can be usefully employed in this respect. The details of analysis and the determinacy of solution need not be explored in this note, since we seek only to demonstrate that collective organization, even if ideally operated, *need not* result in greater total outlay on provision of the final service than that which independent adjustment would generate. This, of course, does not deny that in many cases the satisfaction of the necessary marginal conditions for Pareto-optimality may require greater total outlay. In some cases it will surely do so; in others it will not.

The demonstration is presented in the numerical example shown in Figure 2. The example is presented for the two-person case, but the results can be generalized without difficulty; and, throughout, we use the two-person model as representative of an n-person model, allowing us to eliminate considerations of strategic behavior. Each of two persons in the group, A and B, is presumed to be able to take any one of five separate actions, as indicated by the five-by-five matrix. For simplicity in exposition, an example similar to the earlier one will be helpful. Suppose that the activity in question is that of getting a series of immunization shots that provide partial, but never complete, protection against some communicable disease. Each person can either do nothing, as indicated by the a_0 row and the b_0 column in the matrix, or he may get one, two, three, or four shots.

It is convenient here to measure payoffs in negative terms, that is, in terms of expected costs rather than expected benefits. Hence, players will attempt to minimize the payoffs shown in the matrix. In the upper left-hand corner of each square, we measure the expected value of the costs that catching the disease will impose on each of the two persons, A and B. These are determined by the probability of getting the disease, given the level of immunization undertaken by each person, along with the costs of the disease, if it is contracted. The costs for A are shown without parentheses; those for B are shown with parentheses. Since the two individuals are not assumed to be

---

script, "Some Foundations of Public Expenditure Theory," November 1961, Davis and Whinston utilize game theoretic models similar to those that we introduce here. They do not, however, address themselves specifically to the issue here analyzed.

A＼B	b₀	b₁	b₂	b₃	b₄
a₀ (top)	100 _200_ (100)	60 _120_ (50)	45 _90_ (25)	30 _76_ (16) E	29 _77_ (8)
a₀ (bottom)	0 100 (0) (100)	0 60 (10) (60)	0 45 (20) (45)	0 30 (30) (46)	0 29 (40) (48)
a₁ (top)	60 _140_ (70)	45 _110_ (45)	35 _85_ (20)	28 _81_ (13)	25 _82_ (7)
a₁ (bottom)	10 70 (0) (70)	10 55 (10) (55)	10 45 (20) (40)	10 38 (30) (43)	10 35 (40) (47)
a₂ (top)	40 _110_ (50)	32 _91_ (29)	23 _78_ (15) M	19 _77_ (8)	18 _84_ (6)
a₂ (bottom)	20 60 (0) (50)	20 52 (10) (39)	20 43 (20) (35)	20 39 (30) (38)	20 38 (40) (46)
a₃ (top)	29 _99_ (40)	23 _86_ (23)	18 _82_ (14)	17 _83_ (6)	16 _91_ (5)
a₃ (bottom)	30 59 (0) (40)	30 53 (10) (33)	30 48 (20) (34)	30 47 (30) (36)	30 46 (40) (45)
a₄ (top)	20 _90_ (30)	17 _89_ (22)	16 _89_ (13)	15 _89_ (4)	14 _97_ (3)
a₄ (bottom)	40 60 (0) (30)	40 57 (10) (32)	40 56 (20) (33)	40 55 (30) (34)	40 54 (40) (43)

Figure 2

identical, these costs will differ.[7] Note that as the example is constructed expected costs fall for each individual as either one or both of the two persons get additional shots. Individual behavior exerts external economies throughout the range of action illustrated.

There are direct resource costs involved in securing the services. In the example, immunization shots are available at $10 each. In the lower left-hand

7. These expected costs may be converted into objectively determinate values, at least conceptually, if we think in terms of the costs of purchasing insurance policies guaranteeing complete payments for all damages that might be suffered. This point, as well as several others in the development of this example, we owe to Gordon Tullock.

corner of each matrix square in Figure 2, the total costs of purchasing shots for each individual are shown, again with those for B placed in parentheses. The expected costs of catching the disease plus the costs of getting the shots must be added to provide a single negative payoff for each individual. This addition is indicated in the lower right-hand corner of each matrix square. This total payoff will provide the basis for individual decision under independent adjustment.

Examination of Figure 2 suggests that there exists neither row nor column dominance. Neither A nor B will choose his own level of immunization independent of the action taken by the other. If A gets anything less than three shots, B will purchase two for himself. However, if A gets three shots, B will get only one, and, if A purchases four shots, B will go without immunization of his own. The indicated behavior of A is similar. If B gets no shots, A will get three. If B gets one shot, A will get two. If B gets either three or four shots, A will not seek any immunization on his own account. The matrix is specifically constructed so that a position of equilibrium is attained only when each of the two persons gets two shots; this is shown as the (a_2b_2) box, labeled as M. This is the only position where the independently chosen plans of the two persons are simultaneously fulfilled. Should the private behavior of the two result in any other position being attained, at least one of the two persons would have some motivation for independently changing or modifying his behavior. This is, therefore, the equilibrium position under wholly independent adjustment processes.[8]

It will be useful to examine this equilibrium position more carefully. Note that at equilibrium the behavior of each party continues to impose marginal external benefits on the other. Also, in one of the two cases, this marginal external economy is Pareto-relevant. This is shown by comparing (a_2b_3) with the equilibrium (a_2b_2). If negotiations between the two parties could be introduced, A presumably could compensate B sufficiently so that B would

8. The matrix of Figure 2 is, of course, deliberately constructed so as to include a unique equilibrium position. In the general case, either in the two-person or a larger game, there need not be an equilibrium in pure strategies, and there may also be multiple positions of equilibria. Such questions as these need not, however, concern us here, since our purpose is one of constructing an example that will embody the standard relationships while refuting the orthodox implications concerning resource use.

take an additional immunization shot. The private advantages to B from getting the additional shot are not sufficient to cover the marginal cost of $10, but the combined advantages to both A and B, from B's getting the additional shot, are greater than $10. This is proved by the fact that the figure in the upper right-hand corner of the squares is lower in (a_2b_3) than it is in (a_2b_2). This is the group or collective payoff. Note that although A's action at the position of equilibrium continues to impose marginal external economies on B, there is associated with A's action no Pareto-relevant external economy present. That is to say, the shift from (a_2b_2) to (a_3b_2) cannot be made without damaging at least one of the two parties.

At independent equilibrium, four units of input are being utilized in providing immunization. Total outlay on shots is $40. Now assume that the two persons merge into a collective group for the provision of immunization. If we then assume that the "government" acts perfectly or ideally, the new solution will be located where the total group payoff is minimized. This is shown in the square (a_0b_3), labeled as E. Only in this position, Pareto-optimality is attained with B being given three shots and A none, with both persons sharing the total costs. Total outlay on inputs is now $30, less than the $40 spent under private or market equilibrium. Fewer resources are being devoted to immunization than under the independent adjustment alternative. The position of cooperative or collective equilibrium could, of course, be attained also by the operation of interpersonal markets. That gains from trade could be realized over the change from M to E is indicated by the fact that total group costs are lower in the latter position than in the former.

In the numerical example of Figure 2, Pareto-optimality is attained with smaller total outlay on the service, but also with smaller total "consumption" of final output, in this case, immunization, than under independent adjustment. This is shown by the fact that in E expected costs of catching the disease are $30 for A and $16 for B, whereas these are reduced to $23 and $15 in M. This suggests that under independent adjustment the consumption of final output is overextended.

This conclusion need not, of course, follow, and it is easy to modify the example to produce results similar to those shown for the nonreciprocal case. It is possible that the ideal cooperative result may involve smaller total outlay while at the same time providing a larger quantity of final services consumed. This possibility may be illustrated in Figure 3, which simply sub-

B ⟋ A	b₂		b₃		b₄	
a₀	45 (23)	88	21 (14)	65	20 (8)	68
	0 (20)	45 (43)	0 (30) E	21 (44)	0 (40)	20 (48)
a₁	35 (20)	85	20 (13)	73	19 (7)	76
	10 (20)	45 (40)	10 (30)	30 (43)	10 (40)	29 (47)
a₂	23 (15)	78	19 (8)	77	18 (6)	84
	20 (20) M	43 (35)	20 (30)	39 (38)	20 (40)	38 (46)

Figure 3

stitutes partially new numbers for the upper-right three-by-three corner of the matrix in Figure 2. Remaining parts of the initial matrix remain unchanged and are not reproduced in Figure 3.

Note that, as before, private equilibrium is attained only in the position M, while the position of overall cost minimization is reached in E. However, with the revised numerical payoffs in Figure 3, the quantity of final output is actually increased in the "efficient" solution, despite the fact that, as before, the total outlay is below that attained in the private solution. Note that the expected costs of catching the disease are reduced from \$23 and \$15 for A and B, respectively, in M, to \$21 and \$14 in cooperative or collective equilibrium, even though a smaller total outlay is made.

It should be repeated that the matrix illustration introduced is not designed to show that the "efficient" solution necessarily, or even normally, involves a smaller resource outlay and/or a smaller or a larger consumption of final services than that which independent or private adjustments would produce. The purpose of this analysis, as well as that of the earlier geometrical construction, is primarily negative. It is aimed at showing that the implications concerning aggregate resource use that are normally drawn from the orthodox analysis of collective or quasi-collective goods are not universally correct.

The common-sense explanation of the point made in both the nonreciprocal and in the reciprocal cases is straightforward. The means of producing final output are altered when a shift is made from wholly independent adjustment to cooperative or collective arrangements. Insofar as the utilization of inputs is characterized by relevant external economies which stand in a substitute relationship, the individual can, under cooperative or collective arrangements, in one sense, "purchase" the consumption of others. By contrast, under wholly private adjustments he can only modify his behavior in response to the behavior of others. And whereas here, too, he can utilize the consumption of others as a partial substitute for his own, he cannot, through his own independent efforts, modify the quantity of others' consumption.

If negotiations among all parties to the externality relationship are allowed to take place—that is, if side-payments in interpersonal markets are introduced—the "optimal" solution will tend to be reached through the emergence of private agreements. Such negotiations will surely take place to some extent in any case, and especially when the interacting group is reasonably small. However, when the interactions extend over a large number of persons, the costs of attaining voluntary agreements may become prohibitive, and any approach to the "optimal" solution in this fashion may be precluded. It is in reference to such situations that collectivization arguments are applied. A complete analysis would, however, take into account the costs of reaching collective or political decisions, and, when this set of problems is included, there is no a priori way of determining whether or not the "optimal" solution may be approached through this means.

III. Conclusions

In presenting both the geometrical and the numerical illustrations above, we have referred to the example of health services, especially those that provide immunization from communicable disease. There are several other practical examples that come to mind and reinforce the relevance of the analysis. If a municipal government should cease, forthwith, to provide any collective police protection, individuals would, surely, respond by hiring private policemen, guards, night watchmen. It seems quite likely that in such a situation total resource outlay on providing protection to life and property would be greater than under collectivization. The analysis here suggests that this might be true, even in the absence of scale factors. In other words, even if private policemen should be empowered to arrest thieves on property other than that of their employers, and even if police protection is not provided at increasing returns to scale, collectivization might well reduce total outlay on policemen.

The same broad conclusions apply elsewhere. If there were no municipal fire departments, it is likely that total outlay for fire protection would exceed the costs of maintaining the fire departments. Such general conclusions as these will not be questioned. The difficulty in reconciling them, at least initially, with the standard implications drawn from the Pigovian policy analysis seems to be based on the failure of this analysis to have considered adequately the nature of the externality relationship.[9]

Our interest in the particular comparison was stimulated by an attempt to "explain" the comparative record of Great Britain and the United States in the provision of medical care services in the last fifteen years. Over this period, medical care has been collectivized in Great Britain, while it has remained largely organized under market processes in the United States. Naive extensions of the orthodox economic policy analysis would suggest that under collectivization if decisions are made at all "rationally," total resource outlay on the provision of health services should have been substantially increased over that which might have been generated under market organization. An examination of the comparative performance of the United States and Great Britain over this period does not support this crude hypothesis. Even when adjustments are made for the substantially higher levels of provision in the United States over the whole period, for the relative growth in GNP in the two countries, and for relative price changes, there remains the fact that total outlay on medical services has increased more rapidly in this country, and that the gap has been expanded during the period of the National Health Service.[10] There seems to have been no demonstrable effect of nationalization, per se, on the trend of aggregate medical expenditures in Great Britain in comparison with those in the United States.[11]

---

9. The theory here is being corrected in the light of recent critical contributions. In addition to the papers previously cited, the basic article by R. H. Coase, "The Problem of Social Cost," *Journal of Law and Economics* 3 (October 1960): 1–44, should be mentioned.

10. For an examination of the comparative record, see John and Sylvia Jewkes, *The Genesis of the National Health Service* (Oxford, 1961).

11. "The effect is to channel additional money and resources into health services." This early statement concerning the National Health Service made by Seymour Harris in 1951

There are, of course, other hypotheses that might be developed to "explain" this same experience. We make no particular claims that the consumption of medical services is even approximately described by relationships analogous to those presented in the illustrative analyses of Sections I and II. That some aspects of medical services are of this sort is suggested by the "realism" of the communicable disease examples employed. To some extent, at least, it is surely true that, to any particular individual, the utilization of medical services by others reduces his own private requirements for similar services. Nevertheless, other and more sophisticated hypotheses involving institutional differences between the two countries may prove more satisfactory in "explaining" the comparative record. Minimally, we can say that the facts do not contradict the illustrative analysis presented in this note. The same cannot be said for orthodox Pigovian analysis of external effects.

---

has not been supported by the facts. See Seymour Harris, "The British Health Experiment: The First Two Years of the National Health Service," *American Economic Review* 41 (May 1951): 652–66.

Public Goods in Theory and Practice

A Note on the Minasian-Samuelson Discussion

Practical examples lend both interest and credibility to abstract theory, but these advantages are not without their own opportunity cost. Illustrative applications may be taken seriously, both by the theorist and by his critics, with the result that analytical constructions of value are lost in the fury of policy argument. This seems to have been the case in the recent exchange between Professors Minasian and Samuelson.[1] The attention of both was concentrated on the relative advantages of pay and free TV, with TV signals being one allegedly practical example of a public or collective good. In the shambles, any hoped-for consensus on the theory of public goods itself was made less, not more, probable. In this note, I shall try to reconcile the two positions within the context of a *meaningfully constructed and deliberately* artificial example, still confined to the TV-signal illustration, but explicitly divorced from real-world applicability.

Consider a community of persons living on an island, somewhat outside the normal TV signal range of shore-based stations. By constructing a receiving antenna at the highest point on the island, signals from *one* distant

From *Journal of Law and Economics* 10 (1967): 193–97. Reprinted by permission of the publisher.

1. Minasian, "Television Pricing and the Theory of Public Goods," *Journal of Law and Economics* 7 (1964): 71; Samuelson, "Public Goods and Subscription TV: Correction of the Record," *Journal of Law and Economics* 7 (1964): 81.

station can be picked up, and this can, in turn, be retransmitted to local residents. There is no possibility of local control over program content.

The quantity of output of the receiving-retransmitting facility can be expressed in minutes per day of retransmission, and we shall assume that the total costs of operation are a linear and homogeneous function of this quantity. This simplification eliminates troublesome problems about initial investment and returns to scale.

Let us now examine the results of an ideally operating tax-financed collective facility. The retransmitted signals will be free of direct user charge. Users will finance the services through a set of tax-prices. These will be set so as to equate, at the margin of provision, individual marginal evaluation and individual marginal cost (tax-price). The necessary conditions for Pareto optimality are satisfied when the summed marginal evaluations equal the marginal (average) cost of retransmission. Note that in this ideal solution users are paying the opportunity cost for the service. At the margin, they are required to pay, in tax-price, precisely what they are willing to pay, as measured in money, neither more nor less. Note also that users are "purchasing," through their tax-prices, the services of the facility that are known to be equally and freely available to members of the whole community. They cannot, under this arrangement, purchase divisible units of service.

Once again the artificiality of this illustration should be emphasized. But it is, I submit, this ideal-type situation, or one closely resembling it, that Samuelson initially had in mind in his reference to TV signals as an application of his theory of public goods, although his zeal for stirring practical interest may have led him into the seemingly more general statements of the sort instanced by Minasian in his footnote reply.

Let us now examine an alternative organization of the service in which tax-financing is not employed. Since, by assumption, there can be only one facility, this means a private or a public monopoly. Let us assume that the community grants sole operating rights to a single entrepreneur. Lacking the power to impose tax-prices, the entrepreneur is forced to resort to direct user prices. To collect user prices, he must be able to exclude individuals from the retransmitted signals as the penalty for nonpayment. To avoid additional problems arising from the costs of various excluding devices, let us assume that the community gives the entrepreneur property rights in the signals and allows him to sue for damages all those who use his property without proper compensation.[2] The monopolist faces two related decisions. First, he must determine how much output to supply; in this model, how many minutes per day to transmit. Secondly, he must determine the number of users to whom service will be extended. The first decision involves, on the cost side, a straightforward computation. In our extreme example, service can be extended at a constant average-marginal cost. Conceptually, the monopolist will seek to equate this cost with marginal revenue. But marginal revenue is not so easy to compute, even conceptually, in this model, because each unit of output is *jointly supplied* to a number of users, with this number to be determined. If he is somehow required to charge all users the same price, he can, given a knowledge of all user demand curves, compute a "market" demand curve for his output and reach a joint decision on output and number of users. This solution will clearly violate the necessary conditions for Pareto optimality, as Samuelson initially suggested, since some users will be excluded despite the fact that they can be added at no additional cost to the monopolist. Nor will this inefficiency be eliminated by forcing the monopolist to act as if he were competitive and to equate marginal cost with price, thus reducing net profits to zero. It will, however, be eliminated, and monopoly organization will be fully efficient if the monopolist is allowed to and is able to discriminate perfectly among separate users. In this case, the monopolist will have no incentive to exclude anyone from the service, and he can take into account all of the differences in individual demands. This discriminating-monopoly solution is Pareto-optimal, and is identical with the ideally collective solution, provided we assume away the feedback income effects on the allocative outcome itself. There is, of course, a major distributional difference in the two solutions, and this may, in itself, imply different allocative outcomes if income-effects are allowed. Even here, however, the two solutions represent two separate points on the Pareto-welfare surface.

In either the ideal collective solution (free usage financed by tax-prices) or the ideal "private" solution (perfectly discriminating monopoly), the joint-

---

2. This arrangement is not nearly so farfetched as it might seem in this context. In a decision reached in early 1966, a United States District Court in New York held that televised motion pictures cannot be intercepted by CATV companies without payment of royalties to producers. *United Artists Television, Inc. v. Fortnightly Corp.*, 255 F. Supp. 177 (S.D.N.Y. 1966).

ness or commonality features remain. These are not modified by the form of organization. A single unit of output, a minute of transmission, supplies many persons simultaneously, and each person must adjust to a *single* quantity of output. In essence, the "theory of public goods" is one particular extension of the Marshallian theory of joint supply.

We may now drop some of the extreme simplifications imposed on our example. Suppose that the single receiving antenna can retransmit only one signal at a time, as before, but that it can receive signals from any one of several shore-based stations. The necessary conditions for Pareto optimality in the extension of output of a commonly shared good tell us nothing at all about this choice. The theory of public goods, in this limited sense, is of no assistance in determining which one, from among a set of mutually exclusive alternatives, should be provided. This decision requires a consideration of the total conditions, some conceptual or actual measurement of consumers' surplus. There is, as such, no means of measuring this, and Minasian's point is well taken when he suggests that the ordinary profitability criterion, whether applied by a private or a public monopolist, would be a more instructive guide than the opinions of a governmental authority. The monopolist owner of the antenna, seeking out his highest net revenue, will tend to select that signal (or that mix of signals) which most closely satisfies consumer demand. Care must be taken, however, not to claim too much for the superior allocative judgment of the profit-seeking monopolist. The argument hinges on his ability to discriminate more or less perfectly among users and over quantities. Through this discrimination, the monopolist can secure all of the consumers' surplus. If, by necessity, by convention, or by law, the monopolist is prevented from discriminating and is, instead, required to charge uniform prices, his profitability criterion will no longer serve as an appropriate guide for aggregative allocative decisions. In other words, the perfectly discriminating monopolist may find it profitable to select quite a different signal-mix from that which the nondiscriminating monopolist would find most profitable.

We may modify our initial simplification in one further way. Instead of only one receiving antenna located at the single highest spot on the island, let us now assume that there can be many such antennas erected. Let us further extend this assumption and say that the retransmission of signals can be *competitively supplied.* Many separate retransmitting firms can technically operate with each supplying a different signal to users. Here we confront a model where many *separate* purely collective goods can be supplied competitively if privately organized. These separate goods may be very close substitutes one for the other in the users' utility functions. This is the extremely interesting model that has been fully explored by Professor Earl Thompson.[3] He shows that in this model private organization will violate the necessary conditions for optimality due to an *overinvestment* in facilities, an *oversupply* of the goods.

Many other interesting, and instructive, variations in the initial assumption of the example could be made. In carrying out these exercises, useful theory might emerge. In each case, however, and this is the point I want to emphasize, the example or illustration is *artificially constructed* to be helpful to us in developing our theoretical tools and concepts, and not *vice versa*. We have learned a great deal from Adam Smith's deer and beaver example, much that is helpful in an understanding of real-world market processes, but it is essential that we recognize always the artificiality of the construction. Hard thinking about such real-world problems as the pricing of TV signals can lead to the development of useful theoretical tools, which, we can often illustrate with oversimplified examples depicting idealized conditions. In the critically important discussion about the actual solutions to real-world problems, no set of theoretical tools is likely to be fully adequate. Such problems are, almost by definition, too complex to allow theory to be applied simply and straightforwardly. This acknowledged difficulty should not, however, cause us to reject any set of tools, which may be wholly correct within the context of the models for which they were developed.

Minasian is correct when he states that the modern theory of public goods does not allow us to make institutional decisions about organizational alternatives independent of other considerations, only some of which he mentions. Only the most naive of the theory's advocates should have made this claim, although it seems clear that the theory was interpreted in this sense by some scholars. On the other hand, Minasian extends his criticism beyond acceptable limits when he suggests that the allocative norms contained within the theory are incorrect, within properly constrained models. His demonstration that other considerations may be dominant in certain real-world

3. Thompson, *The Perfectly Competitive Allocation of Collective Goods* (1965).

circumstances has little relevance to the validity or invalidity of the theory of public goods.

It is unfortunate that Minasian failed to separate more fully the theory of public goods from the organizational problems in the TV case. It is equally unfortunate that Samuelson chose to keep the discussion on the same ground. Finally, it is distressing that Samuelson, who could have had the better of the argument, threw his own advantage away by bringing ideological overtones into what should be a reasoned debate. In so doing, he placed an ideological cloud over the whole theory of public goods, to which he has contributed so much. Surely this theory can be, and should be, wholly *wertfrei* in an explicit sense, as Samuelson states in his last sentence. His charges against Minasian may, I fear, prompt the response: "Methinks thou dost protest too much."[4]

4. After completion of this note, I have had occasion to see a more recent paper by Samuelson, in which many aspects of his approach to the theory of public goods are clarified. See Samuelson, "Pure Theory of Expenditure and Taxation" (Massachusetts Institute of Technology, July 1966, mimeographed).

Breton and Weldon
on Public Goods

Professor Albert Breton's paper "A Theory of Government Grants,"[1] along with the subsequent discussion between him and Professor J. C. Weldon,[2] suggests that the modern theory of public goods, often associated with Professors Paul A. Samuelson[3] and R. A. Musgrave,[4] has not yet attained the status of rigid orthodoxy. The Samuelson polar case, the purely public good defined to be equally available to all members of the community, is acknowledged to be of very limited application. To develop his theory of optimal structure for multi-level government, Breton was forced to introduce a category of "non-private" goods, provided publicly but not equally available to members of the inclusive political jurisdiction. Essentially his procedure was that of subdividing the community so that the polar model would apply in each particular case.

Weldon raises objections to Breton's analysis of public goods and, by inference, to the received doctrine. He attempts to bring both purely public and "non-private," or intermediate, goods within a broad theoretical framework based on external economies. I am on record as sharing Weldon's ob-

From *Canadian Journal of Economics and Political Science* 33 (February 1967): 111–15. Reprinted by permission of Blackwell Publishers Ltd.

1. Albert Breton, "A Theory of Government Grants," *Canadian Journal of Economics and Political Science,* 31, no. 2 (May 1965), 175–87.

2. J. C. Weldon, "Public Goods (and Federalism)," *Canadian Journal of Economics and Political Science,* 32, no. 2 (May 1966), 230–38 and 238–42.

3. Paul A. Samuelson, "The Pure Theory of Public Expenditure," *Review of Economics and Statistics,* 36, no. 4 (Nov. 1954), 387–89; "Diagrammatic Exposition of a Theory of Public Expenditure," *Review of Economics and Statistics,* 37, no. 4 (Nov. 1955), 350–56.

4. R. A. Musgrave, *The Theory of Public Finance* (New York, 1959), esp. chap. 4.

jectives in this respect.[5] His discussion is helpful at critical points, but it does not, in my opinion, satisfactorily resolve all of the issues. In addition, Weldon's criticisms of Breton are inappropriate in application to certain problems of interest. Over several years, in the course of developing materials for a graduate seminar, I have, at this point, settled on an approach that provides, in one sense, a synthesis between the positions of Breton and Weldon.[6]

The standard treatment gets on the wrong track when the Samuelson polar model is employed as a means of *classifying* public goods. Helpful suggestions toward some eventual classification are one of the purposes of the whole theory, but, initially, the public-goods model should be used in quite a different fashion. The model supplies allocative norms (and, in certain highly restricted situations, predictions as to political results) for the provision of *any* good or service that happens to be supplied *publicly* rather than privately. Used in this way, the theory derived from the polar case can be applied to all goods along the spectrum, as these may be described in terms of inherent "publicness" characteristics. The Samuelson conditions define norms for optimality which allow us to treat all goods "as if they were public" in the descriptively meaningful sense. My general position here is related to that of Weldon, as expressed in his concluding footnote. I should, however, reverse his emphasis and say that anything which produces public intervention in the supply of a good insures its *public* quality.

To demonstrate this point, I propose to apply the theory to a good that is acknowledged to be purely private in the descriptive sense. In itself, this demonstration would have little relevance, but it will be useful in the later extension to those goods that lie between the polar extremes. Consider "shoes" which are, for some reason, publicly, not privately, supplied. *With the proper definition of units,* the Samuelson model allows us to treat this good as purely public. What is required here is that we identify the final consumer of each item of the good. Once we define the good with which we are concerned as "*my* shoes," the allocative norms hold without question. The necessary conditions for Pareto optimality in the provision of "my shoes" are

5. See my "The Theory of Public Finance," *Southern Economic Journal,* 26 (Jan. 1960), 234–38. This is a review article on Musgrave's book.

6. My approach will be fully presented in my forthcoming book, *The Demand and Supply of Public Goods,* which will, I hope, be published in early 1968.

defined in the equality between summed marginal rates of substitution over all persons and marginal cost. Note that as "*my* shoes" this good is equally available to all members of the group. In the summation process, of course, a whole string of zeroes is added to my own marginal evaluation of the good. The solution is identical to that generated in the competitive market process.

The critical step in the analysis lies in the proper definition of units. The basic distinction that is necessary is one between *units in production* and *units in consumption*. Unfortunately, Weldon slips over this point when acceptance and elaboration would have greatly clarified his own argument.[7] The distinction tends to be obscured, for different reasons, in the two polar cases of the purely private and the purely public good. With the former, a single unit that is produced embodies a unit that is available for consumption, by some *one* person. The total quantity of production units adds up to the total quantity of consumption units. "Shoes" can be discussed without identification, which would be redundant in the normal theory of markets. With a purely public good, the unit of production is equally available to all consumers. The quantity of consumption units available to *each* person is measured by the total production. In this case, the distinction clearly exists, as Weldon recognizes explicitly, but the usefulness of making the identification is not apparent.

In all situations of genuinely joint supply, a unit of production may embody two or more units of consumption, as witness the classic Marshallian examples. A single steer, the unit of production or supply, embodies both meat and hides, two separate consumption components defined on the production unit. Almost by definition, public provision of a good implies that the demands of several persons are met jointly. A single unit of production embodies within it consumption units for all members of the appropriately defined group.

This joint supply approach facilitates the incorporation of the whole range of externalities into a single theoretical framework and makes unnecessary some of the awkward devices resorted to by Weldon in his efforts. Consider now an impure good. Defined in production units, this good will enter the utility functions of several, not necessarily all, members of the po-

---

7. "But it seems to me that at this stage it is not necessary to draw a distinction between production (and possession) and consumption" (p. 237).

litical community. The evaluations placed on this good will vary among individuals, not only because of differences in the utility functions, but also because of differences in the physically measurable service flows to separate
persons, differences in *consumption units*, defined in terms of homogeneous
quality. In his attempts to incorporate such goods in his model, Weldon introduces unnecessary complexity. He states that the arguments in an individual's utility function take on a dimension that measures the total quantity
available *to all persons*, a summation, and not the quantities that are available
to the individual as a particular consumer. My suggested distinction between
units in production and units in consumption provides a more satisfactory
means of getting around the problem with which Weldon is concerned. As
units of production, the total quantities available to the whole community
enter each individual's utility function. The individual's evaluation on any
particular quantity will depend on his own projected utilization. To add an
argument measuring this utilization, as Weldon suggests, seems redundant.

Weldon attempts to bring all of the distinctions between separate categories of goods into individual utility functions, and he explicitly rejects
Breton's proposed separation of "objective benefits" from subjective evaluations. Weldon charges that this proposed distinction is not needed and
that it is non-operational. As earlier paragraphs in this note may have implied, a utility-inclusive approach can be fully general, and it can be applied
to any good. My quarrel with Weldon at this point is limited to the specification of arguments in individual utility functions, not with the essentials of
his approach.

Precisely because of its generality, however, the utility-inclusive approach
does not allow us to tackle problems beyond those already developed in the
standard models. Breton's primary interest lies in a set of different problems,
those relating to the determination of optimal structures of multi-level governments, and he has intuitively recognized the extreme limitations of the
tools of public-goods theory. His attempt to separate "objective benefits"
from subjective evaluations is based in his recognition of the need for a modified set of tools. Weldon's charge that this distinction, properly made, is not
needed and is not operational is, I think, in error once we move beyond the
formal limits of the general public-goods models. Breton's treatment, and
particularly his "objective benefits" language, may be criticized, but I shall

show that a closely related distinction is relevant, and, indeed, is essential, when variability among consumption components in a single production unit is allowed.

Consider fire protection, one of Breton's examples of a non-private good. If a single fire station in a municipality is fixed in location, it will yield differing quantities of consumption services to different persons who live at different distances from the facility. These differences can be measured, in physical terms, by external observers. These differences in physical service flows, measured by the objective probability of fire, can be distinguished from differences in tastes for the service. Even if two persons have identical utility functions, thus insuring that the same evaluation will be placed on equal quantities of homogeneous-quality consumption services, their marginal evaluations of the production unit, the facility, will differ with their distances from the facility.

Weldon is correct, however, in saying that this distinction is not needed under the assumption of the example.[8] If the fire station is *fixed in location,* there is no need of making any distinction between objective service flows and subjective evaluations. Assume, however, that the fixity in location is not present, and, instead, that the community is faced with the additional problem of determining the optimal location of the facility. In this case, a distinction between measurable service flows and subjective evaluations is necessary, and also clearly operational. It becomes possible to modify the mix among separate consumption components by changing the location of the unit of joint supply, the production unit, independent of changes in utility functions. This brief comment is obviously not the place to develop the analysis in detail, but the general validity of Breton's proposed distinction seems clear.[9] In the illustration here, of course, "location" is the only characteristic of the production unit that is allowed to vary. In the real world, many such variables may exist for any one publicly supplied good.

The theory of public goods remains interesting precisely because it has

8. The question of operationality is somewhat different. Conceptually, it would be possible to make the distinction by shifting persons from one location to another and observing their changed evaluations in relation to the measured variations in service flows provided, of course, utility functions could be assumed stable over the process.

9. For further discussion of this analysis, see my "Joint Supply, Externality, and Optimality," *Economica,* 33 (Nov. 1966), 404–15.

not yet attained rigid orthodoxy. No single treatment is likely to stand rigorous scrutiny as the concepts are extended to new problems. This comment applies as fully to the "joint supply–externality" approach that I have advanced as to the models of Breton and Weldon. Both of these scholars have made contributions to an ongoing discussion that will, we hope, eventually produce a "theory of publicly supplied goods" that will, despite the inherently greater complexities, be comparable with the "theory of privately supplied goods."

Convexity Constraints in Public Goods Theory

James M. Buchanan and
António S. Pinto Barbosa

Convexity constraints create problems in the pure theory of public goods that need not arise in the theory of private goods. These problems have not been fully recognized. Aside from a somewhat vague and remotely related discussion by Samuelson himself in his 1966 Biarritz paper, along with a comparable indirect treatment by Bradford in 1970, the point made in this paper has not been explicitly discussed.[1] Specifically, we shall demonstrate that under convexity constraints analogous to those normally introduced in the analysis of allocation in private or partitionable goods markets, the satisfaction of the familiar Samuelson second set of conditions *may not* lead to Pareto-efficient allocations. The analysis suggests, somewhat more restrictively, that even if individual marginal tax prices are equated to individual marginal evaluations of the public good (i.e., a Lindahl tax-share distribution) violations of second-order conditions may generate inefficient solutions.

It will be useful to begin with Samuelson's treatment in his initial 1954 paper.[2] He developed his analysis utilizing two polar categories, purely private

From *Kyklos* 33, fasc. 1 (1980): 63–75. Copyright 1980 by Blackwell Publishers Ltd. Reprinted by permission of Blackwell Publishers Ltd.

1. Paul Samuelson, "Pure Theory of Public Expenditure and Taxation," in *Public Economics*, ed. J. Margolis and H. Guitton (Macmillan, 1969), 98–123. David F. Bradford, "Benefit-Cost Analysis and Demand Curves for Public Goods," *Kyklos* 23, fasc. 4 (1970): 775–91.
2. Paul Samuelson, "The Pure Theory of Public Expenditure," *Review of Economics and Statistics* 36 (1954): 387–89.

goods and purely public goods, which he called "collective consumption goods." Using his notation, the former goods, $X_1, \ldots, X_n$, are characterized by the additive relationship,

$$X_j = \sum_{i=1}^{s} X_j^i,$$

whereas the latter, the public goods, $X_{n+1}, \ldots, X_{n+m}$, are characterized by the equality relationship, $X_{n+j} = X_{n+j}^i$, so that each and every person in the community of persons $(1, 2, \ldots, i, \ldots, s)$ has available for consumption or use the same amount of good.

Samuelson placed what appear to be quite ordinary restrictions on his model as regards utility and production functions. For the former, he states: ". . . I assume each individual has a consistent set of *ordinal preferences* with respect to his consumption of all goods (collective as well as private) which can be summarized by a regularly smooth and convex utility index $u^i = u^i$ $(X_1^i, \ldots, X_{n+m}^i)$ (any monotonic stretching of the utility index is of course also an admissible cardinal index of preference)."[3] (Italics in original.) For the production side Samuelson stated: ". . . I assume a regularly convex and smooth production-possibility schedule relating totals of all outputs, private and collective, or $F(X_1, \ldots, X_{n+m}) = 0$, with $F_j > 0$ and ratios F_j/F_n determinate and subject to the generalized laws of diminishing returns."[4]

Samuelson then proceeds to lay down his set of "optimal conditions," with our particular interest here being, of course, in his statement of his famous set (2) written as:

$$\sum_{i=1}^{s} \frac{u_{n+j}^i}{u_r^i} = \frac{F_{n+j}}{F_r} \qquad \begin{array}{l} (j = 1, \ldots, m; \ r = 1, \ldots, n) \text{ or} \\ (j = 1, \ldots, m; \ r = 1). \end{array} \qquad (2)$$

He amplified his analysis in 1955 in his "Diagrammatic Exposition . . ." paper. In this paper there is only one point of interest to us here. In a footnote, Samuelson states:

> Even though a public good is being compared with a private good, the indifference curves are drawn with the usual convexity to the origin. This assumption, as well as the one about diminishing returns, could be relaxed

---

3. Ibid., 387.
4. Ibid.

without hurting the theory. Indeed, we could recognize the possible case where one man's circus is another man's poison, by permitting indifference curves to bend forward. This would not affect the analysis but would answer a critic's minor objection. Mathematically, we could, without loss of generality, set $X_2^i = $ *any function* of X_2, relaxing strict equality.[5] (Note: here X_2 is the notation for the public good; italics supplied.)

As we shall see, the critic's objections may turn out not to have been so minor, after all. But we shall return to this footnote later, and also notably to Samuelson's 1966 Biarritz paper.

We shall demonstrate that with public goods, it is inappropriate to assume convexity in preference orderings, or more basically, in the consumption set, in a manner analogous to that employed in the analysis of private goods interactions. Nonconvexities may emerge from the "nature of publicness," so to speak, with consequent welfare implications. Even with polar public goods, defined strictly in Samuelson's initial terms, there is no need that the second set of Samuelson conditions insure Pareto optimality. In terms more familiar to some readers, we shall demonstrate that individual marginal evaluation curves may be upward rather than downward sloping, with the welfare implications that may be inferred from this result.

We commence by concentrating on *dimensionality*. Recall the Samuelson definition of his polar case, $X_{n+j} = X_{n+j}^i$. Recall, also, that he assumed a convex utility index $u^i = u^i (X^i, \ldots, X_{n+m}^i)$. There is, of course, nothing wrong in this, but our point is that the convexity assumption here is not so simple as it might seem, and as it has apparently seemed to most economists.

What is in the individual's utility function? The conventional response suggests that in its most general form the utility function describes a person's tastes or preferences for all potentially available goods and services. (The poor man may include an argument for diamonds in his general utility function, despite the fact that his income constraints may keep diamonds forever beyond his reach.) We do not, at least in the conventional models, include in utility functions *only* those goods and services over which actual choices are to be exercised. This distinction becomes important when we look at the role of convexity assumptions in public goods theory.

5. Paul Samuelson, "Diagrammatic Exposition of a Theory of Public Expenditure," *Review of Economics and Statistics* 37 (1955): 350–56, esp. 351.

Buchanan stressed the usefulness of distinguishing carefully between what he called *production units* and *consumption units* in public goods theory.[6] He emphasized that the necessity of making this distinction arises from the central "publicness" feature itself. Consider the opposing polar case, that of the purely private or partitionable good, say, apples. In this case, there is no need to worry about dimensionality, no need to distinguish between an apple as produced and an apple as consumed or available for consumption. An apple is an apple, and we have no qualms about putting "apples" directly into the individual's utility function, the same "apples" that enter directly into the producer's production function. But consider the polar public good. The essential feature of "publicness" is the simultaneous availability of something to all persons in the community. But what is "something"? It is the unit as produced, as made available, the *production unit,* which in itself embodies several consumption services, the consumption unit, that is contained within that which is provided.

For clarification, we may use uppercase X's to define production units and lowercase x's to define consumption units. Hence, a single unit of X has within it several units of x, say $(x_1, x_2, \ldots, x_3)$.

We may introduce an example, Tullock's familiar model of mosquito abatement.[7] In order to get away from possible initial ambiguity involved in differential evaluations, we assume that all persons in the community have identical utility functions. Further, to get away from other complexities, we assume initially that all persons are located at a single point in space. What is the public good in this example? What is it that the members of this community must consume jointly in order to capture the potential efficiency gains? What is it that they must "purchase" from public goods suppliers, or else, produce for themselves? How about *pounds of insecticide per week sprayed on the swamp?* In our terminology, this is a good defined in production units, in uppercase X's.

In "purchasing" this good, however, what are the individuals evaluating? They are indirectly placing values on X, values that are derived from those

6. James M. Buchanan, "Joint Supply, Externality and Optimality," *Economica* 33 (November 1966): 404–15; "Breton and Weldon on Public Goods," *Canadian Journal of Economics and Political Science* 33, no. 1 (February 1967): 111–15.

7. Gordon Tullock, *Private Wants, Public Means* (New York: Basic Books, 1970).

placed directly on the x's, which, in this case, are the *reduced likelihoods of mosquito bites*. To which of these two goods should the standard convexity properties be applied? The appropriate response would seem to be the small x's, the consumption units, the reduction in mosquito bites. An individual's utility function should tell us how much bread, milk, and dollars he would be willing to trade off for reductions in mosquito bites or the probabilities thereof.

But convexity over this set of goods, so defined, need not imply convexity over the X's, over the production units over which fiscal choices must be exercised. To insure that convexity is maintained when the X's are substituted for the x's in individual utility functions, particular restrictions must be imposed on the functional relationship between the production and the consumption units, or $x^i = x^i(X)$. However, there seems to exist no logical or technological basis for imposing the required restrictions. In this case, it must be concluded that individual utility functions, normal over the x's, may be nonconvex over the X's.

We may readily show this by introducing an example. Suppose that for any individual, i, the relationship $x^i = x^i(X)$ is characterized by $\partial x^i/\partial X > 0$, and $\partial^2 x^i/\partial X^2 > 0$. So long as the first derivative of this function increases more rapidly than the marginal rate of substitution between x^i and the numeraire good decreases, individual i's marginal rate of substitution between X and the numeraire will increase rather than decrease. The latter term will embody two separate components, the evaluation of x (the good that enters the utility function) and the numeraire, and the "production" relation between x and X. *Figure 1* illustrates the situation. Holding a person at a specific level of utility, given convex preferences between the lowercase x^i and a numeraire, and given the relationship between x^i and X as depicted, the resulting indifference curve between X and the numeraire is concave to the origin.

The normative welfare implications are clear. Setting the summation of marginal evaluations equal to the marginal cost of providing the public good, defined as the uppercase X, which is the only good that can be "purchased" collectively, may actually describe a minimal rather than a maximal position.

Under the formal conditions of the model presented above, we might restore the standard convexity constraints on utility functions, or, if desired, on consumption sets, defined appropriately on the lowercase x's, the consump-

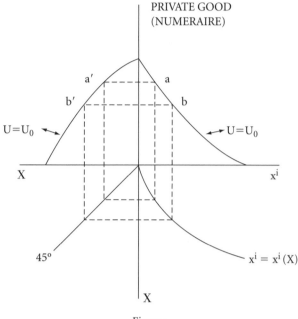

Figure 1

tion units, by the device of incorporating these x's in the production functions in lieu of the X's. If this sort of transformation is accomplished, then
the lowercase x's, the consumption units, are produced under increasing returns, and nonconvexity characterizes the production set with the familiar
welfare implications. That is to say, the consumption units are produced under declining marginal cost conditions throughout the relevant ranges in
question. The question that arises from this procedure concerns the appropriateness of placing consumption units in production functions, which is,
of course, the dual of that involved in placing production units in utility
functions. That which is available for joint or collective consumption is that
which is produced, the composite result of combining inputs. If we think
of the technological basis for the standard assumption of nonincreasing returns, the relevant unit would seem to be that which physically results from
the combination and use of inputs, such as insecticide sprayed on the
swamp. As in its dual, to extend convexity constraints to that which is physically received by consumers seems to be logically-analytically lacking in
foundation.

We should also note that this procedure is available only in the *very special case* that we have postulated in our initial formal model. To demonstrate this, we need change only this one feature. The remaining conditions may be restated. The public good, defined as X, remains purely collective or public in the sense of the equality condition $X = X^i$. We can still retain the assumption that all persons in the group have identical utility functions. And we can assume that there exists only one way, technologically, that the good can be produced. Each unit of X embodies s consumption units, $x^i, \ldots, x^i, \ldots, x^n$, provided simultaneously to all persons in the community.

However, consider the possibility that as between any two persons, i and j, the relationship between $x^i(X)$ and $x^j(X)$ is nonlinear. Specifically, let us assume that for either i or j the conditions previously stated hold. That is, $\partial x^i/\partial X > 0$, $\partial^2 x^i/\partial X^2 > 0$, or $\partial x^j/\partial X > 0$, $\partial^2 x^j/\partial X^2 > 0$, and that the two functions $x^i = x^i(X)$ and $x^j = x^j(X)$ cannot be linearly transformed one into the other. In this setting, there may be no way that the lowercase x's, the consumption units, can be transformed so as to allow them to be entered appropriately into the production functions faced by firms, by producers. The difficulty arises, of course, because a unit of X does not contain within it the same mix of consumption components as production varies.

Note that we have in no way departed from the polar public good constraints. There is no rivalry in consumption; additional consumers can be added at zero marginal cost, regardless of the quantity of X that is produced. There is no "crowding," no "congestion." The range of publicness is unlimited; there is no "local government limit" to efficiency in sizes of the sharing group. Exclusion is not possible. Despite these very severe definitional constraints, we have shown that the familiar conditions deemed to be necessary for allocative efficiency need not produce such results, under plausible assumptions of convexity in utility and production functions.[8]

---

8. There is an analogy, of sorts, between the relationship between dimensionality and convexity constraints in public goods theory and that which emerges in the theory of composite consumer commodities, associated primarily with Gary Becker and his colleagues. ("A Theory of the Allocation of Time," *Economic Journal* 75 [1965]: 493–517; *Economic Theory* [New York: A. A. Knopf, 1971]; "A Theory of Marriage," *Journal of Political Economy* 82 [March/April 1974], part II, 511–53.) In the latter, the person demands a composite commodity, Z, but in order to secure this Z, he must resort to a household production function that allows him to combine inputs, x_1, x_2, x_3, some of which may be

We are surprised that the point made here has not been noticed by those who have worked in formal public goods analysis. To our knowledge, Samuelson himself came closest to a recognition of our point in his 1966 Biarritz paper. Included in that paper is a footnote that warrants citation at some length:

> Whether the same good appears in two utility functions can be affected by definitions and symbolisms used to represent variables. Thus, we may have fireworks in your function and mine; but, without changing the substance of the case, suppose we redefine as distinct variables, fireworks exploded in the sky, y; fireworks observed (or observable) by you, z; fireworks observed by me, v. Then it might be misleadingly said that there are no variables entering literally into more than one utility function and we have here "purely private" goods. However, by such a change in symbolism all public good phenomena could be defined out of existence. This shows the need for some such word as "irreducibly" (enters utility functions) in any formal definition. In the last analysis, we can diagnose the existence of the private good phenomena which can be optimally handled by the market only by a simultaneous scrutiny of the variables and of how they enter in both the utility functions and the technological side constraints.[9]

---

market goods. Each unit of Z, as consumed, therefore, embodies the several x's; seemingly analogous to our X, x^i, x^j relationship. In a sense, the composite-commodities model is the obverse rather than the parallel of the public goods model. That which is purchased in the marketplace is the lowercase "input"; that which is ultimately consumed is the composite of these. Convexity in preferences over the latter need not imply convexity in preferences over the former; in this respect, the analogy holds. However, we do have the broad empirical evidence from individual behavior in markets to suggest that the implied functional relationships between the x's and the Z's are of the appropriate form to insure convexity. There is no such evidence at hand in the theory of public goods. And, indeed, the whole purpose of analysis is different here. The general theory of public goods is not positive; it is explicitly normative. The objective is that of laying down the formal requirements that must be met for the attainment of allocative efficiency. We should perhaps note that some of the writers in the theory of composite commodities have explicitly imposed restrictions on the curvature of the relevant production functions. See, for example, J. Muth, " Household Production and Consumer Demand Functions," *Econometrica* 34 (1966): 699–708, and R. Willis, "A New Approach to the Economic Theory of Fertility," *Journal of Political Economy* 81 (March/April 1973), part II, 514–64. Other writers have not done so. However, the micro-empirical perspective of this body of theory requires relatively less emphasis on formal constraints of the sort discussed in this paper.

9. Samuelson, "Pure Theory of Public Expenditure and Taxation," 108.

Samuelson was really almost there. He was correct in suggesting that a procedure which defined each and every lowercase x as a different variable would result in a model with nothing but "purely private" goods, yet, at the same time, a model that would carry no implications at all for the potential comparative efficacy of institutions. In order for his formal analysis to have implications for market failure, Samuelson was required to stick to the uppercase X's, which we have called production units, as "public goods." In terms of his example, he should, of course, have seen that the fireworks exploded in the sky, y, is the only variable that can enter *both* utility functions, but that the standard convexity properties, which are appropriately applicable for the z's and v's, do not extend readily to the y's without *additional* constraints.

In the Appendix to his Biarritz paper, Samuelson once again, and in a different way, comes very close to a recognition of our point. Here he states that: "Even if, semantically, a variable can be put in more than one individual utility function, we shall not have a *standard* public good case unless it enters the production possibility frontier and industry production functions in the standard way. Moreover, the variable in question may not have the returns and other properties of an ordinary good, private or public."[10] Following this statement, Samuelson proceeds to present an example of a good that has both a separable cost and a joint cost aspect; electricity supplied to summer homes on a peninsula. In this example, he recognizes that there may arise convexity problems. In this, and other examples in the Appendix, however, Samuelson seems to imply that such issues arise only with departures from his polar models, and not with "ordinary public goods."

We now return to the footnote to the 1955 paper cited earlier. By allowing forward-bending indifference curves, Samuelson seems to be saying only that over some ranges marginal evaluations of public goods might be negative for some members of the community, and, if they are, the negative values must be incorporated in any final aggregate solution. But the last sentence of the footnote, in which Samuelson states that "mathematically, we could . . . set $X_2^i =$ any function of X_2, relaxing strict equality," seems highly ambiguous and wholly unrelated to the preceding parts of the note. As our analysis has shown, if the physical flows to all consumers are linearly related, production can be defined on the consumption units, but with the questions

10. Ibid., 115.

raised about convexity in the production set. If the consumption flows are not so related, which seems to have possibly been in the mind of Samuelson's unnamed critic, the possibility of nonconvexities in the consumption set must be recognized.[11]

In his 1966 paper on joint supply, and particularly in his 1967 comment on the Breton-Weldon controversy, Buchanan specifically looked at models in which measurable consumption flows among persons differed, while being produced by commonly available production units meeting all criteria for publicness. But he overlooked the convexity-constraint problem because of his interest in deriving the set of conditions for optimality when the technology allowed for explicit variance in the mix among these consumption components. That is, Buchanan was basically interested in the question: "where should we locate the fire station?" and, as a result, he jumped too readily away from any exhaustive examination of the model which assumes that the location of the station is technologically determinate and not subject to change. Bryan Ellickson seems to have done something analogous in his 1973 paper, in which he stressed the possible nonconvexities that might emerge when "crowding" is allowed on public goods facilities, when the nonrivalry attribute is limited over some ranges of membership. Ellickson apparently failed to note the possible presence of nonconvexities even when no such departures from the polar model are introduced.[12]

To our knowledge, all of those economists who have included public goods pricing in a general equilibria setting have accepted the initial Samuelson formulation without recognition of the significance of the dimensionality issue. For instance, Duncan Foley, in both his early 1967 essay and his 1970 paper, simply postulates an economy that contains both private and public goods, defined analogously to Samuelson's initial statements, and he assumes that preference orderings and production functions over these goods are con-

11. David Bradford ("Benefit-Cost Analysis") indirectly recognized the difference in the convexity assumptions as between private goods and public goods models. His interest was directed toward the instrumental use of benefit-cost analysis, however, and he apparently did not sense the implications for formal public goods theory.

We are indebted to David Rees, who brought Bradford's paper to our attention after we had completed the substantive draft of this paper.

12. Bryan Ellickson, "A Generalization of the Pure Theory of Public Goods," *American Economic Review* 63 (June 1973): 417–32.

vex.[13] In his proof (1970) of the existence of a Lindahl equilibrium, he constructs an all–private goods economy by extending the commodity space so that each person's "bundle of public goods becomes a separate group of commodities." These separate bundles seem to correspond to the lowercase x's in our model. However, in Foley's treatment these bundles must stand in a one-to-one relationship to the public goods, as initially defined. That is to say, there is a perfect mapping between any person's "private goods bundle" in Foley's associate economy and the corresponding public good in the initial model. In our terms, he does not allow for *any* variance between the quantity of X and that of *any* x^i. The nonconvexity possibilities identified in this paper restrict the settings within which sustainable Lindahl equilibria exist below those limits implied by this invariance.[14]

---

13. Duncan Foley, "Resource Allocation and the Public Sector," *Yale Economic Essays* 7 (1967): 43–98; "Lindahl's Solution and the Core of the Economy with Public Goods," *Econometrica* 38 (January 1970): 66–72.

14. Other writers who have made contributions to the general-equilibrium approach developed initially by Foley have not, in our interpretation of their analyses, substantially modified Foley's treatment of this respect.

Public Goods and Natural Liberty

According to the system of natural liberty, the sovereign has only
three duties to attend to; three duties of great importance, indeed,
but plain and intelligible to common understandings: first, the
duty of protecting the society from the violence and invasion of
other independent societies; secondly, the duty of protecting, as
far as possible, every member of the society from the injustice or
oppression of every other member of it, or the duty of establishing an exact administration of justice; and, thirdly, the duty of
erecting and maintaining certain public works and certain public institutions, which it can never be for the interest of any individual, or small number of individuals, to erect and maintain;
because the profit could never repay the expence to any individual or small number of individuals, though it may frequently do
much more than repay it to a great society.

—Adam Smith, *Wealth of Nations,* IV. ix. 51.

Methodological Distance

Adam Smith was an applied welfare economist. He carried with him a conceptual model for the idealized working of the economy, which, although
flawed in some of its particulars, can still teach much to modern students.
Smith did not, however, seek to accomplish his didactic purpose by elabo-
rating his theoretical model. Instead he applied the analysis variously, sometimes repetitively, but always with great skill to the actual economy in which
he lived. The starting-point remained always the institutions that he ob-

From *The Market and the State: Essays in Honour of Adam Smith,* ed. Thomas Wilson
and Andrew S. Skinner (Oxford: Clarendon Press, 1976), 271–86. Reprinted by permission of Oxford University Press.

The writer is indebted to his colleagues Victor Goldberg, Gordon Tullock, Richard
Wagner, and E. G. West, and to Warren Samuels of Michigan State University, for helpful
comments on an earlier version of this paper.

served, the effects of which were to be explained, along with the effects that might be forthcoming under alternative arrangements.

Modern economic theorists proceed quite differently. They analyse abstract and formal models which may bear little or no relationship to the institutions that may exist. (Indeed it is this disparity between the conceptual models and reality that often makes the attempted derivation and testing of empirically refutable hypotheses seem bizarre.) In their elaboration of the formal structures, modern economic theorists have been able to develop precise logical taxonomies that have helped to clear away mental cobwebs. Rigour abounds, even if sometimes in proofs that seem deep in the pure mathematics of conceptual systems.

It is helpful to lay out this methodological distance between Adam Smith and modern economists before getting at the subject matter posed for me in this paper, namely, Smith's conception of public goods and externalities. Given his way of proceeding, we should not expect to find in the *Wealth of Nations* precise definitions of these now-important concepts in theoretical welfare economics.[1] To see whether or not Smith had such concepts embedded in his analytical structure at all, we must approach his work indirectly. We must first ask: what would Smith's major work look like if he possessed no concept of public goods, no idea of external effects? And how would the work that was informed by the equivalent of these modern concepts be different from that which was not so informed?

Libertarian Anarchism

We begin to get an answer to the first of these questions by looking at the analysis of modern economists who explicitly deny the potential relevance of external effects, who see no conceivable agenda for state or collective action emerging from public characteristics of any activities, who reject all attempts to derive an "economic theory of government," an "economic logic of col-

---

1. The distinction between Smith's approach and that of modern economists is stressed by A. Macfie in his comparison of what he calls the Scottish method with the scientific or analytical method. As Macfie suggests, Smith was not "consciously concerned with building a logical model." Instead he was "curious about people, about men at work, about comparative institutions . . ." See A. L. Macfie, *The Individual in Society: Papers on Adam Smith* (London: Allen and Unwin, 1967), 29.

lective action." Modern libertarian anarchists, sometimes called property-rights anarchists, approximate to this description, and they are perhaps best exemplified by Murray Rothbard. His book *For a New Liberty*[2] offers an opportunity for comparison and contrast with the *Wealth of Nations*. Is Rothbard the modern analogue to Adam Smith? Little or no exegesis is required to answer such a question emphatically in the negative. Adam Smith was far too realistic to argue that markets would emerge and would function effectively in the absence of a legal framework.[3] One of the most important lessons of the 1776 masterpiece is the linkage between the *general* security of property (including the enforceability of contracts) and the functioning of markets, a security that could be provided only by the vigilant protection of the sovereign.[4] Smith was a sufficiently good historian and also sufficiently close to the insecurity of the pre-Enlightenment era to avoid the mistake of assuming that property rights and contracts are secure in nature and that they could be preserved through the emergence of voluntary association.

"Laws and Institutions" as Public Goods

We need, therefore, to go no further than Smith's repeated insistence on security to prove that some concept of externality and/or publicness must have

2. Murray Rothbard, *For a New Liberty* (New York: Macmillan, 1973). David Friedman also belongs in this libertarian-anarchist camp, although his analysis is somewhat less extreme than that of Rothbard. See David Friedman, *The Machinery of Freedom* (New York: Harper and Row, 1973).

3. This statement requires no qualification for the *Wealth of Nations*. In his *Theory of Moral Sentiments*, Smith may be interpreted as suggesting that something akin to the idealized libertarian anarchy *could* emerge, if only *all* men would adopt the behavioural norms laid down. However, Smith does not suggest that all men will, in fact, act in this way. And, indeed, he specifically states that government is required because they will not do so. "What institution of government could tend so much to promote the happiness of mankind as the general prevalence of wisdom and virtue? All government is but an imperfect remedy for the deficiency of these." Adam Smith, *The Theory of Moral Sentiments*, with an Introduction by E. G. West (New Rochelle: Arlington House, 1969), 269; IV. i. 2. 1.

4. "It is only under the shelter of the civil magistrate that the owner of that valuable property, which is acquired by the labour of many years, or perhaps of many successive generations, can sleep a single night in security. He is at all times surrounded by unknown enemies, whom, though he never provoked, he can never appease, and from whose injustice he can be protected only by the powerful arm of the civil magistrate continually held up to chastise it." *Wealth of Nations* (Modern Library Edition), 670; V. i. b. 2.

been embodied in the analysis.[5] The following passage makes clear that the "laws and institutions" of a society are directly responsible for the economic well-being of its members.

> China seems to have been long stationary, and had probably long ago acquired that full complement of riches which is consistent with the nature of *its law and institutions*. But this complement may be much inferior to what, with *other laws and institutions*, the nature of its soil, climate, and situation might admit of. A country which neglects or despises foreign commerce, . . . cannot transact the same quantity of business which it might do with different laws and institutions. In a country too, where, though the rich or the owners of large capitals enjoy a good deal of security, the poor or the owners of small capitals enjoy scarce any, but are liable, under the pretense of justice, to be pillaged and plundered at any time by the inferior mandarines, the quantity of stock employed in all the different branches of business transacted within it, can never be equal to what the nature and extent of that business might admit. . . .
>
> A defect in the law may sometimes raise the rate of interest considerably above what the condition of the country, as to wealth or poverty, would require. *When the law does not enforce the performance of contracts,* it puts all borrowers nearly upon the same footing with bankrupts or people of doubtful credit in better regulated countries. . . . Among the barbarous nations who over-ran the Roman empire, the performance of contracts was left for many ages to the faith of the contracting parties.[6]

In this passage, Smith makes several points, directly or indirectly, that are worth noting. The well-being of a society is a function of its basic laws and institutions; these are variable and subject to explicit modification; there is nothing sacrosanct about those laws and institutions that emerge in what may be called the natural process of social evolution;[7] and, finally, the basic

---

5. When we force Smith's treatment into these modern terminological categories, the advantages of clarity must be offset against the necessary losses in generality.

6. *WN* 95; I. ix. 15, 16. Italics supplied.

7. In this interpretation, Smith differs from the position that seems to be taken by F. A. Hayek, who holds Smith up as one of the discoverers of the notion that efficient results need not be willed or planned. This is indeed one of Smith's basic insights into the functioning of a market economy. But, in my view, Hayek extends this notion too far when he applies it to the emergence of law itself. See F. A. Hayek, *Law, Legislation and Liberty,*

laws and institutions must be (or should be) equally available to all persons and groups within a society. These characteristics can be applied with relatively little change to "public goods" in their modern formulation. Such goods (1) enter the utility functions of individuals, (2) can be varied in quantity by the decision-makers for the collectivity, (3) may be provided inefficiently or not at all in the absence of collective action, and (4) must be (or should be) made generally available to all members of the community.

Somewhat surprisingly perhaps, early applications of the modern theory of public goods did not include explicit reference to the legal structure, to the basic "laws and institutions" organized for the protection and enforcement of individual rights and contracts. In one sense, the protection of property is a private good, largely if not exclusively beneficial to the individual whose rights are secured. "Publicness" emerges, however, when protection enforcement takes the form of "law," generally available to all persons, which delineates a structure of reciprocal rights, and which allows the capture of the major scale advantages of joint action.[8] The neglect of this seemingly important aspect of public goods theory is explained, in part, by the same reasons that explain the failure of modern economists to examine legal structures generally. They have implicitly assumed that a well-ordered and functioning "protective State" of a particular sort exists, within which voluntary market arrangements emerge and generate allocative and distributive results. This has allowed attention to be concentrated on the possible "failures" of such arrangements. It is from this "market failure" emphasis of post-Pigovian welfare economics that the modern theory of public or collective-consumption goods emerged, notably in Samuelson's seminal paper in 1954.[9] Early applications and examples were, therefore, designed to demonstrate efficiency limitations of voluntarily organized markets, even when trading arrangements are ideally protected in a well-functioning legal order. Many of the alleged "failures" of markets stem, however, from the inefficient assignment of property rights and not from some inherent charac-

---

vol. I, *Rules and Order* (Chicago: University of Chicago Press, 1973). My interpretation of Smith's position is supported by E. G. West in his Introduction to the Arlington House edition of *TMS*, p. xii.

8. This is recognized by Smith. See *TMS* 501; VII. iv. 35.

9. Paul A. Samuelson, "The Pure Theory of Public Expenditure," *Review of Economics and Statistics*, 36 (Nov. 1954), 387–89.

teristic of the activities in question. David Hume's meadow drainage (a famous "publicness" or "commonality" example which was certainly known
to Adam Smith) does not take place because the meadow is held in common.
There is no necessary "publicness" quality of swamplands. A reassignment
of property rights to bring the interrelated land parcels under single ownership could, in fact, ensure that voluntary action would accomplish efficient
results. In modern public goods theory, attention has been placed on the
costs of exclusion, along with the advantages of joint consumption. The explicit provision of external defence and internal protection is now commonly cited as an example of genuinely public goods, a classification that
would have been accepted directly by Smith, who listed these two specific activities as the first and second duties of the sovereign.[10]

Smith's work was fully informed with an understanding of the concept
that we now call "publicness." There is, nonetheless, an important difference
between the essentially negative emphasis of modern economists on particular instances of market failure, even in a legal order, and Smith's positive
emphasis on the "laws and institutions" required to make markets work.
Smith comes closer than many moderns to the recognition that general law,
itself, represents the best example of "publicness."[11] The commonality or
non-excludability features of law, of the whole legal framework, emerge directly from the very definition itself—rules and regulations that are generally
applicable to all persons and groups in the community. Law may arise from
custom, from conventional modes of behaviour that have become established by usage, but, as noted above, Adam Smith clearly allowed for the possibility of conscious modification and change. Again, almost by definition,
law cannot be changed by voluntary action on the part of one or a few persons. In this sense, law embodies polar or extreme publicness. A person who
voluntarily adopts a rule that restricts his own behaviour secures zero benefits while possibly conferring pure external economies on others in the com-

---

10. See *WN* 653, 669; V. i. a. I, V. i. b. I.

11. This treatment of "law as a public good" has only been recently developed. See, in
particular, William Riker, "Public Safety as a Public Good," in *Is Law Dead?* edited by E. V.
Rostow (New York: Simon and Schuster, 1971), 379–85; Thomas R. Ireland, "Public Order
as a Public Good," typescript (Chicago: Loyola University, 1968). My own book, *The Limits of Liberty* (Chicago: University of Chicago Press, 1975), develops the "publicness" of
law as one of its main themes.

munity. In a formal way, therefore, we might say that "markets fail" in generating the "public good" that law represents, with law here conceived in its widest meaning as the whole set of legal institutions. To Smith, however, this would have seemed a bizarre way of putting a simple point. Without law, markets will not even come into existence, at least in any meaningfully efficient sense. Law is antecedent to market co-ordination, to the economic activity of agents, to the working of Adam Smith's invisible hand.

For those "laws and institutions" which render private holdings secure against both external and internal aggression and invasion, which enforce the performance of contracts, and which facilitate trade, Smith's treatment is wholly consistent with modern public goods analysis. As we move beyond these limits, however, the difference in emphasis mentioned above becomes relevant. Smith's observations led him to recognize the prospect that particular laws, particular rules, applicable to the whole society, might be "public bads" rather than "public goods." His primary attention was turned toward securing a relaxation or removal of the restrictions on the free flow of commerce, on the abolition of the constraints on "natural liberty."[12] By contrast, economists in the early post-Pigovian tradition tended to neglect the "public bads" which political interferences in markets can generate. Only with the relatively recent advent and spread of the theory of public choice, the extension of economic analysis to political choice, has this element of applied welfare economics returned to the corpus of scientific discussion in economics.[13]

12. Smith's position is not wholly consistent with the modern strand of discussion and analysis, which has been called "property-rights economics." In some of the representative works in the latter tradition, "efficient" institutional forms, including the structure of property rights, are somehow predicted to emerge, independent of explicit or conscious collective action. This is related to the Hayek position noted above.

13. I shall not discuss public choice analysis and applications further in this paper. This subdiscipline emerged in the years following World War II, and notably in the United States. In some respects, it is constructed on the failures, analytical and practical, of theoretical welfare economics. It matches its own theory of "government failure" against the traditional welfare economist's theory of "market failure." Public choice theory has gained adherents due to the post-Arrow collapse of "social welfare function" constructions, and due perhaps more importantly to the demonstrable failures of political correctives to market forces.

Agenda for Policy

A comparison between Adam Smith's agenda for economic policy and that of the early post-Pigovian public goods or externality theorist warrants our attention. As we know, Smith's ubiquitous argument called for the dismantling of state interferences with the working of markets. The post-Pigovian, uninfluenced by latter-day public choice analytics, offered arguments, at least by implication, for an extension of state action, for corrections for market failures. To an extent, the real-world setting of 1776 dictated Smith's policy agenda, and any plausible ordering of priorities should have called for a reduction in the scope and range of ill-conceived and often unworkable mercantilist controls.[14] Had Adam Smith lived in a relatively pure *laissez-faire* age, where a minimally protective state confined itself largely to the enforcement of property rights and contracts, it is not difficult for us to imagine him constructing a catalogue of market abuses or failures and calling directly for corrective action. Smith was not a doctrinaire libertarian, and he would have supported legislation for anti-monopoly action, for the definition of the monetary unit, for the regulation of banking, for public utility operation and/or regulation, for minimal public education, for standardized weights and measures, for grade labelling, for limited building codes, possibly for publicly supplied information and support for the arts.

The other side of the comparison is the more puzzling. In the late twentieth century, we do not live in anything that remotely resembles a *laissez-faire* world. We live instead in a veritable maze of governmental rules and regulations, which begin to approach, even if they do not yet exceed, those present in the world of Adam Smith. The intellectual question lies in the general failure of modern-day welfare economists to address more explicitly the "public bads" which political interferences with trade represent. Why have so many modern economists continued to call for an extension in the range of political controls when their demonstrable inefficacies are self-evident?

---

14. Cf. Jacob Viner, "Adam Smith and Laissez Faire," in *The Long View and the Short* (Glencoe, Illinois: Free Press, 1958), 232. The reading of Viner's essay, initially published in 1928 in celebration of the 150th anniversary of *Wealth of Nations,* has the effect of shortening intellectual history on the one hand while dramatically pointing up the changes that have taken place in policy history over the half-century.

What has gone wrong with their agenda for economic policy? Why have so many of them remained relatively silent about minimum wage restrictions, legally protected strike threat systems, rent controls, income policies, price ceilings on crude oil and natural gas, agricultural price supports, publicly subsidized idleness, cartelized transportation networks, restricted licensing for trades and professions, bureaucratic dictation of product quality, product safety, product innovation, hiring practices, educational organization, and countless other restrictions on "natural liberty"?[15]

An Adam Smith returned after two centuries, in 1976, viewing the world as now, and applying his allegedly primitive conceptions of economic order, would surely duplicate his policy priorities of 1776. The *Revised Wealth of Nations* that he might write would probably pay scant if any attention to market failures. It would, instead, contain much criticism of the ineffectiveness of existing and proposed political-governmental nostrums. In careful discussion of example after example, in repetitive application of the elementary verities, such a returned Adam Smith would lay bare the genuine social costs of the interferences with natural liberty. What a challenge this notion of a returned Adam Smith presents! Where is the young economist willing to devote the decade to the task?

Natural Liberty as a Public Good

The restrictions on "natural liberty" surely constitute "public bads," from which it follows that their removal would be equivalent to the production of "public goods." And surely these "public goods" would increase the utility of persons in the community more than the sometimes piddling adjustments that are suggested for correcting minor market distortions. Smith would quickly discern that, now as then, markets "fail" largely because they are not

---

15. A cynical response would be to suggest that many modern economists do not, in fact, fully understand the principle of market co-ordination, and, because of this, have no intellectual faith in the "natural economic order." Macfie suggests that the shift in emphasis here can be traced back to the Benthamites. See A. L. Macfie, op. cit., 157. To state the same point somewhat more charitably, some part of economists' acquiescence can be explained by their implicit, if erroneous, assumption that the restrictions serve as correctives to what they conceive to be relative disparities in the economic power of participants in an unconstrained market order.

allowed to work because of overt political-governmental restrictions. It follows from this that the first steps toward making markets work more efficiently involve removing the restrictions. But are we not forcing the argument somewhat to place Smith's discussion in a public goods context here? Once we accept, with Adam Smith, the publicness attributes of any law, the general applicability to all members and groups in the community, it is relatively straightforward to translate almost all of his discussion into the terminology of public goods analytics. No person or small group can, independently and voluntarily, modify an existing legal rule, but such action can be taken by the collectivity, acting on behalf of all persons.

We may ask why economists have not discussed governmental restrictions on markets in a public goods framework. Why have we introduced the lighthouse, as our classic public goods example, while continuing to discuss the restrictive licensing of taxicabs in orthodox efficiency analysis? In the classroom textbook model, without explicit collective action, no lighthouse will be constructed.[16] But without explicit collective action, an existing restrictive licensing scheme will remain in being. The "public good" that its removal represents will not be produced, making the example analogous in this respect to the lighthouse case.

It will be useful to develop this public goods interpretation of governmental interference with markets in more detail. In so doing, we may be able to identify a source of the economist's frustration with political process. Why does building a lighthouse seem so different, at first glance, from the removal of the licensing of taxicabs? The dilemma of the fishermen seems to be more general; no single person finds himself willing to build the lighthouse, even though, if constructed, *all* fishermen might benefit. Clearly, this is not the case with the removal of taxicab licensing. While this step would surely improve over-all efficiency in the economy, only *some* members of the community will secure benefits; *some* members will clearly be harmed. But the lighthouse example can readily be rigged to make it fully analogous even here. Those fishermen who know precisely where the shoals are, or who

---

16. For a discussion of the economic history of lighthouses and the history of lighthouses in economics, which raises questions about the appropriateness of this stock example in public goods theory, see R. H. Coase, "The Lighthouse in Economics," *Journal of Law and Economics,* 17 (Oct. 1974), 357–76.

might have technically advanced sounding devices, presumably benefit from the absence of the lighthouse, and these persons would possibly be harmed by the production of the public good, which, in itself, would benefit other fishermen, and, in the net, would increase the efficiency of the economy. Public goods analysis can allow for negative evaluations on the part of some of those who must, by definition, share in the quantities that are ultimately provided. In the public goods framework of analysis, however, the presence of negative evaluations on the change that is under consideration implies, at least indirectly, that compensations should be made, as necessary, to secure general agreement. This implication becomes explicit in the Wicksell–Lindahl variant of public goods analysis. By contrast, if the removal of restrictive devices, say a tariff, is discussed in the orthodox manner, the modern economist elevates his efficiency norm into a position of overriding significance, and tends to recommend repeal without mention of potential compensations. It is small wonder that his proposals tend to fare badly in the arena of practical politics. George Stigler has suggested that in these respects Adam Smith was little different from those who have followed him.[17] In Stigler's interpretation, Smith did not present either a positive or a normative theory of public choice, or governmental-political process. This interpretation of Smith has been challenged by E. G. West, who explains Smith's lack of attention to the more direct "politics of policy" by demonstrating his emphasis on constitutional structure, on the basic laws and institutions within which policy measures are taken.[18] West's interpretation is fully consistent with the broadened conception of "public good" attributed to Smith here.

---

17. Stigler argues that Smith did not fully develop a self-interest theory of the emergence and maintenance of governmental restrictions on markets. See George Stigler, "Smith's Travels on the Ship of State," *History of Political Economy*, 3 (Autumn 1971), 265–77; *Essays,* chapter xii.

18. E. G. West, "Adam Smith's Economics of Politics," *History of Political Economy* (forthcoming). Even at the most direct level, however, there is at least one case in which Smith seems to have been fully aware of the necessity to satisfy the self-interests of affected parties. See Smith's interesting letter to Dundas concerning free trade for Ireland, in which the possibilities of compensation to vested interests are indirectly raised. The letter is cited in full in John Rae, *Life of Adam Smith* (1895; New York: Augustus M. Kelley, 1965), 353–55. Letter 201, dated 1 November 1779.

Usury Laws and Market Rates of Interest

To this point, I have suggested that Adam Smith's applied welfare economics was informed by an understanding of the concepts of public goods and
externalities and that, although the order of policy priorities differed, his
agenda for policy action was not dramatically divergent from that of modern
economists. But it would indeed be surprising if the two-century gap, during
which intellectual paradigms have shifted and economic science has developed, produced no specific conflicts in the treatment of particular issues. We
can find one such conflict in Smith's treatment of interest. As we might expect, he was highly critical of legal prohibitions on the payment of interest.
But, surprisingly, Smith was unwilling to allow interest rates to find their
market equilibrium levels. In the markets for money, Smith lost his pervasive
faith in "natural liberty."

His argument warrants serious consideration, especially since it can be
translated into something akin to a modern externality analysis. Smith seemed
to lend support to legal ceilings of money rates of interest, provided that
these rates were set "somewhat above the lowest market price" (*WN* 339; II.
iv. 14), but not greatly above it. He suggested that rate ceilings below the lowest market price would have the same inhibiting effects on trade as outright
prohibitions of interest payments. But why did he support legal ceilings at
all, even if fixed just above the lowest market rates? He did so because, if rates
were allowed to go higher than this

> the greater part of the money ... would be lent to prodigals and projec-
> tors, who alone would be willing to give this high interest. Sober people,
> who will give for the use of money no more than a part of what they are
> likely to make by the use of it, would not venture into the competition. A
> great part of the capital of the country would thus be kept out of the hands
> which were most likely to make a profitable and advantageous use of it,
> and thrown into those which were most likely to waste and destroy it. (*WN*
> 339–40; II. iv. 15.)

If we translate this into modern jargon, Smith is saying that loans made
for productive investment generate external economies because of the effects
on capital formation and on economic growth. By contrast, loans made for
strictly consumption purposes exert no such spillover benefits. As the citation

indicates, Smith predicted that the high-risk *consumption*-loan demanders would be effectively rationed out of money markets. Implicitly, he assumed that high-risk investment loans were not important, an assumption that would surely be questioned in an age of rapid technological change. Even under his assumptions, however, in this instance, Smith may have revealed less sophistication about the pressures of market forces than usual. But, apart from the particulars of his proposal, the basic issue is worth discussion. Does investment generate external economies? Smith was, of course, writing decades before the advent of marginal productivity analysis, before the "wheel of exchange" in an economy was closed by the addition of factor pricing to product pricing. In a fully competitive world, owners of factors receive marginal productivities, including the owner of investment capital. In this pure model, there are spillover benefits from investment activity but these are not Pareto-relevant.[19] In the world that exists, or could exist, however, the rate of investment, and capital formation, that will emerge from private decisions depends on the institutions within which such decisions are made. And whereas there may be no Pareto-relevant external economy exerted by private decisions made at the margins of adjustment within a given institutional setting, the inframarginal changes in behaviour that might be produced by modifying the institutions themselves may well qualify under the Pareto-relevancy criterion. In the impure world where lives are finite, however, where bequests emerge even from rational life-cycle plans, and perhaps more importantly, where collectivities claim increasing shares in incomes generated, the inframarginal external economies from investment and capital formation must be acknowledged. These seem likely to become increasingly relevant for policy in a world now widely characterized as threatened by capital "shortage." Few modern economists would follow Smith in seeking to correct for these by the imposition of legal ceilings on interest rates, but the widespread introduction of subsidies to investment reflects the basic thrust of his argument.

---

19. For a discussion of the distinction between Pareto-relevant and Pareto-irrelevant externalities, see J. M. Buchanan and W. C. Stubblebine, "Externality," *Economica*, 29 (Nov. 1962), 371–84.

Productive and Unproductive Labour

Smith's somewhat confusing and often-criticized distinction between productive and unproductive labour can be interpreted in a manner similar to that applied to his defence of legal ceilings on interest rates. Productive labour is that which is applied to the replacement, or accumulation, of capital or stock, which includes the replacement of, or additions to, inventories of finished consumables. Although he did not specifically discuss it, we may presume that Smith would have also added the labour that goes into the production of human capital here. Unproductive labour is that which produces utility that vanishes upon the instant of its production, where the acts of production and consumption are simultaneous. The externality applies to the act of employing labour. The person who employs labour productively confers external benefits on others in society; the person who hires the menial servant does not. Hence, "every prodigal appears to be a public enemy, and every frugal man a public benefactor." (*WN* 324; II. iii. 25.)

Adam Smith did not, however, use the external economy of investment as a basis for collective interference with the natural liberty of individual choice, as he did in the case of the interest rate. For strictly private decisions, Smith expressed his willingness to allow persons to choose freely, presumably on the grounds that, on balance, the observed rate of capital accumulation was sufficiently high as to warrant a policy stance of inaction.[20] The context of his discussion leaves little doubt, however, but that in some set of circumstances different from that which characterized the Scotland and England of the eighteenth century, he might well have suggested either the subsidization of saving-investment or the penalization of consumption spending. Although he did not expressly examine the bases for taxation in his separate

---

20. It might also be possible to interpret Smith's aversion to abnormally high rates of profit in an externality setting, where, once again, he derived no inferences for policy interferences with natural liberty. While recognizing the allocative function of above-normal profits, Smith emphasized that very high profits tended to generate prodigality in behaviour, to "destroy parsimony." Although he does not apply an externality framework, Rosenberg stresses this aspect of Smith's discussion. See Nathan Rosenberg, "Some Institutional Aspects of the *Wealth of Nations*," *Journal of Political Economy*, 68 (Dec. 1960), 557–70; especially 558.

treatment of taxes, we may conclude from Smith's general argument that he would have looked with favour on proposals to levy general taxes on expenditures or consumption rather than on incomes.

Specific policy implications did emerge, however, from the alleged external economies involved in capital accumulation, even if these did not take the form of interferences with private decisions to save and to spend. These implications stem directly from Smith's admirable propensity to establish his policy priorities in the order of their observed importance, a propensity already noted. The concentration of outlay on unproductive labour was observed to lie in the public or governmental rather than in the private sector of the economy.

> Great nations are never impoverished by private, though they sometimes are by public prodigality and misconduct. The whole, or almost the whole public revenue, is in most countries employed in maintaining unproductive hands. Such are the people who compose a numerous and splendid court, a great ecclesiastical establishment, great fleets and armies, who in time of peace produce nothing, and in time of war acquire nothing that can compensate the expence of maintaining them, even while the war lasts. Such people, as they produce nothing, are all maintained by the produce of other men's labour. When multiplied, therefore, to an unnecessary number, they may in a particular year consume so great a share of this produce, as not to leave a sufficiency for maintaining the productive labourers, who should reproduce it next year. The next year's produce, therefore, will be less than that of the foregoing, and if the same disorder should continue, that of the third year will be less than the second. Those unproductive hands, who should be maintained by a part only of the spare revenue of the people, may consume so great a share of their whole revenue, and therefore oblige so great a number to encroach upon their capitals, upon the funds destined for the maintenance of productive labour, that all the frugality and good conduct of individuals may not be able to compensate the waste and degradation of produce occasioned by this violent and forced encroachment. (*WN* 325 f; II. iii. 30.)

The proclivities of those "who pretend to watch over the economy," who "are themselves always, and without exception, the greatest spendthrifts in the society" impose external costs on all remaining members. Smith strongly infers that check-reins must be placed on those extensions of the public sector beyond those limits which ensure that individuals' "uninterrupted effort to better their own condition" is "protected by law and allowed by liberty to exert itself in the manner that is most advantageous" (*WN* 329; II. iii. 36).

Modern economists may be justifiably critical of Adam Smith's apparent over-emphasis on the prodigality of government. He seemed to overlook the potential productivity of specific collective outlays, although elsewhere in his treatise he clearly allowed for public investment in what we now call "social overhead capital." He recognized the advantages of capital investment in roads, bridges, canals, and other similar projects. His concentrated references here to government profligacy apply to defence outlay, to the maintenance of the bureaucracy, and to the public provision of transfers.

In this age of massive bureaucracy, accompanied by apparently exploding rates of increases in government spending, it seems highly doubtful that a returned Adam Smith would greatly change his policy priorities, even upon a sophisticated understanding of modern public goods and externality analysis. Reluctantly, perhaps begrudgingly, he might acknowledge that the modern technology of war makes the maintenance of a large defence establishment essential. But can we really doubt but that his major animus would be directed toward the bloated budgets which seem to have got beyond the control of the bumbling politicians of our time? The modern economist may reject Smith's central notion that capital accumulation in a setting of natural liberty protected by law provides the key to economic development, or even that such development is, in itself, a desirable objective. What the modern economist cannot do, at least consistently, is to propose further interferences with natural liberty for the avowed purpose of stimulating capital investment while at the same time continuing to ignore the stifling effects of public sector expansion. As Gordon Tullock has remarked, government should take its foot off the brake before it hits the accelerator. Adam Smith would surely have agreed.

PART FIVE

Applications—City, Health, and Social Security

Public Goods and Public Bads

In any behaviorally relevant sense, "goods" and "bads" are reciprocal. Supplying a good eliminates a bad, and destroying a bad produces a good. Conversely, supplying a bad eliminates a good, and destroying a good produces a bad. Until and unless the evaluating and/or choosing agent is specified, however, goods and bads have little or no meaning. Who decides what is good or bad? And for whom? By whom is the choice to be made? In a world where scarcity cannot be ignored, choices must be faced which means, quite simply, that things which are goods for some persons may simultaneously be bads for others. In the particular context to be examined in this paper, behavior aimed at producing good for the individual, as a privately acting independent agent, may be bad for the same individual when he considers himself as a part of a defined collectivity, and vice versa. This elementary fact of life provides the starting point for almost any meaningful discussion of collective or group action, including that of individuals who organize themselves into political units.

The reciprocal relationship between goods and bads has been obscured in much of the modern discussion. A developing literature in a subdiscipline of economic theory concerns itself with "public goods," while the words "public bad" scarcely appear at all. The approach which has become standard emphasizes the failure of voluntary individual behavior in organized markets to produce public goods, more correctly described by the term "collective-consumption goods." The failure to supply such goods in efficient or optimal quantities is, of course, equivalent to a failure to eliminate existing public

From *Financing the Metropolis: Public Policy in Urban Economies,* vol. 4, ed. John P. Crecine (New York: Sage Publications, 1970), 51–71. Copyright 1970 by Sage Publications, Inc. Reprinted by permission of the publisher, Sage Publications, Inc.

bads in efficient quantities, but the mere change in wording may have explanatory significance. More importantly, by indirection the standard approach has concentrated almost exclusively on a presumed once-and-for-all institutional change, the shift of activity from the market to the governmental sector. Almost no attention has been given to the problem of preventing the *erosion* of public goods once these are supplied, an erosion that is generated by the individual behavior of persons producing public bads. A redirection of emphasis is a central objective of this paper. In the development of the argument, many of the problems that are confronted continuously by modern municipal governments will be recognized. It seems clear, for example, that progressive urbanization and economic development reduce the need for collective or governmental financing of public goods in the more traditional context while, at the same time, these increase, often dramatically, the need for collective or governmental action designed to eliminate multiplying public bads. A shorthand, if somewhat inaccurate, way of stating this is to say that municipalities could probably become and remain viable if existing public bads could be eliminated, even if no additional public goods of the standard sort should be provided. In practical policy application, this implies that relatively less emphasis be placed on the financing problem and relatively more emphasis be placed on the problems of enacting and enforcing effective rules for personal and institutional behavior.

Private Goods and Public Goods

Bernard Mandeville, in his famous poem, *Fable of the Bees,* was one of the first social philosophers to demonstrate that the results emerging from the interaction of many persons need not be those intended or planned by any one person or group of persons. Under some situations, he argued, qualities of private individual behavior that might seem vicious or self-seeking may be precisely those required to produce desirable social results when persons interact in a complex environment. Adam Smith, in his *Wealth of Nations,* further developed and elaborated this essential vision, which allows us to predict the emergent results of an interaction process independent of the specific overall plans or objectives of the individual participants. To Smith, social or collective welfare is generated, not by the benevolence of the butcher but out of his regard for his own self-interest in supplying meat for sale. Indeed Smith's genius, and his legitimate claim to be the founder of scientific economic theory, lies precisely in his convincing demonstration that the self-interested, independent behavior of individuals in a competitive market process produces socially desired results. "Socially desired" in this sense is defined strictly in terms of the mutually attainable benefits for all members of the community.

Public good is, therefore, produced by the workings of the competitive market process. Aggregate values, derived from individual choices, are generated and distributed in such a way that all participants secure gains. The predominant share of national produce, even in the mixed economies of the West in the 1970s, is made up of values derived from the production of goods and services through the market, through the so-called private sector. These values are public or social, and the increase in the value of national product and in its rate of growth through time are widely shared objectives for economic policy. These values derived from the market are not, however, those to which the specific term "public good" is normally applied in the postwar discussion. This term, in its current technical and professionally used sense, tends to be reserved for those goods and services that are financed and provided through the governmental-political process, through the so-called public sector. The subdiscipline of economic theory that is now sometimes called the modern theory of public goods is largely devoted to an analysis of why governmental provision of these goods and services may be required, and of how such provision should and does take place.

Private Goods and Public Bads

If we take an economic approach to an analysis of individual behavior, we assume that all persons act so as to maximize utility, whether they act as participants in a market or in a nonmarket setting. In attempting to maximize utility, an individual is, of course, trying to achieve those goods that he values most highly. Indeed, this is merely another way of stating the same thing. The distinguishing feature of the market process is that individuals are allowed, independently and privately, to seek their own private goods, without direct and explicit consideration of the effects of their behavior on other persons in the community. This is the same as saying that in the market process individuals act independently rather than collectively. Decisions are made privately, by the acting individual alone, and he is not required to seek the agreement of anyone other than his partner in the two-way trading that characterizes the market. As suggested above, such utility-maximizing behavior on the part of many persons produces an efficient allocation of economic resources and a maximally valued bundle of goods and services, provided that several important side conditions are either fully satisfied or approximated. Among these conditions, and the only one that is relevant for this paper, must be the *divisibility* of goods and services among separate persons. When it is efficient to share goods and services among several or many persons, the need for cooperative or group action arises. Under some conditions, efficient sharing arrangements may be worked out through an extension of the market process without difficulty (for example, when the sharing groups are relatively small, or when the costs of excluding users are negligible). Under other conditions, however, efficient sharing arrangements may require cooperative or group action organized through the governmental-political process.

When divisibility of goods and services among potential users is not present, and when extended market arrangements are not efficient, the independent or private utility-maximizing behavior of individuals in the market, the pursuit of private goods, yields aggregate results that may be relatively undesirable to all members of the group. The pursuit of private goods may produce public bads in the evaluation of all persons. An inherent conflict emerges between private, utility-maximizing behavior on the part of individuals and the overall results that these same individuals would desire to see achieved. That is to say, individuals may value the results of their private independent behavior, when viewed in an aggregative sense, less than they would value the results of some alternative overall arrangement. When conflict of this sort arises, the competitive market process, by definition, does not produce a maximally valued bundle of goods and services. Care must be taken in all such discussions as this, however, to insure that public or social valuation refers only to that which is derived from individual utility functions. There is no collectivity that exists apart from the individuals, at least in the economist's standard model. Hence, by referring to a conflict between the pursuit of private goods and the achievement of public bads, we mean only that the individuals themselves may be behaving in an institutional framework that produces outcomes that they do not themselves value so highly as possible alternatives. They may be locked in a many-person analogue to the familiar prisoners' dilemma of modern game theory.

The phenomenon has long been recognized and, of course, it has been discussed in many forms. It provides the basis for the contract theory of the state as well as for the modern theory of the public sector. As Hobbes told us long ago, in an anarchic society the life of man is "nasty, brutish, and short." From this, he derived his central argument concerning the need for a voluntary relinquishment of power to a sovereign governmental authority.

The phenomenon is omnipresent in the conurbations of the world in 1970. Traffic, smog, water pollution, urban blight—these are only a few of its familiar manifestations. In each of these familiar examples and in many more (all of which we may summarize under the common rubric "congestion"), the aggregate results of the behavior of many persons who act privately and independently—each one seeking to maximize his own utility given the environmental constraints that he faces, each seeking to secure his own private goods—may be less desirable potentially to all members of the community than alternative institutional arrangements. The untrammelled pursuit of private goods may generate public bads.

A simple nonurban example will be helpful, one that retains considerable relevance in many underdeveloped areas of the world. Assume that separate owners of cattle share grazing rights to common territory. Land is commonly owned, and all cattle owners have grazing rights. In this situation, each cattle owner may have a private incentive to overgraze the common land. Each cattle owner, acting in his own interest, may find it advantageous to behave in such a fashion that all owners are in a worse position than they might be under other forms of behavior or under other institutional arrangements. In economic terms, the result of private utility-maximizing behavior is nonoptimal in the Pareto sense.

General recognition of the inherent conflict between the pursuit of private goods and the generation of public bads has led to many proposals for change designed to eliminate or to surmount the problem. These may be separately discussed.

Proposals for Behavioral Changes

Although economists have only rarely discussed the problem in such terms, the way toward elimination of the conflict that perhaps first comes to mind lies in some modification of the private behavior of individuals. The goods that enter as arguments in individuals' preferences or utility functions are not chosen from on high, and different individuals surely value different sets of goods. If utility functions could be so modified that persons would be led to treat as private goods only those activities that would result in an absence of the conflict, no further action would be required. The conflict between the pursuit of private goods and the generation of public bads simply would not emerge.

Various ethical systems and principles can be interpreted as attempts to formulate behavioral solutions to the problem here. Christian ethics, with its emphasis on love as a guiding principle of human behavior, may be interpreted as an effort in this direction, one that probably must be judged as ultimately unsatisfactory. More germane to the particular problem (because it is less specific) is the system of Kantian ethics. Kant attempted to formulate a fundamental principle for personal human behavior that would eliminate the conflict. His generalization principle, sometimes called the categorical imperative, provides a proposed solution. If, in fact, each person could be induced to act in such a manner that his behavior, if generalized to all members of the community, would produce results that he desires, the pursuit of private good would guarantee the simultaneous provision of public good. Almost by definition, in a purely Kantian world, public bads could not be observed.

At a considerably less sophisticated level, political scientists have often proposed reforms in this same spirit through their emphasis on the political obligation. Upon this principle political leaders are held to be obliged to behave in such a way as to promote the public interest as opposed to their own private interest.

Proposals for Institutional-Organizational Changes

A second approach toward elimination of the conflict is one associated with Adam Smith and the classical economists generally, although its origins extend back to Aristotle's defense of private property. Here an attempt is made to modify the structure of property rights so as to reproduce the harmony between the pursuit of private goods and the generation of overall public good as a result, the potential harmony that Mandeville and Smith both stressed. The simple example noted above can illustrate the approach. An institutional reform that would surely eliminate the overgrazing on the land is the granting of private ownership rights to land, to convert commonly owned property into private property. Once this step is taken, the private owners of the land have an incentive to restrict the usage of the scarce resource to socially optimal levels. Land will be used efficiently; total social product will tend to be maximized by the private utility-maximizing behavior of individuals.

The differences between the behavioral and the institutional approaches to eliminating the problem of conflict should be noted. The first concentrates on modifying the behavior of private individuals in such a way as to make them more conscious of the social or public good. The second accepts the utility functions of individuals more or less as given and attempts to modify institutional arrangements so as to produce the natural harmony that can emerge. In either or both of these approaches, the result, if achieved, is the best of all possible worlds. In either case, the world is transformed so that the pursuit of private goods generates public goods.

Proposals for Specific Collective Action

A third approach comes into play only in those situations where neither of the first two approaches is considered to be practicable. Even under the most plausible assumptions about behavior, and even under an ideal set of private property arrangements, there may still remain inherent indivisibilities such that the conflict between private good and public good will emerge. In such cases, public bads may be observed. It may, for example, be difficult to think either of human behavior being sufficiently reformed or of property rights being so defined as to eliminate such a conflict in the usage of "atmosphere" (generally described). To an extent that economists perhaps do not sufficiently recognize, however, both of the first two approaches are significantly productive of social harmony in any civilized society. Respect for the needs and desires of others surely is a strong motive in individual behavior patterns, and unless this be indeed present to a major degree it is difficult to even imagine how civil life could proceed at all. Also, the traditional arrangements for private property rights allow many potential areas of the conflict to be dissolved without notice. The important areas of disharmony arise only where traditional standards of behavior along with traditional and long-accepted property rights structures allow evident public bads to emerge. Hence, proposals for the production-supply of public goods (the destruction of public bads) arise, proposals that incorporate explicit action on the part of the community acting as a collectivity. This action may take several forms; these will be discussed subsequently. At this point, one first clarifying step must be taken in the argument. The failure of private, independent behavior to produce socially desired results can arise equally from action or inaction. Analytically, these are equivalent. If individuals do not provide, say, an efficient quantity of internal defense through their private utility-maximizing behavior, they create a public bad in precisely the same manner that they do when their private, independent behavior fouls the air with smog. Modern developments in the theory of public goods have concentrated too much on the failure of individuals to act positively in financing or supplying common consumption goods and services, and too little on the excessive negative action of individuals in generating or producing public bads. This analytical bias has been present despite the fact that any given situation can be treated in strictly reciprocal terms. For example, consider once again the overgrazing of common lands. This can be examined as a situation where independent private behavior generates a public bad. Or, conversely, it can be looked at as embodying a failure to create a public good, in this case defined as the effective policing of the usage of the common property. Concentration on the strictly reciprocal nature of all collective-consumption relationships is helpful in clarifying several ambiguities in the analysis.

Implicit Ownership under Collective Action

In a celebrated paper, R. H. Coase demonstrated that under a regime of private ownership and effectively working markets the precise structure of ownership rights need not affect the final allocation of economic resources.[1] So

1. R. H. Coase, "The Problem of Social Cost," *Journal of Law and Economics* 3 (October 1960): 1–44.

long as separate private owners are allowed freely to negotiate trades, one with another, under conditions where transaction costs, as such, are not significant, we should predict that roughly the same allocative results will emerge under any initial assignment of ownership rights. Coase's example was that of two adjacent farms, one of which raised cattle, the other of which raised wheat. The interaction arises because of the likelihood that the cattle will stray and trample the wheat crop. Coase's central point was one of demonstrating that roughly the same allocative outcome emerges regardless of the legal assignment of liability for damages. For economic resource allocation, the assignment of property rights tends, in this model, to be irrelevant.

We may, by analogy if not directly, extend this analysis to what we may call the implicit ownership rights to common facilities and to collective or governmental action generally. Let us assume that all structural changes in property rights which might remove the conflict between the pursuit of private goods and the public good have been made, and that individual behavior is taken as given. Explicit collective or governmental action is indicated. This, in itself, tells us nothing about the starting point, the position from which collective action commences, the structure of the status quo. With the existence of legal titles to private property, the definition of the status quo in terms of rights to exclude others from the usage of defined physical assets is usually not difficult. When we come to discuss common facilities, or those which are potentially common, mere definition of the status quo becomes difficult. There must exist an implicit structure of rights to use commonly shared facilities, but this structure may take several forms.

Who owns the common property? To answer this by saying, "the whole community," becomes operationally meaningless until and unless we specify precisely the rights of individuals to use the property held in common ownership. These rights of action with respect to commonly owned facilities and services define an implicit pattern of ownership, and it is from this pattern that collective action aimed at changing the results must start. Such rights may not, of course, be described specifically in statutes; they may be traditional rights based on the evolution of historical experience. Understanding this structure may, nonetheless, be highly relevant in any discussion of explicit collective action. The reciprocal nature of public goods and public bads can clarify some of the issues here in terms of a familiar municipal example, smog.

There are two implicit ownership extremes, two polar cases. The first is that which has, until quite recently, prevailed in most urban centers, or indeed everywhere else. All persons may possess rights to use the commonly shared resource, air, with no restrictions at all on this usage. At the other extreme, we might think of an implicit ownership pattern in which individuals' rights to use the common resource are severely restricted by outright legal prohibition. This solution seems to be that which is proposed by many of the advocates of pollution control, e.g., Ralph Nader. In this polar extreme, individuals might simply be prevented, by law, from discharging pollutants into the atmosphere.

In the first pattern of rights to usage of the commonly shared resource, we refer to the generation of a public bad in the absence of specific collective action. In the second pattern of rights, we might perhaps be tempted to refer, at least initially, to a public good as the resultant outcome. Surely, it may be argued, since clean air is a good, valued by all members of the community, and since it is commonly available to all, this is a reasonable usage of terms. The emotive strength of this rather simple extension of the standard analysis lends great strength to antipollution campaigns. However, what is overlooked in this facile extension is the necessary presence of private bads in the extreme no-pollution pattern of rights. Individuals are, or may be, prohibited from behaving in ways that they, independently and voluntarily, value more highly than that which the collectively imposed antipollution rules require. The private goods–public bads conflict has merely been replaced by the private bads–public goods conflict. Since individuals place values on both the goods and services through ordinary market processes, the so-called private goods, and on the goods and services generated, directly or indirectly, through the political process, the so-called public goods, it should be clear that the overall public good or social interest, in its more general sense, must involve some balancing off of these two sets of values. If we are limited to a comparison of the two extreme patterns of rights to usage, no restrictions on usage on the one hand and strictly controlled usage on the other, there is simply no a priori means of determining which of the two is the most productive of economic efficiency. In terms of the values that individuals place on results, the smog-laden result of uncontrolled private behavior may well be preferable to that result which would emerge should Ralph Nader be allowed to impose antipollution controls.

The two extreme patterns discussed here are analogous to the different assignments of liability in the Coase problem. In the latter, liability may be assigned to the cattle raiser on the one hand or to the wheat grower on the other. *If no trades were allowed to take place between these two parties, the allocation of resources would be different under the two ownership patterns, and there would be no way of determining,* in the absence of such trade, *which of the two patterns would be most efficient. If,* however, *trade is allowed to take place,* roughly the same results will emerge under either assignment of liability. And, importantly, it seems evident that *the results would not normally be expected to be equivalent to those that would emerge* in either assignment *under the no-trade possibility.*

Geometrical illustration

The analysis can be illustrated easily in a simple diagram. In Figure 1, at the left-hand origin we place completely uncontrolled usage of the air. At the right-hand origin we place strictly controlled usage, with outright prohibition on any discharge of pollutants. Along the abscissa between these limits we measure either air purity or impurity, depending on the starting point and direction of measurement. Along the ordinate we measure values in dollar terms.

In the polluted or smog situation, let us say that the whole collectivity of persons places some positive value on the good or activity that we may call depollution. The aggregate *marginal evaluation* curve is shown by ΣMC. This curve is derived by vertically summing the marginal *evaluation* curves of all

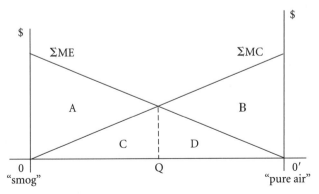

Figure 1. Private goods–public bads balanced against private bads–public goods

persons in the collectivity. In the polluted or smoggy extreme, some measures could be taken which might reduce pollution levels significantly without great cost. This cost could be expected to increase as depollution is extended. The *marginal cost* of cleaning up the air is shown by the rising curve ΣMC in Figure 1. As the diagram is drawn, the most efficient or optimal level of depollution (or pollution) is that shown at Q, where the marginal evaluation placed on depollution, summed over all persons in the group, equals the marginal costs of the same activity, also summed over all persons as required. If we start from the full pollution position, from 0, the net social gain secured from production of the public good (from reducing the public bad) in the quantity 0Q is represented by the triangular area A. Individuals, in their capacities as collective consumers of air, place a value of A plus C on the depollution activity. However, these same individuals, in their capacities as consumers of other goods and services, place a cost of C on the activity. The net gain is limited to A.

If we ignore the feedback effects that may result from different schemes for sharing the net gains,[2] it is relatively easy to see that the same solution emerges if we assume that collective activity commences at the other polar extreme. This equivalence in solution here is the precise analogue to that developed by Coase in his private property–market structure problem. The great difference between the two models is, of course, that the efficient solution emerges in the Coase model from the interaction of traders. In the collective-action model, by contrast, the efficient solution, regardless of the implicit rights structure assumed as the starting point, must be reached through some collective decision-making process. Suppose that at the outset no person is allowed to discharge pollutants into the air. We commence at the right-hand extreme. As drawn on Figure 1, this situation is inefficient; the air is too pure, as determined by individuals' evaluations. The marginal evaluation of additional cleanliness is below marginal cost, or, reciprocally, the marginal evaluation of dirtiness is greater than the marginal cost. As we move leftward from the right-hand ordinate in Figure 1, the analysis is fully

2. These individual marginal evaluation curves, and hence their summation, will not be uniquely determinate until and unless a cost-sharing scheme among individuals is specified or unless income-effect feedbacks are assumed to be absent. This complexity must be recognized, but it need not eliminate the usefulness of the geometrical illustration. For purposes of simplicity, assume that income effects are absent.

symmetrical with the rightward movement previously traced. The ΣMC curve can now be treated as a ΣME curve for the creation of the public bad, whereas the ΣME curve can be treated as the ΣMC curve for the same activity. Once again, moving leftward, the efficient or optimal position is attained at Q, or when an amount 0'Q of the public bad—in this case, air pollution—is produced.

This somewhat unusual manner of looking at the familiar pollution problem prompts the question: Why should individuals place any positive value on the production of a demonstrably public bad? The answer here is that they do so because such production must involve the complementing production of a private good which may outweigh the costs of the public bad as evaluated by the same persons. The inherent conflict between the achievement of public good and the independent utility-maximizing pursuit by individuals of their own private goods is not eliminated at any position along the left-right spectrum of Figure 1. So long as the conflict exists, what is required for efficiency is not the total elimination of public bads (total satiation of demand for public goods), but, instead, a proper balancing off, *at the margin*, between public and private values. It must be kept in mind that in either case the values are those of the individual members of the community and of no external agent. This indicates that the optimal solution is achieved only at Q. If the collective action commences from the rights structure described by the right-hand origin, a net gain from pollution is secured as measured by the triangular area B. The gross gains from pollution are measured by B plus D, but D is the cost that must be subtracted to get the net surplus generated.

A SCHEMATIC MATRIX REPRESENTATION

The geometrical presentation makes clear that efficiency is secured only when collective action incorporates the inherent conflict between private goods and public goods. This is implicit in the standard norms for public goods efficiency, but the reciprocal nature of the problem has tended to be obscured because of the implicit assumption that costs are technologically defined and hence objectively measurable. The standard treatment involves the statement of the necessary conditions for optimality, the equation of summed marginal evaluation with marginal cost. This locates the efficient position, but it *tends to imply,* even if indirectly, *that the conflict is somehow resolved once a financial outlay is made. This causes a major problem in the provision and supply of public facilities and services to be neglected, namely the usage of a publicly provided facility or service once it is financed and constructed.* The erosion of existing and potential public services and facilities has hardly been discussed. In terms of a familiar example, the standard treatment proceeds as if a once-and-for-all installation of smog prevention devices will resolve the problem of pollution.

The importance of recognizing the continuing nature of the inherent conflict can be represented in a simple matrix scheme. In the two-by-two matrix of Figure 2 we place the alternatives for individual, independent behavior in the two rows. The individual, considered here to be a representative for the group, may behave in only two ways. He may act so as to maximize utility, given the constraints that he confronts, that is, he may seek his own private goods. Or, by contrast, he may behave so as not to maximize his own utility. To the economist, this would be irrational behavior if it were voluntary, but constraints may be externally imposed on the individual by the collectivity. In the columns of the matrix of Figure 2, we place the alternative

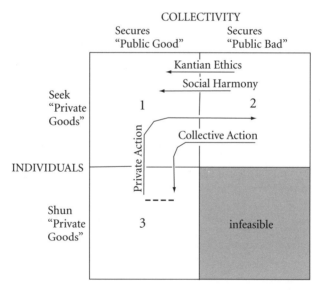

Figure 2. Results of strategies for shifting balance between private and public "goods" and "bads"

results for the collectivity of individuals, as evaluated by a representative individual in the group. These can be either good or bad, as evaluated by the individuals themselves.

The matrix can perhaps be best understood by looking first at the cell numbered 1. This cell is the best of all possible worlds. Through individual behavior aimed at maximizing individual utilities, at seeking private goods, an overall social result is generated that individuals optimally prefer. Public good is secured. The classical economists demonstrated that the working of competitive markets tends to produce results in this cell. In the cell numbered 2, individuals are behaving so as to maximize their own utilities, but the aggregate result is one they do not prefer. Public bad results from the pursuit of private good. This is, of course, the position that we have been discussing in this paper.

Consider, now, the various avenues for reform when this conflict is recognized. First, we mentioned the system of Kantian ethics. The emphasis is on modifying individuals' preferences, or more precisely, the arguments in individuals' utility functions so that individuals will behave differently. The attempt here is to make individuals seek as their own good only those activities that produce outcomes within the first cell of the matrix. Under universal adherence to a carefully defined generalization in principle, final positions in cell 2 are not possible. Second, the institutional-organizational reforms associated with Smith and the classical economists concentrate on modifying the structure of private property rights so as to make positions in cell 1 attainable as replacements for those apparently achieved in cell 2 under less efficient property structures. As suggested earlier, to the extent that either or both of these reform approaches can work, the shift to cell 1 is accomplished.

However, with the explicit collective action designed to produce public goods, or to eliminate public bads, no such shift is possible. If individual behavior does not simultaneously change, and if property arrangements are stable, the elimination of public bad, the shift from cell 2, must necessarily result in a position in cell 3, not cell 1. Conversely, if individuals find themselves for any reason in cell 3, they will have a private incentive to try to shift to cell 1. An individual succeeds in this, however, only to the extent that others do not behave similarly. As more and more persons try to move from cell 3 to cell 1, they will find themselves actually moving to cell 2. There is simply no way that a position in cell 1 can be attained by all participants unless the conflict is eliminated through one of the first two avenues of reform, the ethical or the institutional.

The predominant emphasis in the modern theory of the public sector has been on the demonstration that individuals acting voluntarily through markets will not escape the dilemma position of cell 2. Hence, the argument is made for collective action, for the levy of compulsory taxation to finance publicly supplied goods as a means of overcoming the failures of voluntary market processes. This emphasis is, of course, important and, within its limits, fully appropriate. Where the modern theory of the public sector has been remiss is in its failure to follow up the analysis, and to stress the private incentives for individuals to escape from cell 3. Instead of a successful shift to cell 1, which may have been implied in some of the more naïve presentations, the resultant position in cell 3 should have been more fully recognized. Once this is done, the problem of public goods erosion will have emerged as a natural extension of the analysis. Individuals finding themselves in cell 3 have precisely the same incentives for allowing a public facility or service to erode, to run down, to be destroyed, as they do for failure to provide the goods or services in efficient quantities when they find themselves in cell 2. The failure of individuals, through voluntary channels, to shift from cell 2 is no different from the positive action of individuals in shifting from cell 3. The argument for the levy of compulsory taxes is on all fours with the argument for the imposition of compulsory rules concerning the usage of publicly provided facilities, goods, and services.

The argument of this section may be summarized by reference to the arrows on the matrix diagram in Figure 2. If some Kantian ethics principle is effective, the shift may be made from cell 2 to cell 1, as indicated by the labeled arrow. Similarly, if rearrangements in property rights can convert potential conflict into social harmony, a shift from cell 2 to cell 1 may move along the parallel arrow. If neither of these approaches can be effective, collective action to finance-provide public goods may be undertaken in an attempt to move along the arrow marked "collective action." However, it is impossible to shift from cell 2 and to remain, as might be desired, in cell 1. Inexorably, the process winds up in cell 3. Once in cell 3, however, individuals will necessarily attempt—when and where possible—to move to cell 1 along the arrow indicated by "private action." If and as they succeed, however, and as others adopt similar patterns of behavior, instead of finding themselves in cell 1, as optimally desired by all, they wind up in cell 2.[3]

Municipal Examples

The argument developed here has important applications for many municipal governments. Examples where erosion can take place are familiar. The mere financing and construction of a municipal park is only a first step in guaranteeing that individuals will, in fact, be able to enjoy the services of the park through time. If the collectivity stops short at adequate provision and maintenance of the facility, and if it does not impose and effectively enforce rules on individual usage, erosion will rapidly convert the public good into a public bad. Experience in the financing and provision of housing by govern-

3. Critical readers may raise questions at this point concerning the reasons why changes in property rights are indicated as successfully accomplishing a shift from cell 2 to cell 1, whereas the provision of collective goods or facilities embodies a necessary shift to cell 3. Under any set of private property rights, it may be urged, individuals must adhere to general standards, whether legally or ethically imposed, of respect for the rights of others. In one sense, therefore, they remain in cell 3. If they can secure gains from violation of private property rights (if they have an opportunity to steal), they will do so under strictly defined utility maximization. Why, it may be asked, is the overt violation of private property rights treated differently in this whole discussion than the failure of individuals to preserve public properties?

These are complex issues that have not been sufficiently discussed. To the extent that individuals do not respect the private property rights of others, all property becomes common property when defined behaviorally. When we refer to institutional-organizational changes designed to shift from cell 2 to cell 1, changes in the structure of private ownership rights, we must assume implicitly that these will be accompanied by general acceptance of the new structure in the behavioral standards of persons. It would, of course, do little or no good to modify the property rights structure if individuals refuse to acknowledge it. In this situation, the change in property rights, as a means of moving from cell 2, would generate a situation in cell 3, just as is the case with collectively provided goods and services. Conversely, if the provision of collective goods and services should be accompanied by a shift in behavioral standards that would secure the maintenance and preservation of these, a situation in cell 1 would be achieved. The analysis of the paper, therefore, assumes that the mere financing and provision of goods, services, and facilities collectively or governmentally will not be accompanied by any change in behavioral standards, whereas it is assumed that private property rights, old and new, will be respected. These assumptions seem to be descriptive behaviorally, although, of course, they should be tested empirically.

mental units lends empirical support to the argument here. The investment of capital in slum clearance may lead to very limited long-range improvement value to the community unless the rate of erosion or deterioration is modified. Even more familiar, and empirically observable by everyone, are the effects of the construction of urban freeways. Individual users simply expand traffic volumes to generate additional congestion, producing grossly inefficient usage of the facilities. Traffic congestion can be interpreted in our terms as an erosion of scarce highway-street facilities. Air and water pollution have already been discussed.

A less familiar, but increasingly urgent, example is the erosion and disruption of educational facilities and processes, from lower schools to higher. Vandalism and destruction of physical facilities, violent disruption of traditional classroom instruction, unlawful invasion of public property, and terroristic threats followed by acts against personnel have become characteristics of education in the late 1960s. The argument sketched above concerning the erosion of publicly supplied facilities and services does not fully explain the actions of the terrorists and the lawbreakers, but it does explain the failure of the non-violent and lawful users to defend their common property. Individually and privately, they have no incentive to organize themselves in defense against the militants. This remains true although one and all may recognize that the situation, without effective defense, becomes progressively worse through time.

In all of these cases, and in many others that could be added, individuals behave as the economist predicts. They act so as to maximize their own utility in all of their choices, private and public. The net effect is that publicly or collectively supplied facilities will tend to erode so long as (1) this is technologically possible, and (2) overt constraints against eroding behavior are not embodied in a structure of legally binding rules about usage. It is important to recognize that a behavior pattern equivalent to the "free rider" dilemma is present here. The user of a publicly supplied, commonly used facility or service has no privately valued incentive to protect and preserve the facility or service from deterioration, or at least this incentive tends to be grossly undervalued. The conservation of publicly supplied facilities may require the coercive implementation of rules on usage, and all members of the group, at least conceptually, may approve the adoption of such rules.

Public Financing and Public Order

Cities need financial resources; nothing in this paper is intended to reject this fundamental proposition. Collective-consumption goods must be provided, and the effective range of indivisibility for many of these is limited to the boundaries of single metropolitan units. But all will not be well with mere financing, and the implication that cities could become utopian if only there were (federal) taxpayers willing to provide the billions needed had best be quickly forgotten. The man from Mars who looks at some of the blossoming literature on the urban crisis would surely think that such utopias could sprout everywhere if our cities could only escape their financial straitjackets.

My central objective in this paper has been to show that an alternative and necessarily complementary approach to urban improvement requires more attention, research, and application. In terms of economic value received, the current yield at the margin is surely greater from enforcing more-effective usage of facilities than in enlarging the quantities of the facilities themselves. It should also be noted that the continuing process of expanding public financing and provision, without the accompanying imposition of effective rules concerning use and/or abuse, creates a continuously mounting problem of maintenance. Is it not predictable that many of the ills of the modern city arise precisely because of the shift from private to public property? If this is accepted, the suggested avenue for reform need not be a return to private ownership, although this may, in certain instances, be efficient. The argument of this paper is that an effective avenue for reform may be the enactment and enforcement of stricter rules, preventing the erosion of public goods and services. Public schools require public order; public parks require public policing of usage. The modern theory of public goods demonstrates why it is necessary that the single taxpayer be compelled to pay his taxes. *The theory's extension developed in this paper demonstrates why it is also and equally necessary that the single user of any public good, public service, or public facility be compelled to behave in a manner that will insure that the good, service, or facility so supplied shall be maintained.* The conservation of private property can normally be left to the workings of the market process. The conservation of public property requires explicit public policy.

REFERENCES

Arrow, K. J. *Social Choice and Individual Values.* New York: John Wiley, 1963.

Baumol, W. J. *Welfare Economics and the Theory of the State.* Cambridge: Harvard University Press, 1965.

Black, D. *The Theory of Committees and Elections.* Cambridge: Cambridge University Press, 1958.

Bowen, H. *Toward Social Economy.* New York: Holt, Rinehart & Winston, 1948.

Buchanan, J. M. *Demand and Supply of Public Goods.* Chicago: Rand McNally, 1968.

———. *Public Finance in Democratic Process.* Chapel Hill: University of North Carolina Press, 1967.

Buchanan, J. M., and G. Tullock. *The Calculus of Consent.* Ann Arbor: University of Michigan Press, 1962.

Coase, R. H. "The Problem of Social Cost." *Journal of Law and Economics* 3 (October 1960): 1–44.

Musgrave, R. A. *The Theory of Public Finance.* New York: McGraw-Hill, 1959.

Olson, M. *The Logic of Collective Action.* Cambridge: Harvard University Press, 1965.

Samuelson, P. A. "Diagrammatic Exposition of a Theory of Public Expenditure." *Review of Economics and Statistics,* 37 (November 1955): 350–56.

———. "The Pure Theory of Public Expenditure." *Review of Economics and Statistics* 36 (November 1954): 387–89.

Principles of Urban Fiscal Strategy

I. Introduction

The fiscal incapacity of central cities is a characteristic feature in almost all discussions of urban ills. The demands for expanded public outlays have increased and will continue to increase relative to past and anticipated increases in taxable capacities. Both sides of the urban fiscal account have been adversely affected by the flight of persons and firms to the independently organized suburbs. With this as diagnosis, there seem to be only two directions for reform. The first is the provision of financial relief from external sources, presumably in the form of federal grants. The second involves a widening of the local fiscal base, presumably through the consolidation of central city and suburban governmental units.

In this paper I shall not examine either the prospects for or the consequences of expanded external financial support, whether from the federal government or from the states. Nor shall I discuss specifically the problems or the effects of incorporation and annexation of suburbs. Indeed one implication of the analysis is that attempts to resolve the fiscal plight of cities in this way may be unsuccessful. If the city widens its fiscal base without recognizing the strategic aspects of the fiscal problems that it faces, the result may be more rather than less inefficiency in economic and fiscal locational patterns.

I shall show how a city governmental unit may prevent its fiscal dilemma

From *Public Choice* 11 (Fall 1971): 1–16. Reprinted by permission of the publisher, Kluwer Academic Publishers.

The research in preparation of this paper was supported in part from a Ford Foundation grant on fiscal incentives for rural-urban migration.

from arising in the first place. I introduce the term "strategy" deliberately in its game-theoretic meaning. The decision-makers for the cities must recognize the effects of their own fiscal actions on the behavior of taxpaying and benefits-receiving citizens. Fiscal decisions must be made strategically rather than reactively. Translated into practical policy terms this means that potentially mobile central-city taxpayers who contribute to net fiscal surplus must be deliberately induced to remain in the sharing community by appropriate fiscal adjustments. This simple principle has long been recognized by politicians and by community leaders. It has not, to my knowledge, been explained or interpreted analytically. An essential step in the process is the discarding of familiar cliches concerning the application of standard equity norms.

The analysis is presented in three abstract and highly simplified models. In Section II, we examine a model that compares private (market) and public (collective) organization for the provision of a good or service that embodies no net efficiencies of joint or shared consumption. In one sense, this is the polar case of the purely "private" good, although the model has wider practical applicability. This serves as an introduction to the more complex models of subsequent sections. In Section III, the opposing polar extreme is analyzed: the good or service that embodies complete or total consumption jointness. In one definitional sense, this is the familiar purely "public" or "collective-consumption" good. Section IV expands the comparative analysis by introducing the more realistic set of goods and services that exhibit some net gains from joint consumption but where such gains are not total. Section V explicitly discusses principles for urban fiscal strategy, and summary conclusions are drawn in Section VI.

II. Municipal Provision of Private Goods

I shall use a geometrical construction that was introduced in an earlier paper,[1] and which was itself an extension of a model previously employed by Gordon Tullock and Yorum Barzel.[2] Consider a three-person community. In

---

1. "Notes for an Economic Theory of Socialism," *Public Choice*, 8 (Spring 1970), 29–44.

2. Gordon Tullock, "Social Cost and Governmental Action," *American Economic Review*, 59 (May 1969), 189–97; also, *Private Wants—Public Means* (New York: Basic Books,

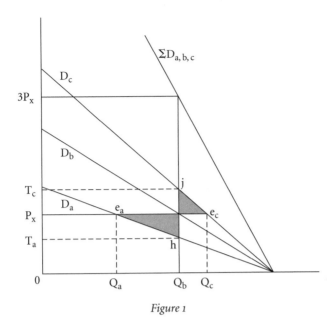

Figure 1

Figure 1, the curves D_a, D_b, and D_c are the demand schedules for the three persons, A, B, and C, for the single good X. If this good is supplied and purchased through ordinary market arrangements, each consumer faces a price, P_x, which, we assume, is equal to marginal cost and constant over quantity. The three persons would be observed to purchase and consume the quantities Q_a, Q_b, and Q_c per period.

Instead of market provision, let us now assume that the provision of the good is organized collectively by the three-person community. The essential feature of collectivist or socialist provision is *equality* in consumption shares. In the community here, each of the three persons must now be provided with access to the *same* quantity of final consumption units. The precise quantity chosen will, of course, depend on the rules for reaching group choices, the political constitution. For purposes of analytical simplicity, we

1970); Yoram Barzel, "Two Propositions on the Optimum Level of Producing Collective Goods," *Public Choice*, 6 (Spring 1969), 31–38.

assume that a simple majority voting rule prevails. Under this rule, the preferences of the median voter will be dominant so long as alternatives can be arrayed in some single-peaked fashion.

We may convert the geometry of market adjustment in Figure 1 into a geometry of collective adjustment through a device that I have employed in two earlier papers.[3] The demand of a single person for the good is presumed to remain unaffected by the method through which the good is provided. Collective provision must embody equal quantities for each person. Hence, collective provision of a three-unit bundle of X becomes equivalent, to the individual demander, with market provision of a one-unit bundle. This allows us to change the dimensions along the abscissa in Figure 1 to three-unit bundles under collective organization and to use the ordinary demand curves of the consumers as the marginal evaluation curves for the collectively provided units.[4] In the initial model, there are no gains to be secured from joint consumption. Hence, the cost of producing a three-unit bundle (with one unit made available to each person) is precisely three times the cost of a one-unit bundle, which we set at P_x. The marginal cost of providing the collective good is $3P_x$.

In addition to the rule for making group choice, the political constitution must also specify some rule for cost sharing. If a poll or head tax exists, each person would be required to pay a tax-price of P_x for each unit of the collective good. Under the set of rules assumed, the median voter, B, would be able to impose his desires on the group. The collectivity would provide the quantity Q_b, and both A and C would be out of budgetary equilibrium. Individual A would want a lower budget, and C would want a higher budget. Dissatisfactions of this sort may, however, be partially or wholly mitigated by appropriate adjustments in the tax-sharing scheme. If we assume that the good exhibits positive income elasticity of demand, and if the underlying utility functions are not substantially different as among the three persons, the demand or marginal evaluations curves would reflect some order of income differentials. In partial, and possibly unconscious, recognition of this,

3. In addition to the paper previously cited, see my "A Public Choice Approach to Public Utility Pricing," *Public Choice*, 5 (Fall 1968), 1–18.

4. This procedure is strictly legitimate only if we assume that income-effect feedbacks on demand are absent.

the fiscal constitution might require, say, proportional income taxation. The tax-prices would be arrayed in relation to income level.

Under this adjustment, assume that the tax-price faced by A is T_a, that faced by B remains at P_x, while that faced by C is increased to T_c. Note that as drawn in Figure 1 these sum to $3P_x$, which is the marginal cost of the three-unit bundle. Further we assume that the tax-prices are uniform over quantities.[5] Again by arbitrary assumption, we allow the new set of tax-prices to bring all three demanders into private budgetary equilibrium, so that each person's marginal evaluation equals marginal tax-price at the same quantity, Q_b, which would then be chosen under any group decision-rule. Under this construction, Q_b would be the apparent Pareto-optimal quantity of the collective good. Summed marginal evaluations equal marginal cost, and each demander is in private equilibrium.[6]

Despite the equilibrium and optimality characteristics of this solution, there is a net welfare loss in shifting from the market to the collective provision of the good X in this model. The measure of this net loss is the two shaded triangular areas in Figure 1, and this loss stems exclusively from the distributional inefficiencies imposed by the uniform consumption constraint. The low-demand (low-income) person is made better off under collective provision than under independent market provision of the good. He secures a fiscal dividend or surplus under collectivization that is larger than his consumer's surplus under market pricing. His net gain from collectivization is shown by $P_xT_ahe_a$. Individual B is, by construction, equally well off under the two separate forms of organization. Individual C, the high-demand (and, by assumption, high-income) person, is made worse off under collective provision. The measure of his net loss from the organizational shift is shown by $T_cP_xe_cj$. Since $P_xT_a = P_xT_c$, it is evident by inspection of Figure 1 that the loss to C must exceed the gain to A. From this it follows that if C should have the option of shifting into some independent market-purchase arrangement, there

---

5. This is an arbitrary assumption that allows us to derive unique marginal evaluation schedules, even without the income-effect feedback assumption noted earlier.

6. Whether or not a position qualifies as Pareto-optimal always depends on the set of constraints that are imposed on adjustments. For Q_b to qualify here, we must assume that retrading of the good among persons after collective provision is either prohibitively costly or is expressly forbidden, and, also, that fundamental organizational change is ruled out.

is no bribe or compensation that A might offer which would induce C to remain in the collective-sharing group.

Despite its extreme simplicity and the arbitrary nature of its assumptions, the relevance of this and subsequent models to the urban fiscal dilemma should be clear. Under the conditions of this initial construction, where the municipality finances and provides a good that can be secured independently with little or no loss in efficiency, the shift of high-demand subgroups into their own purchase units cannot readily be forestalled while sharing gains are retained for remaining groups. Any attempt to impose a central-city tax-price on high-demand users that is above the market or small-group tax-price must fail. On the other hand, if the tax-price on high-demand consumers is reduced sufficiently to induce them to remain within the group, there will be no net gains from collectivization for the low- and middle-demand users. As the construction explicitly shows, these results hold even when the municipality's tax-sharing scheme embodies both apparent efficiency and equity. There is simply no viable fiscal strategy that the city's decision-makers can introduce which will induce potential outmigrants to remain within the group while still making some contribution to the fiscal surplus enjoyed by their fellow citizens.[7]

Because of the three-person limits on the model, the alternative posed is strictly private purchase through the market. The model may be somewhat more generally used, however, and the essential analysis becomes applicable for all municipally provided goods and services that can be secured through independent purchase by relatively small subgroups without undue efficiency losses. In other words, there may be gains from joint consumption over some range of consumers, but so long as these are exhausted within the limits of a potential outmigrant set, the results continue to be relevant.

III. Municipal Provision of Purely Public Goods

Under normal circumstances we should expect that some of the goods and services supplied by municipal governments embody efficiency gains from joint consumption over sizable ranges of population. In this Section, we

---

7. This conclusion would, of course, be modified to the extent that outmigration is costly.

shift to the opposing polar case from that treated in Section II. We assume now that the good provided by the city is purely collective. By this we mean that the cost of providing a unit of good for one person (or subgroup) is the same as the cost of providing units for all members of the community. This is, of course, the familiar Samuelson polar case. Once the good is made available to any one consumer, additional consumers may be added at zero marginal cost.

Figure 2 depicts this model. The marginal cost of the good, say, good Y, is P, and this is the cost that must be paid whether one person or all persons are in the consuming group. Inspection of Figure 2 suggests that under independent or market purchase, individuals A and B would not consume the good, while individual C would consume only Q_c. There are clear gains to the collectivity from organizing for joint consumption, and if the whole group is brought into a sharing agreement, the Pareto-efficient quantity is Q_k. If, at this quantity, tax-prices are uniform over quantities, and if tax shares are arranged so that each person attains full budgetary equilibrium, the tax-prices will be set at T_a, T_b, and T_c. At this set of tax-prices, there is no incentive for any person to withdraw from the collective-sharing arrangement and to consider forming his own independent purchase unit. All per-

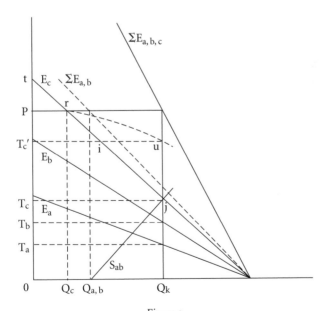

Figure 2

sons are better off in the collective agreement than they would be in any market-like adjustment.

There is, of course, no reason for assuming that relative tax shares will be such that each member of the group attains full budgetary equilibrium, even if the efficient quantity is provided. There is no apparent reason why A and B, as a potential majority, could not increase the tax-price to C, the high-demand person. In so doing, both A and B might improve their fiscal position. They may successfully exploit C through the fiscal mechanism by setting his tax-price higher than his marginal evaluation of the collective good. The construction is useful, however, in suggesting limits to such exploitation.

If the budget is set so that Q_k is provided, the maximum tax-price that may be imposed on C, assuming uniformity over quantities, is T'_c in Figure 2. This maximum is determined at the point where C becomes indifferent between remaining in the group-sharing arrangement and opting out to purchase the good independently. Geometrically, this maximum is found when the area $PriT'_c$, which measures C's gains from collectivization, is just equal to the area iuj, his losses due to budgetary disequilibrium. At this tax-price, C secures a fiscal surplus measured by trP, which is the same as the consumer's surplus he would secure in the market. Under this policy of maximal exploitation of C, both individuals A and B may secure substantially enhanced fiscal dividends by comparison with the nonexploiting solution.[8] As the construction suggests, the limits of fiscal exploitation will depend on C's elasticity of demand for the good over the relevant quantity ranges. If C's demand is highly elastic, he is less vulnerable to potential fiscal exploitation than he would be should his demand be relatively inelastic. Since demand is acknowledged to become more elastic with time, attempts to maximally exploit taxpayers on the basis of short-period considerations may backfire. If this possible shifting in demand is neglected, the combined fiscal dividends to A and B will be maximized in the position noted, with the optimal quantity remaining at Q_k. Since we have neglected the influence of income feed-

8. If the advantages from joint provision are such that even the high-demand members of the community purchase nothing under independent purchase (as would often be true with large-number groups), the limits to fiscal exploitation need not include an adjustment for consumers' surplus achievable under market purchase. In such circumstances, the limits are defined when the taxpayer reaches a position of zero fiscal surplus.

backs on marginal evaluation, the fiscal exploitation of C represents merely a shift on the Pareto-optimality surface.

So long as the limits of fiscal exploitation are not exceeded, the decision-making majority need not be concerned about a strategy for retaining high-demand (and presumably high-income) consumers in the collectivity. Even in this model, however, strategic considerations may emerge at a more complex level. Mistakes may be made either by the exploiters or the exploited. Outmigration may take place, and independent governmental units may be formed. Individual C, who depicts the situation for the representative member of the high-demand, high-income minority, is now assumed to opt out of the collective-sharing agreement. This leaves the smaller two-man community, AB, to provide the good on its own. The optimally preferred quantity is reduced drastically to $Q_{a,b}$. Both A and B are worse off than when C was a full-fledged partner in the fiscal club, although both retain some remnants of fiscal surplus. Individual C, having chosen to opt out, faces the prospect of providing the good independently, in which case consumer's surplus is limited to trP, secured from consumption of the quantity Q_c.

There will now exist, however, clear gains from trade between the newly independent unit, C, and the reduced-size community, AB. All parties may secure gains if an arrangement can be made so that C may now purchase units of the good from AB. If the two-man community, acting as a unit, behaves *nonstrategically*, it will look at its prospect of supplying C in accordance with the curve of marginal supply price, $S_{a,b}$ in Figure 2. This is derived by subtracting the combined marginal evaluations (shown by $\Sigma E_{a,b}$) from the marginal cost P. Faced with this marginal supply curve, treated as a set of price offers, C will extend his purchases to Q_k. This tax-price will be T_c, and the tax-prices to A and B fall back to those that would have been present under three-man budgetary equilibrium.

This seems at first glance to be a satisfactory bargain for all concerned. Both A and B can be better off than they were in the limited two-man club. Individual C is also better off than if he provides the good independently. If we interpret these results naively, they seem to imply that any attempt on the part of A and B to exploit C fiscally will lead to the opting out–trading arrangement which will become again equivalent to the budgetary equilibrium solution. This model will be explanatory, however, only if C behaves strategically while AB behaves nonstrategically.

More sophisticated examination of the model reveals that AB can exploit C equally well as a prospective outside purchaser and as an internal taxpaying member. To accomplish maximal exploitation when C is an outside purchaser, AB must present C with a set of all-or-none purchase offers. Instead of passively allowing C to make his own adjustments along some supply schedule such as $S_{a,b}$, the two-man selling unit, AB, should present C with that set of offers shown by the curve ru in Figure 2. This set reflects the limits of their monopolistic exploitation prospects, given C's ability to produce-purchase the good and gain the consumer's surplus, trP. The limiting set of all-or-none offers presents C with an implicit marginal-price schedule that is identical to his own marginal-evaluation schedule. Under these conditions, C will again be led to purchase Q_k, and he will attain this equilibrium by paying the average price T'_c. The solution is identical with that attained under maximal fiscal exploitation.

The apparent digression on maximal market exploitation has important implications for urban fiscal strategy. Cities may secure increments to internal fiscal surplus from high-demand, high-income consumers whether or not the latter choose to remain within the taxpaying–benefits-receiving group in any direct sense. This can be accomplished, however, only if city decision-makers recognize their position as monopolist sellers and act accordingly.

IV. Municipal Provision of Impure Public Goods

What are the implications for comparative organizational efficiency and for successful strategic behavior by municipalities when goods or services exhibit positive sharing gains but where these are not complete or total? The models developed in Sections II and III above place effective boundaries on the more realistic model considered here. Straightforward extension of the argument suggests that the results depend on which of the two extreme models is most closely approximated. The formal analysis, however, enables us to go somewhat further than this and to indicate direct implications for urban fiscal strategy.

In the construction of Figure 3 we assume that each person in the three-man community can independently purchase the good Z at a price of P_z per unit, which is equal to marginal cost and constant over quantity. The limit-

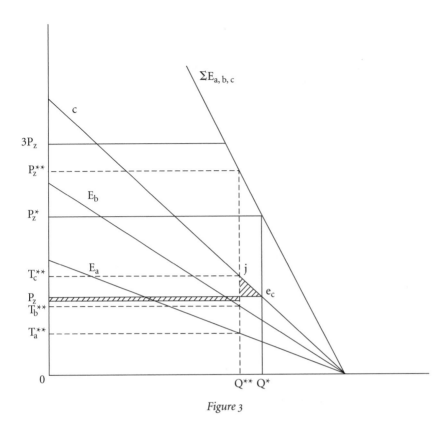

Figure 3

ing cases for the two models already discussed can be established by allowing the relative differential between the marginal cost of supplying one person and the marginal cost of supplying three persons to vary. If the good is purely "private," the marginal cost of the three-unit bundle is $3P_z$; if purely "public," it is P_z. We want to examine cases that fall between these limits.

As the analysis will show, the three-unit bundle price of P_z^* divides the possibilities into two categories. If the marginal cost of providing the three-unit bundle falls between P_z^* and $3P_z$ in Figure 3, we shall call the good "quasi-private." If this cost falls between P_z^* and P_z we shall call the good "quasi-public." There are different results in these two ranges. The dividing point P_z^* is the marginal cost of the three-unit bundle at the quantity where the marginal cost for the one-unit bundle P_z is equal to the marginal evaluation of the high-demand member of the group.

Suppose, initially, that the good falls squarely on the boundary at P_z^*. As before, let us further assume that the three-man community provides this good efficiently in the quantity Q^*, and that tax-prices are adjusted so as to bring each person into budgetary equilibrium. In this situation, individual C is equally well off under the group-sharing arrangement and under independent purchase of Z, while A and/or B secure a sizable fiscal dividend or surplus. Individual C has no incentive for independent purchase, and there is no differential fiscal surplus that he enjoys which allows him to be exploited by A and B.

Consider, however, the situation where the marginal cost for the three-unit bundle falls below P_z^* within the quasi-public range. In these cases, C will secure a differential fiscal surplus at the budgetary equilibrium solution. He will gain something from membership in the sharing community. Over this range, therefore, C may be subject to the sort of fiscal exploitation that was previously discussed.

Things become different, however, when the marginal cost of the collective good falls within the quasi-private range of jointness efficiency, between P_z^* and $3P_z$ in Figure 3. Here the results are not equivalent to those indicated in Section II for the purely private good. In the range considered, effective fiscal strategies can prevent the formation of independent purchasing arrangements. Such strategies will allow the maximal fiscal surplus to be retained by all members of the sharing group. Consider a case where the marginal (average) cost of a three-unit bundle is P_z^{**}. Assume that the community efficiently provides a quantity Q^{**}, and that it sets uniform tax-prices so that each person attains budgetary equilibrium, these being set at T_a^{**}, T_b^{**}, and T_c^{**}. If each person remains in the sharing group, no one will vote for a change in the budget from Q^{**}. In this solution, however, C will be paying more than he would be required to pay under independent purchase ($T_c^{**} > P_z$).

A and B both secure gains from the collective-sharing arrangement, however, and the total gains that they enjoy are more than sufficient to allow overcompensation to C. This is the essential difference between this and the model of Section II. With quasi-private goods, it becomes possible for A and B to work out bribes or side payments that will induce C to remain in the collectivity. Unless such compensations are made, however, C will migrate to the suburbs, with A and B being left in the central city. We have here an apparent example of a Pareto-optimal position that is not stable.[9] In game-theory terminology, the position attained is Pareto-optimal, but it does not qualify as a position in the core of the three-person game. There are gains to be made by a subcoalition in departing from the collective solution.

To be applicable to the urban setting, we should impose the requirement that the compensations take specifically fiscal form. Inducements to C must take the form of tax-price reductions and/or budgetary changes. The construction in Figure 3 allows us to illustrate both the magnitude of the compensations and the means of their provision. Under the collectively efficient solution at Q^{**}, C is worse off than under independent purchase by an amount measured by $T_c^{**} j e_c P_z$. His net surplus is reduced by this total as he enters the collectivity. Hence, inducement must be at least equal to this amount if C is to be retained in the group. One means of compensation would be to accept a larger budget than Q^{**} while also reducing the tax-price that C confronts. He could be allowed to enjoy the quantity Q^* at the tax-price of P_z, placing him in the equivalent position that he attains under the independent-purchase solution. If this were the only alternative, A and B would adopt it since they secure net benefits by comparison to the withdrawal of C from the group. The budgetary expansion beyond Q^{**} is not, however, the least-cost means through which compensation to C might be made. As the construction shows, summed marginal evaluations equal marginal cost at Q^{**}. Hence, there must exist means of securing the desired results while remaining at this level of collective provision.

One part of any fiscal inducement must reduce C's tax-price to P_z, the level at which he may independently purchase the good. If A and B take this step, while holding to the budgetary level Q^{**}, C will find it advantageous to opt out. His losses from collectivization would be those shown by the small

9. Under some relative demand configurations, even with jointness efficiency, the compensation required to keep C in the group may exceed that which A and B can make. The budgetary disequilibrium implied in the apparent Pareto-optimal outcome may not be worth the net gains from joint provision. In this case, the solution outlined in my paper "Notes on the Economic Theory of Socialism" becomes relevant. I am indebted to Prof. R. Williamson of North Carolina State University for calling attention to this point.

shaded triangle of Figure 3. In order to forestall C's departure, further adjustments can be made to reduce his tax-price below P_z. When the small shaded rectangular area is equal to the triangle, C becomes indifferent as between his two organizational alternatives.

Similar results would emerge for any good, the marginal cost for three-unit bundles of which lies between P_z^* and $3P_z$. In all such circumstances, A and B will find it advantageous to reduce the tax-price to C to a level that is *below* his independent-purchase alternative. In addition, note that C's tax-price will fall below his own marginal evaluation of the good. In one sense, this is precisely the opposite to the result reached in Section III. In that model, optimal strategy dictated that C be fiscally exploited by setting his effective tax-price above his marginal evaluation. By contrast, in the quasi-private goods ranges, optimal strategy on the part of A and B dictates that C be subjected to what might be called "negative fiscal exploitation." The tax-prices to A and/or B must lie above his/their own marginal evaluation in the final solution. To secure the fiscal surplus arising from retaining C in the fiscal club, A and/or B must subject himself/themselves to "positive fiscal exploitation."

This part of the analysis has the most interesting implications for fiscal strategy since the required policy steps seem to run afoul of traditional and long-accepted norms for adjusting tax shares. It becomes possible that under some demand-cost configurations the tax-price which C finally confronts may fall below that faced by A and/or B. In many cases, the relative tax-prices that are strategically optimal may embody regression in the tax structure when measured against an income or wealth base. To the traditionalist in normative public finance who thinks in terms of the standard equity norms regression raises red flags. This may apply even more emphatically to the sophisticated analyst who tries to incorporate both traditional tax "principles" and some recognition of the distribution of public-goods benefits. Not only may the "ability-to-pay" principle be violated, the "benefit principle," even when interpreted in marginal terms, may have to be discarded. The equity advocate may not be easily convinced by the public-choice theorist or by the practical politician. Nonetheless, unless he is overruled, those very persons whom he proposes to assist will be harmed. Unless fiscal inducements are made to those who might shift out of the community-sharing group, it is the middle- and low-income demand groups remaining who will suffer the major costs that locational inefficiencies will generate.[10]

V. Principles for Fiscal Strategy

The geometrical exercises may seem remote from the problems of fiscal adjustment actually faced by central-city governments. These units provide a heterogeneous bundle of goods and services, more or less uniformly to all citizens, and finance them with a varied set of tax levies, user charges, and external grants. The demands may be related only in part to income-wealth levels, and the relationship may not extend to particular budgetary components at all. Despite their abstractness and simplicity, however, I should argue that the models are helpful in pointing toward rational urban policy choices. The models isolate and identify features of the fiscal landscape that have long been understood by practical politicians but which have not been incorporated into the public finance theory of local government.

The objective for rational urban fiscal strategy is the maximization of per capita fiscal dividend or surplus. This translates directly into the requirement that all persons who contribute positively to the generation of fiscal surplus be kept within the club. To the extent that persons or groups who do make net contributions are observed to migrate to the suburbs, urban fiscal strategy has failed. Those who contribute most are those who pay the largest share of costs, and these are presumably those whose demands are highest. I have made the standard assumption that the goods provided by municipal governments are characterized by positive income elasticities. If this is accepted, the relative emphasis on retaining the high-income, high-wealth residents becomes obvious. If low- and middle-income-wealth groups withdraw from the fiscal arrangements of the city, net effects on fiscal surplus may be positive rather than negative. This result will depend, of course, on the actual structure of tax sharing. In the models discussed, I have as-

10. This general conclusion is not modified when we allow for some cost of shifting. These costs are included in the construction in the sense that higher costs of shifting reduce the spread between the marginal cost of supplying services to the group and to the potential outmigrant.

sumed that the dominant political majorities are composed of low- and middle-income persons rather than upper-income groups. Because of this, I have concentrated on the fiscal treatment of upper-income groups. If the dominant majority should be from the upper-income-wealth groups, and if this majority attempts to exploit other persons maximally, outmigration might increase rather than reduce fiscal surplus. I can justify my neglect of this possibility empirically. What we observe is the outmigration of upper-income persons and groups; we are not concerned about the formation of slum suburbs. Regardless of just who makes up the dominant political coalition, rational strategy suggests that consideration be given to the suburban migration of those who receive relatively higher incomes and who own relatively higher-valued assets. This arises solely from the self-interests of those citizens who remain in the city. It has nothing to do with the "deservingness" of the high-income or the low-income groups, or with "justice" or "equity" as an abstract ethical norm.

The separate models seem to point toward different strategies, but closer inspection reveals that the essential principle is the same in all cases. The criterion upon which the urban fiscal structure should be based is its relative efficiency in retaining its high-income, high-demand participants. The criterion does not allow the development of norms that apply to all communities at all times. Tax-sharing schemes may range all the way from poll or head taxes on the one hand to confiscatory levies on the other.

We may identify several features that determine the sort of adjustments that will be made under an optimally preferred strategy. These are: (1) the "publicness" of the budgetary bundle that is offered by the municipality; (2) the elasticity of demand for this bundle by the group considered; (3) the costs of outmigration and the formation of alternative purchase-provision arrangements. These factors are controllable to some extent by the municipal decision-makers. An inclusive strategy should, therefore, be directed toward *increasing* the "publicness" of the budgetary items, toward *decreasing* the high-income recipients' elasticity of demand for this bundle, and toward *increasing* the costs of making alternative arrangements.

Since municipalities normally provide a whole set of goods and services, budgetary adjustments should place relatively greater emphasis on those components that exhibit relatively larger sharing efficiencies at the group-size margin. Goods and services that exhibit little or no gains from joint consumption or which exhibit gains which are exhausted before the effective city size is reached should be relatively reduced or eliminated from the city budget. Financing these by direct user charges rather than by taxation may be indicated. Such changes in budgetary composition may seem harmful to low-income consumers. In the larger strategic context, however, these policies, by preserving the fiscal base of the community, may benefit the very groups that seem initially to be harmed.

City governments vary widely in population, in income-wealth distribution, in occupational structure, and in fiscal arrangements. The specific budgetary changes in an optimal strategy will not be uniform from one city to the next. The small city may find it advantageous to extend its provision of goods and services that the large city might find useful to contract. In any case, relatively greater attention should be given to the municipal supply of those goods and services that potential suburbanites might find difficult or very costly to secure independently. To offer practical examples, municipalities should listen more carefully to those who recommend fiscal support for art museums, symphony orchestras, theaters, and parks. Once such services as these are provided, however, appropriate exclusion arrangements, through charges or otherwise, must be introduced to insure that suburbanites who are nonresidents cannot enjoy the "publicness" benefits without making their own net contribution to internal fiscal surplus. The analysis of Section III becomes directly applicable in the city's dealings with suburbanites.

We have found it useful analytically to assume that all persons secure equal quantities of consumption services provided collectively. This rule or institution can also be modified as one tool in an urban strategy kit. One means of increasing the "publicness" of the budgetary bundle may involve differential adjustments on the consumption services side. This is observed to occur in special police details in high-income areas of cities, in better parks in some areas than in others, in better-equipped and better-staffed schools, etc. As with tax-side adjustments designed to accomplish the same purposes, such differentials in public service standards among differing income groups in the municipality may seem to violate traditional equity norms. When strategic considerations are recognized, however, the existence of such differentials may provide evidence that the decision-makers are, in fact, behaving in the interest of the low- and middle-income constituents.

A decrease in the elasticity of demand for the budgetary bundle may be accomplished in part by the steps outlined above. Any adjustment toward increasing "publicness" will decrease elasticity of demand *as faced by the collectivity*. Even among budgetary items with the same degree of "publicness" at the margin, however, demand elasticities may differ. The overall elasticity of demand for the bundle of budgetary items that are tax-financed may be reduced by a shift in favor of those particular items that exhibit relatively low elasticity coefficients.

A third instrumental objective of fiscal strategy involves increasing the cost of setting up alternative provision-purchase arrangements for those who might opt out from the municipal-sharing group. In several respects, these costs are not within the control of the parent municipality. Organizational costs for newly independent suburbs, new fiscal clubs, are subject to relatively little influence, but some steps are possible. Municipal governments from which outmigration has taken place should insure that all sales of goods and services to newly formed suburbs or to private individuals and groups are made on an explicit recognition of the monopolistic powers of the parent unit. If prospective suburbanities are aware of the costs of making repurchase and tie-in agreements with the central city, they may be inhibited from making suburban migrations in the first place. More importantly, even if suburbs are formed beyond city boundaries, suburbanities can be forced to contribute toward the fiscal surplus of city residents by appropriate pricing policies. This aspect of urban strategy has several direct applications, for example, in water line and sewer line extensions, extended fire protection, and police coverage.

VI. Conclusions

Differing environments will indicate differing strategies; no generally applicable rules can be laid down for municipalities to follow. The analysis raises critical questions about the appropriateness of any *general* norm for fiscal organization. Differences in migration potential among subgroups must be taken into account, and intraclass as well as interclass adjustments may be required. Optimal strategies may dictate that economic units which seem comparable in many respects be treated differently by municipal fiscal systems. The familiar practice of allegedly favored treatment accorded high-income residential property owners in assessments may be "explained" as one part of an optimal strategy. If such an explanation is at all accurate, the interests of city residents who are assessed unfavorably may dictate continuation rather than elimination of the favoritism.

To what extent do municipal governments follow the principles outlined? The fiscal plight of cities everywhere suggests either that optimal strategies have not been followed, or, if so, that they have failed. Cities have lost and are continuing to lose high-income residential groups to suburbs beyond their limits. While some of this outmigration might have been prevented, once it has taken place more extreme measures may be required to induce a return. Fiscal pressures may not be the dominating element in an explanation of urban location. If technological, ethnic, and sociological reasons reduce the high-income residents' evaluation of central-city advantages, a successful fiscal strategy might require more blatant fiscal discrimination than political reality would permit. But so long as fiscal values are included alongside nonfiscal values in the utility functions of potential migrants, however, some such strategy must exist.[11]

This elementary analysis has questioned several of the traditional cliches about municipal fiscal structure. It should stimulate further work, both analytical and empirical, which commences from the recognition that the modern city's problem is one of fiscal strategy rather than fiscal frustration imposed by the apparent constraints of nonattainable and false ideals.

11. Throughout the analysis of this paper, I have implicitly assumed that the topography is that of a plane. Insofar as "natural" geographic limits exist to urban-unit size, extension of municipal boundaries to these limits may, of course, reduce the need for fiscal strategy. Without such limits, however, attempts to extend boundaries may actually increase locational distortion.

The Inconsistencies of the National Health Service

Introduction

To a detached observer in 1965, Great Britain's 17-year experiment in providing "free" health services exhibits many signs of failure. In July 1965, an overwhelming majority of the delegates to the Swansea meeting of the British Medical Association supported a resolution calling for the introduction of privately collected fees from patients, recoverable from the state, to be included as one method of remuneration in the "doctors' charter" at present under negotiation with the Minister of Health. Even before this unpredicted and unexpected expression of professional opposition, the Association held the undated resignations of nearly 18,000 family doctors (out of a total of 23,000) pending the outcome of negotiations on many points with the Minister. Relatively fewer numbers are entering the medical profession each year, and the emigration of British-trained doctors continues.[1] The number of practising doctors declined by 300 from October 1963 to October 1964 in the face of a substantial net increase in population. Resident staff in British hospitals has come increasingly to be composed of immigrants, mostly from India and Pakistan. Hospital facilities are overcrowded, and long delays in securing treatment, save for strictly emergency cases, are universally noted.

What are the reasons for these apparent failures in the system for which

From Occasional Paper no. 7 (London: Institute of Economic Affairs, 1965). Reprinted by permission of the publisher.

1. See J. R. Seale, "Medical Emigration: A Study in the Inadequacy of Official Statistics," in *Lessons from Central Forecasting*, Eaton Paper 6, IEA, October 1965.

so much was hoped in 1948? Why do the ideals of the late 1940s remain so far out of reach, even after 17 years? Some such understanding is essential if anything other than gimcrack reforms are to be introduced. Recent events in the United States and in Canada make it additionally important to evaluate and interpret British experience correctly. In 1965, also in July, the United States embarked upon its own programme of national government financing of medical care for the aged. The Canadian government is actively considering proposals to provide major federal aid to provincial health-service systems. Can similar failures be predicted in these two cases?

There are three possible explanations of the apparent failure of the National Health Service. Are the undesirable features observed in the British system due to mistakes in administering the health services, mistakes that "wiser" men or parties could have avoided? Are these difficulties due to the very structure of the institutions through which health services are provided, and which could, therefore, be removed only after major reforms in this institutional structure? Or, finally, are these difficulties inherent in the nature of the health services themselves? Can services that are privately valued by individuals—"personal" services—be provided "free" by governments?

I shall argue that only the second of these questions needs to be answered affirmatively. The observed failures of the NHS can be explained by the *structure of the institutions*. This suggests that, at best, improvements in administration can provide only short-term palliatives. Explanations are not to be found in either wrong-headed decisions by ministers or short-sighted policies of political parties. Governments that remain broadly democratic can be successful in providing "free" services, but only if they do so within institutions that promote general consistency in the social decision-making process. In models that approximate to the British structure, I shall explain the observed results by showing that in their *private or individual choice* behaviour as potential users or demanders of health-medical services, individuals are inconsistent with their *public or collective choice* behaviour as voters-taxpayers who make decisions on supplying these same services. The individuals who are the demanders and those who are the suppliers are, of course, basically the same persons acting in two separate roles, and the facts themselves suggest the inconsistency. My central point is that this inconsistency does not in any way reflect irrationality on the part of individual decision-makers, but that it arises exclusively from the institutional setting for choice on the two sides of the account. Once this relatively simple point is recognised and accepted, the directions for possible constructive reforms become clear.

My discussion is limited to institutional theory. I shall not discuss either the historical development of the NHS or its descriptive characteristics at present. The discussion is also positive; I shall not be concerned here with the normative question as to how health services "should" be organised, privately or publicly. In what follows, I shall first review briefly the traditional principle of neo-classical public finance that is relevant for the analysis of the NHS. The implications normally drawn from the application of this principle will be noted, emphasising the contrast between the inferred neo-classical predictions and the British experience. The reasons for the refutation of these predictions are shown to lie in economists' failure to analyse political choice processes. The individual and the collective settings for individual choice behaviour are examined in some detail, and models that seem to typify the British example will be presented. Finally, brief attention will be given to alternative institutional arrangements that might eliminate the fundamental inconsistencies.

The Elasticity Principle

If the price elasticity of individual demand, i.e., the responsiveness to a (small) change in price, is significantly higher than zero over the applicable range, governments cannot efficiently "give away" goods or services. This is one of the most widely accepted principles in the theory of public finance. It is found in most modern textbooks, but it also finds authority in such respected neo-classical writers as Pigou and Wicksell.[2] Within its traditional setting, the principle is valid. If government tries to supply goods or services that are privately divisible among separate persons at zero prices to users, the quantity demanded by all individuals in the aggregate will be significantly larger than the quantity that would be demanded at prices set by (marginal) cost, except where the price elasticity approaches zero.

For some goods and services, this required elasticity condition is satisfied. For example, the government could, without undue losses in efficiency, pro-

---

2. A. C. Pigou, *A Study in Public Finance,* Macmillan, 1928; Knut Wicksell, *Finanztheoretische Untersuchungen,* Gustav Fischer, 1896.

vide "free" funeral services, for the very simple reason that each person dies only once; a zero price does not produce a larger demand for funerals than a high (or even a low) price. For other goods and services, "free" provision would obviously be impossible, for example, beefsteaks, motor cars, and minks. Between such extremes as these, various goods and services may be arrayed in terms of predicted elasticity coefficients over the relevant ranges of prices. Education, for example, can within limits be made available free of direct user charges because each child can "demand" only one year's quantity of service per year.[3] Medical-health services clearly fall somewhere along the spectrum between education and motor cars. For certain types of medical care, price elasticity may be low indeed; there should be approximately the same number of broken legs treated under zero and under marginal-cost prices. For other types of health service, however, price elasticity may be relatively high. The British experience suggests that the demands for drugs[4] and for consultation by general practitioners and possibly for hospital care fall into this category. For medical-health services taken as an undifferentiated whole, individuals will be led to demand significantly larger quantities at zero user prices than they would demand at positive prices.[5] This part of the neo-classical principle amounts to nothing more than a straightforward application of the first law of demand.

But there is more to be said about the principle. It states that governments cannot *efficiently* give away goods and services that do not satisfy the required elasticity condition. In this form, the principle says nothing at all about the manner in which the inefficiencies will be generated when this condition is not met, or about the final incidence of such inefficiencies. Economists have normally assumed that these inefficiencies would take the form of relatively excessive investment in supplying the services in question.

---

3. For such services as funerals and education, individual demands for improvements in *quality* under zero user pricing replace, to some extent, the more direct individual adjustments in *quantity* that are possible with goods and services falling along the opposite end of the array suggested. At best, however, these demands for quality improvements become pressures upon governments for change; they cannot, in themselves, consume resources.

4. Since the 2s. charge for prescriptions dispensed under the NHS was abolished on 1 February, 1965, Ministry of Health figures show that prescriptions have risen 20 per cent in number and 28 per cent in cost compared with the same period of 1964; by comparison, certified sickness rose by only 7 per cent.

5. This is the economic theory behind the vague allusions by some sociologists to a "price-barrier."—*Editor.*

This assumption represents a simple extension of consumer-sovereignty models in which supply is expected always to adjust to demand over the long run. The presumption has been that, should governments try to give away services that fail to meet the required elasticity condition, they will find it necessary to extend supply to meet expressed demand, even at the expense of relative over-investment in the services. In responding to "needs" criteria at zero user prices, governments would have been predicted to devote relatively too much public outlay to the provision of such divisible, personal services as medical care, "too much" being measured against the standard criteria for allocating resource use of consumer preferences as expressed in the market. The alternative response that governments might make in such situations seems rarely to have been considered. They may make decisions on the supply of the service independent of the demands for the service, and on the basis of quite different considerations. As a result, the inefficiencies may take the form of deterioration in the *quality* of the services themselves, including congestion of available facilities.

External Economies

A second, and, to some extent, independent, principle has emerged from theoretical economics and finds its origin in Pigou's discussion of external economies and diseconomies.[6] When an activity generates significant external economies, individual or private organisation has been held to generate relative under-investment. The standard Pigovian inference is that a lower-than-optimal amount of the activity will take place. Medical-health services have been classified by many economists as being such that private or individual organisation produces significant external economies. This is, of course, the argument that has been thought to provide the economic rationale for a shift from private organisation to public or collective organisation. Under the latter, presumably, the relevant external effects can be internalised in the collective-decision process. The orthodox Pigovian prediction would be that such a shift in organisation, from private to public, would result in substantial increases in outlay on providing the services.[7]

---

6. A. C. Pigou, *The Economics of Welfare,* third edition, Macmillan, 1929.

7. In a paper previously published, Milton Kafoglis and I examined this hypothesis within the standard model of post-Pigovian welfare economics. We showed that total in-

The Neo-classical Prediction

The two strands of economic analysis sketched above become mutually re-inforcing when prediction is made concerning the direction of change in the total resources used in medical services that would result from substituting a socialised or nationalised service for a privately organised service, in whole or in part. The welfare economist, concentrating his attention on the predicted presence of external economies and ignoring problems of collective decision-making, predicts that such a change in organisation will increase the resources invested from sub-optimal to optimal levels. The traditional public finance theorist might agree with the welfare economist, but, being somewhat more sophisticated as regards attention to political decisions, and recognising the elasticity conditions, he predicts that governments will tend to expand investment *beyond* optimal limits. In trying to meet expressed "needs" for or demands on the available facilities, substantial over-investment might take place. The sophisticated neo-classical economist, taking both of these considerations into account, would have seemed on quite safe grounds in predicting that after 1948 total outlay on health-medical services in Great Britain would increase substantially *relative to that which would have been made under the alternatives.*

Experience in Great Britain so far does not corroborate such neo-classical predictions that might have been, and were, made.[8] Since 1948, total outlay on medical-health care has increased less in Great Britain than in the United States, where it is supplied largely in the market, even after all of the appropriate statistical adjustments for income-wealth levels, population, etc., are

---

vestment in supplying a service may not be increased by a shift from private to public organisation, even when the presence of relevant external economies is acknowledged. Our discussion centred on the necessity to distinguish inputs and outputs. We demonstrated that under certain assumptions about the substitutability between private and public provision in individuals' utility functions, overall efficiency might be increased without expansion in investment, even on the presumption that government decisions are fully correct. See James M. Buchanan and Milton Z. Kafoglis, "A Note on Public Goods Supply," *American Economic Review*, June 1963, 403–14. The argument developed in this earlier paper and its relationship to the discussion in the present paper are summarised in the Appendix, pp. 357–60.

8. For example, Seymour Harris, "The British Health Experiment: The First Two Years of the National Health Service," *American Economic Review*, May 1951, 652–66.

made.[9] The task before us becomes that of "explaining" why these predictions failed. For this purpose, it is not necessary to discuss further the theory of external economies and its possible application to the organisation of medical-health services. Such discussion becomes relevant to the normative question concerning the efficient method of organising the services and to the comparative results of alternative structures. The aim here is much more limited; we seek only to understand the broad pattern of results that are observed under the British experiment of collectivising the health services, results that are at variance with the neo-classical predictions. We can do this by concentrating on elementary analysis.

The central part of the elasticity principle seems to be corroborated. At zero levels of user price, individuals are observed to demand relatively large quantities of health services, and we may presume that these quantities would be substantially reduced upon the establishment of positive charges. (Experience with drug fees alone suggests this result.) The neo-classical prediction relating to *individual* or *private* responses to the provision of "free" health services does not therefore seem to be challenged by the evidence.

It is in relation to the *public* or *collective* responses to these demands that predictions seem to have gone astray. Responsible *collective*, i.e., governmental, decision-makers have not expanded investment in supplying health services to the levels of expressed *individual* demands. The inefficiencies that have arisen are clearly not in the form of excessive total outlay on the health services. The British experience strongly suggests that rather than responding to "needs" through increases in aggregate supply governments have chosen to allow the quality of services to deteriorate rapidly, both in some appropriate, physically measurable sense[10] and in terms of congestion costs imposed on prospective consumers.

The failures of the NHS are not exhibited by a disproportionately large

9. See John and Sylvia Jewkes, *The Genesis of the British National Health Service*, Blackwell, 1961.

10. Physical measurement of quality is, of course, difficult in any setting, and notably so when research advances are as rapid as in medical care. Nevertheless it seems clear that quality of service, for example in British hospitals, has been allowed to deteriorate relative to that which would have been predicted to be present under a nationalised scheme.

fraction of British resources being drained away through investment in supplying it; the failures are exhibited by breakdowns in the quality of the services themselves due to the disparity between the facilities supplied and the demands made upon them.

Democratic Choice Process

Could this combination of results have been predicted by a more satisfactory model of choice behaviour? Can the observed pattern of results be explained? I shall show that explanation becomes possible when a plausible model for democratic choice process is added. We must extend the standard theory so that we can say something about the predicted responses of individuals in their capacities as participants in *collective* or group decisions. Only when this step is taken can we make some elementary predictions about the reactions of governments to privately expressed demands on health facilities and services.

The evidence suggests that the neo-classical inference that governments respond straightforwardly to "needs" is invalid. Economists have not examined either this inference or that of theoretical welfare economics (that governments act "optimally") carefully because analysis of the political-choice mechanism has been held to be outside their range of competence. Institutional and policy analysis in both neo-classical and Keynesian economics has suffered because of this implicit refusal to extend the model of individual choice behaviour. The result has been a sharp distinction between the choice behaviour of the individual in market processes and his behaviour in political processes. Implicitly, analysis has presumed that governmental decisions are divorced from the preferences of individual citizens. The first requirement for a more sophisticated explanation of observed experience is an explicit construction of a model for the political-decision process.

In any system that is properly described by the much-abused word "democratic," political decisions must ultimately be made by the individuals who hold membership in the politically or collectively organised group. Individuals make choices in two separate capacities, as buyers-sellers in ordinary markets for *private* goods and services, and as buyers-sellers of *public* goods and services in the political process. Only within recent years has rigorous analysis come to be applied to the second type of individual choice behaviour.[11] An economic theory of collective decision-making remains in its infancy, but, even with the rudimentary models that are available, significant advances in an understanding of the general results of democratic political systems can be made.

At any general level, analysis of political process must take some account of the rules and the institutions through which separate individual choices, whether directly or indirectly expressed, are combined so as to produce results that, once selected, are uniformly imposed on all members of the political unit. Obviously, different rules can produce decisively different results, even should the underlying structure of individual preferences remain unchanged. Economy in explanation at the very beginning of analysis, however, may be gained by neglecting the necessarily complex examination of alternative rules. Such an examination should not be introduced until the explanatory potential of simpler models has been exhausted. In certain cases it may be possible to explain phenomena of the real world satisfactorily through reliance on single-person models, that is, through an analysis limited to the choice behaviour of a single, isolated individual as he participates in political process. If such an analysis works there is no need to resort to more complicated interactions under collective-decision rules, despite the possible emergence of additional explanatory potential.

I hope to show that the observed experience of the NHS can be satisfactorily explained by analysing the behaviour of the individual citizen, as a demander of health services on the one hand and as a potential voter on the other. Considerations of the way in which his preferences are translated into government policy in the political process are not needed. In other words, the results are those that would emerge from the rational calculus of the individual as private or individual demander and as public or collective supplier of health services. For clarity, the model to be discussed could be assumed one in which all individuals are identical to the single person, or, alternatively, one in which the single person is genuinely "representative" of the whole community.

---

11. For a list of some of the relevant works here, see "Suggestions for Further Reading" on page 360, particularly Section I.

Consider now a single individual. He participates in both market decisions and political decisions. In the former he chooses the quantities of private goods and services he will buy or sell, demand or supply. He will do so individualistically and privately, and the divisibility of the goods and services ensures that he can act separately and independent of other persons. The individual can select his own most preferred level of consumption of, say, beer, without in any way deciding or even affecting what any one, or all, of his fellow citizens shall consume. In the second capacity, as a participant in the political process, the individual also chooses the quantities of public goods and services that he will demand and supply. But here he will do so as a member of a group. Although his own preferences will determine the manner of his voting, the outcomes must be applied to *all* members of the group. A choice implies, therefore, a willingness to finance stated quantities of a good or service for all members of the group through appropriately chosen taxes also levied on all members.

Nothing more than a cursory examination of the institutions of the NHS is required to recognise that an individual is placed in the position of demanding medical-health services in a market-like choosing capacity. The "market" he confronts presents him with opportunities of selecting preferred quantities of services at zero prices. He chooses individualistically and privately, and, on the *demand* side, "free" health services are treated in much the same way as "free" beer, that is, the demand would swell more or less rapidly. At the same time, however, the individual as a participant in collective-political choice, as a voter-taxpayer-beneficiary, must indicate his decision on the aggregate quantity of medical-health services to be supplied to the community as a whole. In this capacity he cannot select an outcome for himself that will not also be applicable for everyone else. On the *supply* side, medical-health services are not "free" in any sense of the word; on the contrary, they are severely limited by consideration of all the other alternatives—more schools, better housing, larger pensions—that would have to be sacrificed if they were expanded solely in response to demand at zero prices.

Once this essential splitting of the individual's decision is recognised, the inconsistency in results is not at all strange. Indeed, this inconsistency is precisely what careful analysis would lead us to predict.

The Individual as Private Demander
and Public Supplier

Why will the individual demand more services privately than he will supply publicly? This is the kernel of the internal conflict in the NHS.

We may first concentrate on his behaviour in demanding services made available to him by the community at zero user prices. What will determine the quantity demanded? One of the first lessons in elementary economics provides the answer. The rational person will extend his demands on such services to the point at which the marginal utility becomes zero: that is, so long as additional services promise to yield positive benefits, there will be no incentive for the individual to restrict his "purchases." But, one may say, this sort of behaviour will be "malingering," the word commonly heard in 1965 British comments on the health service. Should not the individual consumer, or prospective consumer, recognise that when he extends his own private demands to such limits he uses up resources that are valuable to the community and for which the community must pay?

The individual who is well informed may well recognise that his own behaviour in this respect will commit valuable resources.[12] This point is not in question, and our explanation does not depend on ignorance to explain the observed results. Accurate recognition and measurement of the social costs of health-medical services will in no way modify the behaviour of the individual in demanding such services. Faced with no direct user charges, he will not find it personally advantageous to restrict his own demands, although he may fully appreciate that the value of these services to him is less than the cost imposed on the whole community in supplying them. The individual's behaviour in this case is precisely equivalent to that of the person who refuses to contribute voluntarily to the financing of a mutually desired purely

---

12. Survey data indicate that individuals tend to be grossly uninformed about the costs of publicly supplied medical services in Great Britain, and that there is a consistent tendency to under-estimate these costs. This direction of error tends to accentuate the behavioural inconsistency discussed in this paper. By contrast, there seems to be a consistent tendency for individuals to over-estimate the costs of publicly supplied education. See *Choice in Welfare*, IEA, 1963. *Choice in Welfare, 1965,* also indicates the degree of knowledge or ignorance of the taxes paid and social benefits received by households of varying income and size.

public or purely collective good (the "free-rider" who benefits whether he pays or not).[13]

In either of these two situations, the individual, indeed each and every individual, may recognise full well that he, along with *all* of his fellows, would be better off if *everyone*, in practice, behaved differently. But there is nothing he is able to do, individually and voluntarily, to affect the way in which others behave.[14] If he decides, privately and personally, to reduce his own demands on the services, for reasons of "social conscience," he will be acting irrationally. But since his behaviour will not, in itself, modify the behaviour of others in the aggregate, he will be foregoing opportunities for personal gains, however slight, without benefiting others to any measurable extent. Under choice conditions such as these, it is not at all surprising that what is called "malingering" is widely observed.

Let us now shift our attention to the behaviour of the same individual, who is assumed to be both informed and rational, as he participates directly or indirectly in the political-choice process. We may consider his participation in decisions on the supply of health services independent of his participation in decisions on other issues for collective action. He must indicate his preferences, in some voting or quasi-voting process, among alternative health-service budgets, each of which embodies a specific quantity of services to be made available for the whole community, and each of which, in turn, embodies an implied levy of taxes sufficient to finance the matching quantity. How much taxation will the individual prefer in combination with how much total outlay on the health services?

To the extent that he is well informed, the individual can make some reasonably accurate translation between the tax or cost side and the level of health-service benefits that may be provided. He will know, roughly, what level of tax rates will be required to finance each level of health-service budget and, in turn, what quantity of aggregate services each budget will supply. But what will determine his own choice among budgets? The individual's

13. In the modern theory of public finance, the individual behaviour in this situation is discussed at length as the "free-rider problem." See the references to this discussion in "Suggestions for Further Reading," on page 360, Section II.

14. He finds himself caught in an n-person analogue to the familiar prisoners' dilemma, much discussed in modern game theory. See R. Duncan Luce and Howard Raiffa, *Games and Decisions*, Wiley, 1958, 94–102.

own preferences will be controlling here as they are in private choice, but here he cannot choose between positions for himself independent of or in isolation from the positions of all others in the political group. Here choice involves indicating a preference for one *group* outcome over the others, even though this choice may be largely determined by the individual's own position in this outcome. Each alternative for choice embodies results not only for the participating or "voting" individual but also for all others. Each budget defines a specific expected level of services along with a specific expected level of taxation, along with a distribution in both cases.

This is a choice setting that is categorically different from that which characterises the demand side. In his capacity as a participant in collective choice, the individual must *balance costs against benefits.* He will try, as best he can, to estimate the tax costs that various levels of service will impose on him, and he will weigh these against estimates of benefits that he will secure from these various levels. Clearly any choice on the individual's part here to extend supply to the point where the marginal utility from the services becomes zero would be foolish because the sacrifice of alternatives would be relatively enormous. The individual will quite rationally indicate a preference for an aggregate supply of services that falls below such satiation levels. His choice, in a political-decision context, will be for a quantity of gross investment in health services much lower than that which would be required by a policy of providing constant-quality services to the extent indicated by privately expressed "needs."[15]

Application to British Experience

I suggest that the observed breakdown in the NHS can at least be partially explained by the theory of institutional choice outlined above. The politicians who have made the decisions on investment in the health services have been simply responding to the preferences of individual citizens. The ob-

---

15. In this second choice situation, the individual is not in the n-person analogue to the prisoners' dilemma at all. Here the analogue would be the individual prisoner's voting choice for a standard "policy for confessing" to be applied for all prisoners. The difference in the two choice situations for the individual creates inconsistency in results. There is no need for us to extend the analysis beyond the level of the single individual. We need not call upon the more complex models of group-choice for explanation.

served results are precisely those that the theory would have enabled us to predict. Alternative hypotheses concerning the behaviour of politicians can, of course, be advanced, and some of them might be of explanatory value. My emphasis is on the point that no supplemental hypotheses are required; the experience can be explained by postulating that politicians behave "as if" they transmit the preferences of citizens into political outcomes.

As indicated at several places, the first half of the theory is a straightforward application of one of the most elementary of economic principles, about which there will surely be little or no debate. The novelty or innovation in this analysis lies in its extension of what is essentially economic reasoning to political decisions. This economic theory of politics remains unfamiliar territory, but we are fortunate here in that no complex models seem to be needed to explain satisfactorily the health-service experience. There has been no need to resort to models of majority rule, of parliamentary systems of government, of political parties, of political leadership. This is not to deny that some such models might provide equally satisfactory explanations of real-world results. One of the fundamental methodological principles for all science, however, is that of accepting the simplest possible hypothesis when a genuine choice among explanations is possible. All that has been necessary here is a simple acknowledgement that individual preferences are influential in determining political outcomes. The results suggest that the transmission of these preferences into outcomes does take place, quite independent of the particular way in which this process operates.

This is merely another way of stating that the British political order is assumed to be effectively "democratic." The theory cannot be used simultaneously to explain the results from a democratic political model and to prove that the system is, in fact, democratic. If a *dirigiste,* non-democratic political structure is postulated, explanation of the observed results would necessarily be different.

Directions for Reform

If the explanation advanced in this paper is accepted, the directions for reform in the institutions of the NHS are indicated. The inconsistency between demand-choice and supply-choice must be eliminated, and the individual, as the ultimate chooser, must be placed in positions where the two parts of what is really a single decision are not arbitrarily separated. This can be accomplished only if an explicit decision on demand is allowed to call forth or to imply a specific supply response, or if an explicit decision on supply embodies a specific demand response. The splitting into two parts of what must be, in the final analysis, a single decision must be removed.

To illustrate that any arbitrary splitting of the demand-supply decision will create inconsistency, we may examine the various alternatives other than the one found in practice. Suppose, as our first example, that an attempt should be made to provide health services "free," as currently, but that, also, an attempt should be made to cover the costs of these services through "free" contributions, without the imposition of coercive taxes. In this situation, individuals would have health services freely made available to them, but they would also be allowed freely to make whatever contributions they choose toward financing them. Predicted results of this institutional combination are obvious. Relatively little would be collected in contributions, since all individuals would be placed in "free-rider" positions. The system would be characterised by gross under-supply and gross over-demand, with resulting deterioration in quality in all respects. The institutional combination in being embodies only one-half of this worst possible system.

As a second illustrative example of a split-decision structure, let us suppose that, as in the preceding case, individuals are asked to make voluntary contributions but that on the demand side decisions are made publicly, not privately. The government would, in this situation, place restrictive limits on the use of the health services, but there would be no collective decision on the total amount to be supplied. This structure need not exhibit quality deterioration due to excessive individual demand, but the aggregate quantity of health services would be grossly inadequate and much below that quantity which would satisfy criteria for the optimal use of resources. This institutional combination is mentioned here only because it represents the exact reverse of that which is in being; here there would be public or collective demand decisions and private or individual supply decisions. The inefficiencies would take a dramatically different form from those currently observed.

Any reasonably workable set of institutions must bring demand decisions and supply decisions into the same framework for individual choice. There are only two alternatives here. The first is to allow individuals to make both demand decisions and supply decisions privately. This amounts to treating medical-health services as private and allowing the ordinary institutions of the market to operate. Individuals would be allowed, as they now are, to adjust demands privately and independently, but not at zero prices. Instead, prices would be set by competitive forces, and the services finally made available would be determined not through a collective-political decision but by the private decisions of many suppliers responding to expressed demands. This structure would be an efficient one in the restricted sense that no apparent shortages or surpluses would be observed.

Market organisation may not, however, take adequate account of the external economies in certain types of medical-health services. In addition, the distributive results of market organisation may not prove broadly acceptable and direct transfers of income-wealth to mitigate them may not be feasible. For either or both these reasons, or others, the market organisation of health services based on the distribution of income that emerges from a market economy may be rejected.

The alternative institutional structure is one in which both the demand side and the supply side are joined in a collective or public choice process. If the market solution is rejected, this becomes the only avenue of reform. The institutions through which individuals are allowed to adjust demands privately and individually to zero-price health services must be eliminated, and a specific collective decision on aggregate supply or quantity of services must be made to embody a specific quality of final services distributed in a specific manner among individuals. This means that the government must decide, collectively, how much health services each member of the group shall have available to him. There must be some determinate allocation of final services among persons, either in physical quantity units or in more-flexible units of general purchasing power. In the first case, each individual would be allowed to utilise specific maximum quantities per year: x visits to the surgery; y minor operations; z days in hospital. In the second case, each individual would be allowed to utilise a total "value" of service of P pounds per year as he chooses among the various health services. This scheme would allow for a somewhat wider individual range of choice among health-service facilities, but it would require, of course, the assigning of specific "shadow prices" to the different services made available. Either of these two schemes would, however, eliminate the institutional inefficiencies that are currently observed. There need be no congestion of available facilities and no continuing deterioration in service standards. The allowable demand on the facilities would be limited by the supply decision, and that would be that.

The objections to these modifications in existing institutions stem from the failure to allow for individuals who may desire, privately and personally, to utilise more health-medical services than any collective or political determination of allowable limits would provide. Such a desire, or need, may be due to fortuitous circumstances, and it may be largely independent of user price in many instances. If a collective limit of 30 days in hospital is imposed, what about the person whose illness requires 60 days?

Considerable improvements may be made in overcoming such objections if the many separate categories of health services are differentiated and treated separately. In general terms, however, this genuine problem of above-limit demands under any publicly financed system of health services can be met only by allowing for a market or market-like set of institutions to emerge which supplements the publicly financed, publicly supplied facilities. The advantages of such a system are that there need be no limits placed on the total amount of health services to be utilised by any single person or family; the necessity for limits applies only to the total amount of health services that shall be *publicly* financed and/or *publicly* supplied for him. Over and beyond these limits, the individual may be allowed to choose as much or as little as he desires, and for any reason.

Any detailed discussion of the particular features of the combined institutional structure that seems indicated as relatively efficient would require a second paper. One implication of the argument may be noted. Consideration should be given to an institutional structure that replaces, in whole or in part, direct public or governmental supply and operation by *public financing* of privately organised operation. This structure would allow for greater flexibility in individual adjustments, while, at the same time, it would facilitate bringing the demand side and the supply side more closely into coordination, in both public and private choices. On the basis of externality, equity, or other arguments, a political or collective decision can be made on the aggregate quantity of health services that will be *publicly financed*, and this decision can include a set of maximum limits, defined in purchasing power units, that will be made available to each person. These need not, of course, be equal among separate persons and groups. Individuals could be provided with vouchers for these indicated limits, which they could then utilise in purchasing health services as they chose. To the extent that their demands exceeded the amounts that could be purchased for such limits, individuals would be able to extend utilisation by privately financed supplements, these being financed directly by paying fees or charges or through various possible private insurance schemes.

My concern is not with recommending the institutional structure that Great Britain "should" adopt. The various institutional reforms above are mentioned to illustrate that an efficient NHS *can be organised* once the inconsistencies are recognised. Under a continuation of the existing structure the observed inefficiencies are likely to become more and more serious over time.

Appendix

Criteria for Aggregate Investment in Health Services

There are two distinct elements of the British experience that seem to refute the normative implications of neo-classical welfare economics. These are the failures of total investment in health services to rise demonstrably above that which would have been forthcoming under private organisation, and the willingness of governments to allow apparent quality deterioration including increasing congestion of available facilities. This paper has been limited to an explanation of the second of these elements.

In a paper published in 1963, written jointly with Milton Kafoglis of the University of Florida, an hypothesis was advanced that can partially "explain" the first of these two characteristic elements of the British experience. National Health Service data were cited as illustrative of the more general argument. It may be helpful here to summarise the argument of the Buchanan-Kafoglis paper and to relate it to that which this paper advances.

The Buchanan-Kafoglis analysis was concerned with comparing total outlay on a service under private and under public organisation when, at the margin of private extension, there are significant external economies. Whether or not such external economies characterise medical care in general need not be discussed in detail here. Some types of service, notably prevention of communicable diseases, seem clearly to exhibit such external economies, and, if necessary, the argument can be restricted in application to them. The orthodox Pigovian and post-Pigovian theorems about the divergence between marginal private and marginal social products suggest that an organisational shift from the private sector to the public sector would result in an increase in total resource commitment to the service in question. Implicitly, the whole analysis assumes that collective decision-makers would invest "optimally." The Buchanan-Kafoglis argument did not modify this implied assumption about collective decision-making. The argument showed, however, that a distinction between resource inputs and consumption output is required. The presence of significant external economies implies that outputs should be increased but, if "efficiencies" in utilising inputs are produced by a shift from private to public organisation, total resource commitment may not be increased by this shift from a sub-optimal to an optimal position.

The argument was illustrated by a medical-care example. Consider the case of a highly communicable disease the spread of which can be prevented only by improved sanitation measures. In this situation, the community may find that collectivisation of the service, with the component change in *distribution* of total resource investment, provides for a greater than one-for-one substitute for individuals' previously undertaken outlays. The superior efficiencies may be such that the optimally distributed investment generates optimal outputs with fewer resources than private investment. This result need not, of course, be present, but the analysis suggests that organisational-institutional changes that effectively internalise external economies need not imply expanded overall resource commitment.

What does this analysis signify for the experience of the NHS? It suggests that the relatively limited total outlay on the provision of medical-health facilities since 1948 does not, in itself, imply that the aggregate investment is sub-optimal. To the extent that external economies characterised the pre-1948 organisation of the services, the change in distributional efficiency achieved under general collectivisation may have been sufficient to guarantee optimal supplies at observed levels of outlay. On the other hand, to the extent that relevant external economies did not characterise pre-1948 experience, no such increased distributional efficiency should have taken place. But, in this case, there is no economic argument, as such, for collectivisation, and the private or market organisation tends to generate optimal levels of supply. The analysis suggests, therefore, that regardless of the extent to which relevant external economies might have been present under private organisation no implication can be drawn concerning relative levels of outlay required for "optimality."

If comparative levels of overall investment in medical-health care since 1948 tell us nothing at all about the attainment of the socially desired or optimal provision, how can the "wisdom" of collective decision-makers after 1948 be evaluated? Here we resort to the second element that is observed, namely, congestion on the available facilities. Does this congestion, in itself, tell us anything? Does it suggest that total investment is sub-optimal? No such inference is possible. The congestion that is observed indicates only that the supply of medical-health services at a standard quality is not sufficient to meet demand at zero user prices. But, since zero user prices are not demonstrably optimal in themselves, there is no implication that the supply of standard-quality services sufficient to meet all demands at these prices would produce optimal levels of investment.

Therefore, if we look at the experience of the NHS in the framework of theoretical welfare economics, we can infer nothing at all concerning the "correctness" or "incorrectness" of the collective decisions that have been made as regards overall or aggregate levels of provision. The observed facts are consistent with either non-optimal or optimal levels of investment since 1948.

The distribution of the services made available must be sharply distinguished from the aggregate levels of supply. It seems highly unlikely, of course, that this distribution has been "efficient" or "optimal," since, as the analysis of the present paper shows, the results depend on the private adjustments of many separate persons. The collectivisation of demand decisions might or might not involve a larger resource commitment; it would almost certainly involve a modified pattern of distributing the services that are made available.

Applied to the economics of health services, the emphasis of the earlier Buchanan-Kafoglis paper was on the question: What do the observed facts tell us about the level of total resource usage as measured in terms of the standard criteria of theoretical welfare economics? The answer is: Nothing at all.

The emphasis of the present paper has been quite different and is on the question: Can the observed facts be explained satisfactorily in terms of simple models of private and public choice?

The dominant weakness of the NHS is not the inefficiencies of public or collective decisions. It is rather the inconsistency between these decisions and the private or individual decisions on the demand side.

SUGGESTIONS FOR FURTHER READING

I. The following works are selected examples of an economic-analytical approach to political decision-making:

Downs, Anthony. *An Economic Theory of Democracy.* Harper, New York, 1957.
Black, Duncan. *The Theory of Committees and Elections.* Cambridge University Press, Cambridge, 1958.
Buchanan, James M., and Tullock, Gordon. *The Calculus of Consent.* University of Michigan Press, Ann Arbor, 1962.
Riker, William. *The Theory of Political Coalitions.* Yale University Press, New Haven, 1962.

II. The "free-rider" problem is central to the modern theory of public goods. The following works are suggested:

Samuelson, Paul A. "The Pure Theory of Public Expenditure," *Review of Economics and Statistics,* November 1954, 387–89; "Diagrammatic Exposition of the Theory of Public Expenditure," *Review of Economics and Statistics,* November 1955, 350–56.
Musgrave, Richard A. *The Theory of Public Finance.* McGraw-Hill, New York, 1959.
Olson, Mancur. *The Logic of Collective Action.* Harvard University Press, Cambridge, Mass., 1965.

III. The models suggested in the Buchanan-Kafoglis paper are extended in:

Buchanan, James M., and Tullock, Gordon. "Public and Private Interaction under Reciprocal Externality," Second Conference on Urban Expenditure Decisions (to be published by the Committee on Urban Economics, Resources for the Future).

IV. For specific discussions on the National Health Service that analyse relevant aspects of the problem the following works are suggested:

Jewkes, John and Sylvia. *The Genesis of the British National Health Service.* Basil Blackwell, Oxford, 1961, and *Value for Money in Medicine.* Blackwell, 1963.
Lees, D. S. *Health Through Choice.* Hobart Paper 14, Institute of Economic Affairs, 1961; reprinted with a Postscript in *Freedom or Free-for-All?* I. E. A., 1965.
Monopoly or Choice in Health Services? Occasional Paper 3, Institute of Economic Affairs, 1964.

Technological Determinism Despite the Reality of Scarcity
A Neglected Element in the Theory of Spending for Medical and Health Care

Introduction

In the United States, a large and ever-increasing share of total economic value is directed toward outlay on medical or health care services. This final end-use of value, along with its rate of growth, is of major concern to anyone who understands the elementary reality of scarcity. The finitude of the resource base, the labor force and its complement of accumulated and natural capital, guarantees that the share of total value directed into medical services cannot continue to grow without limit.

It has proven to be very hard, however, to get analytical "handles" on the fundamental issues here, "handles" that will allow us to sort out just where the problem is and to begin to identify ways and means of dealing with some central elements. I propose to make yet another effort, this time from the perspective of a constitutional political economist who is expert neither in the economics, the technology, nor the ethics of health or medicine. I want to suggest that perhaps, just perhaps, the listing of causal sources has been incomplete. In particular, I want to suggest that the central problems may not be those that emerge directly from the institutional structure described by the mix of public (governmental) and private financing, may not be those that

From University of Arkansas Medical School, Little Rock, 1990, 3–17. Reprinted by permission of the publisher.

emerge directly from the moral hazard that accompanies any large-scale in-surance arrangement, may not be primarily because of the explosion in medi-cal malpractice litigation, and may not be those that emerge directly from the organization of the supplying industry. These familiar problems may, them-selves, become apparent sources of concern only in the presence of a more fundamental relationship. I want to suggest that an ultimate causal source of difficulty emerges from the singular nature of the "demand" for medical ser-vices, at least for some major portion of these services, and that economists who analyze this "demand" as if it were analogous to other final or consump-tion service end-uses of economic value may have confused the whole policy discussion. Let me qualify my argument by acknowledging that I am offering one insight or perspective; I do not claim all-inclusive explanatory power.

I shall clarify the discussion first by analyzing the "demand" for medical services in terms of elementary economic principles. In this early part of the lecture, I shall resort to highly abstract and admittedly partial models of the medical health characteristics of the population. The analysis is designed to demonstrate why the advancing technology of medical-service delivery tends to drive the whole "machine," thereby "exploiting" peculiar features of the "demand." In this sense, my title is accurately descriptive; my analysis ex-plains why resource outlay in medical services tends to be technologically de-terministic, despite the elementary reality of scarcity.

Once having gotten the elementary economics out of the way, I shall then turn to the ethical issues that necessarily emerge. I shall address these issues from a constitutionalist perspective that will allow us to establish a forum for dialogue, even if the perspective remains silent on the ultimate normative choices that we must make, either directly or indirectly.

Utility and All That

Presumably, individuals produce value in order to spend it on final end-uses or consumption. And the professional economist models the rational choice behavior of individuals as utility maximization. Individuals spend or use their scarce resources so as to maximize the flow of utility or satisfaction that they can achieve. From this simple model of choice behavior, an important principle emerges. The scarce resource yields a maximum flow of utility only if it is allocated among uses in such fashion that a unit of that resource yields the same return in all of the uses to which it is put. Applied to the individual who considers spending alternatives that are possible under given income or wealth constraints, this principle suggests that a dollar spent must yield the same utility return in all uses. If this result is not present, then clearly it would be rational to shift spending from the use that yields less to the use that yields more, again as measured in increments of utility or satisfaction.

This elementary model of choice behavior, which is part and parcel of any economist's tool kit, suggests that rational choice requires spending on any valued end-use be made at the margin, in terms of "more or less" rather than in terms of comparative total outlay. From this emphasis on the calculus of margins, which is itself consequent from the maximization framework, there follows the implication that in the economic sense there is no differentiation to be made between the separate potential end-uses of value. A dollar is a dollar is a dollar, and the dollar spent for medical services at the margin yields a return equal to the dollar spent on popsicles. From this elementary model of choice behavior, the generalized principle of consumers' sovereignty in a market economy emerges. The preferences of consumers ultimately determine the mix of valued end-items produced by an economy's scarce resources.

Technological development affects this mix only as it may modify relative costs of goods that may be produced and, through such changes in costs, may modify relative prices confronted by consumers, and, hence, relative quantities of differing goods purchased.

I want to suggest here that this elementary model may be a source of misunderstanding at the point where it conflates all potential outlays as withdrawals from an exogenously determined income or wealth constraint. I want to suggest that the economist's categorical distinction between the constraint set and preferences may be misguided, and that the dividing line here may be endogenous in itself to the choice calculus of the individual. That is to say, there may exist categories of spending that are treated by individuals to be withdrawals from income or wealth *prior to* the standard calculus of utility maximization. One way of stating this is to say that the demands for any such potentially valued items are *lexicographically* related to other end-uses.

I suggest, specifically, that the preferences for or the demand for medical and health care services tend to fit this classification, at least in important respects. No one would spend willingly on medical services if it were not that one feels it necessary. I make an exception for the "little old ladies"—of both sexes—who literally enjoy trips to the clinic. The individual purchases medical services, directly or indirectly, in order to be able to restore, or preserve, that level of well-being attainable by a rationally selected outlay on nonmedical goods and services. In this sense, medical services are categorically distinct from other end-uses of value, with the partial exceptions of services such as emergency plumbing, hurricane or earthquake damage repairs, automotive towing, and a few others. In a very real sense, outlay on medical services does not compete with other outlays constrained within an exogenously determined budget; medical service outlay comes "off the top," so to speak, and becomes a determinant of rather than determined by the budget constraint. The difference here is recognized indirectly by the presence of medical outlay deductions under general income taxes.

When we pose the question of how much is to be spent on medical and health care services, whether this question be put to the individual who spends privately in the market or to the public chooser (voter, legislator, or bureaucrat) who spends publicly in the governmental sector, the answer is: "Whatever is necessary." By comparison and contrast, consider how this answer would sound if asked in the context of spending on food, clothing, entertainment, travel, or housing. Suppose we ask an individual how much should be spent on clothing. If he or she responds by saying, "whatever is necessary," we should dismiss the response as meaningless. By contrast, there tends to be a target level of well-offness that outlay on medical services purports to restore, before consideration of other outlays.[1]

---

1. As noted, economists' concentration on utility maximization subject to exogenously determined constraints has neglected the possibility that some potential outlays themselves may affect the constraint set. By contrast and comparison, psychologists, who do not work within the economists' model of choice behavior, have examined the problems involved in ordering potential demands hierarchically. Economists reject all such attempts in terms of failure to understand marginal adjustments. My argument here is that for a limited subset of potential uses of outlay the approach taken by psychologists may yield helpful insights that the economist's model tends to leave out.

I remain almost a total illiterate in psychology, but the discussion of motivation by Abraham Maslow has been helpful here. See Abraham Maslow, *Motivation and Personality* (New York: Harper and Row, 1954).

The Attenuation of Consumer Sovereignty

The elementary fact that we demand and purchase medical and health care services (or, at least, a substantial share of these services), either privately or publicly, lexicographically before the exercise of choices among other valued end-uses tends to reduce the user's interest in the process and manner of delivery of the services relative to that exercised in the purchase of other goods and services. Because the objective sought is "whatever is necessary to keep one healthy" so that once in such a state we can get on with life, we tend to be much less concerned about just how the required services are supplied. The individual, as final user, tends to abrogate his choice-making role, and to allow the suppliers, themselves, to select among alternative means of delivery. Analogues are present in these situations noted above; when our car breaks down, we tell the mechanic to "fix it," and we rarely inquire specifically and directly into the means through which the repairs actually are to be carried out.

With medical service delivery, this feature often is discussed in terms of an asymmetry of information between the final user and the supplier; we defer to the doctor because we accept that he knows better than we do just what services are needed to restore or preserve our well-offness. I am not questioning the empirical reality of some differential in information here. My analysis does suggest, however, that the apparent acquiescence of the final user in the alleged "expertise" of the supplier stems, at least in part, from the absence of the user's direct interest in the consumption flow of services, as such. The combined unwillingness and inability of final consumers-users of medical services to monitor suppliers may produce results that are value-wasting rather than value-economizing. Again, and as with the alleged informational asymmetry, the fundamental causal element may be the peculiar nature of the demand for medical services rather than the incentive structure.

Technological Dictatorship

So long as the resource requirements dictated by the current technology are severely limited relative to the total potential value generated in the economy, the lexicographic character of the demand for medical services may be accommodated without serious concern. Persons in varying decision capacities can continue to treat medical services outlay lexically before other end-uses of economic value without calling necessary attention to the ultimate contradiction between such an ordering and the finitude of the resources base.

Suppose, however, that advance in technology expands the public's definition and conception of "well-offness." Suppose there arise prospects for a reduction in the probability of premature death from disease and for an extension in longevity. Suppose further, however, that these prospects can be realized only by commitment of significantly large increments in resource cost. The continuing public response that medical care supply be extended to meet the demand described as "whatever is necessary" becomes an engine through which relatively enormous demands on resources can be mobilized. And this technologically driven allocative result will tend to emerge under almost any arrangement for the organization and financing of the medical service delivery, although these aspects, of course, may retain secondary relevance.

Let me clarify the discussion by introducing a highly simplified example, which is in no way intended to be descriptive but is constructed exclusively to convey the principle at work. For all ages, there were 315,000 broken arms reported in the United States in 1978, presumably resulting from a variety of causes. Each person so injured demanded restorative treatment, and, within limits, each person presumably was provided with basically the same essential services, as determined by the then-available technology. For illustration, let us say that, on average, an arm fracture required a resource outlay of $300. Recall the data are from 1978, not 1988.

This demand was lexicographic, by which I mean that this total outlay on repairing broken arms was largely independent of the potential demands for nonmedical services and of the costs of treatment. The outlay on repairing broken arms depended, first, on the number of fractures, which was stochastically predictable, and on the available technology. And, so long as this technology was such as to keep the overall resource requirements within tolerable bounds, there need have been no conscious awareness of the conflict with overall availability of resource.

Now, however, let us assume, strictly for purposes of making the argument here, that a new and totally different technology of bone repair had become available, a technology that almost miraculously would have repaired a broken arm quickly, so that full usage was restored after only one day. Assume further, however, that this new technique involved a resource cost one thousand times that of the old technology or $300,000 in this illustration.

If the same set of user-consumer attitudes should have carried over, attitudes that required the outlay that was "necessary" given the technology available, there would have resulted a threshold shift in total resource commitment to arm repairs. And this result would have emerged under almost any organization of the delivery system. If we assume that all members of the population were insured fully through private or public schemes against broken arms in 1978, and that the outlay per fracture under the old technology was $300, each person would have faced, on average, an insurance premium (ignoring administrative costs of the insurance system) of roughly $0.42. This premium now would increase to $420, under the introduction of the new technology, for insurance against broken arms alone.

The example indicates that as technological advance is generalized over *all* categories of medical care the resource commitment may become extremely large relative to the size of the economy, and note also that the resource commitment depends strictly on the technology. It is important to recognize that the causal influence runs from the technology directly to the resource use, without the intervening "filter" through expressed preferences, as would be the case with resource usage on ordinary goods and services. To the extent that the demand for medical services, in the aggregate, is lexicographic, the total resource outlay depends strictly on the rate of technological advance. And the self-interest of suppliers acts both to accelerate technological change and to promote uniform rates of adoption of new technology over all sectors and regions of medical-service delivery. The socio-institutional "engine" seems capable of generating levels of outlay that are far beyond those already attained. It becomes relatively easy to think of a share of one-quarter of the total value produced in the economy being devoted to medical and health care services by the century's turn.

Efficiency Considerations

Economists have tended to concentrate attention on changes or reforms that will insure that the medical services supplied in response to demand are delivered efficiently. Their focus has been on the perverse incentives faced by suppliers in the face of informational asymmetry, on the moral hazard present under any large-scale insurance scheme, on the free-rider behavior of users under public financing arrangements, on the cost-increasing results of effective cartelization of delivery systems. The reforms advanced by medical economists take the form of suggestions for increasing the competitiveness among suppliers, both among separate "firms" and among separate professional practitioners across the industrial group, for requiring co-payment by users under insurance systems, whether these be governmental or private, and for regulatory political-bureaucratic intervention when organizational rearrangements fail to produce desired results.

As an economist, I do not challenge the arguments advanced by those of my colleagues who concern themselves with the efficiency gains promised on successful implementation of those and other possible reforms. My emphasis is, however, quite different, in that I suggest that even in the ideal-utopian world where each and every one of the economists' recommendations is adopted, where medical service delivery is ideally efficient, the lexicographic nature of demand insures that the central allocative issue will remain. As a society, we will still be devoting what appears to be an excessively large share of total value produced in the economy to outlay on the medical and health care sector.

The Ethics of Lexicographic Preferences

As an economist, I have reached the end of my tether when I have explained the results that we observe, speculated a bit about alternative futures, and advanced or supported proposals for reform designed to increase efficiency in medical-service delivery. If I am to go further and criticize the allocative results that I predict to occur, I must shift to more controversial subject matter. If there is no efficiency-based criterion to be mounted, and if the results still seem to "appear to embody an excessively large commitment of resources to medical services," I must examine the basis for such an intuition. The "ethics of lexicographic preferences" cannot be avoided.

Let me clarify again the meaning of lexicographic preferences, especially in application to medical services. I have suggested that as an empirical generalization persons demand the outlay on medical services that "is necessary to maximize survival and longevity," and that such a target level of medical care comes to be determined technologically, relatively independent of the manner in which the delivery system is financed or organized. If we are to question this working-out of lexicographic preferences on ethical grounds, it is necessary to isolate and to identify just who is damaged or harmed; in some comparative sense, who suffers as a result of lexicography in preferences for medical services?

I do not want to concentrate on distributional differences that may violate canons of simple justice when all persons do not share the preferences in question. If those with lexicographic preferences for medical services make up a dominant majority coalition, and if the industry wholly or partially is organized and financed publicly, those persons who do not share these extreme preferences may be coerced into financing and ultimately consuming medical services beyond preferred levels. In this case, claims that the system is unjust or unfair may become ethically legitimate.

However, I want to concentrate on the more difficult question that may arise when *all* persons in the society share lexicographic preferences for medical services. If the delivery system is tolerably efficient, and if participants know the relationship between total resource commitment and the state of technology, can there then be any objection raised to the allocative results, even if very large shares in total value seem pre-committed to the medical sector of the economy?

This question becomes especially difficult for an individualist-cum-contractarian, as I often classify myself in all such discussions as this. The individualist cannot invoke the existence of some external source of value that would produce criteria with which to evaluate alternative sets of individual preference patterns. By adopting the individualist philosophical stance, one is thereby committed to a denial that such external sources of evaluation exist. Any criticism of individual preference patterns must be derived, therefore, from the evaluation of some individuals themselves. But if by presumption here all persons in a society hold lexicographic preferences for medical services, how can there possibly be any ethical grounds for criticism?

One intellectual ploy that might be suggested is to adopt the familiar contractarian procedure and examine the choice calculus that might emerge from behind an appropriately drawn veil of ignorance and/or uncertainty. This procedure does allow some escape from the constraints imposed by identifiable self-interest while it preserves the individualistic character of the choice setting without invoking external evaluation, as such. This exercise is helpful in forcing some further clarification in the meaning of lexicographic preferences for medical services.

In his private, individually identified capacity as a present or future consumer-user of medical services, the individual may exhibit strict lexicographic preferences. That is, for himself or herself, as an identified user-consumer-patient, the individual may demand that "which is necessary to maximize survival and longevity." At the same time, the same individual, if placed behind the appropriately drawn veil of ignorance and/or uncertainty, may not have such extreme preferences. In this latter setting, the person is forced, essentially, to choose that supply of medical services that is to be made available to anyone (everyone) in the relevant group of participants. And it is surely plausible to suggest that no inconsistency arises between the presence of lexicographic preference in the private-individualized setting and the absence of such preferences in the veil-of-ignorance setting. The presumed differences between choices made in the two settings are directionally predictable. Clearly, the working-out of privately identified lexicographic preferences for medical services may generate a larger commitment of resources to the medical sector than the commitment that would be generated under institutions that, directly or indirectly, force persons into some veil-of-ignorance stance. There arises, in this case, an interesting argument for governmental or socialized decision making, one that is almost counter to those that were advanced traditionally. Governmental or collectivized decision making may require, at least in some ideal sense, that participants make choices as to resource commitments in something that resembles veil-of-ignorance settings. Governmental or collectivized arrangements become, therefore, instrumental means to *limit* overall resource commitments to the supply of services to meet demands that are lexicographic when exercised privately.

The above discussion of the possibility that preferences tend to be lexicographic if exercised privately but non-lexicographic if exercised and expressed publicly or through collective decision structures is, in one sense, a digres-

sion from my main argument, because my presupposition is that lexicographic preferences are present in the demand for medical services, regardless of the institutional-structural setting within which individuals exercise
demand choices. This empirical presupposition that lexicographic preferences for medical services exist in the veil-of-ignorance choice setting as well
as in the privately identifiable choice setting should be tested, of course. And
the existence of differences in the basic preferences in the private and the
collectivized setting may explain, in part, the relatively smaller resource
commitment for medical services in fully socialized systems than in quasi-
privatized systems.[2] But casual empiricism also suggests that even in collectivized structures preferences tend to be lexicographic. It seems plausible to
suggest that the resource commitments in the collectivized delivery systems
are as dependent on the rate of technological advance as are the commitments in quasi-privatized systems.

In any case, for purposes of my argument here, I want to presume that
lexicographic preferences characterize choices as to medical services demands in all settings. That is to say, whether persons purchase their own
medical services, either directly or through voluntarily chosen insurance
schemes, or whether persons participate, directly or indirectly, in collective
decisions as to the collective demands for medical services, the lexicographic
character of the demand is presumed to be descriptive. This presumption allows me to return to the central ethical question in its strongest form. If persons in a society share the lexicographic preferences for medical services,
how can there be anything "wrong" with whatever result that emerges, regardless of the size of the resource commitment that the exercise of such
preferences may involve?

As noted earlier, the working out of the lexicographic preferences for
medical services becomes equivalent to the taking of a share of total value
(income) "off the top," so to speak, with this share itself being determined by
the state of current technology. The effect is as if the income available for
disposition over all utility-enhancing uses is reduced as medical technology
advances. There is presumably no clear relationship between the potential

2. See my "The Inconsistencies of the National Health Service," Occasional Paper
No. 7 (London: Institute of Economic Affairs, 1965).

supply of work effort and disposable income. But because saving is itself one use of income that is available for disposition after the "necessary" outlay on medical services, we can predict that there will be an inverse relationship between the rate of technological change in medicine and the absolute level of saving, and through this, of capital formation in the economy.

It is plausible, therefore, to envisage an economy in which an ever-increasing outlay, both in absolute amount and relative to total product value, is devoted to the medical care industry while the rate of saving and capital formation falls, again both in absolute amount and relative to total value of product. In the limiting case, we can imagine society with a low income level but with most of the income produced devoted to the medical service industry.

If we invoke an intergenerational veil-of-ignorance construction, we may suggest that such a society will be less preferred than one in which the total outlay on medicine and health care is restricted through the use of some intergenerational rule. An intergenerational veil-of-ignorance construction has the following property: an individual is presumed to be unable to locate himself or herself generationally. That is, the individual cannot know whether, in actuality, he or she will be born in 1990, 2010, 2030, 2050, or some generation thereafter. Suppose, however, that behind such a veil, the individual is allowed to choose between (1) a regime that would leave the working out of lexicographic preferences undisturbed and (2) a regime that incorporates some explicitly chosen limit to the total outlay. It seems plausible to suggest that the individual in such a choice setting may prefer the second of these regimes, which would predictably involve a higher level of income in later periods, but at the expense of some restriction on the full satisfaction of the lexicographic preferences for medical services in earlier periods. The actual choice here would depend, of course, on the predicted rate of advance in medical technology, as well as on the cost and other characteristics of this technology over the extended number of periods.

If we shift out of the strict individualist-contractarian normative framework and adopt a more evolutionary perspective that places an independent value on the viability of a complex socio-economic–political interaction through time, an argument in support of collectively imposed constraints on the total resource commitment to medical care might be developed. The regime that allows for a higher rate of capital formation would have survival value relative to the regime that devotes its potential for saving to outlay for currently used medical services.

Summary and Conclusion

I deliberately have confined the discussion in this lecture to the implications of a single element in the economics of medical services, an element that may not have received sufficient critical attention by economists. I have suggested that preferences for medical and health care services tend to be lexicographic, in the sense that the full satisfaction of these preferences takes priority over other possible end-uses to which economic value might be put. This feature or characteristic of the demand for medical services creates a direct linkage between the rate of advance in medical service technology and the total resource commitment made by society in meeting this demand.

My concentration on this single relationship should not be taken to represent any relegation to secondary importance of those other features of the complex institutional structure for delivery that have been stressed by others who have examined the basic economics of the medical industry. I have suggested, however, that these complementary features tend to be made more serious in their impact by the existence of the underlying lexicographic preferences. Further, I have suggested that even if these familiar complementary features of the complex structure of medical care delivery should be adjusted or reformed in full compliance with economists' dictates, the technology-dependent resource commitment implied by the lexicographic preferences would remain problematic.

The derivation of an ethical criticism of the exercise of lexicographic preferences, if such do indeed exist, is not, however, an easy task, especially for the individualist-contractarian, even if there arises some strongly felt intuitive sense that something may be "wrong" with such preferences, as exhibited. In order to mount any ethical criticism that seems at all defensible, it becomes necessary to introduce an intergenerational perspective. In this very long-range view of things, a regime that collectively adopts some rule that effectively places restrictions on the size of the overall resource commitment to medical services, and perhaps especially the share of the aggregate commitment that involves maintenance and extension of nonproductive lives, may well be preferred to the regime that incorporates no such rule among its complexity of institutional arrangements.

Critics of my thesis in this lecture may attack me as a Cassandra who raises unnecessary fears about prospects for excessively large resource commitments to the medical and health care industry. They may bring this charge on either one of two separate arguments. There may be critics, especially economists, who remain wedded to the rational choice models of the formal analysis in the textbooks, models that implicitly deny the possible existence of lexicographic preferences, especially as applied over large potential changes in resource commitments. Persons will reduce, or so it may be argued, the outlay on medical services in the face of technology-driven quality improvement as costs accelerate beyond certain limits. Hence, so long as the delivery system is financed and organized so as to incorporate incentives that are broadly compatible with the furtherance of standard efficiency norms, there is little cause for worry.

A second, and perhaps less effective, criticism may be mounted that acknowledges the possible existence of lexicographic preferences but suggests that the technological advances to be expected will increase quality of care greatly, relative to the accompanying increases in cost. This criticism, which is likely to emerge from participants in the medical care industry itself, implies that ultimate users-consumers indeed will get "value for money," and, therefore, need not express concern for any comparative wastage of value through overextension of resource outlay.

Of course, no one can predict the rate of technological development in the medical care or any other industry, but the dramatic research successes over the whole area of related research programs in genetics, molecular biology, biochemistry, and related areas in applied medicine offer little evidence that mitigates against the widely shared concerns about overextendibility, especially in the face of observed dramatic increases in outlays over recent decades.

I conclude, therefore, with this question: How much can we as a body politic "afford" to spend on medical and health care? The *laissez-faire* response emergent from the mixed private-public delivery system now in place does not offer, for me, a satisfying resolution to this question. But these unsatisfactory results under the mixed system of delivery are surely no basis for any argument to the effect that a more collectivized structure, under lexicographic preferences, would accomplish net improvement.

"The fault, Dear Brutus . . ."

The Budgetary Politics of Social Security

Social security is off limits for serious political discussion and debate. When crisis threatened in the early 1980s, both an independent commission and a genuinely bipartisan agreement were deemed necessary. But were the proposals that were developed and legally incorporated into the system exposed to sufficient scrutiny? Many are now concerned that the reforms failed to take into account important macroeconomic and macropolitical implications. This chapter addresses some of the rather obvious problems that emerge when political spillovers between social security and the comprehensive federal budget are acknowledged.

The second section presents a stylized model of social security financing as it is—was—supposed to work under the reforms enacted in 1983. In describing this model, I shall emphasize the restrictiveness of the conditions that must be satisfied to ensure the desired results. The third section then examines the difficulties raised by the interdependence of the revenues and the outlays of the social security account and non-social-security components in the comprehensive federal budget. The impact of the 1983 reforms on the budgetary politics of the late 1980s and the 1990s assumes center stage in this discussion. The fourth section examines the institutional sources of possible interdependence and analyzes the prospective effects of taking social security out of the comprehensive federal budget. In the fifth section, I try to

From *Social Security's Looming Surpluses: Prospects and Implications,* ed. Carolyn L. Weaver (Washington, D.C.: AEI Press, 1990), 45–56. Reprinted with the permission of The American Enterprise Institute for Public Policy Research, Washington, D.C.

I am indebted to my colleague Richard E. Wagner for helpful discussions.

place the system in the larger political context, and I make some predictions about future developments.

For convenience, I ignore the nontemporal redistributional elements in the social security tax and benefit formulas and make no efforts to analyze impacts on aggregate economic variables. My comments refer only to the Old-Age, Survivors, and Disability Insurance (OASDI) part of the social security structure, which excludes Medicare.[1]

Sufficient unto Itself—The Idealized Postreform System

Assume that in a stylized prereform setting the social security account operated on a purely pay-as-you-go intergenerational transfer basis. There was no trust fund accumulation, but the participants were ensured a return on tax-financed "investment" at least equal to the growth rate of the economy, which in turn was approximately equal to the real rate of return on private investment.

This fully operational pay-as-you-go system of intertemporal transfer is then shocked by a dramatic and unpredicted shift in demographic patterns. An unanticipated surge occurs in the rate of increase in population over a limited period of years, which is then followed by a return to slower rates of increase. The projected impact of this demographic shift on the operation of the pay-as-you-go transfer system comes to be widely recognized. As the baby-boom generation reaches retirement, the rate of tax on productive income earners must be increased sharply if, indeed, the implicit contract with members of the baby-boom generation is to be honored. Failing reform, the present value of future social security liabilities will exceed, and by a large order of magnitude, the present value of anticipated revenues.

---

1. For presentations of the results of simulation models that examine those effects under several sets of assumptions, see Joseph M. Anderson, Richard A. Kuzmak, Donald W. Moran, George R. Schink, Dale W. Jorgenson, and William R. M. Perradin, "Study of the Potential Economic and Fiscal Effects of Investment of the Assets of the Social Security Old-Age and Survivors and Disability Insurance Trust Funds: Final Report to the Social Security Administration" (May 1988, mimeographed); and Henry J. Aaron, Barry P. Bosworth, and Gary T. Burtless, "Final Report to the Social Security Administration on Contract No. 600-87-0072 (1988, mimeographed).

At some point, the "crisis" could have been expected to provoke attempts at reform. To forestall the dire predictions about possible default on the implicit intergenerational contract in future decades, suppose an attempt was made—as in 1983—to shift from the purely pay-as-you-go system to one that embodies some elements of a funded system. Rates of tax on current income earners are increased beyond those rates that would have been dictated by strict pay-as-you-go accounting integrity. In the late 1980s, the trust fund accounts start to accumulate surpluses, and these surpluses are programmed to accelerate dramatically over the decades of the 1990s, 2000s, and 2010s.[2] These surpluses, invested at interest in government debt claims, are designed to meet the pension commitments to the baby-boom generation during the drawdown decades of the next century, without unduly onerous tax increases on the workers at that time. In a real sense, the members of the baby-boom generation are subjected to current taxes sufficient not only to finance the pensions of those who are now retired or who will retire in the 1990s but also to finance a portion of *their own* retirement in the third, fourth, and fifth decades of the next century. The period of trust fund accumulation is to be followed by an anticipated period of depletion, which is to be financed from the previously accumulated surpluses.

The central difference between a pay-as-you-go system of intergenerational transfers and a fully funded system lies in the fully funded system's investment of excess revenues in income-earning assets. These assets, in turn, generate returns sufficient to finance the future obligations that are currently incurred. For future income streams to be higher than they would be under the pay-as-you-go system, the rate of capital formation must increase. But social security trust fund surpluses are invested exclusively in claims against the U.S. government. These claims earn interest, which accrues to the account; but since the federal budget is in deficit, the funds collected from payroll taxes are used directly to finance current outlays by the

2. See intermediate II-B projections contained in the Board of Trustees of the Federal Old-Age and Survivors Insurance Trust Fund and the Federal Disability Insurance Trust Fund, *1989 Annual Report of the Board of Trustees of the Federal Old-Age and Survivors Insurance Trust Fund and the Federal Disability Insurance Trust Fund* (Washington, D.C.: GPO, 1989).

federal government. Can we say, then, that the shift to a partially funded system increases the rate of capital formation in the economy?

The answer is affirmative, if we impose the economists' *ceteris paribus* and consider the social security account in isolation. The actual use of the tax revenues is irrelevant in this setting. The debt claims against the government earn interest, and the account, therefore, grows precisely as if the funds had been invested in private income-earning assets in the economy. But how can we be assured that the net result is an increase in the rate of aggregate capital formation? This result is ensured if social security, in fact, operates independent of the rest of the budget. If choices made outside the social security system are not themselves affected by the trust fund accumulations (a relationship to be discussed at length later), then the rate of capital formation in the economy must increase, because as the social security trust fund "purchases" debt claims from the Treasury, there is a dollar-for-dollar reduction in the private sector's purchase of Treasury obligations. This increases purchases of private sector securities, those issued by private borrowers who, in turn, use the funds to purchase income-earning assets that can provide returns sufficient to amortize the obligations.

As trust fund surpluses grow over the next three decades, the *ceteris paribus* scenario will ultimately require that social security "purchase" not only the debt claims issued by the government to finance Treasury deficits but also a portion of the outstanding debt claims held by the public. That is to say, some share of trust fund surpluses will go toward retiring privately held public debt. The effects of this operation, of course, are no different from those involved when the trust fund surpluses replace private purchases of Treasury securities to finance a Treasury deficit. In either case, private funds are freed for additional investment in income-yielding assets.

In the drawdown period (projected by the social security board of trustees to commence in the second third of the next century), the social security account will find it necessary to call its debt claims against the Treasury to meet its implicit obligations to the baby-boom retirees. To honor these calls against it, the Treasury will find it necessary to increase its sale of securities to purchasers other than the social security account. As lendable funds are shifted to the purchase of government debt instruments, the rate of investment in interest-earning assets in the economy will be reduced. The period of trust fund shrinkage will affect the aggregate rate of capital formation in precisely the opposite way from that generated during the period of trust fund accumulation.

Social Security Trust Funds and the Federal Budget

As many critics of Marshallian (partial equilibrium) economic method have noted, *cetera* are seldom, if ever, *paribus*. This criticism applies particularly to the stylized scenario of social security independence sketched earlier and which arguably served as the basis for the reforms enacted in 1983. As has been the case with many other ill-advised ventures into economic policy, however, the reforms failed to reckon with the elementary realities of democratic politics. A small dose of public choice theory might have dampened the enthusiasm of those who sought to ensure the integrity of the system.

The fact is that the social security fiscal account is not, and cannot be, *politically* independent of the income and outlays that describe the more inclusive fiscal operations of the federal government. There is no necessary economic interdependence here; there is no internal contradiction, in a general equilibrium sense, involved in treating the social security account as if it were separate and apart from remaining components of the comprehensive federal budget. The interdependence is political rather than economic, and it emerges from the predicted behavior of political decision makers who are ultimately responsive to the demands of voting constituencies.

Budgetary complements to social security independence

To understand the potential effects of the projected trust fund accumulations over the decades of the 1990s, 2000s, and 2010s, we should carefully define the budgetary discipline that political agents would have to follow to ensure full social security isolation. As noted, the operation of the system *as if* it were independent would require that the partial derivative of the reform-induced changes in non-social-security revenue and outlay streams over the half-century be zero. That is to say, the path through time of non-social-security revenues and outlays could not vary with shifts in social security financing from periods of pay-as-you-go, to trust fund accumulation, and later to trust fund depletion.

Note that the genuine independence here does not require specification of any particular relationship between non-social-security revenues and outlays, either early, middle, or late in the projected temporal sequence. The non-social-security portion of the budget may be in deficit, in balance, or in surplus, and shifts among these three possible sets of relationships may occur over time as dictated by political forces. All that is strictly required for independence is that this time path of the budget deficit (positive or negative) not be affected directly by what happens in the social security account itself.

How would the required invariance reveal itself in the comprehensive federal budget? The comprehensive budget deficit would be observed to move toward budget surplus during the period of social security trust fund accumulation and to move below the non-social-security time path toward budget deficit during anticipated periods of trust fund shrinkage. If we state this requirement more simply as part of the measured budget deficit, the comprehensive deficit must be reduced, dollar for dollar, with increases in social security trust fund balances and increased, dollar for dollar, with decreases in trust fund balances in later periods.

INTERDEPENDENCE IMPOSED BY AGGREGATE BUDGETARY TARGETS

This requirement for social security independence and isolation will be violated under any and all policy regimes that involve aggregate targets for the revenue-outlay relationship in the comprehensive federal budget. Suppose, by way of a simple and unreal example, that there existed a rigidly enforced rule for comprehensive budget balance under the pay-as-you-go period for the social security account and later. In operation, this rule would prevent the necessary generation of a comprehensive budget surplus during the periods of social security trust fund accumulation. Conversely, it would facilitate an expansion in other outlays or a reduction in nonpayroll taxes, while at the same time allowing the budget balance target to be met. Alternatively, suppose that the comprehensive budget was in deficit during the period of pay-as-you-go social security financing but that medium-range legislative targets were established to reduce and then eliminate the comprehensive budget deficit; this is the setting under Gramm-Rudman-Hollings. In this case, surpluses in the social security account allow the deficit-reduction targets to be satisfied, while still allowing for *increases* in the non-social-security deficit. Much the same results emerge under any scheme for deficit control that uses balance or imbalance in the comprehensive budget as a criterion for policy achievement. As a final example, suppose that a decision is made to keep the relationship between the measured comprehensive budget deficit and the gross national product constant. Again, satisfaction of this norm would allow non-social-security deficits to increase during the period of trust fund accumulation.

Social security surpluses and budgetary ease

What will be the effects of any of the predicted violations of the strict independence requirement? Suppose that social security, in fact, runs surpluses and that these surpluses serve merely to relieve pressures on politicians to reduce the deficit in the rest of the budget. Outlays in the rest of the budget increase relative to tax revenues, and the non-social-security deficit increases despite the apparent decrease in the comprehensive budget deficit. This scenario, which is almost certain to be descriptive of fiscal and political reality in the 1990s, implies that the 1983 reforms will not accomplish their ultimate purpose, which was to relieve pressures upon income earners when the baby-boom generation reaches retirement age.

It may be useful to trace the steps in the analysis here. Suppose that the generation of a trust fund surplus (payroll tax revenues and other income in excess of current program payments) causes politicians to expand outlays on other government programs. This policy combination negates the funding purpose of the 1983 reforms, because no funds are released for an increase in private capital formation. No displacement of private lending to government takes place. As before, the social security account "purchases" claims against the Treasury with the enhanced payroll tax receipts; but the government now uses these revenues, *not* to replace funds previously borrowed from the private sector but to expand outlays on other government programs. There is no release of funds that can be made available to private investors in income-earning assets.

One feature of this politicized interdependence scenario deserves special notice. If the trust fund surpluses are used to expand other government spending, this will not be reflected in an increase in the measured comprehensive budget deficit because the added spending is financed by the payroll tax revenues that generate the surpluses in the first place. The deficit is simply higher than it otherwise would have been. But because surplus social security receipts are used directly to "purchase" claims against the Treasury, the measured national debt will increase, and, with it, interest obligations.[3] This apparently paradoxical feature stems, of course, from the accounting conventions that allow for the dual counting of payroll tax revenues, both as the source for the "purchase" of the internally held social security claims against the Treasury and as the revenue offset to general outlays in the comprehensive budget. Payroll taxpayers think of themselves as paying for the future benefits that the social security claims against the Treasury measure. But who then is paying for the expansion of other outlays? This payment must finally rest with future taxpayers, who must finance the amortization of the social security claims.

As noted, to the extent that the trust fund surpluses are offset by expansions in other spending, there will be no induced increase in the rate of private capital formation in the economy. There will be no direct or indirect "funding" of the future pension obligations. The social security account, treated as an administratively separate unit, will accumulate claims against the Treasury, and hence the general taxpayer, but there will be no increase in future income that will allow such claims to be more easily financed, either through taxation or debt issue.

---

3. It may be suggested that there is no increase in the size of the debt, properly measured. If retirement benefits are promised in future periods, the present value of these benefits is a liability of the federal government that should be included in properly measured debt totals. The "funding" process serves merely to make these real liabilities explicit.

In the strict independence scenario, by contrast, there will be an explicit reduction in the size of the debt, properly measured, as trust fund surpluses emerge.

POSTSURPLUS POLITICAL CONSEQUENCES

The independence and interdependence scenarios described above are dramatically different in their relevance to macroeconomic policy. The first embodies an increase in private capital formation as a result of the 1983 social security reforms, independent of the movements in the rest of the federal budget. The second, and more realistic, scenario involves a dissipation of the social security trust fund buildup through politicized profligacy in the rest of the budget. However, and this is a point worthy of some emphasis, the political consequences in the postsurplus period need not be so great as the economic differences in the two models might suggest.

In either case, at the beginning of the drawdown period, social security will call in its claims against the Treasury, and the Treasury will stand obligated to advance the funds that are required to meet the emerging social security deficits. This demand on the Treasury can be met by increases in the sale of government securities to the private sector, by taxation, or by a reduction in other government spending. The Treasury will face this fiscal choice regardless of whether it has maintained the discipline dictated by the independence scenario during periods of the trust fund buildup. And under either scenario social security advocates can argue that payroll taxes have indeed been sufficiently high to "finance" the drawdown of the trust fund accumulations, quite apart from the presence or absence of fiscal discipline in other sectors of the comprehensive budget. Conversely, under either scenario, social security critics can argue that program changes are necessary because of the large deficits in social security, regardless of fiscal policy in the predeficit period.

A fully symmetrical interdependent fiscal stance over the whole buildup and drawdown cycle might suggest that during the surplus period the non-social-security deficits would be higher than under the independence scenario, but lower during the drawdown period because of the increased fiscal pressures. But there would seem to be no behavioral basis for predicting such symmetry. The social security surpluses can, as noted, facilitate a hidden increase in the deficit in the rest of the budget, an increase that is consistent with the natural proclivities of constituency-responsive politicians. The later social security deficits present politicians with much less desirable options. Unless otherwise constrained, they will finance the social security deficit with additional borrowing from the private sector, thereby producing explosive growth in the size of the comprehensive budget deficits over the entire draw-down period. This resort to the private sector for sale of bonds would, of course, be more appropriate under the independence model, since public borrowing from the private sector would have been reduced and possibly eliminated during the surplus period.

Sectoral Independence

Would the independent integrity of social security be more likely to be respected with accounting separation from the other revenue-outlay components of the comprehensive federal budget? That is to say, for purposes of Gramm-Rudman, should earmarked payroll taxes be excluded from federal budget revenues, and should social security payments be excluded from federal expenditures? There exists a well-grounded public choice argument for sectoral separation of elements in the comprehensive budget, especially if revenues from particular sources are earmarked for and limited to spending on particular programs and, further, if the financing of such programs is limited to the defined sources of revenues. The rationality of the political decision-making process is enhanced if the costs and benefits of particular programs can be more readily identified and if the institutional structure is such that it encourages politicians to make choices on a program-by-program basis. If the social security structure could be removed from the comprehensive federal budget, there would seem to be less likelihood that the surpluses over the next three decades would facilitate increases in deficits in the rest of the budget, thereby reducing or eliminating the economic advantages of "funding."

There is an institutional difficulty of major proportions, however, in removing the social security account from the comprehensive federal budget, a difficulty that may negate the apparent advantages to be gained in overall fiscal responsibility. The payroll tax and the revenues therefrom finance both retirement and disability payments *and medical payments* under the Hospital Insurance (HI) account. It seems unlikely, therefore, that the social security account could be meaningfully separated from the HI account, or that one account could be removed from Gramm-Rudman without the other. And so long as the HI account faces prospective deficits, politicians would have a natural proclivity to use the buildup in the social security trust funds to finance the mounting deficits in the HI trust fund, rather than to increase net purchases of securities from the Treasury. Because the two accounts would seem likely to be included in any institutional or administrative sectoralization of the comprehensive budget, little would be gained by attempts to accomplish social security's independence by this route.

A somewhat different argument can be advanced against removing the social security account from the comprehensive federal budget, which relates to the politics of social security itself. Throughout most of the history of social security, benefits have increased well beyond the limits justified by actuarial standards. This suggests that surplus revenues in the account are politically vulnerable. If the social security and the HI accounts are removed from the comprehensive budget, political pressures to use emerging surpluses to fund increases in non-social-security deficits would tend to give way to comparable or greater pressures to fund unjustifiable increases in program benefits.[4]

Prospects, Politics, and Predictions

Application of elementary public choice theory to the current social security financing arrangement yields relatively straightforward predictions, especially over the medium term extending through the mid-1990s. The much-heralded reforms enacted in 1983 have commenced to generate the anticipated trust fund surpluses. These surpluses will not, however, be allowed to reduce the size of overall federal deficits, as would be required if the funding purpose of the revised tax structure were to be achieved. Instead, it seems almost certain that the trust fund accumulation will become one of the primary means through which the comprehensive budget deficit will be kept within the limits defined by deficit-reduction targets, such as those embodied in Gramm-Rudman. As I noted earlier, non-social-security deficits, including those in the HI account, will likely be increased rather than decreased over the interim. In particular, because of the political and accounting links between the various social security programs, the surpluses will provide the politically

4. See Carolyn L. Weaver, "Controlling the Risks Posed by Advance Funding—Options for Reform," in this volume for more on this.

justifiable source of financing for the increasing deficits in the HI account. To the extent that the social security surpluses exceed the HI deficits, they will allow for still further increases in federal spending outside the social insurance system.

To appreciate the full impact of the reforms and the inclusive budgetary politics of the federal government, we should recall the fiscal setting of the early and mid-1980s. By 1983, it had become clear that some of the extremist supply-side projections were not within the realm of the possible; the tax changes of 1981, the unsuccessful attempts to reduce nondefense federal spending, and the increase in defense spending combined to ensure an explosion in the size of the comprehensive budget deficit. A constitutional amendment to require budget balance gained support, both in several states and in the Congress itself. Prospects for the adoption of such an amendment became very real in 1983. While this was taking place, Congress itself began to acknowledge that its own procedures were seriously flawed; there was an emerging recognition that the proclivity to generate ever-increasing and permanent deficits must, somehow, be curbed.

First in 1985 and again in 1987 after judicial rejection of some features of the 1985 legislation, Congress enacted the Gramm-Rudman-Hollings budgetary reforms that incorporated specific targets for deficit reduction over a five-year period, the first version dictating budget balance by 1991 and the second by 1993. This phase-in feature of the legislation was grounded, apparently, on the conviction that taxpayers and beneficiaries in the late 1980s were unwilling to accept the fiscal austerity that would be required to move more directly to budget balance.

The public did not recognize that the earlier-enacted "reforms" in social security would make the achievement of the Gramm-Rudman targets much easier than if pay-as-you-go financing had been maintained. The increases in the social security tax rates virtually guaranteed that there would be a substantial excess of social security revenues over payment obligations in the interim. From the standpoint of social security alone, these reforms did indeed incorporate the fiscal austerity that was deemed politically impossible if undertaken directly.

If we view all this cynically, the wage earners subjected to the increased payroll taxes were tricked by the illusion created by dual counting into financing the targeted reduction in the comprehensive budget deficit. Beneficiaries of other government programs and nonpayroll taxpayers will enjoy unchanged, and even enhanced, benefit flows at the expense of payroll taxpayers. In a very real sense, the fiscal crisis that appeared on the way to resolution was simply postponed for up to three decades by the changes enacted in social security.

The social security account will, to be sure, accumulate very substantial nominal claims against the general taxpayers and beneficiaries of the federal government. There will have been no "funded" increase in the tax base, however, that will facilitate the financing of these claims when due. After the first two decades of the next century, when these social security claims are called, wage earners will be able to make a plausible case against further payroll tax hikes to help finance these system-held claims. But by that time, the events of the 1980s will be bygones, and the democratic politics of the 2020s will not respect the good intentions of the reformers of the 1990s.

What are the conclusions? Were the 1983 reforms a mistake? Did they foster fiscal illusions that will make ultimate reform in fiscal procedures more difficult? I shall not answer these questions directly here. But the analysis does allow me to identify the gainers and losers from the changes that were made. In any resource or commodity dimension, current payroll taxpayers lose; they are required to sacrifice current consumption and investment opportunities. These losses need not be matched in a subjective psychological dimension if payroll taxpayers think of themselves as "purchasing" a more secure funding of their own future retirement payments. Current nonpayroll taxpayers and non-social-security program beneficiaries gain in an opportunity cost sense. They are not required to reduce the benefits they get from the spending flows that generate the current deficit. Future taxpayers, generally payroll and other, along with future beneficiaries of other government programs lose relative to their positions under either a continuation of the pay-as-you-go system combined with nonprogram sources of comprehensive deficit reduction or the genuine "funding" of the surpluses. In either case, future taxpayers and beneficiaries would have available a larger income base from which to meet social security payment obligations. Alternatively, future social security claimants may themselves lose benefits if their claims are not honored.

The result seems clear. The pattern of gains and losses, among groups within the current generation and between groups in the current and future generations, is not what motivated the 1983 legislation. The National Commission on Social Security Reform (the Greenspan Commission) and its advocates may have produced a fiscal chain of events that was no part of their intention. Would they have been so enthusiastic in support of the changes and so self-satisfied with their apparent accomplishments if they had looked more realistically on the working of modern democratic politics?

The predictions made here have implications, on the one hand, for the playing of budgetary politics in post-Reagan Washington, and especially in the 1989–1993 term of the president. On the one hand, the "deficit issue," which is discussed almost exclusively in terms of the measured comprehensive budget, will be less acute because of the trust fund accumulations and will therefore be less acute politically unless major increases in domestic spending take place. There need be no major tax increase unless such spending increases do, in fact, occur. On the other hand, the machinations of politicians should never be neglected. Especially in the period 1990–1992, residues of the deficit issue from the mid-1980s may be used to justify broad-based tax increases and (non-revenue-enhancing) increases in upper-bracket income taxes. This pattern of revenue enhancement together with the social security tax increases underpinning the trust fund surpluses would allow for a shift upward in the share of income returned to the government in taxes. Such a scenario will not, of course, embody genuine funding of social security. After Reagan, we may face a political reality that simultaneously embodies a continuing deep mistrust of both politicians and institutions and a return to the public sector growth pattern that has characterized almost the whole of this century.

Social Security Survival

A Public-Choice Perspective

I. Introduction

Economists are professionally trained to search out and to discover alleged inefficiencies in institutional arrangements, public and/or private. Further, once alleged inefficiencies are located, economists have an impulsive proclivity to propose reform. I am no different from my peers in these respects; on several occasions, I have joined the ranks of those who have advanced proposals for reform in the Social Security system.[1] As I have emphasized in earlier papers, however, the task of designing reforms that meet the test for Pareto superiority, even when considerations of practicability are totally neglected, is by no means an easy one. But, of course, unless some such reforms can be demonstrated to be possible, the existing system must be judged to be Pareto efficient. Note carefully what such a judgment would and would not imply. It would not imply that everyone could not have been made better off by a series of different decisions made over a historical sequence of periods. Clearly, we could all be in an improved position today if

From *Cato Journal* 3 (Fall 1983): 339–53. Reprinted by permission of the publisher.

The author is indebted to his colleagues Geoffrey Brennan, Loren Lomasky, Jonathan Pincus, and Gordon Tullock for helpful comments.

1. See Buchanan, "Social Insurance in a Growing Economy: A Proposal for Radical Reform," *National Tax Journal* 21 (December 1968): 386–95; "Comment on Browning's Paper," in *Financing Social Security*, ed. Colin Campbell (Washington, D.C.: American Enterprise Institute, 1979), 208–12; and "Dismantling the Welfare State," paper presented at the regional meeting of the Mont Pelerin Society, Stockholm, Sweden, September 1981.

Americans, privately and collectively, had invested more in capital formation in the 1950s, 1960s, and 1970s. And the incurrence of "social insurance" debt, even if implicit, without the creation of offsetting assets, is the same thing as negative capital formation. But to regret the loss of what might have been if a different series of decisions had been made is not to say that there must be inefficiencies in the set of institutional arrangements that is now in existence. Nor would a judgment that the existing institutional structure is Pareto efficient imply that it satisfies criteria of equity or justice. The intergenerational transfer may be widely held to be grossly inequitable although it meets the test for Pareto efficiency.

So much for preliminaries, which I advance here for two purposes: to indicate what I shall not discuss in this paper, and to provide background for what I shall discuss. I want to resist the temptation to analyze proposals for structural reform, whether they are my own or those advanced by others. Aside from a slight departure in section X, I shall remain within predictive public-choice theory, and I shall attempt to explain public-choice aspects of the existing Social Security system that the economists-as-reformers have often found puzzling. Specifically, I want to explain the *survival* of what seems to be neither a viable intergenerational social insurance system nor an efficient welfare system. Why does what seems to be an n-person, n-period social dilemma have such staying power?

II. The Sacred and the Profane

I commence with a simple empirical observation. Elected politicians, at all levels, treat the existing system as sacrosanct. It is widely presumed that any pronounced challenge to the basic structure of the system is equivalent to political suicide. The "reforms" that have been proposed and/or implemented are widely acknowledged to be temporary patches on the rips around the edges of the structure. There is no apparent support for basic institutional change.

If these politicians, over all persuasions and in all parties, are to be credited with ordinary precepts of rational behavior, the implication seems clear. There is no widespread support for basic structural reform, among *any* membership group in the American political constituency—among the old or the young, the black, the brown, or the white, the female or the male, the rich or the poor, the Frost Belt or the Sun Belt. The absence of support for structural change among the old, the disabled, the low-wage earners, and possibly some other constituencies, requires no sophisticated explanation. For these groups, self-interest considerations are sufficient. But why is there not more opposition to the system observed among the ranks of the young? Why is the support for the system so universal?

Why do young and even prospective employees support the system when plausible computations of the expected rates of return to "investment" within the system suggest that these rates may be significantly lower than rates of return on comparable investment in individually purchased, privately marketed retirement-disability schemes? Must we finally explain the absence of even so much as nascent opposition among the ranks of the young by resorting to the naive belief that the Ponzi scheme is never-ending? Must we blame failures of information and communication, illusions, altruistic impulses, and rational ignorance? Or are there rationally derived reasons for the near-universal support[2] for the system—reasons that have somehow been overlooked by most economist-critics?[3]

III. Comparison of Relevant Alternatives

To begin to answer these questions, it is best to begin with a skeletal summary of the existing system. It is an unfunded transfer scheme that imposes payroll taxes on currently employed persons and utilizes the revenues from

2. By "rationally derived," I mean in line with the demonstrated self-interest of participants, strictly in keeping with public-choice orthodoxy. I shall, in this paper, ignore the whole set of problems introduced by the absence of individual *responsibility* for political decisions in democracy, and the effects of this absence on precepts for individual rationality in the specific acts of expressing political "choices." On these problems, see Geoffrey Brennan and James Buchanan, "The Logic of the Levers: The Pure Theory of Electoral Preference," mimeographed (Center for Study of Public Choice, Blacksburg, Va., January 1983); and Geoffrey Brennan and Loren Lomasky, "Large Numbers, Small Costs: The Uneasy Foundations of Democratic Rule," mimeographed (Center for Study of Public Choice, Blacksburg, Va., March 1983).

3. It may, of course, be argued that the prevalent political attitudes toward the existing institutional structure will soon undergo very substantial change as the financial plight of the system comes to be more widely recognized. For such an argument, see Carolyn Weaver, "The Long-Term Outlook for Social Security—Continued Political Turmoil," mimeographed (National Commission on Social Security Reform, October 1982).

such taxes to finance payments to qualified nonemployed recipients (retirees, dependents, survivors, and the disabled). The system is not, however, a simple interclass transfer mechanism operated on in-period differentiation between qualified taxpayers and qualified recipients. Eligibility claims for benefit payments are established by an employment record, applicable over all classes and wage levels of covered employees, rather than by direct means-test criteria. Through their own payroll records, employees accumulate claims against the system—claims that must be met in accordance with designated criteria for eligibility.

Financially, the system as a whole is best understood as an unfunded liability of the national government, an implicit, indexed national debt—a debt that exceeds by several times the nonindexed public debt that is nominally measured. The implicit debt of the existing (early 1980s) Social Security system is estimated to be roughly $8 trillion, by comparison with a nominally measured debt of something over $1 trillion.

It would be redundant to extend the discussion of these features of the system. The skeletal summary is useful, however, in any discussion of structural reform—discussion that becomes meaningful only when it involves comparing *relevant* alternatives. Critics and reformers of the existing structure have often faltered at precisely this point. In particular, the proposal for reform that would allow individuals to voluntarily opt out of the system has been treated as a relevant alternative when it is not. Such treatment reflects a crude fallacy of composition.

It is, of course, easy to show that many potential and actual participants in the existing system could substantially improve their positions if they were allowed to withdraw and invest voluntarily in their own preferred, privately marketed insurance plans. If a young employee, say at age 25, were allowed to withdraw voluntarily from the system, to relieve himself of all payroll-tax obligations (levied both against his wage directly and against his employer) and at the same time were to renounce all claims to future benefits from the system, he would be able to secure a rate of return under privately purchased insurance that would yield either the same level of expected benefits at substantially lower costs or substantially higher benefits at the same costs. Acknowledging this apparent comparative advantage of privately purchased insurance leads naturally to the inference that such a person, on grounds of economic self-interest, would cease to support the existing structure politically—hence, there should be a potential for organizing a political constituency to support the opting-out alternative.[4]

My central argument in this paper is that no such inference can be drawn. The disparity between individualized rates of return on "investment" within the system and outside it does not in itself provide a basis for political opposition to the existing structure. It does not do so because individualized opting out, or voluntary withdrawal, is not a relevant alternative and participants in the system do not treat it as such.

IV. Debt, Demos, and Default

People recognize that any structural reform that introduces the alternative of opting out would necessarily lead to the abandonment and breakdown of the intergenerational transfer scheme that exists. Therefore, when they face the question of supporting or opposing the proposal to opt out, individuals must model or estimate the alternative system that would replace the present one. The relevant alternative is the institutional structure that would emerge in lieu of the existing intergenerational transfer scheme. The relevant alternative is *not* the existing transfer scheme only with the individual having been removed from all tax obligations and all claims.

What alternative institution would emerge? To answer this question, the individual must try to predict how the democratic process will operate. If one predicts that the existing structure will be abandoned without any governmental-political-institutional replacement, then the attractiveness of the opting-out alternative to young and prospective employees might remain. But it is at this point that the summary description of the existing system in terms of the implicit national debt becomes helpful. Will individuals

4. In some extreme models, the paradox of support analyzed here does not arise, because there is no basic difference between debt and tax finance. The young person, by opting out, may secure a higher rate of return on private investment, but because future tax liabilities are reduced, he will expect lower bequests than would be expected in the system. Hence, the apparent advantages of opting out are not clear, except insofar as changes in the distribution of net burden can be accomplished. See Robert J. Barro, "Are Government Bonds Net Wealth?" *Journal of Political Economy* 82 (November 1974): 1095–117.

My explanation of system survival does not in any way invoke a Barro-like model of intergenerational interdependence.

seriously consider default on the Social Security debt obligation to be an alternative?[5] Will government dishonor all of the claims to benefits from the system? Or will some means be found to finance at least some considerable share of the claims that individuals hold against the structure?

In making predictions here, each person must, willy-nilly, become his own public-choice economist. Moreover, in the calculus of politics, each individual must consider the following factors. First, the individual must recognize that his own normative position on the legitimacy or illegitimacy of claims against the existing system is not directly relevant, although some generalized prediction about normative attitudes over the whole citizenry must be made. That is, an individual may personally dismiss all claims on Social Security as being morally irrelevant. However, unless this personal attitude is generalized to others, some estimate must be made about how citizens in general feel about the moral status of existing claims.

Moral legitimacy aside, the individual must also recognize that members of several constituencies in the political community will support payment of Social Security claims, in full or in large part, on the basis of straightforward self-interest calculations. Those who would not find it advantageous to opt out of the existing system voluntarily, even if they could do so in isolation, will have self-interested reasons to support some other scheme of meeting the obligations of the system in the event that the system collapses. These individuals will never support default on the implicit national debt that the claims represent. These groups will of course include all those who are currently receiving benefits, as well as those who expect to collect benefits in the near future. Roughly speaking, the self-interested supporters of some replacement scheme that will meet the outstanding debt obligations will tend to include all participants over some critical middle-age limits (about age 40).[6]

---

5. The Social Security debt is singular in that the claims (the "bonds") are universally held by all past and present employees. Default on such widely held and uniformly distributed debt becomes much more difficult politically than default on nominal debt instruments. The latter, even if held internally, would tend to exhibit concentrated ownership, and, if held externally, would not have direct internal political representation. The potential effects of ownership patterns on prospects for debt default have not, to my knowledge, been carefully analyzed.

6. Browning has analyzed the age-profile breakdown in support of continued increases in levels of benefit payments. Much the same sort of analysis could be used here

Quite apart from both the moral legitimacy of existing claims and the self-interested motivations of individuals for receiving transfers, there is also the direct welfare obligation that would emerge in the absence of the existing system. Even if few people adhere to the notion that claims against the system are morally legitimate in some quasi-legal sense of entitlements, some individuals will recognize that the aged poor and disabled, now within and supported by the system, must be kept alive. And while a strictly administered, means-tested welfare structure may require substantially less revenue than the generalized benefit system now in existence does, little support could be predicted for total disregard for those who would be unable to find minimal subsistence without the Social Security umbrella as it is currently administered.[7]

Finally, the participant must include some estimate for increased support payments that might be necessary for the members of his own family who may be current recipients of Social Security benefits, but whose funds might be reduced under an alternative arrangement.

Moral attitudes concerning the legitimacy of claims, self-interest, welfare, and own-family obligations (along with other considerations relating to citizens' potentially supporting or opposing any financing of a welfare scheme as a replacement for the one that exists) must be somehow estimated and then interjected into a model of how the politics of American representative democracy actually work. What constituency's pressures would be likely to be more influential? Elementary public-choice theory suggests that the more concentrated interests of potential beneficiaries are likely to carry somewhat more weight than the diffused interests of taxpayers, particularly if the beneficiaries' interest is accompanied by moral argument, whether on the grounds of default on debt or on the grounds of commitment to welfare.

It is difficult to imagine any rational calculus that would predict the total absence of political response to a breakdown and collapse of the existing so-

---

to predict what groups would support meeting the system's debt claims, even in the event that the system collapses. See Edgar K. Browning, "Why the Social Insurance Budget Is Too Large in a Democracy," *Economic Inquiry* 13 (September 1975): 373–88.

7. The revenue requirement of the welfare obligation is mentioned as an offset in a somewhat different context by Gordon Tullock in *The Economics of Income Redistribution* (Boston: Kluwer-Nijhoff, 1982), 114.

cial insurance system. It can be predicted that under almost any set of circumstances, major financing requirements will continue to exist regardless of the fate of the existing structure. The government is not likely to default on the implicit real debt that the mistakes of past generations have created.[8] The effective and relevant alternative to the existing system is a tax-transfer scheme that may not be substantially different, in essence, from the one that exists.

V. From the Aggregate to the Individual

In order for an individual to calculate whether he will be better off by switching to a replacement system, he must translate the public-choice predictions about the alternative tax-transfer scheme into individually identifiable tax obligations. The participant must estimate the present value of his future tax obligations under the existing structure, along with the present value of the benefits he can expect to receive under the alternative structure. The in-system estimates will not, of course, be easy to make, since here, too, some political modeling will be required. How will tax rates and benefit levels be adjusted as the political system responds to recurring short-term crises? Will the base for payroll taxation continue to be increased? Will elements of progressive taxation be increased or decreased? Will the retirement age be changed? Will benefits be subjected to income taxes? Will benefits be overindexed, underindexed, or ideally adjusted? These questions will tend to be answered differently by different people, and even if there should be some similarity of political predictions, the age, income, and family status of an individual will make his estimates unique.

Assume now that a particular participant does go through the required estimation procedures and that the present values for taxes and benefits are predicted. These estimated present values then will provide the benchmark

---

8. Because the implicit debt of the system is indexed, default via inflation is not possible, as is the case with nominal public debt. Furthermore, the measure of nominal debt may include a significant component for expected default, whereas no such component is included in real debt. Hence, the real debt overhang of the social insurance system may be considerably more than eight times as burdensome as the nominally measured debt, as is indicated by the ratio of $8 trillion to $1 trillion.

for comparing the existing system to the relevant alternative, the tax-transfer scheme that some predict will emerge.

My overall purpose is to explain why individuals who could be expected to find structural change advantageous nevertheless continue to support the existing system. Hence, I shall focus on the calculus of the young participant who under the structural change would renounce all claims to future benefits and who at the same time would be relieved of all payroll-tax obligations, present and future (whether levied on employee or on the employer). Such a person would normally expect to be required to pay taxes to finance some share in the replacement tax-transfer scheme that emerges. The critical relationship is that between the present value of this young participant's anticipated tax share and the present value of payroll taxes and benefits anticipated under the existing system.[9]

To the extent that payroll-tax obligations are reduced and are *not* offset by increased taxes under the replacement scheme, the individual in question will have additional funds to invest in private insurance. Critics and would-be reformers of the existing system have often overlooked the tax cost of any replacement scheme—a cost that the participant must always consider in any realistic comparison.

The calculation of an individual's tax obligation under the replacement institution will depend, of course, on the expected total cost of the new system. This cost is normally thought to be somewhat less than the projected cost of the existing system. Beyond such aggregate estimates, however, the individual must determine his own share of the cost. This estimate will depend first on a prediction of the tax or tax array that will be used to finance the replacement scheme (value-added tax, increased income-tax rates, broad-based consumption tax, and so on). Second, the estimate will depend on the individual's theory of incidence for the particular tax set predicted. Finally, the estimate will depend on some predictions about the individual's own position in the possibly relevant age, income, family status, consumption pattern, and other profiles that determine tax liabilities.

---

9. For simplicity, I shall assume that the individual making the calculations does not expect to receive any welfare benefits under the alternative system.

VI. The Individual's Simple Algebra of Institutional Comparison

No claim is made here that the individual estimates of the present values for tax obligations and benefit claims will be simple. Any such estimates necessarily involve possibilities for major miscalculations. Nonetheless, it is essential to reduce the analysis of individual institutional choice to such specific detail if we are to understand the apparent near-universal support for the existing structure. This section, which is in many respects the core of the paper, develops the simple algebra of the comparison that the individual participant must make.

Initially, I shall define some terms, all of which are assumed to be dated as of the time that the individual participant confronts the institutional choice.

T_S^i Individual i's estimate of the present value of the tax obligations faced under the existing institutional arrangements, as these arrangements may be nonstructurally modified in future periods.

T_A^i Individual i's estimate of the present value of the tax (and personal) obligations faced under the alternative tax-transfer arrangements that will be predicted to emerge as a structural replacement for the existing system if it is abandoned or repealed.

$\dfrac{T_A^i}{T_S^i} = t^i$ The share (of his present-value tax obligations under the present system) that the individual anticipates will be drained away by taxes and personal outlays under the replacement system.

$(1 - t^i)$ The share of each dollar's worth of present-value tax obligations under the existing system that individual i anticipates to be made available for private investment if the existing system is dropped.

r The market-determined real rate of return on private investment.

Note that $(1 - t^i)$ also defines the present value of a dollar's worth of present-value tax obligations that is withdrawn for private investment. Since $(1 - t^i)$ is available for investment at a rate of r per period, this stream of returns (discounted at r) is simply $(1 - t^i)$.

B_S^i Individual i's estimate of the present value of the benefit payments expected to be received under the existing system, as these arrangements may be nonstructurally modified over future periods.

$\dfrac{B_S^i}{T_S^i} = c^i$ The share of each dollar's worth of present-value tax obligation that individual i estimates to be offset by present-valued benefits.

For individual i to be indifferent toward the two institutional alternatives, the following condition must hold:

$$(1 - t^i) = c^i \qquad (1)$$

Several familiar relationships may be derived from (1). First, if $B_S^i = T_S^i$, or $c^i = 1$, *any* positive tax or personal outlay expected under a replacement institution is sufficient to cause the individual to prefer the existing structure. Second, if $B_S^i < T_S^i$, then $c^i < 1$. In this case, the individual may prefer the existing system if $t^i > 0$. The critical relationship is the one between t^i and c^i. If $t^i > c^i$, the individual will prefer the existing system; if $t^i < c^i$, the individual will support abandoning the existing system in favor of the alternative.

It may be helpful to redefine c^i in (1) as the ratio between the annualized stream of returns in perpetuity g, equal to the expected benefits of the system, and the market-determined rate of return (or the rate of discount) r. This yields:

$$(1 - t^i) = g/r \qquad (2)$$

The situation that is of particular interest is the one present when $t^i > c^i$ in (1), or when $g^i < r$ in (2), and when $t^i > 0$. Suppose $t^i = .6$, or $(1 - t^i) = .4$; the individual anticipates that his dollar's tax obligation under the existing system, computed in present-value terms, will be reduced to \$.60 by a shift to the alternative tax-transfer scheme. From (1) it is clear that c^i needs only to be greater than \$.40 in order to ensure that the individual in question will support continuation of the existing structure. That is to say, the present value of the expected benefits can be as low as four-tenths the present value of expected tax payments without causing loss of support for continuation of the present system. In terms of (2), the annualized return of expected benefits (g) need only be four-tenths the rate of discount (r) in this setting.

If, for example, given the value for $(1 - t^i)$ of .4, with a rate of discount $r = .06$, any value for g above .024 will ensure support for the existing structure.[10]

The simple algebra of institutional comparison suggests that support for the existing system may persist even if individuals recognize that their "investments" of tax payments in the system are much less advantageous than their opportunities for investment in the market.[11] The algebra incorporates the recognition on the part of the individual that he is locked into a socioeconomic-political structure in which the exit option is effectively closed. The overhang of the implicit public debt that decisions of decades have created cannot be neglected. The simple algebra is helpful, however, in suggesting that support for the existing structure has limits. If, for any reason, the ratios defined in (1) and (2) reach critical levels for many people, popular support for the existing structure may rapidly erode. The near-universality of support now observed suggests only that the ratios have not yet attained such "subversive" levels.

VII. Parameter Shifts

The parameters that enter into the individual's comparison may be (1) exogenous to the system and exogenous to the individual's own calculus, (2) exogenous to the individual participant but endogenous to the system, or (3) endogenous to the participant.

Consider, first, the market rate of return (or rate of discount). How will an increase in this rate affect the representative individual's institutional

---

10. Note that g is *not* the internal rate of return to "investment" in the existing system. So long as a participant anticipates any positive return of benefits, then $g^i > 0$. And, of course, expected benefits may well be positive even if internal rates of return on system "investment" are negative. With any given value for g^i, there may be many internal rates of return, depending on the time profile of expected benefits.

11. I have assumed throughout the analysis that the individual can secure the real rate of return, r, in the market. During periods of expected inflation, this assumption may not be warranted—especially if there exist legal restrictions on the private issue of indexed bonds. If any private investment must embody an inflation-risk premium, the individual may have an additional reason, over and above those discussed, for supporting the fully indexed pension scheme, regardless of its annualized rate of yield in relation to the riskless real rate of return.

comparison? Assume, first, that r (the real rate of return on capital) increases exogenously because of a technological change.

The time profile of taxes expected under the two institutions will differ in that the future taxes will tend to be "bunched" under the replacement tax-transfer scheme during the period in which the outstanding claims against the system are met. The numerator of the ratio T_A^i / T_S^i will tend to fall by less than the denominator as r increases. On the other side, the expected value of any fixed stream of benefits, B_S^i, will carry a lowered present value as r increases, and this value will fall by more than that of T_S^i. Hence, t^i will increase and c^i will decrease as r increases. The effects work in offsetting directions, although it seems plausible to suggest that c^i will fall more than t^i rises, hence making support for the existing system fall. This effect may be countered, however, if expected benefits increase as the real return on investment increases.

To the extent that the whole system, through time, acts to reduce the rate of capital formation, r will tend to increase endogenously to the system, and will ultimately reflect a reduction rather than an increase in the income base upon which taxes must be levied. In this case, expected benefits may fall. This effect, plus the differential capitalization effects of the separate time streams, would allow us to predict that support for the structure will fall.

The remaining parameters are all endogenous to the system, even though they may be exogenous to the participant. Consider a shift upward in the retirement age (say from 65 to 68) that is not offset by any other change in the system. If this change is made effective only after some time lag, the effect is unambiguously to reduce the value of c^i, without any noticeable effect on t^i. Hence, the existing institutional structure necessarily becomes less attractive to young participants.

Consider now a straightforward increase in the rate of tax on payrolls, with no change in the upper limit for the tax. The denominator in both of the relevant ratios, T_S^i, will increase, reducing the values for both t^i and c^i. The alternative replacement scheme would necessarily become relatively more attractive for all people who face tax obligations under the existing system. An increase in the upper limit for levying the payroll tax without increasing the basic rate will exert a similar effect, but only on those who will thereby face higher expected tax obligations.

Treating Social Security benefits as part of taxable income, wholly or partly, with revenues returned to the system, will make the system less attractive to those who expect to have above-average incomes. If the alternative tax base for the replacement tax-transfer scheme is a broad-based consumption tax or value-added tax instead of an income tax, the group that is directly affected would become more interested in abandoning the present Social Security system.

Internal changes in the benefit/payout ratios made to increase the internal progressivity of the overall system will have effects similar to those caused by making benefits taxable. The support of upper-income participants for the system may be eroded as internal progressivity is increased.[12]

Shifts in the parameters endogenous to the individual's own estimation process are more difficult to discuss analytically. The estimates for expected benefits and expected taxes within the system, and for expected taxes under the replacement system, are necessarily subjective. These estimates depend on the individual's modeling of politics as well as on his judgment about underlying demographic trends.

VIII. Strategy for Support

Having established the individual's algebra of institutional comparisons, we can now trace the familiar strategies of support for continuation of the existing structure. Those who are differentially advantaged by such continuation—the administering bureaucracy along with those who are net beneficiaries, present and future—will seek to influence (in specific directions) the estimates that present and prospective participants make. Clearly, it will be useful to try to get individuals to place a high value on both t^i and c^i, since a high value for both ratios lends support to the existing system.

A strategy that will act on both parameters is one that stresses the contractual basis for the claims of the existing structure. If it is convincing, this strategy will assure all prospective beneficiaries that the present values of expected benefits are indeed positive and high. At the same time, however, this

12. See Tullock, pp. 130–35, for a somewhat different direction in discussion of the effects of shifts in parameters on support for the system.

strategy suggests that because the claims are contractual obligations, there will be a large carryover tax burden under any replacement scheme that might be politically viable.

It is also important to influence the values that are subjectively estimated for taxes expected under the system. From the earliest years of the system, the false argument that employees do not really bear the incidence of the employers' portion of the payroll tax has been used to make participants think they get more than any proper economic calculation would suggest. It is clearly in the interests of all supporters of the existing system to foster this fallacy.

Supporters of the system will tend to oppose increases in the retirement age (because such increases unambiguously make the system less attractive to all nonretirees) and also to oppose straightforward increases in the payroll tax. Faced with short-run emergency adjustments, supporters will tend to favor increasing the upper limit for applying the tax, as well as including the benefits in the income tax, provided the system secures the return of revenues. Supporters will not desire to push the internal progressivity of the system so far that it loses the support of large numbers of high-income payroll-tax payers.

IX. Strategy for Opposition

For those who seek to undermine the existing structure and who recognize that the simple algebra of participants must be influenced to do so, the primary argument must be one that opposes the contractual basis for claims against the system. To the extent that people can be led to think that they personally have no legitimate claim against the system on retirement, the expected value of benefits is necessarily reduced. At the same time, the erosion of the notion of legitimacy of claims reduces the tax overhang that would be anticipated under some replacement tax-transfer scheme. Both effects tend to make abandonment of the system look more attractive.

When short-run "reforms" are needed, those who seek to undermine the support of the system (over the longer term) would do well to propose increases in the retirement age and increases in payroll taxes. These groups also should support proposals aimed at increasing the internal progressivity of the system. To the extent that participants come to perceive the system as a

complex transfer scheme between current income classes instead of strictly between generations, the "insurance contract" image will become tarnished.

X. System Survival and Pareto Efficiency

The observed behavior of politicians suggests that there is no serious threat
to the survival of the existing institutional structure of Social Security in the
United States (in 1983), despite the sometimes anguished howls of the system's critics. The analysis in this paper explains the apparent paradox. To say
that the system survives, however, is not the same thing as to say that it is
Pareto efficient. An inefficient institution may survive until and unless ways
can be found to secure political support for reform.

As the analysis has shown, the existing system may enjoy the support of
participants who may expect significantly lower returns inside the system
(compared with what they might earn outside the system) because such participants fear the tax burdens that are associated with the overhang of national debt that the system embodies. In order to generate political support
for a replacement system from those who expect relatively lower in-system
returns on "investment," it would be necessary to reduce (perhaps dramatically) the anticipated tax costs of the alternative tax-transfer scheme that is
predicted to emerge.

At this point, it is useful to recall that there would be a specific time profile of the outlays required to pay off many or all of the existing claims that
have accumulated within the existing structure. If the Social Security system should collapse in 1984, with no further collection of payroll taxes and
no further accumulation of benefit claims, a commitment to meet its existing claims would require massive outlays over a two- to three-decade period,
with substantial reductions beyond that time. It is this massive and time-
bunched revenue requirement that creates the high values for t^i among many
participants.

In order to reduce t^i, it would be necessary to assure participants that the
burden of bailing out would not be allowed to fall disproportionately on the
particular generation that would pay taxes immediately after the institutional
reform takes place. To this purpose, I suggested elsewhere[13] that accumulated

---

13. See Buchanan, "Comment on Browning's Paper."

claims be met by issuing new debt intended specifically to ensure that *all* future generations, along with the present one, share equally in the costs imposed by the mistakes of almost half a century. I shall not discuss my own proposal here. Suffice it to say only that unless proponents promise some stretching out of the revenue requirements for bailing out, the calculus of participants will presumably remain such that despite its apparent inefficiencies the existing structure will continue to survive.

As I have already suggested, however, and as the simple algebra indicates, there are limits beyond which the existing Social Security system is unlikely to survive, even in the presence of the continually growing debt overhang. If the patchwork pattern of "reforms" is such that major support constituencies are lost, the system that has seemed politically sacrosanct may quickly become subject to intense intergroup distributive struggle. In that case, winners will win and losers will lose, with no guarantee that a replacement system will be any more efficient or equitable than the one that disappears.[14]

14. As noted earlier, some observers predict that we are already in the beginning stages of such political turmoil. See Weaver, "The Long-Term Outlook for Social Security."

Social Insurance
in a Growing Economy
A Proposal for Radical Reform[1,2]

By any of the accepted standards for evaluation, the United States social security system is in a mess. If it is considered in the image of an actuarially based
insurance system, the account has long since been financially unsound. The
reserves of Old-Age, Survivors, and Disability Insurance (OASDI) amount
to only $24.5 billion, slightly more than the benefits payments in 1967 alone.
Reserves were not accumulated to cover benefit obligations to those who
have already retired, and no attempt is being made to accumulate reserves
sufficient to finance the pensions of those who will retire in future years.
Current policy aims at setting payroll-tax rates at levels that will provide
sufficient funds to cover current benefits; each time benefit levels are raised
or coverage is extended, tax rates must be raised accordingly. Alternatively,
when the system is considered in the image of an orthodox and straightforward tax-transfer mechanism in which some persons are taxed to provide other persons with benefits, most of the traditional principles of fiscal

From *National Tax Journal* 21 (December 1968): 386–95. Reprinted by permission of
the publisher.

1. At the outset I should acknowledge that this proposal was directly stimulated by the
reading of a more abstract analytical discussion by Asimakopulos and Weldon. Although
they employ a welfare framework quite different from mine, some of their discussion provides a basis for my specific reform suggestions. See A. Asimakopulos and J. G. Weldon,
"On the Theory of Government Pension Plans" (mimeographed, McGill University,
1967).

2. Professor Colin D. Campbell of Dartmouth University provided helpful suggestions
for revisions of an earlier draft of this paper.

equity are crudely violated. Taxes imposed on currently productive young workers finance payments to pensioners who may be, and often are, financially more able. Benefits are directly, if not perfectly, related to earnings record and not to needs, which is precisely the reverse of the relationship that equity norms would dictate.

In the welter of discussion about practical reforms it is no wonder that a genuine insurance system and a tax-transfer system seem to have been posed as either-or alternatives. Pulled simultaneously in both directions, the existing system seems to provide a clear example of a modern Buridan's ass. Operation of a bona fide social "insurance" system would require the continued separation of the trust-fund account from general revenues of the government, the continued reliance on earmarked taxes levied on payrolls, further strengthening of the eroded concept of individualized claims to expected benefit payments, a more specific relationship between tax payments and actuarially computed benefits, and, finally, the introduction of provisions that would allow individuals to opt out of the governmental system upon presentation of evidence concerning adequate private pension coverage. In sharp contrast, the operation of an explicit tax-transfer system incorporating orthodox fiscal principles would eliminate the need for separate trust-fund accounting, would be financed by general taxes rather than from earmarked charges on payrolls, would altogether eliminate the concept of benefit rights or claims in an individualized sense, would relate benefits strictly to needs, and, finally, would make the system universally applicable to all persons.

In one sense, the system that we have seems the worst of both worlds. It is compulsory, inequitable, and unsound. Reform in either one of the two directions might seem indicated. In a previous article, Professor Colin D. Campbell and I suggested one avenue of reform that would allow the immediate conversion of the current structure into one that could embody genuine insurance principles.[3] Our proposal for reform involved the shifting of the social security system in the direction of the insurance pole. Other recent critics, notably Pechman, Aaron, and Taussig in a forthcoming Brookings

---

3. James M. Buchanan and Colin D. Campbell, "Voluntary Social Security," *Wall Street Journal*, 20 December 1966.

study, suggest reforms leading in the opposite direction, toward an avowed tax-transfer mechanism.[4]

This paper advances a compromise or synthetic program for institutional reform. It embodies an acceptance of the sophisticated analytical defense of central elements characteristic of the current system, the defense suggested by Professor Paul Samuelson and others.[5] The proposal goes beyond this, however, and incorporates specific emendations of the existing system that will secure many of the advantages of genuine insurance. These involve the vesting of individualized rights to benefits based on earnings, the provision for opting out of the governmental system and choosing a private program, and the replacement of payroll taxes by compulsory purchases of a new type of bond (here called "Social Insurance Bonds"), which will have a potential yield equal to the rate of growth in Gross National Product (GNP), however rapid this may be. The various policy steps will be discussed in some detail in Section II. Before this, Section I examines briefly the whole set of issues raised in social insurance.

I. Social Insurance in a Growing Economy

It may be agreed at the outset that there is a genuine collective interest in guaranteeing that each person make some provision for his own income support during retirement years. If an individual fails to do this, support for his subsistence in his old age becomes a general charge against the whole community, given modern standards for poverty relief. To protect itself against the need to incur such charges, the collectivity of individuals may rationally enact legislation that will, effectively, coerce individuals to make the necessary provision for their own retirement-income support. If a pension system

4. J. Pechman, H. Aaron, and M. Taussig, "Social Security: A Tax and Transfer System" (mimeographed, Brookings Institution, September 1967).

5. Samuelson has provided both the initial theoretical foundations for the position and the most widely circulated statement. See his "An Exact Consumption-Loan Model of Interest without the Social Contrivance of Money," *Journal of Political Economy,* 66 (December 1958), 467–82; and his "Social Security," *Newsweek,* 13 February 1967.

See also H. Aaron, "The Social Insurance Paradox," *Canadian Journal of Economics and Political Science,* 32 (August 1966), 371–74, along with the Asimakopulos and Weldon paper previously noted.

were organized on orthodox insurance principles, a simple law requiring all persons to purchase adequate pension protection from private firms might be sufficient here, but there is no reason why supplemental governmental programs should not also be introduced. In either case, the individual would be required to pay for his own future benefits, discounted and actuarially based. Competing private and public schemes could exist side by side and considerations of personal preference along with comparative efficiency would determine the individual's choice between these.

The objective of providing all persons with a minimum income as part of an overall welfare program must be separately considered. This is not equivalent to the social insurance objective, and the analysis of the two must be kept distinct. One of the chief sources of crisis in the existing social security system is the observed tendency of politicians, especially in recent years, to confuse the achievement of social insurance objectives with the relief of primary and secondary poverty and to load the same set of institutions with these quite different burdens. If some persons do not earn incomes adequate to provide for their own retirement support, through either public or private pension plans, adequate as considered by the majority of voters in a democracy, there will emerge some welfare program for insuring general public financing of income payments to these persons during retirement. But this is a wholly different problem, one that properly belongs to poverty relief generally considered, from that which has as its objective only that of guaranteeing that income-earners above the poverty line put aside enough to provide for their own income support during retirement years. The discussion in this paper, along with the specific reforms that are suggested, is limited to the social insurance objective.

Each year the GNP of the United States increases both as a result of rising real output and of higher prices. This simple fact of economic growth plays havoc with the logical niceties of insurance models that are based on the assumptions of a stationary economy. The growth in real GNP results in part from population growth, and this implies that the labor force increases over time and also that the age composition of the population changes. Real output also expands as capital accumulates and as technology advances. Growth in real output causes money incomes to increase over time, even without inflation, and, of course, inflation makes the growth in money incomes even greater. This growth in the national economy, as measured by the standard methods of valuation, causes orthodox insurance programs to become grossly inadequate as time passes.

Any actuarially based system, public or private, must accumulate reserves against future obligations. These reserves can be invested so as to yield a normal return, one that is equal to that earned on comparable-risk investments in the economy. But such a system cannot accumulate its reserves at a rate of return that is equal to the rate of growth in the national economy if the latter rate should exceed that on ordinary investment. But, as Samuelson has shown, if the social security system is conceived as an *intergenerational* tax-transfer system, it may then allow young workers to "invest" at rates that are equivalent to the rate of economic growth. In such a system, young persons finance the pensions of the aged rather than their own. A particular advantage of this system is that no reserves are accumulated. The "return" on this investment made by currently productive income earners must be the higher benefits that they expect to secure from the levy of comparable payroll taxes on the next generation of young workers. Because of the growth in the labor force, and in the level of income generally, the base for the payroll tax in the next generation will be higher than it is today, and the young worker today, by this argument, may legitimately expect that his rate of return on "investment" will approximate the rate of growth in the national economy. He can, in other words, expect to fare at least no worse, and probably better, than he would under any strict insurance system.

At a purely formal level of analysis, this argument cannot be challenged, but some of its implications must be kept in mind. Perhaps the most significant concerns the absence of any assurance or guarantee that current contributors will, in fact, secure the "returns on their investment," individually or collectively, that the idealized scheme indicates to be possible. The argument shows how a rate of return equal to the rate growth in GNP would be possible; it does nothing by way of demonstrating that this possibility will be transformed into practical reality. Currently, the total value of taxes scheduled to be paid in by young workers exceeds the value of the benefits they are scheduled to receive. For example, a married man who started to work in 1967 at age 22 and retires in 2010 and who earns throughout his working life the maximum wage base is now scheduled to accumulate over $54 thousand in taxes for old-age insurance alone. The value of the pension that he and his wife are scheduled to receive is only $33 thousand. The currently productive young worker, earning income now, is asked to subject himself to a payroll tax, with an accompanying benefit schedule that is actuarially not a paying proposition, in exchange for the implicit promises that future legislators will impose payroll taxes on the next generation of workers sufficient to produce the differentially larger return that economic growth makes possible. To the young worker faced with this prospect, it seems little wonder that it carries a touch of "pie in the sky." If given the opportunity to choose between the two, he might well opt for a genuine insurance scheme which allows for considerably greater certainty about rates of return on what is genuine investment, both for the individual contributor and for the group of contributors collectively. He may do so even if he fully understands and accepts the argument that in the rapidly growing economy the intergenerational tax-transfer mechanism may possibly secure for him a net advantage. The uncertainties may outweigh the differential in possible returns.

It should be emphasized that the argument for the intergenerational tax-transfer system involves a specific structure of taxes and transfers. In effect, it is highly misleading to discuss the idealized structure of charges and benefits under this rubric at all. Strictly interpreted, the system is not one of taxes and transfers in any ordinary sense. The currently productive young worker must, it is true, pay a tax levied compulsorily on him, the proceeds of which are used directly to finance pensions for the aged of the present generation. He makes no investment as such. But the scheme can best be understood by thinking of the young worker as making an investment in his own retirement through his indirect "purchase" of the implied public obligation. It is this indirect insurance feature that seems to provide justification for the continued reliance on payroll taxes, in themselves regressive, as the major financing source and for the continuing usage of the term "social insurance" to refer to the whole system.

As American legislation has suggested, however, once the tax-transfer terminology begins to be used, and once the nation's policymakers come to think of the whole system as one that is based on taxes and transfers, levied and provided at the whims of the national government, rather than on sound insurance principles, a Pandora's box is opened. Liberal policy advocates immediately ask, and understandably, why regressive payroll taxes need be used. Why should these not be replaced by general taxes levied on more equitable grounds? More importantly, they will also ask why benefits should be earnings related. Why should those in need be excluded, even if they have not been prior contributing participants in the system? Why should we not add other features to the tax-transfer system, such as Medicare? Recent experience makes clear that the sophisticated defense for the indirect insurance scheme, using intergenerational taxes and transfer as surrogates for real investment in order to secure the possibly higher rates of return promised by economic growth, will not likely produce a politically viable institutional structure.

If and when he recognizes all this, and if he should be given the opportunity for effective choice, the young worker would almost certainly choose the straight-forward insurance scheme over the current system. The "pie in the sky" aspects of existing institutions loom larger, and he can, in fact, foresee that increasing political gimmikry can produce a collapse of the whole structure.

II. A Program for Radical Reform

In this section, I shall take a quite different approach. I shall suggest specific reforms that will allow the existing system to be modified in such a way as to embody the advantages of an intergenerational tax-transfer program while *at the same time* incorporating most of the desirable features of a genuine insurance system. On their face, the proposals seem radical, but they are designed to provide a synthesis of the two quite different approaches to social insurance. Hopefully, the proposals, if adopted, could lead to the "best of both worlds," whereas currently existing institutions come close to being the obverse.

1. Repeal the payroll tax on both employees and employers. The first and most radical proposal involves the outright repeal of payroll taxes, both those levied on the employee and on the employer. One subsidiary advantage of this proposal is that it would dispel the illusion that the employer portion of this tax falls somehow on other than the employee. Some defenders of current institutions argue that the tax on employers should not be considered a charge on employees even though it is based on their wages. Actually, whether nominally imposed on employee or employer, the current tax is on payrolls. It increases labor costs directly and hence the wage earner pays the employer as well as the employee portion of the tax. The elimination of all

payroll taxes would have the additional advantage of removing the current discrimination in favor of the self-employed, who are now required to pay only three-fourths the rate of tax paid by other workers.

2. Require all income-earners to purchase Social Insurance Bonds, to be described below, with the amount of this purchase proportionately related to income earned.

The essential difference between a tax and the compulsory purchase of bonds must be emphasized. The taxpayer secures no explicit claim in exchange for his payment. With a bond, however, the purchaser receives a claim in return for his payment, an obligation against the government. This feature remains even with the compulsion of bond purchase. The presence of this identifiable claim on the government, to be held by the individual, a claim of entitlement to retirement-income support, is an extremely important part of the whole program suggested. The contributor holding such a claim can legitimately expect it to be honored. Contrast this with the absence of any identifiable claim in an intergenerational tax-transfer system, where the taxpayer must hope future legislators will, in fact, carry out the implicitly agreed obligations to increase overall benefit payments.

3. Utilize proceeds from bond sales to finance current pension payments to the extent possible. Finance any excess current payments from general revenues.

The major source of financing current pension outlays should be the revenues secured from bond sales. But there is no necessary reason why these proceeds should match precisely the total of current payment obligations which have been incorporated in existing legislation on the basis of other considerations. There seems to be no justifiable excuse for loading currently productive income-earners with these charges, and these seem properly borne by the whole community. Upon the implementation of the whole reform package suggested here, current income-earners would contribute, through their compulsory bond purchases, a sum estimated to be sufficient to finance their own retirement-income support. These purchases will provide a source of revenues to the government, and these may conveniently, but not necessarily, be used to finance current obligations. The attempted matching of the two sides of the separate account is not, however, characteristic of the program suggested.

4. Allow individuals who desire to do so to purchase additional Social Insurance Bonds, over and above the percentage of income required.

This is an important feature that the program allows to be accomplished without difficulty. Individuals need not be limited in the amounts of their purchases to the required totals that their incomes indicate. Those who desire additional income-retirement protection should be allowed to supplement compulsory purchases with voluntary purchases, perhaps within certain agreed-on maximum limits. It seems clear that this feature would produce a relatively larger provision for retirement-income support in the aggregate.

5. Allow individuals to purchase Social Insurance Bonds from private firms if they so desire, as an alternative to purchases from the federal governmental agency.

Nothing inherent in this program requires a governmental monopoly. If private firms are able and willing to market the type of bonds proposed, and if these firms can demonstrate appropriate insurance protection against their own bankruptcy, there is no reason that all persons must patronize the governmental agency. In order to be able to provide the return which the Social Insurance Bonds carry, a private firm might, of course, find it necessary to function differently from an ordinary "insurance" operation. Competition between privately organized institutions and a governmental insurance agency can serve as an effective guarantor against gross bureaucratic inefficiency.

6. Equate the return on Social Insurance Bonds to the higher of the following two rates: (1) the rate of interest on long-term U.S. Treasury bonds, or (2) the rate of growth in GNP.

This characteristic of the proposed bonds is the key to the reforms advanced. These bonds should carry no explicitly stated rate of yield. On the face of each bond the explicit value of the purchase amount should be noted along with the date of purchase. The bond certificate should then contain an explicit statement that the bond will mature upon the owner's retirement at age 65 and that there will be credited to the holder on that date an amount equal to the face value accumulated at the higher of the two proposed rates of return. The bonds should be nontransferable, and when a bond-owner qualifies for retirement he should convert the total amount of the claim into an annuity that would guarantee him a stream of benefit payments during his retirement years.

An example will be helpful. Suppose that the required rate on annual income is 10 per cent. For a worker earning $10,000 this implies an annual bond purchase of $1,000. He would be required to purchase such a bond each year, from the public agency or from a competing private firm. Let us suppose that he does so in 1968. He is then guaranteed that when he retires, say in the year 2011, this bond will be converted into an annuity which will be computed by accumulating the $1,000 paid in 1968 at the *actual* rate of growth in GNP over the period or at the rate on U.S. Treasury bonds over the period, whichever is the higher. Each year's bond will be converted in a similar fashion. After retirement the individual will then receive a pension payment computed on this accumulated value of his payments and on life-expectancy tables.

The percentage of annual income that should be devoted to compulsory bond purchases should depend on prevailing views concerning the time patterns of spending and saving income for retirement support, as well as on observed behavior regarding other sources of retirement income such as home ownership, private pensions, and personal saving. Under the present social security program, a person retiring in 1968 who has recently earned an annual income of $6,600, the maximum wage base in 1966–67, is entitled to a social security pension for himself and his wife in the amount of $2,828, which is about 43 per cent of his preretirement annual income. Persons with lower incomes receive proportionately larger pensions relative to their pre-retirement incomes.

A 10 per cent rate, used in the example, will allow an individual whose income remains wholly stationary over a whole working life to receive a pension that is roughly equal to annual income, provided that we use a 4 per cent rate of yield. But there is nothing "sacred" or "scientific" in either the current ratio of pensions to preretirement income or in the ratio implicit in the 10 per cent example. The required rate of bond purchases can and should be determined through the workings of the political process; no one rate is "better" or more "efficient" than any other.

How would the proposed program work if the national economy were stationary? There would, in this case, be no growth in GNP. The yield on the Social Insurance Bonds would then be the rate on U.S. Treasury bonds. This rate would closely approximate that which could be earned on reserves accumulated under standard insurance plans. The individual participant in the proposed system would fare neither better nor worse than he would fare under the more familiar orthodox insurance system.

If the economy grows, either for real or monetary reasons, the rate of growth may exceed the rate at which government can borrow in the long-term bond market. In this case, the Social Insurance Bonds would accumulate in value as determined by this rate of growth. The individual participant clearly would fare better than he would under the orthodox insurance system, while at the same time most of the protective features of the latter system would be retained.

If the labor force expands, the yield on the Social Insurance Bonds will increase along with GNP; the same holds for increases in the capital stock and for technological advance. Also, and this provides one of the most attractive features of the program, the participant is amply protected against inflation. The rate of yield on the Social Insurance Bonds automatically adjusts upward to take account of purely inflationary growth. There is no need for the schedule of benefits to be politically juggled to retain some relationship to cost-of-living indices, as the existing system has required. Nor is the participant forced to bear a major share of the incidence of secular inflation as he would be forced to do under a more orthodox insurance system.

III. Practical Implementation

One of the most important advantages to be secured from the changes suggested lies in the wider acceptability that such a new system would carry because of the incorporation of individualized claims to benefits. Another important advantage arises in the protection offers against political interference, the most probable source of crisis in the existing set of institutions. In effect, both of these advantages are derived from an orthodox insurance system, and these are translated or transformed into the dynamic compulsory bond purchase program in the reforms outlined here. Finally, the advantages to be gained from allowing individual participants some freedom to supplement voluntarily the compulsory purchase limits along with some freedom to choose private rather than public agencies of supply are not insignificant.

I have concentrated on the social insurance objective, but even within this limitation many of the complexities have been deliberately ignored. Obviously provisions would have to be included to deal with disabilities, with benefits to dependents and survivors, with possibly differential treatment of persons with differing family status, and other similar problems. These seem capable of being incorporated into the basic reforms without undue difficulty.

Two more fundamental sets of problems remain, however, one involving initial implementation of the reforms, the other involving changes in desired pattern of saving over a person's life span.

From what we have to what is proposed

Payroll taxes could be repealed tomorrow, and the compulsory bond purchases placed in their stead. More difficult adjustment problems arise on the side of current and projected benefit obligations under existing institutions. At present, these obligations have little or no connection with individualized shares in taxes paid into the system by current contributors. Tax payments of persons retiring in 1968 amount to between 10 and 30 per cent of the present value of benefits that they have been led to expect. Of course, the obligations for payment of benefits should be honored, but there seems to be no excuse for imposing the burden of payment on currently productive income earners.

One means of accomplishing the shift from the existing system to the one that has been proposed embodies a variation on the plan advanced by Professor Colin Campbell and me in our earlier paper. Persons who are current claimants, or who expect to be claimants in the near-term, can simply be *given* Social Insurance Bonds on the inauguration of the new system. Effectively used, this scheme can eliminate all discrimination between those who entered the old system and those who enter the new one. It will also eliminate all need for continuous political juggling with benefit schedules.

An example may be helpful in clarification. Consider the person who is to retire in 1968 after having paid the legally required taxes into the OASDI account, along with his employer, since its inception. These tax payments, even as accumulated, bear little or no relationship to the present value of the benefits that this person has been led to expect. Initiation of the new system could proceed *as if* this person had been a participant in the *new* system for all of his income-earning years. Data could be assembled that indicate the level of his earnings in each year over the period, and he can be assumed to have purchased the required total of special bonds over the whole period. He will not, of course, hold these claims, but he can be made a "present" of such claims in the indicated amount immediately upon inauguration of the new system. These claims would then be converted directly into an annuity that he could start receiving in 1969. The person who retires in 1968 becomes, in this way, a full-fledged participant in the new system immediately, and he is treated precisely like the person who enters the system in 1968 and who plans to retire in 2011. Similarly, all persons who have spent a part of their income-earning careers under the old system could be given Social Insurance Bonds upon the start of the new system to make them full-fledged participants. For this group, all remaining income-earning years would, of course, require the compulsory bond purchases. By this means of making gratuitous transfers of bonds to all who have participated in the old system, the transition to the new system could be made without difficulty.

The example presumes, however, that benefit payments under the new system would be equal to or exceed those under the existing system. The level of benefits will, of course, be dependent on the required rate of bond purchase from income. If the presently determined structure of benefit payments under existing institutions should, for any person or group, be in excess of that forthcoming under the "as if" assumption of long-term membership in the new system, the current obligations would necessarily have to be met, and, for these persons, they would be accorded differentially favorable treatment.

Protection against inflation is provided over the income-earning period, but, in the simple form discussed above, no comparable protection is provided against inflation that may occur during the period of retirement itself. This is, of course, a much shorter span of years, but some protection against inflation may also be desired for this period. Here a variable annuity related to the rate of growth in GNP during the period in which benefits are received is suggested. There seems to be no apparent reason why the accumulated value of payments could not be converted into a variable annuity of this sort should this additional protection be desired. For comparable accumulated values, the variable annuity would be necessarily lower during the years immediately following retirement than the fixed annuity. This feature might itself be undesirable, but it, too, could be adjusted by adding other bases for variability.

The agreed-on rate of bond purchase from annually earned incomes need not remain stable over time. After some initial phase, people may decide on a higher ratio of retirement income to preretirement income. In order to prevent discrimination among different age levels upon change in the required rate of bond purchases, all prior contributors' claims may be adjusted to the new rate (presumably higher than the old) by the gratuitous transfer of supplemental bonds, along lines similar to those discussed. For such prior contributors, pension payments will be in excess of accumulated values of actual money contributions made, even when computed at the indicated rates of yield. But these pensions will not be in excess of what these monetary contributions *would have been,* in accumulated value, had the new rate of purchase been effective throughout the earning careers. This sort of adjustment is fully compatible with the social insurance structure as here proposed. What would not be compatible would be any attempt to increase the present-value of pension payments to prior contributors to some level in excess of the accumulated value of his taxes or charges, assuming that the new rate had been applicable throughout their earning careers. It is precisely this sort of tampering with the system that is likely to be destructive.

IV. Conclusions

There are probably many analytical and institutional loose ends involved in the program for reform that I have advanced here. These should obviously be discussed in any more detailed examination. None seems to present insurmountable difficulties, and it seems reasonable to limit consideration here to essential principles. Most critics agree that the existing system needs reform. From this basis, I have tried to outline a set of changes that seem to be improvements. But here, as in most discussions of institutional change, we should proceed pragmatically. There is nothing sacrosanct about my suggestions; but neither is there anything sacrosanct about the institutions that happen to exist. Effective social policy, in this or any other area, requires a continuing critical examination of the institutions that we observe and which should be designed to serve our objectives.

Commentary

Like most of those at this conference, I receive perhaps hundreds of papers in the course of a year, in the form of early drafts, working papers, preprints, reprints, offprints, or whatever. I read relatively few of these on receipt. Most of them accumulate on the floor of my office until, one day every few months, I get a burst of enthusiasm to clean up, at which point I glance hurriedly at the papers, perhaps as many as ten or fifteen in an hour. But anything I receive from Martin Feldstein is a clear exception to this rule; anything I receive from him I open immediately and read, and I almost always learn something. I make this exception because I know that a Feldstein paper will, first of all, be readable—that it will not require the wholly wasted effort of translation from esoteric mathematics into straightforward economics. Secondly, I know that a Feldstein paper will be relevant—it will address an issue or issues of current policy interest and importance.

At this point I am tempted to say that a Feldstein paper also reflects a basic intellectual honesty or integrity. This is, of course, a true statement, but it does not convey precisely the meaning I want to convey here, and to make a categorical distinction in this respect would be unfair to the others. But I do want to take a shot at the question, why do modern economists seem to have been so reluctant to apply straightforward economic theory to the central policy issues Feldstein notes? Why have so many of our intellectual peers chosen, instead, to launch off into the never-never land of abstruse mathematics on the one hand and the tedious detail of empirical rigor on the other?

From *Income Redistribution,* ed. Colin D. Campbell (Washington, D.C.: American Enterprise Institute, 1977), 99–101. Reprinted with the permission of The American Enterprise Institute for Public Policy Research, Washington, D.C.

The most plausible hypothesis suggests that many modern economists do not really want to face up to the rather direct policy implications that emerge from a straightforward application of their logic. They are essentially escapist; they maximize personal utilities by divorcing their subject matter and method from reality. They can, in this way, join their fellow intellectuals in quasi-serious policy dialogue without jeopardizing their "progressive" role. It is to members of this group, who surely dominate our profession today, that Feldstein's work must appear most disturbing. They can reject neither his analysis nor his empirical results, and he challenges them to earn their keep as economists.

Feldstein's strictures do not apply so directly, or at least in the same way, to those of us in the minority of economists who have worked within the classical paradigm, who have incorporated the spontaneous coordination of markets into our thinking about economic policy at all levels. Members of this minority do not really need empirical proof that "water runs down-hill"—to borrow one of Frank Knight's phrases. We do not need convincing by numbers that compensation payments increase unemployment rates, that graduated income taxes affect work incentives (the more so the more progressive the rate structure), that transfers reduce work effort, that social security induces early retirement, that an unfunded public pension system reduces private saving. When I see sophisticated efforts by professional economists to disprove such elementary verities, my own reaction is one of cynical amusement, based on a long-held suspicion that truth is not really the motive force behind the fanciful facades. In a sense it is a mark of the disintegration of the economics profession that the considerable talents of Professor Feldstein must be concentrated on convincing his fellows that the elementary principles are, in fact, valid ones.

But let me shift quickly away from my general comments on the efforts of my fellow economists. I have only one minor technical criticism of Feldstein's paper. He notes that when a person is taxed directly for the payment of benefits he expects to receive, the income effect washes out, leaving the directionally predictable substitution effect. This is, of course, correct, but Feldstein seems here to imply that there is no comparable washing out of the income effect when such a fiscal quid pro quo is absent. However, so long as income effects are roughly symmetrical over all persons and groups in the community, there will always be a netting out over the whole group, provided only that the governmental transfers or provision of services are valued by those who receive them.

My main criticism is a general one and reflects my public-choice perspective, as opposed to the perspective of an orthodox price-theory economist. Throughout his discussion in this paper, Feldstein seems to imply that the institutional reforms in social insurance that he calls for can be made if only our political decision makers will get their ideas straight, if only they will recognize the inconsistencies in existing programs, if only they will, indeed, act in the "public interest." I recognize the need for a division of labor here, and it is perhaps desirable that Feldstein should concentrate his energies on the strict economics of policy. But neither he nor anyone else should be so naive as to expect that policy reform will follow directly upon an understanding and appreciation of the economics of the matters at issue.

The politics are also important. The political setting within which policy decisions are made can influence the outcomes that emerge, no matter what their economic content. To illustrate this, let me take a single example, admittedly the one that allows me to make the strongest case. Consider the development of the unfunded public pension system, along with Feldstein's suggestion for a needed shift toward fund accumulation. Even if we fully recognize the peculiar historical circumstances of the 1930s, the collapse of the financial structure in the Great Depression, and the subsequently influential ideas of Keynes and the Keynesians, should we not also recognize the institutional biases that democratic politics itself might have exerted and might have been expected to exert on observed results? Elected politicians like to spend, and they do not like to impose taxes. Is this not enough to suggest that we should hardly have expected democratic decision making to produce a funded system which would, of course, have required the collection of current taxes in excess of current outpayments? Congress acted consistently with the most elementary public-choice model when projected tax increases were postponed until these seemed necessary to keep the system on a pay-as-we-go basis. The system that we now observe is "explainable" at least in part by public-choice theory, quite apart from economic ignorance or economic error.

The conflict that seems likely to emerge over ensuing decades is not, however, so amenable to elementary public-choice analysis. As Daniel Orr has suggested, it seems likely that the whole social security issue will dramatically shift from one that has embodied apparent political consensus to one characterized by sharpened conflict when legislators recognize that commitments coming due require additional current financing.[1] The choice between reducing the rates of return on the intergenerational investments made by workers who have legitimate expectations and increasing rates of tax on currently productive workers will have important economic effects. But the political interplay of alternative coalitions will do as much toward determining the final outcome as the underlying economic analysis.

We can rely on elementary public-choice theory to predict that a modern Congress will not go beyond minimal pay-as-we-go requirements. It is not likely to change its stripes suddenly and commence to accumulate a positive fund balance in the OASDI account, as Feldstein urges, and despite evidence to the effect that the economic results might be beneficial. Even the most sophisticated and effective congressman could scarcely return to his constituents with the news that he supports an increased payroll or income tax in order to benefit future pension recipients, with spillover benefits for the economy as a whole. In a wisdom that we have almost lost, James Madison and the other founding fathers knew that democracy can effectively make only a limited number of nonsophisticated decisions. Until economists relearn this lesson, they will continue to seem quixotic in their discussions of policy.

My criticism in this respect is not, of course, directed at Feldstein in particular. It becomes, finally, a plea for more research and more analysis of the institutional processes through which economic policy is made—research and analysis which will necessarily draw attention to the potential for reform of these processes, as such, rather than in the particular pattern of outcomes generated.

---

1. Daniel Orr, "Social Security and Social Values," University of California, San Diego, April 1, 1976.

PART SIX

Distributive Norms and Collective Action

What Kind of Redistribution Do We Want?[1]

In two recent contributions, Mr. Lucien Foldes has challenged a central proposition in the liberal theory of economic policy, the proposition "that interference by the government with the distribution of real income should normally
be confined to transfers of general purchasing power, leaving the allocation of
specific goods to the competitive market."[2] I share Foldes' dissatisfaction
with the prescribed policy separation between allocation and distribution.
My own criticism is a methodological one that carries with it certain empirical implications. Foldes' analysis is technical and is subject to the same
methodological objections as the work that he criticizes. Before outlining
my own position, however, I shall briefly examine Foldes' two critical arguments. I shall demonstrate that his first argument holds only with respect to
a limited sort of redistribution; more general methods, but with transfers still
limited to the numeraire good, can be found that will accomplish the objectives specified. With respect to his second argument, I shall show that the
liberal policy proposition in question can be interpreted so that the difficulties stressed by Foldes will not arise. In these preliminaries, covered in Sections I and II, I shall accept the methodological setting employed by both
Foldes and those whom he criticizes.

From *Economica* 35 (May 1968): 185–90. Copyright 1968 by London School of Economics and Political Science. Reprinted by permission of Blackwell Publishers Ltd.

1. I am indebted to P. T. Bauer, Nicos Devletoglou and Lucien Foldes for helpful comments.

2. Lucien Foldes, "Income Redistribution in Money and in Kind," *Economica*, vol. 34
(1967), 30–41; "A Note on Redistribution," *Economica*, vol. 34 (1967), 203–5.

I

Foldes bases his first objection on the absence of a one-for-one correspondence between a pre-trade and a post-trade allocation of goods in those situations where all of the conditions for perfectly competitive markets are not
met. There exists no single point on the welfare surface that corresponds to a
point off the surface; the distribution of the gains from trade is not uniquely
settled by the distribution of initial endowments. When this is recognized, it
follows that if the ultimate objective is the attainment of a given point on the
welfare surface, defined by a vector indicating the amounts of all goods in
the final possession of all persons, no *initial* set of transfers in the single numeraire good can be found that will guarantee the post-trade attainment of
the desired point.

Although he recognizes it indirectly, Foldes does not explicitly examine
the possibility of allowing trade itself to provide data which can then be utilized to modify the initial set of transfers by further shifts, still limited to the
numeraire. Once such subsequent transfers are allowed, any desired point on
the welfare surface can be reached.[3]

This may be illustrated in a simple two-person, two-good exchange model
that is essentially equivalent in results to Foldes' more complex geometrical
constructions. A two-person model cannot, of course, be identical with the
many-person model of competitive adjustment. The simpler model does,
however, extract from the more complex one precisely those elements of indeterminacy which generate the problems that Foldes examines.

The numeraire good in Figure 1 is measured along the abscissa. The heavy
line between 0_a and $0'_b$ represents the contract locus which is presumed
known. Suppose that the "social welfare function" dictates a final allocation
at R, while an initial pre-trade allocation of the two goods is shown at M. It
can be seen readily that no set of transfers between the two persons in the
numeraire alone, initially and before trade, will guarantee the post-trading

3. In private conversation, Foldes justifies his neglect of this method of redistribution
on grounds of practicability. He suggests that initial transfers may be the only ones that
are at all feasible. At such a level of discourse I should go much further. Rather than redistribution, as such, practical reality may limit policy to modifications in institutional
arrangements which will, in turn, generate changes in distributional outcomes. In the text
of this section, my concern is strictly with the technical aspects of Foldes' propositions.

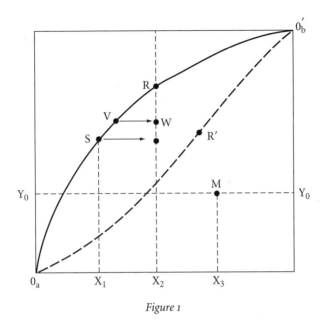

Figure 1

result at R. For any point along the horizontal line, Y_0 Y_0 (other than its intersection with the locus), there must exist a multiplicity of trading outcomes. Assume, however, that trade is allowed to take place without an initial transfer in the numeraire, and that S is reached. The next step is the transfer of an amount, $X_1 X_2$, of the numeraire good from A to B, producing the distribution at T. Trade again generates a re-adjustment, and V is reached. Again a transfer in the numeraire takes place, shifting the distribution to W. This process can be continued until R is attained. Clearly, R must be on the contract locus for it to qualify as a position on the welfare surface in the first place.

II

The second criticism advanced by Foldes is based on the ignorance of individual preference functions. Different distributions of goods may be desired under differing configurations of preferences. If, indeed, the contract locus is that shown in Figure 1, the point R may represent the "socially desired" allocation. However, should the locus be like that traced by the broken dotted curve, some other position, R', might be desirable. Foldes argues that in such a case, if the government knows nothing about preferences, no set of transfers in the numeraire can be fully effective. He then develops interesting geometrical devices which indicate that transfers in all goods can be found which will guarantee the reaching of the desired point, whichever it turns out to be.

Much the same objection can be raised to this argument as to the earlier one. If the market is allowed to provide data, the ignorance about individual preference functions is soon dispelled, and the desired point attained. At this stage, however, I want to enter a different objection, one that might be called a defence of the traditional proposition. Foldes admits that his model is "extreme in some respects," but he does not suggest that the problem he discusses could not arise under one plausible interpretation of the liberal policy dichotomy that he criticizes. This interpretation embodies a different sort of redistribution from that contained in Foldes' treatment. One form of the "social welfare function" might simply include general purchasing power in the hands of different persons (families) as its central argument involving no specification as to the detailed distribution of all real goods.

This version may be stated in either a pre-trade or a post-trade form. In the first case, even if preferences are fully known, there need be no final point on the welfare surface that is preferred, and any one of the sub-infinity of points corresponding to the initially desired distribution of the numeraire good is equally satisfactory. In the geometry of Figure 1, the specified objective may be limited to insuring that whatever the initial allocation redistribution should take place until some position along the vertical from X_2 is reached. This clearly involves a set of transfers in the numeraire only as the policy device: a transfer from B to A in the amount X_3X_2 if the initial position is M. This interpretation is probably that which has been implicitly accepted by most economists who have advanced the allocation-distribution policy dichotomy.[4]

Alternatively, a post-trade distribution in the numeraire may be the limited objective that is specified. Here the method sketched in Section I will insure that some position along the vertical from X_2 is finally attained, this being de-

---

4. Neo-classical utilitarian economists in particular seem to have had this sort of welfare function implicitly in mind.

termined by the intersection of the contract locus with this vertical. There is no need here to know anything at all about individual preference orderings.

III

My criticism of the traditional allocation-distribution dichotomy is quite different from that of Foldes. It seems to me methodologically inconsistent to derive criteria for optimality in allocation from individual evaluations and to call upon external, non-individualistic weights for deriving distributive norms. If the economist is willing to introduce his own, or anyone else's, arbitrary notions about distribution into his policy analysis, disguised by the fiction of a "social welfare function," then it would appear equally legitimate to introduce comparable notions about allocation in specific goods. The orthodox supporter of the policy dichotomy may respond by saying: If the aim is purely redistributional, individual ranges of choice are most widely extended when transfers are limited to the numeraire. My question is: Why should the aim be purely redistributional? What is the logic of the traditional position? Allocational aims, derived from the same sort of external value scale as the distributional ones, would seem equally worthy of discussion. Economists seem to have been willing to use one set of norms for one-half of the policy dichotomy and quite a different set for the other. If they must use the approach of a "social welfare function" to problems of policy, the arguments that they include are those of their own choosing, and there seems no reason for limiting these only partially to individually derived evaluations. The standard approach does, admittedly, involve *less* reliance on non-individualistic norms, and this may be deemed desirable in itself. But the practice of dividing analysis sharply along the allocation-distribution boundary seems to be arbitrary and inappropriate.[5]

In my view, a consistent methodological position does not allow the introduction of non-individualistic norms in *either* allocation *or* distribution.[6]

5. The origins of the arbitrary dividing line are probably to be found in the peculiar inconsistencies of the utilitarians, who were simultaneously individualists and collectivists. Individuals were judged best able to act in their own interests, but aggregate utility was somehow held to be comparable among persons.

6. When non-individualistic norms are introduced, the domain of economics, *as I define the discipline,* is abandoned. This statement cannot be challenged. It may, of course,

It will be objected that my approach amounts to an "opting out" of the discussion of many interesting and highly important issues of applied economic policy. So it does, but I can see no personal excuse for joining other economists in an attempt to hoodwink the public into thinking that we make more sense out of these issues than analysis allows, or that economists have a hot line to God. By opting out of discussions where explicitly normative statements lie at the very beginning of the analysis, economists might leave themselves more time for the positive theory of political economy. By this I refer to the examination and analysis of the behaviour of individuals under various institutional structures as they attempt to achieve *their own* redistributional objectives. The interesting question here becomes: What kind of real income redistribution do people seek?

The answer is an empirical one, and it is here that I think adherence to the traditional policy dichotomy has blinded otherwise competent practitioners to the observed facts of political life. Although they rarely use the same terminology, most liberal economists join their *dirigiste* colleagues in prescribing policy rather than limiting their efforts to the examination of the manner in which policy is chosen and implemented. Libertarian economists remain reformers; they merely want different reforms. Guided in this by the allocation-distribution dichotomy, they have suggested measures that stand almost no chance of achieving that for which they are proposed. I refer here explicitly to the proposal for the negative income tax. This is currently the focus of much attention in the United States, and it is associated widely with the name of Professor Milton Friedman. He, among others, has proposed the adoption of this scheme as a means of transferring general purchasing power to low-income receivers *as a substitute* for the many transfers in kind that are currently reflected in varied governmental programmes.

What libertarian backers of such proposals do not fully appreciate is the

---

be argued that even within the discipline as defined, value judgments cannot be avoided. At this point, I shall not enter into debate on this issue. But it must, I think, be acknowledged that a categorical shift is made when one moves from individualistic to non-individualistic models of analysis. In other words, the existence or non-existence of a genuinely *wertfrei* economics may be debatable, but it could hardly be argued that the introduction of norms derived from external and non-individual evaluations does not substantially move the discussion away from the purity extreme of the spectrum.

lack of interest on the part of the public in real income redistribution as such. One must search diligently to find much "social" concern expressed for the prudent poor whose lives are well ordered and stable. The evidence seems to indicate that general redistribution of purchasing power, or even general change in relative levels of well-being, is not widely desired. Instead members of the public want, and express through their behaviour patterns, relief for specific spending patterns.

This expression of individual preferences can be brought within general analysis of externalities. The mere fact that some members of the community are poor does not, in and of itself, normally impose an external diseconomy on many of the remaining members. What does impose such an external diseconomy is the *way* that certain persons behave when they are poor. It is not the low income of the family down the street that bothers most of us; it is the fact that the family lives in a dilapidated house and dresses its children in rags that imposes on our sensibilities. And we are willing to pay something to remove this external effect; it is relevant for behaviour. Ordinary citizens are probably quite unwilling to finance substantial transfers of general purchasing power to the poor in their communities. But they are probably willing to finance specific transfers, either directly as income-in-kind or indirectly in purchasing power that is earmarked for specific items of spending (vouchers).[7]

My position carries with it some of the same implications for economists as that expressed by Foldes. The externalities model could readily be extended to cover the illustrative examples he cites. Economists should devote more attention to redistribution in specific non-numeraire goods. The contrast in method should, however, be stressed. While Foldes is saying that distribution-in-kind may be an efficient means of achieving externally derived policy objectives, I advance the refutable hypothesis that distribution in kind is the predictable outcome of the political process.

---

7. It should be noted that the externalities model allows the derivation of specific transfers-in-kind solely from individual evaluations. There is no need to introduce paternalistic motivation. In practice, of course, paternalistic elements cannot be distinguished easily from other elements in choice behaviour.

Distributive and
Redistributive Norms
A Note of Clarification[1]

In this chapter I want to clarify the distinction between distributive and re-distributive norms, a distinction that has not always been kept in mind by social philosophers who analyze issues of distributive justice. By a "distributive norm" I refer to an individual's idealized distribution in a community. To describe a situation where this norm would become directly relevant for choice, we can imagine an individual confronting the prospects of living in any one of many alternative communities, each of which embodies a different predicted distribution but all of which have the same total product. In order to avoid the particularization of the norm to a defined position, we can also imagine that the individual remains totally ignorant as to the specific position he himself will occupy in the distribution of the community that he selects (or any other community that he might select).

Despite appearances, this choice is *not* that which is confronted by an individual in a Rawlsian-type constitutional calculus. In the first choice-setting posed above, the individual is restricted to the selection of a single community from among a set of prospects, a community that is described by a specified predicted distributional pattern. By comparison and contrast, the Rawlsian-type choice problem invokes *re*distributive norms. By a

From *Liberty, Market and State: Political Economy in the 1980s* (Brighton, England: Wheatsheaf Books, 1986), 159–64. Copyright 1986 by James M. Buchanan. First published in Great Britain in 1986 by Wheatsheaf Books Ltd, Brighton, Sussex. Reprinted by permission of Pearson Education Limited.

1. I am indebted to Geoffrey Brennan and Bruce Chapman for helpful discussion and criticism.

"redistributive norm" I refer to an individual's idealized distributive pattern for a specified community, *after* redistributive adjustments have been made from some initial distribution. Again, it is presumed that the individual does not know his own position before or after adjustment; he chooses behind the veil of ignorance. The individual's redistributive norm need not be, and indeed normally would not be expected to be, equivalent to that distributive norm that informs the first and quite different choice problem. Put differently, the conceptually observed distributive pattern in the community selected by the individual in the first choice-setting will not be the same as either the pre- or post-adjustment distributive pattern in the specific community in which the individual finds himself when the second choice-problem is posed.

Such possible differences in conceptually observed results may be widely acknowledged, but these tend to be attributed to production-incentive problems created by the operation of the adjustment process itself. To the extent that the implementation of any redistributive adjustments involve feedback incentive effects on the size of total product, we should not of course expect the individual's most desired post-adjustment pattern in a specific community to match his idealized distribution in a community that requires no corrective adjustments. My central point in this chapter, however, is that, *even in the total absence of all production loss,* the distributive norm and the redistributive norm differ for the individual whose "values" remain invariant as between the two conceptualized choice settings.

Consider a highly stylized setting where persons are distributed locationally over a featureless plain in each of several communities. In every case there is a single all-purpose consumption good (manna) which is nonstorable and which remains scarce regardless of quantities made available to any person. In each of these communities, the same total quantity (in pounds) is dropped from the sky each period, distributed in some fashion among the different locations on the plain. We want to look at the choice of a single person who can choose among these separate communities under the veil-of-ignorance constraint; he cannot predict which position (location) he will occupy in the community that he chooses. I shall refer to this as the first choice-setting.

Under these conditions, it is plausible to suggest that the individual will select the community that will be described by equal distribution of the good among all of the locations (individuals). By presupposition, one such community will exist in the choice set, and, also by presupposition, there will be no redistribution required or allowed. My argument does not require that the individual's choice be that community characterized by full equality, but it is helpful to think of this for expository reasons.

I want to compare and contrast this first choice-setting with a second and different one. Suppose now that the individual knows that he must remain a member of a given community, one that is predicted to have the same total product, or total amount of the all-purpose good, as each of the communities in the first choice-setting. Again there is to be a drop of the good from the sky at the beginning of each period, but, in this second setting, this drop is known to involve a distribution among locations (individuals) in accordance with some predicted pattern, one that will involve significant inequalities. The individual is, as before, behind the Rawlsian veil of ignorance; he does not know which of the locations or economic positions he will occupy in this community. The choice that he faces is that among alternative corrective adjustment schemes, redistributive arrangements, all of which are assumed to "work perfectly" in the sense that there is no effect on the size of total product. The same amount of the all-purpose good will be available, in total, regardless of the redistributive scheme selected.

My argument is that if we assume that the individual selected the community with an equal distribution in the first choice-setting, he will *not* select a corrective adjustment scheme that will generate full equality in the second choice-setting. Such a scheme will not represent a plausible choice for the same person who selects the equal-distribution community in the first choice.

The difference lies in the fact that in the second setting *re*distribution must take place in order to secure the results that may be preferred. Quite apart from predictable effects on incentives, emphasized by economists, redistribution will be predicted to involve utility losses inherent in the process of transfer itself. The transfer of units of the all-purpose good from those persons who initially receive relatively large endowments to those persons who initially receive relatively small endowments will be predicted to generate a perceived utility loss to the transferors that will, beyond some limits, exceed the perceived utility gains to the transferees.

We must of course keep in mind just what sort of utility comparisons are being made here. We are not concerned with interpersonal comparability of utilities among separate members of the community at the post-constitutional stage when the transfers are actually made. The relevant comparison for our purposes is that which takes place, within the calculus of the single person at the moment of constitutional choice among the alternative redistribution schemes. In this choice, the individual must somehow assign utilities or utility weights to himself in each one of the set of possible positions in the post-constitutional distribution, both pre- and post-adjustment. This assignment will presumably involve some predictions as to the utilities that will be perceived post-constitutionally, but that which the individual maximizes in making the selection among institutions is his own utility at the moment of choice.[2]

In the highly stylized example introduced here, there is no basis for the emergence of ethically respectable claims or rights in the initial endowments received by individuals at the separate locations in the community and hence no reason why predictions of the relevance of such rights or claims should enter into the individual's constitutional choice calculus. No arguments about "finders-keepers," "just desert," "just acquisition," or the like, would seem to be worthy of consideration. Despite the acknowledged arbitrariness in the initial distribution of endowments of the good, however, "possession" of a sort does exist (or will be predicted to exist), at least for the moment between initial receipt of endowments and the corrective adjustments. The reduction from the initial endowment received by any individual will be viewed, in some sense, as a "taking," which will, in itself, be predicted to create a utility loss over and beyond that which would be measured by a simple difference between before and after sizes of endowments. That is to say, the person whose post-adjustment endowment is reached by a "taking

---

2. It seems inappropriate to model any Rawlsian-type choice in social welfare function terms. For example, Cooter and Helpman examine the implications of seven separate social welfare functions, one of which they label "Rawlsian," and defined as that which maximizes the utility of the least advantaged. Presumably, the government is to be assigned the task of acting in accordance with the instructions of this function, which would in this case require some attempts to measure the utilities of persons in the post-constitutional period during which transfer schemes are implemented. But this is wholly different from the problem of the individual, behind the veil of ignorance, who chooses among separate redistributive institutions and who may be modelled as maximizing *his own utility*, at that moment; see Robert Cooter and Elhanen Helpman, "Optimal Income Taxation for Transfer Payment," *Quarterly Journal of Economics*, 88 (Nov. 1974), 656–70.

away" from his initial quantity of good will tend to be at a lower level of utility than the same person would be whose initial endowment requires no adjustment and which remains equal to the post-adjustment endowment in the other situation.

In the second choice-setting, given the assumed absence of any effect on total product, any person faced with the constitutional choice as posed, will select a transfer or adjustment scheme that will shift the distribution very substantially towards equality in the post-adjustment imputation. That is to say, the post-constitutional setting selected will embody major *re*distribution in the model postulated here. My point in this chapter is limited to the suggestion that even after "costless" redistribution in the sense of production loss, the results will fall short of the ideal distribution that would be selected by the same person in the first choice-setting.

The difference between these two conceptually observed final distributions may depend, in part, on the predicted pre-adjustment distributive pattern in the second choice-setting. The more unequal this distribution, the more transfers that will be required to generate any given post-adjustment distribution. The question of interest becomes whether the desired post-adjustment distribution is or is not modified by the predicted pre-adjustment pattern. If the utility loss predicted to occur in the process of transfer itself, that loss consequent on "taking" and not matched by "getting," per se, increases, and at an increasing rate, with the amount of transfer, the more unequal the predicted pre-adjustment distribution then the more unequal the post-adjustment distribution; hence, the more different the redistributive norms from the distributive norms emergent under the first choice-setting. Differing functional relationships between the size of transfers and predicted utility loss involved in "taking" may remove this effect of pre-adjustment distributional patterns on post-adjustment norms.[3]

In some more general sense, my argument demonstrates that the famil-

---

3. In an extreme and limiting case where such a utility loss is acknowledged but is assumed to be of a lump-sum nature independent of the predicted size of transfer, we get the interesting result that, if any adjustment at all is selected, the redistributive norm does become identical to the distributive norm. Only in this extreme case will the general results of my argument fail to hold, and even here the argument suggests that there may exist many pre-adjustment distributive patterns embodying some inequalities that would remain undisturbed in that the individual would opt for no redistributive scheme while, at the same time, the distributive norm for the individual might remain that of full equality.

iar and much-discussed equity-efficiency trade-off depends on the institutional structure of the society. I have quite deliberately restricted analysis to models in which no production loss takes place in order to show that the equity norm will vary with the choice setting. In the stylized example for my second choice-problem, we may convert the results into those of the first choice-problem by allowing someone to advance a proposal for a scheme that will collect all of the manna in a net above the plain, and *before* the initial individual endowments are identified. This prior collectivization of all income-wealth, if it could be done without production loss, would eliminate the predicted utility loss of the transfer process itself and would make the individual's constitutional choice one among final distributions not among redistributive institutions.

This variation on the simple example suggests that, given egalitarian objectives and totally ignoring production efficiency considerations, there may have been some vaguely plausible argument on behalf of the traditional socialist proposal for collectivization of the "means of production." If, through such a shift in institutional ownership arrangements, it could somehow become possible to amalgamate individual productive shares, so as to forestall "possession," a distributive norm might be possible that would embody more equality than would be the case under market-like arrangements, with private ownership, where overt "taking" is necessarily required to achieve any desired final distributive results. Whether or not collectivization arrangements could effectively accomplish such a divorce between productive contributions and distributive claims is, of course, highly questionable on empirical grounds.

The assumption throughout this chapter of zero production losses under redistributive schemes is of course totally unrealistic. As such losses are predicted to occur, and as they are taken into account in the individual's constitutional choice calculus, we should predict that the preferred post-adjustment distributive patterns will depart significantly from idealized distributive norms.[4] My point in this chapter has been limited to the demonstration that even when production efficiency losses are assumed away distributive and redistributive norms will differ, even within the calculus of a single individual.

---

4. In another work, Geoffrey Brennan and I attempt to identify the several sources of possible efficiency loss, and notably those that arise due to the necessity that any redistributive arrangement must be politically implemented; see Geoffrey Brennan and James M. Buchanan, *The Reason of Rules* (Cambridge: Cambridge University Press, forthcoming, 1985), Ch. 8.

Government Transfer Spending

If the society were annually to employ all the labour which it can
annually purchase, as the quantity of labour would increase greatly
every year, so the produce of every succeeding year would be of
vastly greater value than that of the foregoing. But there is no country in which the whole annual produce is employed in maintaining
the industrious. The idle everywhere consume a great part of it;
and according to the different proportions in which it is annually
divided between those two different orders of people, its ordinary
or average value must either annually increase, or diminish, or continue the same from one year to another.

—Adam Smith, *Wealth of Nations*

Horror stories about public spending and its growth emerge directly from
almost any cursory look at the subject. No great amount of thought is required on anyone's part to describe plausibly predictable scenarios that almost no one could desire, regardless of his ideological position. I shall not
spend much time here on such constructions.[1] But a minimum initial dosage
of data may establish a frame of mind that is necessary for a hard-headed

From *Governmental Controls and the Free Market: The U.S. Economy in the 1970s*, ed.
Svetozar Pejovich (College Station: Texas A&M University Press, 1976), 122–40. Reprinted
by permission of the publisher.

I am indebted to my colleague Gordon Tullock for his helpful comments on an earlier
draft of this essay.

1. For a series of papers that present and analyze the data in some detail, see Thomas
Borcherding, ed., *Budgets and Bureaucrats: Sources of Government Growth* (Durham,
N.C.: Duke University Press, 1976).

analysis of our situation. As Samuel Johnson is alleged to have remarked, men constantly need reminding about things they already know.

In 1975 total government spending in the United States economy amounted to more than one-third of the gross national product (GNP). More than one dollar out of every three dollars of value produced was spent through public or governmental channels and was directed in patterns of outlay determined by some collective decision process rather than by the choices of individuals in their private capacities. (And this statistic does not include the effects of government regulations in modifying private behavior.) The formally computed share of total public expenditure in United States GNP increased from 27 percent in 1960, roughly a 25 percent change between 1960 and 1975. Extrapolation alone suggests that by the year 2000 public spending will approach one-half of the GNP. And we must, of course, keep in mind that governmental activities are included, valued simply at cost. But, of course, simple extrapolation becomes highly misleading, since the productive bases upon which any growth in real output depends may become so eroded that the very increase in the formal public-sector share of the nominal GNP will be accelerated long before 1990 or even 1984.

Perhaps even more disturbing than the increasing and absolutely large public-sector share in the GNP is the relatively sudden change that has occurred in the effective composition of this share since the 1960's and that shows no signs of tailing off. I refer here to the shift within public spending itself away from use of resources or so-called productive outlays, in proportional terms, and toward transfer or nonproductive governmental outlays. For the so-called productive public expenditures, the outlays on the purchase of real goods and services that are provided through government, an argument can be made, within limits, to the effect that these goods and services are themselves indirect inputs for the generation of national product.[2] The

---

2. This seemingly straightforward statement requires specific assumptions in order for it to hold. In a world where real goods and services are provided publicly through pure Niskanen bureaus, each one of which successfully extracts all of the potential fiscal surplus through oversupply, there is no net addition to value generated by the public sector. On the other hand, if the goods and services so provided are genuinely nonexcludable, and hence impossible to provide through markets, and, further, if public supply necessarily implies pure Niskanen bureaucracy, there is no net inefficiency generated because

movement of goods is facilitated by publicly provided highways; public education supposedly increases the supply of productive human capital; policemen protect private property and make the economy more efficient thereby. The list could be extended. No such argument can be adduced with respect to transfer spending. Resources are not, of course, "used up" directly in the pure transfer process, but purchasing power must be drawn from payments made to productive resource owners and shifted to individuals and groups in ways unrelated to productivity. The effects on overall economic productivity in the economy must be unidirectional; the increase in transfers can have only the net effect of sapping the sources of economic growth. Another way of putting this point is to say that within limits an argument can be made for the efficiency of productive outlays of governments, but no comparable efficiency basis justifies transfer outlays.[3] For the most part, the transfer outlays must be justified on grounds of nonefficiency, and the conflict between the objectives for transfers and efficiency must be squarely acknowledged.

Let us look briefly at the data on the increase in the transfer share of federal spending. In 1960 this part of the budget amounted only to 5.6 percent of the GNP, having changed relatively little over the 1950's, up only from 5.3 percent in 1950. By 1974, however, total transfer spending by government exceeded 10 percent of the GNP. In absolute totals, transfer spending doubled between 1970 and 1975 alone, moving up from under $80 billion to almost $160 billion. No one would dare predict a leveling off, or even a deceleration, of the rate of increase. It seems well within the realm of plausibility that by 1984 we shall be devoting one-fourth of our GNP to transfer payments alone.

In this chapter I want to concentrate attention on the effects of these increases in transfer payments on the national economy. I shall simply leave

---

of the existence of the public sector. At the limit, the community secures neither net gains nor net losses from supplying public goods and services to itself. For description of the Niskanen bureau, see William A. Niskanen, *Bureaucracy and Representative Government* (Chicago: Aldine-Atherton, Inc., 1971).

3. A limited amount of transfer activity can be rationalized on grounds of efficiency if utility interdependence exists. This aspect of transfer policy has recently been widely discussed under the rubric of Pareto-optimal redistribution. For the basic paper, see Harold Hochman and James Rodgers, "Pareto Optimal Redistribution," *American Economic Review* 59 (Sept., 1969): 542–57. Even if this argument is accepted, however, it does not seem wholly comparable to that which may be adduced to support nontransfer activity.

out of the account the growth in nontransfer spending which exerts different and perhaps equally important effects.

Basic Social Security

We may look first at the basic component of the social security system in the United States, the OASDI program of retirement, survivors', and disability benefits. For fiscal year 1976, these payments alone will approximate $75 billion, or roughly 5 percent of the GNP. This figure represents an increase from a mere $1 billion in 1950 and from a low $11 billion in 1960, and it is a near doubling of the $38 billion of 1970. What has been the economic effect of this explosive growth in these transfer payments, and what will be the effect of the predicted continued acceleration of this growth?[4]

In order to analyze these questions systematically, it is useful to construct a model that isolates specific features of the program. Consider the following model. Suppose that there are only two age groups (generations) living at any particular time: a retired group and a working group. All members of one generation are productive workers, and we may, for purposes of simplification, assume them to be equal. No members of the other generation work; they live off past earnings, gifts from the working generation, or receipt of public transfers. We suppose here that a political decision is made, in period T_0, to implement a public retirement program only after a time lag, only in, say, T_{30}, when all members of Generation 2 will have become retired and the work force will be made up of the succeeding Generation 3. This assumption means that members of Generation 1, the retired persons at the time of the initial legislation, are totally unaffected; they secure no retirement benefits. We may, through this device, concentrate on the behavior of members of Generation 2, who remain working in the periods before the transfers commence but who will all be retired when these payments start. How will the members of Generation 2 react? I shall present two differing hypotheses which yield contrasting results, and I shall then attempt to determine which of the two seems more in keeping with observed empirical reality.

4. For a general discussion, see Colin Campbell, "Social Insurance in the United States: A Program in Search of an Explanation," *Journal of Law and Economics* 12 (Oct., 1969): 249–66.

Ricardo-Barro model

We may label the first scenario after its classical originator and its most modern expositor.[5] A central assumption in this scenario is the existence of strong family ties between succeeding generations; that is, between 1 and 2, between 2 and 3, between 3 and 4, and so on. When the public or governmental retirement program is announced to be effective in the future, members of Generation 2, those who are currently working and who will themselves be the first recipients of the publicly provided retirement benefits, will act as if they hold legitimate claims against the community. These claims will come due on retirement, and it is assumed that they will be fully honored by the community. The present value of these claims will be included as a part of the net wealth of Generation 2 during their working years. Holding these claims against the government, members of Generation 2 will act to reduce their own private saving aimed directly at supporting their own income needs during retirement years. In the limit, the latter can be reduced dollar-for-dollar with the present value of the public claim.

But who is to pay off the claims when they come due? Who is to pay off the implicit public debt that is created by the announcement of the governmental retirement program? The only productive group in existence during the time when Generation 2 retires will be Generation 3. In the Ricardo-Barro model, members of Generation 2 will fully recognize the future obligations that the retirement program places on members of Generation 3, and members of Generation 2 will adjust their planned bequests, positive or negative, to just offset those obligations. In this scenario, therefore, Generation 2 will simply replace the accumulation of assets for their own retirement support with accumulation of assets for enhanced transfers to members of Generation 3. The net saving of Generation 2 is not affected by the introduction of the public pension scheme. As a result of Generation 2's behavior, members of Generation 3 will have direct ownership of a larger capital stock and hence a larger income than they would have in the

5. David Ricardo, *Works and Correspondence,* vol. 1, *Principles of Political Economy and Taxation* (Cambridge: Cambridge University Press, 1951), 244–49; Robert J. Barro, "Are Government Bonds Net Wealth?" *Journal of Political Economy* 82 (Nov.–Dec., 1974): 1095–118.

absence of the public transfer obligation. Thus, members of Generation 3 can meet the commitment for financing the pension payments to members of Generation 2 as the latter retire and shift out of the productive labor force. The aggregate stock of private capital is essentially unchanged by the introduction and operation of the public or governmental retirement scheme, and upon the full implementation of the program, the set of public transfers simply replaces the drawing-down of privately accumulated claims by recipients.

FELDSTEIN MODEL

The contrasting model may be associated with Martin Feldstein, its most articulate modern proponent.[6] In this scenario, the members of Generation 2, the productive group at the time that the future benefit program is announced, will treat the newly created claims to future payments as net wealth. They will reduce the private accumulation of assets designed to finance their own retirement income support. To this point the two analytical models are equivalent, but in the Feldstein construction, members of Generation 2 will not, as a result of the introduction of the public pension scheme, modify their planned bequests to members of Generation 3. Essentially, persons behave in accordance with a life-cycle model for rational choice, and family ties with Generation 3 are such that planned bequests are not affected.

In the Feldstein scenario, therefore, the important announcement effect of the public pension scheme is to reduce aggregate private saving. When the retirement claims come due, when prior commitments must be honored by the government, members of Generation 3 find themselves with a capital stock no larger than they would have had in the absence of the transfer system. As a result, the transfers to members of Generation 2 represent a deadweight burden, so to speak, against the income receipts of the productive members of the community, in this case Generation 3.

6. Martin Feldstein, "Social Security, Induced Retirement, and Aggregate Capital Accumulation," *Journal of Political Economy* 82 (Sept.–Oct., 1974): 905–26.

EVALUATION

The two models produce dramatically differing results, even in the extremely simplified setting that is postulated, one that is designed to eliminate many of the familiar effects. Any assessment of the present social security structure depends critically on which of the two scenarios is accepted in broad and general terms. At base, the choice between the two must be made on empirical grounds. Feldstein attempts to support his analysis with empirical estimates based on time series data from the United States. He estimates that the social security system has reduced total private saving by roughly 38 percent. This reduction will, over the long term, exert roughly similar effects on the level of private capital stock. Barro makes no attempt to support his contrasting analysis with empirical estimates.

I am not competent to examine critically Feldstein's empirical tests of his analysis. But without resort to complex data or to the intricacies of econometrics, straightforward empirical observation seems strongly to support the Feldstein rather than the Ricardo-Barro scenario. To establish this conclusion it is necessary to look at the historical record in a public-choice framework.

By 1975 the United States social security system had gone through forty years of history. Careful examination of the political decisions made over this long period should shed some light on the economic incidence of the institutions. I should note that the United States system, as it was introduced and as it has operated, is not equivalent to that analyzed in the simplified model above. Benefit payments were commenced immediately and not after a generation's lag, as in the simplified setting used above. But we may still get some general results by staying with the simplified model while extending it with care to the actual institutions in existence.

Under the setting postulated, suppose that at the time that the public or governmental pension system is enacted members of Generation 2, those who are scheduled to be the first benefit recipients, are taxed at sufficiently high levels to offset fully the present values of the benefit claims which they secure. In other words, assume that strict actuarial funding is followed from the outset of the system; genuine insurance principles are followed. The tax revenues during the periods before Generation 2 retires would then be accumulated in a special pension fund or reserve which would be invested in public or private debt instruments or capital assets. Under this scheme, the fund balances would just be sufficient to finance the pension transfers to members of Generation 2 as they retire and present their claims. In recognition of this fund accumulation, members of Generation 2, at the time of enactment, will have no motive to modify the rate of private bequests to Generation 3, regardless of family ties, since there will be no net burden imposed on Generation 3 by the whole scheme.

The important conclusion, for purposes of differentiating between the two scenarios sketched out above, is that the fully funded and actuarially sound system of public or governmental pension transfers is not different, in effect, from the nonfunded system described in the Ricardo-Barro scenario. Members of Generation 2 put aside, in both sequences, funds that are just sufficient to finance their own retirement, in the one case (Ricardo-Barro) via the enhanced bequests to Generation 3 and in the other case (full funding) via the system's fund balances. Members of Generation 3 secure no net increment to private assets under the funded pension scheme, but they incur no offsetting obligations to pay direct transfers to Generation 2.

This basic equivalence may be acknowledged, but what does this tell us about the explanatory power of the two scenarios? It suggests that *if* the Ricardo-Barro model is descriptive of the behavior of persons of Generation 2, those persons should be roughly *indifferent* to a fully funded scheme for public pensions or the unfunded scheme outlined above. Evidence for such indifference would consist in roughly equal political support for the alternative structures.

But the political record offers the contrary. Despite much initial discussion about the social security system being based on "sound insurance principles," and despite the continued misuse of the word "insurance," the observed political decisions about the system have never reflected a willingness on the part of decision makers to adopt full funding. Over an initial period, almost by necessity, a fund was accumulated, but it was never sufficiently large to offset the present values of future benefit claims. By the 1950's the absence of fund accumulation appropriate for general insurance principles came to be widely acknowledged, and the system was transformed into a straightforward transfer mechanism, with taxes being maintained roughly in balance with the benefit payout required. The net indebtedness of the social security system, treated actuarially, has been estimated at roughly $2.4 trillion, although the specific estimates here are difficult to compute. The main point is, however, clear. Political decision makers, who have presumably been responsive to the desires of constituents, at least indirectly, have definitely preferred the unfunded to the funded system. In the context of our simple two-generation construction, therefore, this suggests that members of Generation 2, the working group, elect politicians who refrain from imposing taxes for the purpose of accumulating fund reserves. The historical record indicates that politicians impose taxes only as required to meet current benefit obligations that the system has incurred. The evidence could scarcely be stronger in support of the essential Feldstein hypothesis. Over the forty-year period of its existence, the social security system has embodied the creation of claims against incomes of later periods, claims that have been treated as net wealth by potential beneficiaries and which have not been offset by the accumulation of either private or public assets.

One component of the so-called crisis in the system is the fact that these claims are coming due in ever-increasing magnitude, as the figures noted earlier suggest. Those who produce incomes currently are being called upon to transfer increasing shares of those incomes to those who have what they consider to be legitimate claims. Private saving in the economy is lower than it would be without the public transfers for three reasons. First, current taxpayers are led to expect that they, too, will be qualified to receive social security benefits on retirement. These future claims substitute for private saving that might be designed to provide retirement income support. Second, because private saving has been lower over the period of the system's existence, the capital stock is lower than it might have been. Thus, income before transfers, income from which private saving might be made, is lower. Finally, private saving that might be forthcoming for other purposes, over and beyond basic retirement income support, is reduced because disposable income is curtailed by the necessity to meet the increasing transfer burden.

DEMOGRAPHIC SHIFTS

These results emerge even if we project that the population will maintain a constant age profile, with the ratio between the working population and the retired population remaining unchanged. If major changes in this ratio occur, the analysis must be modified. Consider our model of separated generations again. Suppose that Generation 2 arrives at retirement and that its claims for support are financed by taxes on Generation 3. The latter, in its turn, anticipates support from Generation 4, which will be the productive group upon Generation 3's retirement. But let us now assume that Generation 4 is substantially smaller than Generation 3; the birth rate falls between Generation 2 and Generation 3. In that case, Generation 4 will find its transfer burden increased for yet another reason. And with this increased burden there will be still further reductions in disposable income, from which private saving and, ultimately, private capital formation must be made. These demographic shifts are of major importance in assessing the viability of the United States social security system beyond the 1980's. Because of the sharp curtailment in crude birth rates that occurred after the late 1950's, fear is now increasingly expressed about the ability of those who will be economically productive in the years after the turn of the century to finance the transfers that will be required to meet the claims of those who are members of the "baby-boom" generation and who will reach retirement in that period. If the Ricardo-Barro behavioral hypothesis should be correct, it should be possible to observe a major shift in the savings habits of the baby-boom generation as it moves into the income-producing stages of its life cycle. Accompanying the decline in the crude birth rate there should be observed an increase in private savings motivated by the recognition of the transfer burden that this generation will place on the next via the social security system. Has such a change been noted?

Early retirement

The analysis to this point has assumed that individuals have no choice about which generation or which group they belong to. If we modify the basic model slightly to allow for some degree of individual choice between working and receiving pension support, we can add yet another dimension to the transfer problem. If a person may, on his own option, choose to retire early and to qualify for income support, even if at some reduced level, such behavior exerts a double effect. By shifting out of the work force, a person reduces the overall income base from which transfers are made, even if he does not qualify for a retirement pension. But, if he does so qualify, he will add to the transfer burden from the reduced income base. The inducement for such behavior will, of course, increase as the level of transfer taxes increases.[7]

Nongenerality in the Social Security System

In its idealized form, the most important feature of a basic social security system is its generality. Potential beneficiaries include a very large proportion of the total population, and actual beneficiaries qualify for the receipt of transfers largely on the basis of age. That is, each person becomes old, and the aging process is something that cannot be individually controlled.

This feature of generality is important for both the financing and the political support of the system. To the extent that almost every member of the productive working population can anticipate the receipt of transfers on his own future retirement, taxes to finance payment to those currently retired may be rationalized on some basis of "intergenerational transfer" instead of on the more questionable criteria of equity or efficiency applicable for more general levies. In this context, individuals who pay taxes can plausibly accept the total tax-benefit structure as an "exchange" of sorts. Comparisons can be made between present values of tax obligations over a period of a person's working years and present values of future benefits over a period of anticipated retirement years. In the framework of our earlier example, members of Generation 3 may finance the retirement benefits for members of Generation 2, when they come due, on the expectation that they are indirectly "purchasing" claims against members of Generation 4, who will, in subsequent years, be called upon to finance Generation 3's retirement. In an idealized and fully mature system, there would be a present-value equivalence between a person's payments into the system and the transfers he secures from the system, computed or estimated on genuine actuarial principles. To the extent that a system approximates this ideal, it can be treated as an intergenerational exchange of sorts, and there is no need to raise issues of equity about the financing.[8]

---

7. For an analytical and empirical study which indicates that retirement is strongly influenced by the current social security system, see Michael J. Boskin, "Social Security and Early Retirement," mimeographed (Stanford University and National Bureau of Economic Research, Mar., 1975).

8. This was the model upon which my proposal for the issuance of Social Security Bonds was based. Compulsory purchase of such bonds, in lieu of the payroll tax, would

As it has developed, and as noted above, however, the United States system has not approximated this ideal. Persons who have qualified for retirement income transfers, and persons who anticipate retiring before the mid-1980's, have secured extremely favorable "bargains" from the system. The value of the benefits secured from the system far exceeds the value of payments made to the system, appropriately computed. This bargain will not, however, continue for those who commence retirement in the late 1980's and beyond unless benefit levels are increased above those now anticipated. And such real increases in benefits seem increasingly unlikely, given the observed demographic shift already mentioned. For young workers in the 1970's and beyond, the "exchange" of present taxes for future benefits that the system promises is a bad bargain, and possibly a very bad one, indeed.

To the extent that large numbers of workers recognize this fact, the political support for the whole social security structure may be threatened. Young workers in the 1970's may properly ask: Why should I pay taxes to support old people who have got a fine bargain while I am almost certain to get a bad deal? The young workers in the 1980's can ask this question much more emphatically. If the implicit intergenerational exchange comes to be treated as not offering "mutual gains," the system of payroll taxes becomes vulnerable. And the generality features of the structure will seem to be increasingly replaced by overtly discriminatory features. If those retiring before the mid-1980's secure such a better deal than all those who come after them, what is the "justification" for the observed differential treatment?

These issues would be present even if there were no additional discriminatory features embodied in the United States system. But there are many other departures from an idealized general system of retirement benefits than the failure of Congress to adjust tax rates in past years. Even with a

---

cause purchasers (potential benefit recipients) to treat future claims more clearly as net wealth in their personal portfolios and, at the same time, create more definitive obligations on the part of the system to meet such claims. My proposal involved the usage of funds from bond "sales" to finance current pension claims; no creation of assets was implied. Thus, the effects on real capital formation, under my scheme, might even be more severe than those under the present scheme, because of the enhanced security of future claims. The Feldstein concern about real capital formation would be increased. For my proposal, see my "Social Insurance in a Growing Economy: A Proposal for Radical Reform," *National Tax Journal* 21 (Dec., 1968): 386–95.

single-age cohort group, the structure of taxes and benefits tends differentially to favor the low-wage earner, the self-employed, and the worker with dependents who do not work. The structure tends to penalize the high-wage earner, the single worker, and the working wife or husband of a working marriage partner.

These discriminatory features, of both sorts, prevent the developing opposition from being contained and controlled by the introduction of a private pension option. If a system meets the idealized pattern of generality, persons could be allowed to opt out, to select private pension schemes, insuring thereby that the overall objective of social security for the aged would be met. But because of the departures from generality, the United States system must remain a compulsory one, with opting out disallowed. If such an option were opened up, there would be an immediate exodus of young workers, single workers, and working married couples—precisely those groups who anticipate the unfavorable intergenerational exchanges. This exodus would, of course, leave the older workers, the self-employed, and the low-wage earners in the system, tending thereby to accelerate the necessity of reducing project benefit levels or of increasing tax rates, steps which would, in turn, accelerate the exodus from the system.

If provisions for opting out are not possible, how is the political response to the mounting criticism of the social security transfer system to take shape? What plausible predictions can be made for policy change in the 1980's? Support has continued to increase for general treasury financing of at least some part of the system's obligations. In early 1975 the official advisory council on the system recommended that those transfer payments not strictly retirement-related, such as medicare payments, should be funded from general revenue sources and not from payroll taxes.

Steps in this direction will probably be taken as the system's transfer budget balance comes to be increasingly threatened in the late 1970's and early 1980's. But resort to the financing of social security transfer from general tax monies, even if it is only partial, must necessarily exert major policy consequences. The pretense of an independent financial entity incorporating an intergenerational exchange through a "trust fund" would be destroyed, and the distribution of transfer benefits would have to be evaluated against orthodox criteria of "need" instead of automatic or general eligibility. The general tax financing of benefit payments would lead directly to demands for means tests for recipients. Potential beneficiaries could no longer anticipate transfer payments as "rights" in the trust-fund context. General-fund financing would probably guarantee that persons who own assets valued above some cutoff level would be denied benefits, regardless of their record of payroll tax payments through their productive earning period. The cutoff level here will tend to be somewhat above the asset holdings of the median beneficiary, at least in some anticipatory setting. To set the cutoff level to insure that only those persons at the lower extremes qualify for transfers would lead to political abandonment of the whole system.

The introduction of any means test for receiving benefits will, however, tend to accentuate the effect on private saving and private capital formation emphasized by Feldstein. If a person anticipates that he will qualify for retirement income support only if the value of accumulated assets falls below defined limits, rational behavior will, of course, dictate that asset accumulation be held within these limits. It is difficult to conceive of a more direct discouragement to private saving for the middle-income earners. And this impact on the behavior of middle-income earners would more than offset the opposing effects on the very-high-income earners, who may be led to increase rates of private saving because they can no longer place positive discounted values on social security claims.

As the social security system shifts away from its independent financial status and toward incorporation into the general budget account of the federal government, there will also arise tax-side pressures for change. Allegations about the regressivity of payroll taxes remain wholly irrelevant as long as the fiction or mystique of intergenerational exchange is maintained and as long as the system is treated as a benefit-tax package on the individual level of consideration. Once this nexus is dropped and means tests are introduced on the receipts side of the ledger, there must arise intense demands for modifying the structure of taxes, for removing the limits on earnings subject to the tax, and for dropping the proportional rate structure itself. Political experience has demonstrated the willingness of the Congress to increase the income bases for the tax, and quite independent of the relationship to potential pension receipts. As the benefits side is further modified by means tests, attempts will be made to introduce progressive elements into the payroll-tax structure.

The most plausible prediction suggests that the United States social secu rity system will come increasingly to resemble a "welfare" or "discriminatory transfer" system and decreasingly to resemble an idealized general system of retirement-income support. But there is one vital difference between them that might be projected for the social security system and the standard program of discriminatory transfers to be discussed briefly below. Because the existing institutions were developed from, and the acceptance of the institutions was based on, the conception of a general system of retirement-income support, massive quantitative significance seems insured. Attempts to maintain a large part of the widespread political support that the program secured over the first forty years of its existence will guarantee that at least a majority of workers can anticipate the receipt of transfer benefits on retirement. But, with the effective divorce of the level of these benefits from the payment of taxes, both individually and for the system as a whole, there will be little, if any, pressure for containment. The system can, therefore, become the institutional means for massive income and/or wealth transfers from the upper-income receipts to those who expect to qualify for benefits. The social security system can well become the institutional vehicle through which a majority, acting in its own self-interest, "legitimizes" its direct exploitation of the high-income minority, something that it cannot do either with respect to the progressive-tax financing of genuinely public goods and services or with the provisions of welfare benefits to differentially favored minorities.[9]

The particular scenario might be sketched in somewhat more detail. Congress will face continuing pressures from the current and future claimants under the social security system for an increase in the level and range of benefits. At the same time, Congress will face pressures from current taxpayers, as taxpayers, against rising real-tax burdens. To the extent that the set of effective taxpayers can be reduced to a minority by introducing progressivity in the rate structure and by increasing the wage-salary base, the political weights are shifted toward expansions. As the Goldwater episode demonstrated in 1964, which politicians will not quickly forget, social security is a sacred cow in the United States. Recognition of political reality suggests

9. In this context, the social security system may approximate the institutional embodiment of the limiting set of transfers discussed in my paper "The Political Economy of Franchise in the Welfare State," in *Essays on Capitalism and Freedom*, ed. R. Seldon (Charlottesville: University Press of Virginia, 1975).

that it is not the "bankruptcy" of the system that threatens future benefit recipients, but instead the "political transfer potential" of the system which threatens to sap the productive strength of the national economy.

Welfare Transfers

Any analysis and discussion of the explosive growth in federal transfer payments over the 1965–1975 decade must give primary attention to the basic social security system. But account must also be taken of other transfer payments which, in total, are of roughly equal quantitative significance. The set of transfers which might be discussed under the single "welfare" rubric amounted to somewhat more than $17 billion in fiscal year 1975.

These transfers include those made under the Supplemental Security Income Program, covering direct assistance to the aged (not covered under OASDI), the blind, and the disabled—roughly $5 billion for fiscal year 1975. The second major component of the welfare transfers is the aid to states for maintenance payments to families with dependent children (AFDC). This program was roughly $5 billion in size in fiscal year 1975. Housing subsidies amounted to another $2 billion, and food stamp outlays, to more than $3.5 billion. Child nutrition programs added a final $2 billion to the welfare payments total.

In contrast with the transfers made under the social security program, certain components of the welfare system arouse significant political and public opposition. Survey data suggest that welfare spending is among the least desired of budget outlays on behalf of the voting public. Nevertheless, we observe a continued increase in the levels of welfare spending in almost all categories and regardless of the rate of growth or the prosperity of the national economy. How is this growth to be explained?

Welfare transfers may, for this purpose, be classified into two distinct groups: those made to persons who qualify on the basis of criteria that are not behaviorally induced, and those made on eligibility criteria that are within the control of the recipient. The first set includes payments made to the aged poor not covered by OASDI payments, to the blind, and to the disabled and could be extended beyond the strict set of welfare transfers to include at least some of the payments to veterans. The welfare payments which arouse the main public clamor are those for which persons can become eligible by modifying their own behavior. These include AFDC transfers to women who qualify for welfare payments when their male cohorts "desert" them, payments which also increase as they increase the number of children. The income criteria determining eligibility for food stamps are so loosely drawn that both students and strikers can qualify. Transfer programs of these types are essentially open-ended, with the outlays coming to be largely uncontrollable. And at this juncture in the discussion the role of the federal bureaucracy cannot be overlooked. Evidence is accumulating to indicate that the bureaucracy plays a major role in the rate of growth in federal spending of all sorts, and this bureaucratic influence seems notably true with respect to welfare spending. Bureaucrats in the welfare agencies are rewarded in terms of the case loads that their agencies carry; it is to their own advantage to see eligibility lists increased, not reduced.

Nonetheless, and despite the extremely rapid rates of increase that have been observed in the whole set of welfare transfers, this sector of the federal transfer program seems ultimately more manageable than the social security sector. This conclusion is based on the political- or public-choice reasons already noted above. By the nature of the case, welfare transfers will tend to benefit differentially favored minorities of the population. And although these minorities may, through such agencies as the welfare rights organizations, exert considerable direct political pressures, the budget increases must still secure the implicit sanction of the political spokesmen and representatives of the majority of the population. Explicit espousal of vastly expanded programs for welfare transfers is the path to political suicide, as George McGovern found out in 1972, and proposals for replacing the piecemeal separate program with a general program of income maintenance, the so-called negative income tax, meet relatively stiff opposition, as Richard Nixon found out in 1970.

Transfer Payments and National Economic Growth

Space does not permit a discussion of remaining major elements in the set of federal transfer programs, among the most notable of which are payments to veterans and payments to the unemployed. It will, however, be useful to examine, in very general terms, the impact of increasing transfer payments, both in relative and absolute terms, on the national economy. As we have noted, the rate of private saving and private capital formation has been substantially reduced because of the social security system's failure to accumulate a reserve fund. More directly, any transfer payment must reduce the income left for the free disposition of the primary income earner. To the extent that the income earner retains options which allow him to shift to nonpecuniary sources of utility, some reduction in work effort must accompany every increase in transfer spending. Incentives to work and to save out of income earned from work are necessarily related directly to the differential between retained or disposable incomes and the level of transfers made.

Insofar as a larger and larger share of the taxes required to finance transfers comes to be placed on capital, there will be differential effects on the rate of capital accumulation. Those who are competent in the manipulation of growth models can probably offer useful insights on alternative scenarios. I can make only some general suggestions here. Suppose that the rate of capital accumulation depends on disposable income left in the command of productive income earners. Suppose, further, that the national economy is in some long-run dynamic equilibrium; it is on a steady growth path. There will exist a specific relationship between the size of the aggregate capital stock and the level of income generated. Onto this steadily growing economy let us impose a reduction in disposable incomes of the productive income earners because of the transfer of funds to specific groups in the economy, groups which do not make current economic contributions. This reduction in disposable income will, of course, reduce the rate of private saving. But note that there will also be produced a disequilibrium between the size of the capital stock and the level of current income that is disposable. Owners of capital will have an incentive to draw down stocks in order to maintain incomes above the levels which would be possible in the absence of capital withdrawal. For a transition period, it seems quite possible that there would take place a net reduction in the aggregate stock of capital. At the end of this transition, the capital stock would be reduced to a level commensurate with the lowered level of income that is sustainable, given the continuation of the transfer policy.

I have discussed with my colleagues a parable that was intended to illustrate this situation, at least in part. Suppose that somewhere in a remote mountain valley there lives a farmer who produces apples for sale on the market. His only capital is standing apple trees, which he can also market for firewood if he chooses. He has gone along for years replacing his trees as they die out and adding a few new seedlings each year, thus expanding his orchard and, ultimately, his apple crop. Now, lo and behold, one year a thief appears who steals x percent of the apples from the trees. The farmer may react by reducing the rate at which he expands his orchard, but he also may sell off his standing trees for firewood. For the thief there is a genuine maximization problem: What is the optimal percentage of the crop to steal, given his predictions about the responses of the farmer?

This is about where we are with transfer policy. Concern has been expressed about the response of saving, investment, and labor supply to the increasing taxes required to finance transfers to the nonproductive members of society. Implicitly, economists have examined the maximization problem for the transferees, based on the fear that they might overshoot the proper target as defined by the transferees' own interest. But this position overlooks the possible secondary or strategic reactions of the apple farmer. When will he begin to behave strategically? When will he take one of the other options open to him? He can, of course, quit farming and become a thief. And he can (or can he?) decide that the way to protect his apples is by catching and punishing the thief. As applied to transfer policy, when and how will those who earn incomes from productive activity react explicitly against the increasing drainage coercively imposed on them by government? But what if there are more thieves than farmers? How near have we come to Plato's definition of "democracy"?

This is nothing more than a rough-and-ready sketch of the sort of analysis that could be carried out, starting from an empirically relevant basis, on the observed dramatic increases in the levels of transfer spending by government. It is time that economists commenced to apply their learned expertise to such issues as these. Whether or not such applications would result in a change in the direction of budgetary emphasis, including a possible reduction in the rate at which government spending, overall, is increasing, may be questioned. Honest assessment must yield pessimistic predictions about the maintenance of the private sector in the national economy. Government cannot continue to grow at the rate it did over the decade between 1965 and 1975. But the way in which Leviathan is contained becomes all-important for the preservation of the ideals of liberty and freedom that the United States has historically represented.[10]

10. For a general discussion of the problems of controlling Leviathan, see my book *The Limits of Liberty: Between Anarchy and Leviathan* (Chicago: University of Chicago Press, 1975).

Who Should Pay for
Common-Access Facilities?

I. Introduction

This paper challenges one of the "principles" of public finance that seems to have been accepted implicitly rather than examined explicitly. I demonstrate that the efficient means of financing certain common-access facilities *may* involve the imposition of taxes that are inversely rather than directly related to the income-wealth positions of potential users, at least at the margin. The analysis suggests, further, that the adoption of such tax rates may be in the interest of those persons who are subjected to the relatively high levies. The paper adds to the mounting evidence that traditional public-finance precepts often lack analytical bases and that these require continuing critical appraisal.

II. Common Access without User Prices

For many facilities adequate financing from direct user pricing is inefficient in an institutional sense. The costs of excluding users on a unit-of-service basis may be prohibitive. In such cases, usage of the facility may be opened to all. Access to the services of the facility may be made commonly available to all members of the relevant community without payment of a user charge. To finance such a facility requires resort to some means other than direct

From *Public Finance/Finances Publiques* 27, no. 1 (1972): 1–8. Reprinted by permission of the publisher.

I am indebted to my colleagues Charles Goetz and Gordon Tullock for helpful discussions on this paper.

pricing of services as used. These means may take the form of initiation fees, annual club dues, membership subscriptions, or season tickets in the case of privately owned facilities (golf and swimming clubs are good examples), or taxes in the case of publicly owned facilities (examples are municipal swimming pools and museums). The organizational arrangements, as such, are not directly relevant to the question to be examined here. The discussion is limited to the ordering of such "nondirect" prices among members of a potential user or consumer group. Somewhat paradoxically, the analysis suggests that for some common-access facilities, low-income users "should" be charged higher "nondirect prices" than high-income users.

An example

Consider a simple example which we place in a collective-choice context. Suppose that there are acknowledged advantages to a small community of nearby residents from the maintenance and upkeep of a beach facility. Furthermore, assume that the charging of direct user prices in the form, say, of daily or hourly fees, involves unduly high collection and enforcement costs. The facility may be maintained at differing levels of quantity, which can be measured continuously in square yards of sand beach. The decision as to the quantity to be maintained is to be collectively made. Income-wealth levels differ as among members of the community of prospective consumers or users, but, for simplicity, we assume that underlying preference functions are identical for all persons.

The question is: How "should" the community of users finance the beach-maintenance charges, and how much maintenance (measured in square yards) "should" be undertaken? Conceptually at least, the second part of this question can be answered without difficulty by anyone familiar with the modern theory of public or collective consumption goods. A necessary condition for the attainment of an optimal or efficient quantity of the "good," in our case, the beach facility, is equality between marginal evaluations summed over all potential users and the marginal cost of providing the "good." In terms of this example, optimality is reached when the value placed on slightly larger beach area, summed over all persons in the community, is equal to the added maintenance cost involved in the slightly larger area. As noted, this is a conceptually satisfactory answer rather than an instrumentally helpful one. The criterion tells us next to nothing about how the marginal evaluations of the members of the community may be determined.

III. Wicksell's Criterion for Efficiency

Knut Wicksell's approach to the problem of financing publicly provided facilities provides more instrumental assistance in this respect.[1] The costs of financing differing levels of beach maintenance may be presumed to be known in advance. If we disregard, for now, the costs of organizing for political decisions, we may suppose that some arbitrarily chosen small initial level of beach maintenance, say for X square yards, is proposed along with a whole array of differing tax-sharing arrangements. Among the community of N persons, total tax payments, T, must be equal to the known costs of financing the initial level of maintenance, X. Individual tax shares may, however, range from zero to T, or, if we designate an individual's share as t_i, the condition to be met is that $0 \leq t_i \geq T$.[2] *Any* tax-sharing scheme that meets this condition qualifies for inclusion in the array that is matched against the proposed outlay.

In some way, say at a town meeting, the outlay proposed is presented for a vote in the form of a series of motions, each one of which embodies simultaneous approval of the outlay *and* a specific tax-sharing arrangement for financing it. So long as unanimous consent is not secured, no decision is reached. The decision stage stops when *some* tax plan for financing the outlay secures the agreement among all members. For the small, initially proposed quantity of maintenance, there may, of course, be many tax schemes that could generate unanimous support. Suppose that one such scheme is adopted. From this point, a second proposal is made which embodies the

---

1. See Knut Wicksell, *Finanztheoretische Untersuchungen,* Jena, Gustav Fischer, 1896, major portions of which are translated as "A New Principle of Just Taxation" and included in *Classics in the Theory of Public Finance,* edited by R. A. Musgrave and A. T. Peacock, London, Macmillan, 1958, 72–118.

2. This assumes that no member of the community considers beach maintenance a "bad"; that is, no member places a negative evaluation on the proposed change. In this case, t_i might, of course, be less than zero; that is, negative taxes might be required.

financing of some increment to *X*. The same voting procedure is followed, with unanimous approval being the criterion for final decision. In this way, the community proceeds by a series of finite steps to determine the appropriate quantity of beach maintenance to be provided and, simultaneously, the tax-sharing of the costs of the facility will be determined.

The Wicksellian collective-decision model conceptually provides us with a meaning of efficiency in financing, a meaning that might be revealed by individual behavior under a set of idealized conditions. Even Wicksell recognized, however, that these conditions could hardly be realized in any real-world decision process. Group decision-making takes time and hence involves costs. Furthermore, the existence of an unanimity rule creates strong incentives for unproductive investment in bargaining strategy on the part of individuals. On balance, the Wicksellian framework provides little more than a benchmark from which departures may be measured. In a larger institutional sense, efficiency in collective choice making may require violations of the conditions that are required to guarantee efficiency in the narrowly allocative sense.[3]

IV. Tax Institutions and Collective-Decision Rules

To this end, modifications on the Wicksellian scheme have been variously proposed. Relatively little support may be found for application of a unanimity rule, but public-finance scholars have recognized that properly chosen tax-sharing schemes may partially substitute for the inclusiveness of rules. To the extent that tax-sharing institutions can be selected and imposed independent of the collective-decision process, and to the extent that the tax shares embodied in these institutions accurately reflect the strength of individuals' desires for the facility to be financed, the inclusiveness of choice-making rules may be relaxed without generating predicted departures from efficiency in outcomes. As an extreme example to illustrate this relationship between tax shares and decision rules, consider a community of equals in which a tax-sharing institution requires equal payments. In this case, if the

---

3. For a generalized discussion, see James M. Buchanan and Gordon Tullock, *The Calculus of Consent*, Ann Arbor, University of Michigan Press, 1962.

facility to be financed is of the extreme polar type that benefits all members of the community equally, *any* decision-making rule will yield the same result as any other, from single-person dictatorship to unanimity.[4]

The tax institutions that are observed to exist normally relate individual tax shares positively to income-wealth positions of individuals, and ethical norms for tax-sharing embody this relationship. To the extent that these institutions are interpreted to embody efficiency at all, the relationship between income-wealth criteria and tax shares is taken to indicate a positive income-wealth elasticity of demand for the services provided by the publicly provided facility. Since this is characteristic of so-called "normal" goods in the private economy, the extension of the assumption to apply to goods and services that are publicly provided seems to be fully acceptable. If publicly provided goods are characterized by a positive income elasticity, certain bounds would be set on the inefficiency of public goods provision, almost independent of consideration for the actual rules for reaching collective or political decisions or for the practical workings of these rules. That is to say, so long as individual tax shares are positively related to income-wealth positions, and so long as the goods in question satisfy criteria for "publicness," the inefficiencies generated by less-than-unanimity rules for decision may not be excessive. Something of this sort, at least, may describe what we might call the "conventional wisdom" among modern public-finance specialists.

I shall demonstrate, however, that there is a major error in the line of reasoning traced out briefly above. When this error is corrected, it is relatively easy to show that for the sort of facilities examined in this note there need not be a positive relationship between income-wealth level and tax shares for individual members of the community, even if, under some conditions, the services of the facilities should be characterized by a positive income elasticity of demand. Efficiency may require that low-income–low-wealth recipients pay somewhat larger tax shares than their high-income–high-wealth counterparts, and failure to allow this in fiscal institutional structures may, in fact, impose differential harm precisely on the low-income–low-wealth users of the facilities.

---

4. For a complete discussion of the relationship between tax institutions and decision rules, see my *Demand and Supply of Public Goods,* Chicago, Rand McNally, 1968.

V. Dimensions of Evaluation

Let us return to the beach-maintenance example introduced earlier. If their underlying preferences are essentially identical, how could it be possible that a low-income member of the community might place a higher marginal evaluation on some given extension of the facility size than his high-income neighbor? Once the question is put in terms of this sort of example, the answer seems intuitively plausible. The *marginal* evaluation that an individual user places on an extension of the *facility* is the increment to total value that he anticipates to derive from this extension, an increment that is dependent on his anticipated *total* usage of the facility. If it can be plausibly argued that the low-income consumer uses the services of the common-access facility more than the high-income user, it becomes logically possible that the marginal evaluation which he places on the extension of the facility is relatively larger. This will be possible even if, over wide ranges of equal service levels, the evaluation of the high-income user is relatively greater.

For a market-supplied good or service, income elasticity is defined to be the percentage change in quantity demanded divided by the percentage change in income. But this definition obscures the assumption of a fixed price. Implicitly, the adjustment that takes place in consumption consequent on the change in income is in quantity demanded. Hence, individual persons at different income levels are presumed to consume or use *differing* quantities. For a public good, however, the characteristic feature is precisely the absence of quantity adjustment. That quantity which is available to one user is, by definition, equally available to all users. In our example, the beach, in whatever quantity provided, is equally available to all members of the community. The common measure of income elasticity is scarcely relevant until and unless we specify a price. In this case, however, it is precisely the "price" differentials, in this case tax-share differentials, that we seek to establish. To say that the publicly provided good exhibits a positive income elasticity of demand is meaningless without some specification of the demand price.

But the commonly available facility may be used *variously* by different members of the community. Usage of the services of the facility, the beach in our example, depends on the action of the individual in availing himself of the privilege. And it is in this respect that the low-income or low-wealth consumer may be motivated to use the services of the facility to a relatively more intensive level than his high-income counterpart.

It will be helpful to think of a common-access facility, in whatever quantity provided, as being made available to users at a zero direct price, although the analysis would be unchanged if some nominal user fees should be charged. At a zero price, why should we predict that the consumer with relatively low income would utilize the services of the facility more than the user in a more favorable economic position? If usage were genuinely "free," we should predict that with comparable utility functions the intensity of usage would be approximately the same for all persons. But, despite a zero money price, the actual usage of a facility cannot be "free" in a utility sense. Consumption takes time, and facilities of the sort discussed here are likely to be relatively time-intensive when compared with other consumption goods and services. As Gary Becker has emphasized, it is necessary to consider "time prices" as well as money prices in any complete theory of individual consumer adjustment.[5] The time price, unlike money price in market transactions, will not be uniform as among separate consumers because of the differing opportunities for using time in other ways, either in the production or in the consumption of income. Almost by definition, these opportunities are relatively greater for the potential user who receives the relatively higher income. The services of the publicly provided facility, available at zero user prices, are, therefore, "cheaper" for the low-income person than for his high-income cohort because of the differential in time price. From this it follows that there will be a difference in the intensity of usage of the facility as between income levels, and that the relatively low-income user will consume more services of the facility. In our example, the number of trips that the relatively low-income user will make to the beach each year may be predicted to be greater than the number made by his high-income counterpart, assuming similarity in underlying utility functions. The potential user who has a relatively high income can spend his time in alternative ways, either by consuming substitute services (he may go to the mountains), or by earning more income.

The relationship between usage and alternative opportunities can be empirically observed and is, of course, widely recognized. The "beach boys" are

5. See Gary Becker, "A Theory of the Allocation of Time," *Economic Journal,* Vol. 75, September 1965, 493–517.

those who do not have either income or alternative employment opportunities readily available. The only point that is at all novel in this analysis involves the implications of this for tax-share adjustments and for determining the efficient quantity of facility to be provided. To examine these implications more carefully, let us return to the Wicksellian collective-choice process introduced above. Suppose that the community is currently financing a quantity of beach maintenance, say Y square yards of beach area, and that this is being financed from the levy of equal-per-head taxes, regardless of the fact that persons with differing incomes are among the group of users. An increment in quantity is now proposed, say a shift from Y to Z in quantity, with the unanimity rule in force. The cost of financing the increment is known, and the proposal to add this quantity is placed before the group, along with a whole array of tax shares arranged so as to cover the outlay that is required.

Consider the positions of two separate members of the decision-making group, A and B. The first person, A, uses the common-access facility, say, six times per year, and he places an evaluation on the incremental change in quantity based on this anticipated usage. The second person, B, who has fewer opportunities for alternative consumption and for productive employment, uses the beach, say, twelve times per year, and his evaluation on the incremental change in quantity proposed is based in this anticipated usage. It is surely possible, indeed it is plausible to think, that individual B may place a somewhat higher valuation on the incremental change in beach-maintenance quantity than individual A. To the extent that he does so, the Wicksellian decision process might attain unanimous agreement on the extension only through B's expressed willingness to pay more than one-half of the tax costs involved in the extension under consideration. If institutional rigidities or incorrectly derived norms for the allocation of tax shares prevent any negative relationship between tax shares and income levels, inefficiency would characterize the final outcome. And the incidence of this inefficiency may well cause more harm to B than to A.

VI. Real-World Applications

It seems possible that the factors emphasized here may be a relatively significant source of public-sector inefficiency in the real world, although detailed empirical investigation would be needed to support this as a generalized hypothesis. Municipal governments are alleged to be in financial crises every-where, but crises are defined with respect to traditional and orthodox sources of tax revenues. Widespread discussion of reform includes the replacement of traditional tax sources by direct user pricing when and where this may be at all applicable. Objections to user pricing can be, and are made, on distribu-tional grounds. Those who are likely to be harmed are low-income benefici-aries of what are now largely "free" services, that is, free of direct user prices. In light of these quite legitimate distributional arguments against direct user pricing, consideration should perhaps be given to the replacement of tradi-tional taxing sources by unorthodox ones. It seems quite possible that the relatively poor members of many communities would secure net benefits from the levy of taxes that are actually related to incomes *negatively* rather than positively. If such a negative relationship seems bizarre, the limiting case of equal-per-head taxes might be considered. The distinction between equal-per-head taxes and direct user prices should be noted. Direct user prices are *uniform* for all persons, per unit of service demanded. Equal-per-head taxes are uniform for all persons, but services of the facility consumed may vary as among these persons. Hence, to the extent that low-income persons utilize the services of a common-access facility more intensively, the final money "price" per unit of service remains lower for them than for their high-income cohorts.

Unless some such fiscal devices are introduced, common-access facilities in existence may be allowed to deteriorate rapidly as their usage by high- and median-income residents of municipalities continues to fall. Low-income central-city residents can secure genuine advantages from municipal provi-sion of additional common-access facilities. But higher-income residents who have privately available substitutes may be unwilling to finance added municipal facilities through orthodox taxing formulae. If they are forced to do so, they may continue to migrate to independent suburbs in increasing numbers.[6] The introduction of imaginative tax devices that are designed to reflect the realities of common-facility usage and evaluation rather than out-moded norms of traditional public finance may allow additional common-access facilities to be financed which would otherwise be impossible.[7] Rather

6. The possibilities of "voting with their feet" through outmigration effectively shifts collective-decision processes in the direction of a unanimity rule.

7. This conclusion is in the Wicksellian tradition. Although his proposals for intro-ducing a unanimity rule or a relative unanimity rule in fiscal choice making has often

than opting out through migration, relatively high-income members might be willing to contribute to the fiscal surplus potentially available to all members of the community, even if this surplus should be differentially enjoyed by low-income members. Even the resident who has his own private swimming pool may be willing to pay some tax share in the financing of a municipal common-access pool. He may, however, be unwilling to pay a tax share that is dictated by the orthodox tax institutions which relate payments, not to relative evaluations, but to an income-asset base.

VII. Generalizations

The argument of this paper should not be interpreted as a general attack on particular tax institutions. The analysis has been limited to common-access facilities that are publicly provided. The argument does lend support for multi-sector budgets which would allow differing components of a public-goods mix to be subjected to differing fiscal choices. Tax institutions that may provide some approximation to efficiency in the array of tax shares for certain categories of publicly provided goods and services may be quite inappropriate for other categories. Methodologically, the argument re-emphasizes the importance of separating efficiency and distributional norms in the analyses of fiscal institutions. In the attempts to make all fiscal institutions incorporate distributional objectives, important potential efficiency gains may be neglected, which, themselves, might have *desirable* distributional by-products.

VIII. Privately Owned Facilities

As suggested at the outset, much of the analysis applies to privately owned and organized facilities as well as to publicly organized governmental facilities. Only the latter have been discussed in detail here. Consider a privately organized cooperative swimming club, which is confronted with a decision concerning whether or not to construct an addition to the facility. There seems to be no apparent reason why the incremental subscriptions required

---

been interpreted as restricting the scope of approved projects, Wicksell himself interpreted his proposals as means of securing political approval of public projects that could not otherwise secure support. Wicksell's emphasis was on introducing greater variability in tax-sharing arrangements.

from members need to be uniform, and, indeed, it seems likely that for many situations nonuniform subscriptions would secure approval more quickly. Members or potential members who are anticipated to use the services of the common facility more intensively may place differentially higher evaluations on the proposed extension in size. And these members may, on balance, be classified below other members on income-wealth criteria. To restrict subscriptions to uniform levels per member may inhibit construction of the proposed extension, with the resultant concentration of opportunity loss on those who stand to benefit most from the incremental addition.

Who Should Distribute What
in a Federal System?

It is frequently asserted that redistribution, as a governmental function, can be properly assigned only to the central or national government.[1] The remaining half of this assertion implies that allocative functions can, by contrast, be performed by local governmental units if the appropriately defined "publicness" ranges are spatially limited and if interjurisdictional spillovers are not significant. I want to examine this "principle" of modern public finance theory in some detail and in some depth.

It is difficult to separate positive and normative strands in the orthodox discussion of this principle. If redistribution is interpreted exclusively in terms of coercively imposed transfers of income and wealth from some persons to others, discussion concerning the possibility of carrying out this activity at various levels of government reduces to a single positive proposition. The ability of any person, agency, or governmental unit to coerce another depends on the range of alternatives open to the one to be coerced. If an individual has available to him multiple options that offer substantially the same utility prospects, no other person exerts much power over him. In the limit, the perfectly competitive market minimizes man's power over man or, conversely, maximizes man's freedom from coercion by other men. It should

Republished with permission of the Columbia University Press, 562 West 113 St., New York, NY 10025. *Redistribution through Public Choice,* ed. H. H. Hochman and G. Peterson, 1974, 22–42. Reproduced by permission of the publisher via Copyright Clearance Center, Inc.

James M. Buchanan is indebted to his colleague Charles Goetz for helpful comments.

1. For a statement to this effect, see R. A. Musgrave, "Economics of Fiscal Federalism," *Nebraska Journal of Economics and Business* (Autumn, 1971), 10.

be evident that the power of any government to extract income and wealth coercively from a person is related inversely to the locational alternatives that are available to that person. For this reason alone, a local governmental unit in a national economy is severely limited in its strictly zero-sum redistributive activity. It is constrained by the ability of individuals to shift among alternative locationally separated jurisdictions, and this constraining influence operates even when the existence of relevant and sometimes significant decision thresholds is acknowledged. Since persons do not have comparable abilities to shift readily across national boundaries, the power of a central or national government to enforce imposed redistribution policies is clearly greater than that possessed by local authorities.

If this is all there is to the "principle" that the redistributive function must be performed centrally, extended discussion would hardly seem to be warranted. In what follows I assume that those who advance the principle have something more than this in mind, and especially that attention is not exclusively focused on the strictly zero-sum redistributive activities of governments. In Section I, I discuss the sharing of gains-from-trade from the provision of collective consumption of public goods at the various governmental levels. In Section II the related but analytically separate category that is commonly called "Pareto-optimal redistribution" is examined. In this setting income-wealth redistribution is itself treated as a public good. In Section III the Pareto-optimality approach is extended to apply to the whole set of institutions or processes that generate specific distributional outcomes. As will become evident, the discussion in this section is most closely related to the explicitly normative or value-laden treatment that is accorded distribution by many scholars. In both Sections II and III an attempt is made to restrict discussion to those aspects of the analysis that bear directly on the functional location of redistribution in a hierarchical governmental system, that is, in a federal polity.

I. Distribution of Gains-from-Trade

GAINS-FROM-TRADE IN PRIVATE GOODS

Modern economic theory is somewhat misleading in its distributive implications. Given an initial set of individual resource endowments, including capacities or skills, this theory implies that there is a uniquely determinate position on the utility-possibility frontier that tends to be produced through the operation of the market process. The final distribution of the gross gains-from-trade seems to be determined independent of the path or process through which it is reached. In one sense this suggests first the solving of the simultaneous equations of the whole complex system and second the inference from solution to that unique set of initial endowments that might have been required to generate it. This has always seemed to me to turn things around. The market process tends to generate an equilibrium, but the location of this equilibrium on the "social utility surface," that is, its distributional characteristics, depends on the path through which it is approached. It seems unreal to postulate the perfect recontracting that is required to produce a one-for-one correspondence between an initial set of endowments and a final distribution of utility or welfare among individuals. Any plausibly realistic model must allow exchange to be made, and implemented, before equilibrium is finally, if ever, attained. Trading at prices that are different from those that might characterize the potentially attainable final general equilibrium solution must be allowed to take place. Once this is done, however, the path toward the utility-possibility frontier delineates the set of positions attainable on the frontier.[2]

Markets do not work perfectly, and there are numerous constraints on the freedom of trading among individuals and groups. If we drop the formalism of modern general-equilibrium theory, we can discuss the market process within any given set of externally imposed constraints. It becomes meaningful to talk about the characteristics of the equilibrium that will tend to emerge within the set of institutional limits postulated, and we can utilize the concept of a feasible or attainable utility-possibility frontier, the location of which will be dependent on such limits.

I can illustrate this point geometrically and in such a way as to introduce the central elements of this paper. Figure 1 is drawn in a two-man utility space. I want to use this two-man construction, however, both here and later,

---

2. For a sophisticated critique of modern general-equilibrium theory that expresses much of my own, and largely intuitive, dissatisfaction, see Maurice Allais, "Les théories de l'équilibre économique général et de l'efficacité maximale," *Revue d'Économie Politique* (May, 1971), 331–409.

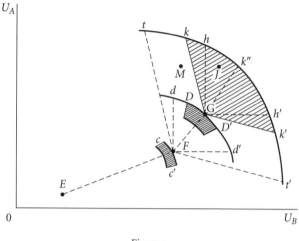

Figure 1

to depict situations faced by individuals in many-person settings. Hence, to each person in the construction, the "other person" is conceived to be the whole environment that he confronts, including the behavior of many other persons, an environment that he considers to be beyond his own power of control or influence, at least in any direct sense.

In a Hobbesian world, where life is indeed "nasty, brutish, and short," and where neither property rights nor trade exists, the utility positions attained by the two persons, A and B, are shown at *E* in Figure 1. This position depicts reaction-curve equilibrium in the savage and anarchistic "society." The distribution of utility, which reflects the instrumental distribution of real goods, depends strictly on the relative abilities of persons to survive and prosper in the hostile environment of potential conflict.

Once property rights are defined and legally protected, market-type exchanges become possible, and these allow dramatic gains to be secured by all parties. Modern microeconomic theory implies that movement takes place along a unique price vector, which could be indirectly represented in Figure 1 by the heavily dotted line extending from *E* to point *F*, a position on a utility-possibility frontier under the institutional structure that allows voluntary exchange. As noted above, the one-to-one relationship between *E* and *F* exists only in a regime of perfect recontracting, which requires, in its turn, the presence of a large number of traders on both sides of all markets, along with an absence of all barriers to the consummation of trade. If we drop any of these requirements, the one-to-one correspondence vanishes, and the initial position, *E*, along with a practically workable market order may produce a position along or near a finite and narrowly defined segment of a frontier. The shaded area between and below the points *c* and *c'* depicts this set of positions. Regardless of the particulars of the institutional process, we can think of the market or exchange system as insuring that one position in this set will be attained.

It is important to understand the basic reason for the relatively narrow limits within which the final distribution of the gains-from-trade is bounded. These limits are a direct consequence of the ability of single traders to select among alternatives. In the extreme and formal model each trader is a pure price-taker in all markets. There is no room for bargaining, as such, despite the presence of mutual gains in each two-party contract. We need not impose the severe restrictions of the formal model, however, to confine the utility or welfare distribution within relatively narrow limits, as shown.

GAINS-FROM-TRADE IN LOCAL PUBLIC GOODS

We may now introduce localized collective-consumption or public goods and services. Suppose that the existing technology along with existing individual preference functions makes possible the efficient joint consumption of certain goods and services that are spatially limited and that are non-excludable among beneficiaries. Local governmental units emerge to finance and to provide these goods and services. We assume, as before, that the central government exists only to enforce property rights, to insure against fraudulent contracts, and to guarantee freedom of resource flows throughout the national economy.

If there are efficiency gains to be secured from the provision and consumption of such localized public goods, the utility-possibility frontier is shifted outward from that which is attainable in the setting that allows only for the provision of purely private goods.[3] In Figure 1 the introduction of

---

3. For purposes of discussion here, I assume that local public goods will not be provided through ordinary market processes. This is not a realistic assumption. In the absence of local government, entrepreneurs would find it profitable to organize arrangements through

these goods allows positions to the northeast of the set bounded by c and c' to be attained.

How are the gains-from-trade in localized public goods to be distributed? If we assume that private-goods equilibrium is attained at F, any position within the inclusive limits defined by F, d, and d' would reflect mutual gains, or in the many-person setting, gains to all parties. In a regime of spatially competitive governments, however, we should predict that the range of attainable utility or welfare distributions would be considerably more confined than the set indicated. The reason is identical with that shown to impose bounds on the distributions of the gains from private-goods trade. If there are alternative sellers and buyers, the power of any one to impose terms of trade on market participants is restricted. This principle applies directly to the competition among local governmental units. Consider a single local government that provides a public good to its citizens. Can this unit extract from an individual citizen-taxpayer-beneficiary all the fiscal surplus that the enjoyment of this public good represents? It can do so only if and to the extent that he has no alternatives available to him, if there are no better "deals" in other locations, taking into account the costs of making a move. But it seems clear that the prospects of "voting with the feet" that individuals face in a regime of spatially competitive local governments in a federal system insure results that are broadly comparable in kind to the operation of effectively competitive markets.

This process of adjustment involves both distributional and efficiency dimensions. The distribution of the gross gains-from-trade in local public goods is restricted. At the same time these gains tend to be fully exploited, insuring that the equilibrium finally attained will fall along or near the utility-possibility frontier itself rather than inside it. The results are comparable in kind to those produced by workably competitive markets, but this is not to suggest that either the distributional or the efficiency con-

---

which local public goods would be provided, even those that are nonexcludable. In some circumstances, and especially where tie-in arrangements can be introduced that effectively reinstate excludability, market organization may prove even more efficient than local governmental units. In other circumstances, where exclusion cannot be introduced even indirectly, market arrangements may emerge, but these may remain seriously inefficient in supplying the local collective goods.

straints are nearly so confining as those that open-ended market adjustment tends to guarantee. The Tiebout adjustment mechanism does not offer a wholly satisfactory analogue to market competition, despite its directional effects.[4]

For purposes of illustration in Figure 1, the provision of local public goods through a regime of spatially competitive local governmental units tends to narrow the set of attainable outcomes to the shaded area between and below the segment DD'. As drawn, this set is not so narrowly confined as that shown to be attainable from trade in purely private goods, although outcomes are still restricted to a subset of those positions that exhibit nothing more than mutual gains to all parties.

It is important to emphasize that these results do not depend in any way on the collective decision-making rules in local governments. These rules may range all the way from Wicksellian unanimity or quasi-unanimity, through the direct democracy of the New England town, the representative democracy of a city council, to the effective dictatorship of Boss Crump. Within any specific jurisdiction, the rule or institutions for reaching local fiscal decisions and the levy of taxes along with the selection of the size and mix of the expenditure budget will determine the final distributive outcomes, although these will rarely be unique. Conceptually, we can think of the distributional position attained by an individual, say A, as ranging over the whole set of possibilities represented by the shaded area between and below D and D' as this person shifts from one local jurisdiction to another and/or as the decision rules vary. If A should be dictator, a position at or near D might be secured, and if B replaces him, A might find himself at D'. But the point to be stressed here is that regardless of the decision rules the migrational or locational alternatives that are potentially available to all citizens in the federalism insure that the distributional set of outcomes attainable within any single local unit is narrowly bounded.

4. The now-classic paper here is Charles M. Tiebout, "A Pure Theory of Local Expenditures," *Journal of Political Economy* (October, 1956), 416–24. For a critical assessment of the Tiebout adjustment process, under its most favorable assumptions and in terms of efficiency-optimality criteria, see James M. Buchanan and Charles J. Goetz, "Efficiency Limits to Fiscal Mobility," *Public Economics* (April, 1972), 25–44.

Gains-from-trade in national public goods

Assume that a position, shown by G in Figure 1, is attained through the operation of market competition in supplying private goods and through spatially competitive local governments in supplying localized public goods. But we now assume further that there remain new welfare or efficiency gains to be exploited through the allocation of some resources to the production-provision of collective-consumption goods that are not confined geographically, at least not within the boundaries of the national government's jurisdiction. For purposes of analysis, we assume that neither local governments nor market institutions will devote resources to the provision of such goods.[5] Furthermore, we assume that all collective-consumption goods and services fall into one or the other of the two distinct categories examined here, the strictly local or the strictly national.[6] The effect of introducing the existence of national public goods is to shift the utility-possibility frontier outward.

If the central or national government in the federalism accepts the responsibility for organizing the provision of these goods, how will the gross gains-from-trade be distributed, and how efficient will the production-provision be? There is a major difference between this and the two earlier models examined, a difference in kind and one that should be immediately apparent. Since there are no competing "sellers" of the national public goods, there are no effective constraints on the range of distributional outcomes that are comparable to those demonstrated to be present both under private-goods market process and under localized public-goods provision through local governments. Alternatives always exist, and these will define the extremes of potential distributive outcomes. The individual can migrate across international boundaries, and he can join others in revolutionary uprising against the national government. In the United States in the 1970's, however, these

5. As noted with reference to the market supply of local public goods, this is an unrealistic assumption. It is made here only for the purpose of simplifying the exposition.

6. Much the same applies here as in the preceding footnote, although genuine problems emerge when we allow for the existence of public goods whose efficiency jointness-nonexcludability ranges are geographically limited but not sufficiently to allow for effective competition among spatially defined collective bodies.

can scarcely be considered effective alternatives, and especially for individuals who are "representative" members of the national citizenry. And such extreme limits surely will not confine the distributional outcomes even within the set of positions that dominate the initial or no-trade position (G in Figure 1) in the standard sense. There is no external constraint that insures against central government distributions of gains-from-trade that fall outside the set of positions that exhibit gains to all parties, that is, outside the area bounded by h, h', and G. One, some, or even many persons in the economy could be made worse off with than without central-government provision of national public goods.

It seems plausible, however, to postulate some broad limits on central-government or federal-government fiscal power. Constitutional restrictions do exist, despite Supreme Court confusion between constitutional order and "social justice." Elements of a fiscal constitution remain in being, and these prevent arbitrary and discriminatory exercise of the taxing power by the federal government. Although the extension to the spending side of the budget is not symmetrical, there are also some legal limitations on overt discrimination in the allocation of governmental benefits. Within existing constitutional constraints, and so long as the model is restricted to one where the central government supplies and finances only genuinely national public goods and services, as reasonably classified, we can talk meaningfully about some bounded set of distributional outcomes. In terms of our illustration in Figure 1, we postulate that such constraints will insure outcomes within the shaded area defined by G, k, and k'. Note that this allows for some positions outside the set that dominates G for all persons in the group (the set Ghh') but that these nonintersecting positions are restricted in range. In the real world, of course, there are no necessary restrictions of the sort depicted in the construction.

The broader range of possible outcomes here than in the two earlier models is apparent, but a second feature should also be noted. In both earlier models the existence of effective alternatives serves to insure not only the limited range of distributional possibilities but also the approximate achievement of the utility-possibility frontier. That is to say, alternatives also generate pressures toward efficiency. The absence of effective alternatives to national public-goods provision eliminates such pressures. There is no force tending to push the system to positions along or near the kk' boundaries, and final positions well within the shaded area seem equally if not more likely to emerge.[7] The implications of the analysis for the relative efficiencies of local and central government are clear. It is directly predictable that central or national government will be less efficient than local units.[8]

In order to bound the set at all, we have found it necessary to resort to constitutional-legal constraints, a step that was not required in the discussion of local-governmental provision of public goods. Within the set, as now bounded, the position actually attained will depend on the particular operation of the decision-making process at the central-government level. Since the set is relatively more inclusive, and by a wide margin, than the comparable one in the earlier or local-government model, the analysis suggests that the structure of collective decision-making rules is much more important in central-government or federal-government affairs, more important for individual participants, than in local-government matters or in the market. The reason, of course, is again the relative absence of effective alternatives. Without alternatives, the individual is a necessary party to the outcome collectively selected even if he, personally, remains strongly opposed or is even harmed in the process.[9] At the central-government level, alternatives remain,

---

7. William Niskanen has presented plausible arguments to the effect that central-government bureaus, possessing monopoly powers in the provision of particular public goods and services, "sell" these services, in effect, at all-or-none terms to "buyers," that is, to legislatures. In this case, all the fiscal surplus is squeezed out as bureaucratic waste, at least in the limit, and net gains-from-trade vanish. In terms of our model, the Niskanen hypothesis suggests that with many central-government goods the actually attainable utility-possibility frontier does not extend beyond G. See William A. Niskanen, *Bureaucracy and Representative Government* (Chicago: Aldine, 1971).

8. This prediction may seem bizarre in the face of popular mythology about local-government corruption. Local governments have their own equivalents of Bobby Baker and the Rayburn Building, but governments at this level cannot, by the nature of their situations, have their own Tulsa ship canals, Florida barge canals, maritime and farm subsidies, HEW bureaucracy, F-111 airplanes, or, even, their own Vietnam wars.

9. In the market, the individual need not be at all interested in the "decision rules." In fact, these are rarely discussed. He does not "vote" on the prices that he confronts in the marketplace. He has no need to do so because his protection is provided, ideally and conceptually, in the presence of alternative sellers and buyers. The individual in a local government may vote, directly or indirectly, on tax and budget matters, but the possible increments or decrements to his utility that such choices can produce are con-

at best, potential. In working democracies significant departures by governments from outcomes desired by majorities or even by intense minorities will, of course, provide incentives to nonincumbent parties and politicians to offer more-efficient and more-preferred alternatives.

The construction of Figure 1 allows us to depict the distributional consequences of a transfer of local government functions to the central government. Suppose that local units are abolished and that the central government assumes the responsibility for providing localized public goods throughout the area of what becomes a unitary political system. The range of possible outcomes, under the same constitutional-legal constraints, is expanded to the area bounded by F, t, and t' in Figure 1. Clearly, opportunities now exist for sharing the total gains from "public-goods trade" that were not present under the genuinely federal system. The central government may now, under certain decision-making processes, produce an outcome such as that shown at M, which lies wholly outside the set that was previously attainable. Furthermore, this position becomes attainable under the same rules. Note, also, that the new position, M, might lie farther inside the utility-possibility locus than J, which we may assume to have been the position attained under the federal organization. This reflects the reduced pressure toward efficiency in the structure characterized by less-effective alternatives for individual choice.

The effects of shifting the dividing line between local and central government are clear. Centralization tends to widen the set of possible distributional outcomes and, simultaneously, to reduce the institutional pressures for efficiency in public-goods provision. In the analysis to this point we have assumed that there is a clear-cut distinction between localized and central public goods and services, that the efficient jointness-nonexcludability ranges are sharply delineated. As we know, however, these ranges are nearly always fuzzy, and intergovernmental spillovers exist for almost all localized public goods. The argument for central-government takeover often hinges on the relative significance of these spillover effects. Centralization allows for the internalization of the intergovernmental externalities that these spillovers represent;

---

fined in value by his migrational prospects. The basic difference between the importance of decision rules at the central-government and local-government levels seems to have been wholly ignored in the Supreme Court reapportionment decisions, which were apparently based on bad economics as well as on naive political science.

this, considered in isolation, can increase overall efficiency in public-goods supply. Against this must be placed the offsetting efficiency drain that centralization makes possible through its elimination of effective alternatives. The accompanying widening of the range of distributional possibilities may or may not be considered a desirable attribute in its own right.

As indicated earlier, to place any plausible restrictions on the set of outcomes produced by central-government action we found it necessary to resort to constitutional-legal constraints. In this context, and as the construction of Figure 1 suggests, central-government takeover of local functions becomes equivalent to a relaxation of such constitutional limits. The elementary point developed in this and preceding paragraphs should not be excessively belabored. Perhaps it is obvious to everyone that the amount of redistribution of welfare that the federal government can accomplish under a budget of, say, 50 billion dollars is significantly less than that which becomes possible with a budget of 250 billion dollars. Even with extreme progressivity in rate structure, with the general tax base, and with accompanying redistributive elements in spending patterns, the distributional possibilities in the former case may fall far short of those in the latter, even if, in shifting to the larger budget, the tax base is seriously eroded, the rate structure is made less progressive, and the pattern of spending becomes, in itself, somewhat less redistributive.

II. Pareto Optimal Redistribution

In the discussion of Section I, individual utility functions were implicitly assumed not to contain arguments for either the income-wealth characteristics of others (flows or stocks) or for their specific commodity and service characteristics (flows or stocks). If this assumption is dropped, and interdependence among persons in any or in all of these respects is introduced, redistribution may emerge as a specifically chosen objective in an idealized voluntaristic choice process. In the terminology of welfare economics, redistribution may involve Pareto shifts to the Pareto-welfare surface. This surface may be unattainable without redistributional activity. And this activity may be, but need not be, over and above the results forthcoming from the sharing of the gross gains-from-trade in private and in orthodox public goods and services.

REDISTRIBUTION AS A PRIVATE GOOD

I shall use a threefold classification and examine redistribution as (1) a purely private good, (2) a local public good, and (3) a national public good. If interpersonal interdependence exists, itself an empirical question, the form of this interdependence must be empirically ascertained since these alternative descriptive categories embody differing implications.

If an individual secures utility from the act of making income transfers to other persons but secures no utility from increases in the income or wealth levels of others apart from his own act of giving, or secures no utility from other's acts of giving, redistribution becomes analogous to the consumption of a purely divisible or private good.[10] There are no "public" properties; neither nonexcludability nor joint-consumption efficiency is present. We should observe this sort of redistribution to take place in the wholly voluntary sector. In the construction of Figure 1 this purely private redistribution would be embodied in the attainment of the market equilibrium somewhere in the set bounded by c and c'.

REDISTRIBUTION AS A LOCAL PUBLIC GOOD[11]

Our emphasis now shifts to those situations where individual utility functions include arguments for the income-wealth characteristics of others, as such, but where these "others" are residents of spatially defined local communities or jurisdictions. Individuals are wholly uninterested in the incomes of those beyond the confines of the local community. Furthermore, we assume that for those potential transfer recipients within the local jurisdictions specific identification is either not possible or not relevant for choice. That is to say, potential taxpayers in the local community are interested in the in-

---

10. This motivation may, of course, be mixed with others. For a discussion that emphasizes this aspect, see Thomas Ireland, "Charity Budgeting," in Thomas Ireland and David B. Johnson, *The Economics of Charity* (Blacksburg: Center for Study of Public Choice, 1971).

11. This subject has recently been discussed in some detail by Mark Pauly. My discussion is confined to only a few of the models that he develops. At certain points, however, my results diverge from those suggested by Pauly. See Mark V. Pauly, "Redistribution as a Local Public Good," paper presented at COUPE meeting, Cambridge, October, 1971.

come level of the "local poor," but they make no identification of the members of this group, as such.[12]

Initially, we may examine a submodel in which taxpayers in the separate localities are immobile; they do not shift among communities in response to differential fiscal pressures. The potential welfare recipients are, by contrast, assumed to be fully mobile as among localities, and they respond directly to the level of welfare payments or income transfers.[13] If we ignore costs of migration, one condition for equilibrium in this model is that the transfer payments per person be equal in all localities. The potential recipients will distribute themselves among the communities to insure that this condition is fulfilled. The system of interaction between welfare or transfer recipients on the one hand and local taxpayers on the other generates an equilibrium that is Pareto optimal, despite the interdependence between the level of "bad" in a given community and the community's own efforts at eliminating this.

The interaction becomes more complex when we allow a Tiebout-like adjustment among potential taxpayers to accompany the migrational adjustments of welfare recipients. The equilibrium that will be produced retains Pareto-optimality characteristics, however, since persons will tend to locate themselves among the spatially competitive local governments in accordance with their own preferences for redistributive activity. Although the migrational adjustments of potential recipients insure that transfers per person are equal in all localities, the net transfers away from taxpayers may differ among separate communities, with the trade-off being made in terms of the number of recipients.

In the geometry of Figure 1 local-government action in providing income-wealth redistribution that can be classified as a strictly local public good becomes no different from the action involved in supplying any other local public good. The utility-possibility frontier is shifted outward, and the equilibrium will tend to fall in the area bounded by D and D', as before.

---

12. In this model the making of income transfers becomes analogous to the removal of a "bad" rather than the purchase of a "good." In some respects, these two acts are behaviorally equivalent, but here it seems useful to make a conceptual separation between them.

13. This model seems realistic because nonfiscal elements may well dominate the fiscal in taxpayer locational decisions.

REDISTRIBUTION AS A NATIONAL PUBLIC GOOD

If individual utility functions include arguments for the income-wealth positions of other persons throughout the national economy without spatial
distinctions, local governments find themselves in what appears to be the familiar public-good dilemma. Since the single unit cannot exclude others
from the benefit of its own action, investment in the activity of redistribution
will be suboptimal. There are, however, differences between this and the
standard public-good case. To an extent, redistribution as an activity that
generates utility is divisible. The local community that carries out redistribution transfers income to specific local residents; it cannot, by the nature of
the production process here, generate benefits that spill over equally to all
persons in the nation. Hence, despite the assumed national scope of the utility interdependence that motivates the activity, the "production divisibility"
restores at least elements of excludability. Local communities find themselves
in a reciprocal-externalities interaction. This suggests that the suboptimality
in result will be less than that indicated to be present in the pure public-good
interaction and may, under some conditions, vanish.[14]

If a case for federal-government or national-government redistributive
activity is to be based on the grounds of strict utility interdependence, evidence should be available to indicate that the sociocultural environment is
such that the effective limits are, indeed, those determined by national
boundaries rather than those more limited in space on the one hand and
those more extensive on the other.

III. "Constitutional" Redistribution

Those who have advanced the "principle" that the redistribution function
must be performed at the central-government level in a federal system need
not accept either of the models developed above. In rejecting such models
many scholars have, however, been too quick to resort to externally derived

14. The "distribution of redistribution" among separate local units may be nonoptimal, while at the same time the total amount of redistribution may be larger than that
which would be generated under fully centralized redistribution by the central government. For a discussion of the general model, see James M. Buchanan and Milton Z. Kafoglis, "A Note on Public Goods Supply," *American Economic Review* (June, 1963).

ethical norms. This step tends to remove the discussion from the realm of scientific discourse with predictable results.

To a partial extent the analysis of redistribution can be shifted to another plane, and without explicit value commitment, by examining what I have called "constitutional" redistribution.[15] This approach begins with the empirically valid proposition that explicit distributions of income are not, in fact, objects of choice for collectivities at any level. The relevant choices to be made are those among rules or institutions that, in turn, operate to generate probability distributions of distributive outcomes or allocations. At the stage of genuine "constitutional" choice, it is not appropriate to include the standard arguments in individual utility functions, nor is it at all appropriate to introduce explicit utility interdependence in the sense discussed in the preceding section. Conceptually at least, individuals engaged in "constitutional" choice remain uncertain about their own income-wealth positions in subsequent periods during which the rules to be adopted will remain in force.[16]

To clarify the argument here, it will be useful to compare and contrast allocation and distribution. At the "constitutional" stage market institutions may be chosen along with a decision to enforce contracts made under these institutions. Resources will be allocated, and it becomes meaningful to discuss the process under the "constitutional" rule that insures that these market institutions will remain in being. In the allocative process final products will be distributed in accordance with the rules. To this extent, distribution accompanies allocation. But the distributive pattern that accompanies market process, the distribution of the gross gains-from-trade, may not embody characteristics that are fully acceptable at the "constitutional" level of decision. The "game" may not seem "fair," quite independent of identification of particular recipients during specific market periods. If this is generally accepted, attempts may emerge, at the "constitutional" level, to introduce what

15. In more general terms, the shift to "constitutional" levels of choice or decision making, and especially when collective alternatives are involved, allows many of the standard tools of welfare economics to be used in what would otherwise seem value-laden territory. On this, see my "The Relevance of Pareto Optimality," *Journal of Conflict Resolution* (December, 1962), 341–54, and also James M. Buchanan and Gordon Tullock, *The Calculus of Consent* (Ann Arbor: University of Michigan Press, 1962).

16. The similarity between this approach and that of John Rawls should be apparent. See John Rawls, *A Theory of Justice* (Cambridge, Mass.: Harvard University Press, 1971).

we may call redistributive institutions, which are aimed to modify the distributive outcomes of market process.

This elementary logical derivation is not substantially changed when we allow for public-sector allocation, either at the central-government or local-government level. Constitutionally, a set of institutions may be established that determines the appropriate functions for the market, for local government, and for central government. Operating within these limits, the separate units allocate resources and distribute final goods and services. Over and beyond this pattern of results, however, explicitly redistributive institutions may also be constitutionally introduced.

The advantage of the "constitutional" approach is that it allows for a conceptual derivation of redistributive institutions in terms of Wicksellian efficiency, without resort to explicit value norms. Once redistributive institutions are constitutionally adopted, and as these operate, the actual redistribution that they produce must be zero-sum. Hence, at this stage, it becomes conceptually impossible to derive the unanimous support required for Wicksellian efficiency without introducing the utility interdependence of the type discussed in Section II.

Whether or not such explicitly redistributive institutions will emerge constitutionally, for any of the several reasons that might be adduced,[17] is an empirical question. Also, even if these do emerge, the criteria for efficiency may or may not be satisfied. These questions are not directly relevant to my purpose in this paper. The "principle" that redistribution must be performed at the central-government level may be restated as follows: If redistributive institutions or rules are to be selected at the "constitutional" level, these can be enforced only by the authority of the central or national government because of the zero-sum characteristics of the actual redistributions attempted during subsequent periods of application of these rules.

We may use an elementary example to demonstrate the validity of the principle as interpreted. For expositional simplicity only, assume that no public goods exist, and that the market has been constitutionally selected as

---

17. I have, in earlier works, discussed some of these. See Buchanan and Tullock, *The Calculus of Consent*, and also my *Public Finance in Democratic Process* (Chapel Hill: University of North Carolina Press, 1967). For further discussion, see Richard E. Wagner, *The Fiscal Organization of American Federalism* (Chicago: Markham, 1971), 4–6. Also, see paper 9, by Mitchell Polinsky, in this book.

the allocating process over a well-defined national economy, which includes local-government as well as central-governmental jurisdiction. Suppose that those persons living within a geographically defined subarea of the national economy should decide, again at some constitutional stage of deliberation, to modify the market-determined distributive pattern toward greater equality. Such rules are put into being for the single subarea government. As the rules are applied, however, individuals who are subjected to net taxes will find it advantageous to shift to other local jurisdictions, and potential recipients of net transfers will find it advantageous to shift into the redistributive jurisdiction. The Tiebout adjustment, by both groups, will make accomplishment of the intended distributive results impossible for the local community. This analysis is relevant even if it is acknowledged that those very persons who might have supported the imposition of the redistributive rules at the constitutional stage will themselves shift location when these rules come into operation. Effective enforcement of redistributive rules or institutions that are aimed at modifying the distributive outcomes in the market, or in the combined market–public sector process, must be carried out by the governmental jurisdiction that is itself coincident with the market in the geographical area.

There is, of course, nothing inconsistent in the combined presence of redistributive institutions, in the constitutional sense, and Pareto-optimal transfers, as chosen in the operational working of political process. A "constitutional" decision may be made to finance a major portion of central-government budgets with a progressive income tax, quite independent of and in advance of knowledge about the public-good mixes that describe such budgets. As these budgetary-mix choices are made, however, one of the components may well be the transfers of income designed for poverty relief.

As the analysis of Section I demonstrated, there is more range of variation in the distribution of the gross gains-from-trade in the central government's provision of public goods and services than there is in the distribution of such gains from the provision of goods either through the market or through local governments. When this is recognized, and if a sizable central-government sector exists, the institutionalization of redistribution may be limited largely if not wholly to tax-side constraints on central-government fiscal structure. If a "fiscal constitution" is designed to insure a substantial role for progressive taxation, regardless of the demand pattern for publicly supplied goods, marginally or inframarginally, the final distribution of welfare may be constrained to fall within specific limits. (In Figure 1 such constitutional restriction may insure that the final distributional outcome falls between, say, the rays terminating at k and k''.) The institutionalization of redistribution in this manner will, necessarily, distort the in-sector allocative process of the central government. The satisfaction of the necessary marginal conditions for optimality in the provision of goods and services becomes more difficult and, in practical reality, may become impossible. These allocative inefficiencies may be offset against the distributional "efficiencies" that progression in the fiscal structure is predicted to generate.

IV. Conclusions

Methodologically, this paper contains one tautological proposition and two sets of predictive hypotheses in political economy. The proposition states, quite straightforwardly, that zero-sum transfers, defined in utility dimensions, are limited by the extent of individual alternatives. The first set of hypotheses concerns the existence and the importance of utility interdependence as among specifically definable persons and groups, within the context of an operative political process. Individuals are observed to perform private charities, to join voluntary groups with charitable objectives, and to support redistributive transfers at local, central, and international governmental levels. The overall division of distributional responsibility among these separate institutional structures that might be required to meet Pareto criteria for optimality can be determined only empirically. The second set of hypotheses concerns the existence, actual or potential, of consensus among individuals on the establishment and maintenance, constitutionally, of rules of fiscal structure that embody income-wealth redistribution.

It is important to emphasize that nowhere in the discussion has it been necessary to introduce external ethical norms, either my own or those arbitrarily derived from some fanciful "social welfare function." In this sense, I have not answered the "should" question posed in the paper's title. Indirectly, my answer is: *The redistribution that "should" be performed at various levels of government is that which individuals, acting through their collective entities, local and central, expressly prefer.* Idealized outcomes that reflect some "true" amalgamation of individuals' preferences are not, of course, possible to attain. Political outcomes emerge from the workings of institutions, themselves imperfect, that exhibit stochastic variety and, on occasion, internal inconsistency. This makes the task of the political economist especially difficult; he cannot "read" the genuine preferences of individuals from the revealed political outcomes that he observes. The empirical testing of the hypotheses derivable from either of the two analytical models requires sophisticated and highly imaginative research. The potential for the central government to effect zero-sum transfers, derivable from no plausible model of consensus, and reflecting the will of a dominant political coalition, breaks any direct connection between observed governmental behavior and the Pareto conditions for efficiency, at the operational or constitutional level. Within certain carefully drawn limits, this obstacle could be handled in the simpler of the two models, that of straightforward Pareto-optimal transfers. For genuine constitutional choice, however, observed opposition to the actual operation of redistributive institutions cannot, in itself, provide evidence of an absence of "efficiency" in the more comprehensive choice of social institutions.

Despite such problems, the discussion of what we may call the "political economy of redistribution" has been substantially advanced in recent years.[18] There is no cause for retreat into obscurantist ethics, which does little more than embroil us, one with another, over just whose personal set of values "should" be selected by that nonexistent yet subservient elite through which too many of us seek in unconscious willingness to subvert ordinary democratic process.

18. For a paper that summarizes much of this discussion, see Harold M. Hochman, "Individual Preferences and Distributional Adjustment," presented at the New Orleans meeting of the American Economic Association, December, 1971.

Name Index

Aaron, Henry J., 377n. 1, 408–9
Adams, T. S., 81
Allais, Maurice, 474n. 2
Anderson, Joseph M., 377n.1
Aristotle, 306
Arrow, Kenneth J., 288n. 13
Asimakopulos, A., 407n. 1

Barone, Enrico, 59n. 1, 68, 70, 71, 79–80, 97, 99, 100, 101, 105
Barro, Robert J., 394n. 4, 445n. 5
Barzel, Yoram, 322, 323
Bator, Francis, xii
Bauer, Peter T., 428n. 1
Baumol, William J., 175n. 2, 239n. 12
Becker, Gary S., 277n. 8, 467
Benham, F. C., 60
Bhagwati, Jagdish, 161n. 6, 162n. 7
Black, Duncan, 360
Blum, Walter J., 79n. 17
Bohm, Peter, 188n. 5
Borcherding, Thomas, 441n. 1
Borgatta, Gino, 69–70, 73, 97, 101, 102n. 49, 105
Boskin, Michael J., 378n. 2, 451n. 7
Bosworth, Barry P., 377n. 1
Boulding, Kenneth E., 156n. 1, 170n. 5
Bowen, Howard, 104n. 51
Bowman, R. T., 40, 48
Bradford, David F., 271, 280n. 11

Brennan, Geoffrey, xviin. 11, 392n. 2, 435n. 1, 440n. 4
Breton, Alfred, 265–70, 280
Browning, Edgar K., 395n. 6
Burtless, Gary T., 377n. 1

Campbell, Colin, xviin. 10, 390n. 1, 407n. 2, 408, 418, 421n., 444n. 4
Chammah, Albert M., 227n. 2, 228n. 3
Chapman, Bruce, 435n. 1
Chipman, John S., 167n. 16
Clarke, Edward H., 188n. 5
Coase, Ronald H., 122n. 10, 124–25, 132n. 6, 169, 173, 174n. 1, 176, 201n. 8, 218n. 10, 257n. 9, 291n. 16, 308–9, 311, 312
Cohen Stuart, Arnold J., 79
Commons, John R., 61
Conigliani, C. A., 97, 98
Cooter, Robert, 438n. 2
Cosciani, Cesare, 70, 71, 74, 97, 100
Crecine, John P., xviin. 10, 301n.

Davis, Otto, 125n. 15, 127n. 1, 166n. 13, 169, 237n. 10, 250
del Vecchio, Gustavo, 73n. 11, 103, 105
de Viti de Marco, Antonio, 59, 64–66, 69, 70, 73–78, 84, 85–92, 97–98, 100, 105
Devletoglou, Nicos, 428n. 1
Dosser, Douglas, 40n. 3, 223n. 16
Downs, Anthony, 67n. 8, 360

Subject Index

anarchy: libertarian, 283–84; rules under, 4–5

bads. *See* public bads
benefits: in externalities, 16; individuals sharing public goods, 227–43
benefits, Social Security: exceed value of payments, 452; favoritism and penalties in, 453
bureaucracy: decision making and spending of, 33–35; defined, 33
bureaucracy, federal: role in growth of spending, 457

choice: democratic, 347–49; in laissez-faire economy, 9–11; utility maximization in, 362–63. *See also* collective choice; individual choice
clubs: optimal size, 205n. 11; quantity of goods with different sizes of, 202–3; total cost and benefit per person in, 200–202
club theory: of cooperative membership, 193–94; determining membership margin, 194–207; optimal exclusion theory in, 208
Coase theorem, 174–75
collective action: based on individual choice (Ferrara), 63; broad definition of and justification for, 4; competition in, 35–37; to control monopoly practices, 23–24; explicit, 29–35; against external

diseconomy, 184; externalities as basis for, 17–19; for externalities within the law, 20–21; implicit ownership under, 308–18; under majority voting, 30–32; market adjustment to external economies of, 130–32; origin of, 5; political economy of, 25–37; proposals for specific, 307–8; with reciprocal external economies, 138–43; to reduce transaction costs, 13–14; without relevant externality, 134–35
collective choice: contribution of Italian theorists to concept of, 97–100, 104; as problem of fiscal theory, 104
collective-consumption goods. *See* public goods
collective-decision model, Wicksellian, 463–64
collective services. *See* public services
consumers: availability of public good units of production, 267; sovereignty in market economy, 363
consumption: ownership-consumption in club theory, 194–207; in private exchange of goods and services, 211; of services with external economies, 245–56
consumption units: cost of joint supply of, 213; emergence of external economy or diseconomy in supply of, 216–17; in Marshallian joint supply theory, 212–13,

This book is set in Minion, a typeface designed by Robert Slimbach specifically for digital typesetting. Released by Adobe in 1989, it is a versatile neohumanist face that shows the influence of Slimbach's own calligraphy.

This book is printed on paper that is acid-free and meets the requirements of the American National Standard for Permanence of Paper for Printed Library Materials, z39.48-1992. ⊚

Book design by Louise OFarrell, Gainesville, Fla.
Typography by Impressions Book and Journal Services, Inc., Madison, Wisc.
Printed and bound by Worzalla Publishing Company, Stevens Point, Wisc.